The Art of Coercion

A VOLUME IN THE SERIES

Cornell Studies in Security Affairs

Edited by Austin Carson, Alexander B. Downes, Kelly M. Greenhill, and Caitlin Talmadge

Founding editors: Robert J. Art, Robert Jervis, and Stephen M. Walt

A list of titles in this series is available at cornellpress.cornell.edu.

The Art of Coercion

Credible Threats and the Assurance Dilemma

Reid B. C. Pauly

Cornell University Press

Ithaca and London

Thanks to generous funding from the Stanton Foundation and Brown University's Watson Institute, the ebook editions of this book are available as open access volumes through the Cornell Open initiative.

First published 2025 by Cornell University Press

Library of Congress Cataloging-in-Publication Data

Names: Pauly, Reid B. C., 1988– author
Title: The art of coercion : credible threats and the assurance dilemma / Reid B.C. Pauly.
Description: Ithaca, New York : Cornell University Press, 2025. | Series: Cornell studies in security affairs | Includes bibliographical references and index.
Identifiers: LCCN 2025001691 (print) | LCCN 2025001692 (ebook) | ISBN 9781501782688 hardcover | ISBN 9781501782787 paperback | ISBN 9781501782695 epub | ISBN 9781501782701 pdf
Subjects: LCSH: Nuclear arms control—Case studies | Ultimatums (International relations)—Case studies
Classification: LCC JZ5675 .P384 2025 (print) | LCC JZ5675 (ebook) | DDC 327.1/74—dc23/eng/20250312
LC record available at https://lccn.loc.gov/2025001691
LC ebook record available at https://lccn.loc.gov/2025001692

GPSR EU contact: Sam Thornton, Mare Nostrum Group B.V., Mauritskade 21D, 1091 GC, Amsterdam, NL, gpsr@mare-nostrum.co.uk.

For Natalie

Contents

Acknowledgments

Early on in my career, I was advised that good mentors are not found but earned. Taking stock of the immense support that I have received in bringing this book to fruition, I suspect an imbalance between my assets and liabilities. I will be earning the mentorship afforded me for years to come, and I am resolved to pay it all back, or forward.

This book began at the Massachusetts Institute of Technology (MIT) Security Studies Program (SSP), where I was fortunate to have Barry Posen as an adviser. He encouraged me to ask big and important questions about the world, the answers to which matter to people who make decisions. I have endeavored to bring this ethos to all of my projects since. Vipin Narang and Frank Gavin were responsible for bringing me to MIT in the first place. Each graciously helped me at different moments to find the time, the funding, or the networks I needed to pursue my research. I appreciate their mentorship and friendship.

In SSP's unique and dedicated intellectual community, I followed good advice from Owen Coté, Taylor Fravel, Ken Oye, Dick Samuels, John Tirman, Steve Van Evera, and Jim Walsh. Elina Hamilton, Laura Kerwin, Paula Kreutzer, Lynne Levine, Harlene Miller, Joli Divon Saraf, Janine Sazinsky, Laurie Scheffler, and Susan Twarog helped me to navigate the university. I shared ideas with Dan Altman, Lena Andrews, Mark Bell, Chris Clary, Fiona Cunningham, Mayumi Fukushima, Brendan Green, Phil Haun, Peter Krause, Sameer Lalwani, Marika Landau-Wells, Nina McMurry, Andrew Miller, Nick Miller, Aidan Milliff, Rachel Odell, Kelly Pasolli, Sara Plana, Erik Sand, Rachel Tecott, Tim Wright, and Ketian Zhang. And I have yet to produce any work without sending it first to Phil Martin, Tim McDonnell, or Cullen Nutt.

At the Harvard Kennedy School's Belfer Center for Science and International Affairs, I thank Matt Bunn, Aditi Kumar, Sean Lynn-Jones, Marty Malin, Steve Miller, John Park, and Steve Walt for their support. I also benefited from the advice of Nick Anderson, Aaron Arnold, Alex Bollfrass, Mariana Budjeryn, Rebecca Gibbons, Francesca Giovannini, Ayako Kobayashi, Chris Lawrence, Sahar Nowrouzzadeh, Frank O'Donnell, Nick Roth, Mahsa Rouhi, Nina Silove, Cameron Tracy, Ben Zala, and many other exceptional scholars and practitioners.

I have also had the great privilege of working for Scott Sagan at Stanford University's Center for International Security and Cooperation (CISAC). His unbounded energy continues to be an inspiration. Over manuscripts, cigars, and baseball games, it was in California that I decided to pursue a career in academia. What an honor it was to return to CISAC, among my favorite places on earth, for a Stanton postdoctoral fellowship. I thank Lynn Eden, Rod Ewing, Gabrielle Hecht, Sig Hecker, Tracy Hines, David Holloway, Colin Kahl, Herb Lin, Steve Pifer, Harold Trinkunas, and Amy Zegart for their support. I also received great feedback that year from Debak Das, Mariya Grinberg, Asfandyar Mir, Andrew Reddie, Michal Smetana, and Lauren Sukin.

I have been fortunate to be invited into several professional networks in which I continue to find friends and mentors, including the Carnegie International Policy Scholars Consortium and Network, Bridging the Gap, and the Schmidt Futures International Strategy Forum. Through these communities I received helpful advice from Peter Feaver, Lee Feinstein, Jim Goldgeier, Peg Hermann, Bruce Jentleson, Kori Schake, Jim Steinberg, Marc Trachtenberg, and Philip Zelikow. I was also thankful to be affiliated with the RAND Corporation under the supervision of Karl Mueller and Paula Thornhill. Through these and other programs, I met David Arceneaux, James Cameron, Matthew Cebul, Jennifer Erickson, Dani Gilbert, Adam Liff, Erik Lin-Greenberg, Rebecca Lissner, Julia Macdonald, Dani Nedal, Brad Potter, Jackie Schneider, Jane Vaynman, Tristan Volpe, Rachel Whitlark, and James Wilson.

When I was just starting out, I was lucky enough to meet Tom Schelling. Over teas and lunches at his home in Bethesda, Maryland, we would discuss nuclear strategy, American foreign policy, and the politics of coercive diplomacy. Tom never got to see this book, but I see him in its pages.

Several other scholars were gracious enough to read the manuscript, in whole or part, including Målfrid Braut-Hegghammer, Austin Carson, Andrew Coe, Dale Copeland, Alex Debs, Charlie Glaser, Stacie Goddard, Robert Jervis, Elizabeth Saunders, Ken Schultz, Todd Sechser, Alex Weisiger, and Jessica Chen Weiss. And I benefited from advice and encouragement from Jim Fearon, Matt Fuhrmann, Avery Goldstein, Kelly Greenhill, Jeff Knopf, Ed Mansfield, Nuno Monteiro, Robin Möser, Daryl Press, Josh Rovner, Beth Simmons, and Caitlin Talmadge.

I am grateful to be a faculty member in Brown University's Political Science Department and Watson School for International and Public Affairs. I work alongside uplifting colleagues—Peter Andreas, Mark Blyth, Corey Brettschneider, Jeff Colgan, Rose McDermott, Eric Patashnik, Wendy Schiller, David Skarbek, Rich Snyder, Ed Steinfeld, Nina Tannenwald, and Ashutosh Varshney—and a caring cohort of junior colleagues—Danny Choi, Gemma Dipoppa, Aditi Sahasrabuddhe, Paul Testa, and Marques Zarate. I especially thank Tyler Jost for reading multiple chapters of this book. Olivia Falkenrath, Alex Kung, Lachlan MacKenzie, Casey Monyak, Sofia Yee-Wadsworth, and Isabella Yepes were excellent research assistants. Every year I am reminded of the exceptional quality of Brown University students.

To complete this book, I received generous research funding from the Stanton Foundation, the Smith Richardson Foundation, the Simons Foundation, the Tobin Foundation, and the James Martin Center for Nonproliferation Studies. I am especially privileged to be among the new generation of nuclear scholars that the Stanton Foundation has nurtured. This book is open access because of their support.

Portions of chapters 1 and 5 were previously published as Reid B. C. Pauly, "Damned If They Do, Damned If They Don't: The Assurance Dilemma in International Coercion," *International Security* 49, no. 1 (2024): 91–132, portions of chapter 2 were previously published as Reid B. C. Pauly, "Deniability in the Nuclear Nonproliferation Regime," *International Studies Quarterly* 66, no. 1 (2022), and portions of chapters 2 and 4 as Cullen G. Nutt and Reid B. C. Pauly, "Caught Red-Handed: How States Wield Proof to Coerce Wrongdoers," *International Security* 46, no. 2 (2021): 7–50.

At Cornell University Press, I thank Jackie Teoh and Alex Downes. It is another echo in my career to be publishing this book with my alma mater far above Cayuga's waters.

Finally, my deepest debts are to my family. My parents, Caryl Clark and Louis Pauly, inspired me to be curious about the world. Tessa, Brian, Barrett, and Oscar ground me in the best parts of life. Aris is always ready with a pep talk. And I have found in Dave, Carol, Hayley, and Sam seemingly endless reserves of unconditional love. To my teammate Natalie and our two incredible children, Winifred and Clark, you are the source of all my dreams and plans. Thank you.

Abbreviations

AEB	Atomic Energy Board (South Africa)
AEC	Atomic Energy Corporation (South Africa)
AEOI	Atomic Energy Organization of Iran
ANC	African National Congress
Armscor	Armaments Corporation (South Africa)
CAAA	Comprehensive Anti-Apartheid Act
CAATSA	Countering America's Adversaries Through Sanctions Act
CBI	Central Bank of Iran
CIA	Central Intelligence Agency
CISADA	Comprehensive Iran Sanctions, Accountability, and Divestment Act
CRRC	Conflict Records Research Center
E3	France, Germany, and the United Kingdom
E3 + 3	France, Germany, and the United Kingdom, plus China, Russia, and the United States
EU	European Union
FBIS	Foreign Broadcast Information Service
FRUS	*Foreign Relations of the United States*
HEU	highly enriched uranium
IAEA	International Atomic Energy Agency
IAEC	Iraqi Atomic Energy Commission
IDF	Israel Defense Forces
INARA	Iran Nuclear Agreement Review Act
IRGC	Islamic Revolutionary Guard Corps (Iran)
ISIL	Islamic State of Iraq and the Levant
JCPOA	Joint Comprehensive Plan of Action

JPOA	Joint Plan of Action
LEU	low-enriched uranium
MI6	Secret Intelligence Service (UK)
MOP	Massive Ordnance Penetrator
NARA	National Archives and Records Administration
NATO	North Atlantic Treaty Organization
NIC	National Intelligence Council (US)
NIE	national intelligence estimate
NNPA	Nuclear Non-Proliferation Act
NPT	Treaty on the Non-Proliferation of Nuclear Weapons, or Nuclear Nonproliferation Treaty
NSC	National Security Council (US)
NTI	Nuclear Threat Initiative
P5+1	United States, United Kingdom, France, Russia, and China, plus Germany
PMD	possible military dimensions
PNE	peaceful nuclear explosive
SWIFT	Society for Worldwide Interbank Financial Telecommunication
TASS	Telegrafnoye agentstvo Sovetskogo Soyuza
U-235	uranium-235
UF6	uranium hexafluoride
UNGA	United Nations General Assembly
UNMOVIC	United Nations Monitoring, Verification and Inspection Commission
UNSC	United Nations Security Council
UNSCOM	United Nations Special Commission
WMD	weapon of mass destruction

The Art of Coercion

Introduction

When Do Threats Work?

Coercion is the practice of convincing a target by the use of threats to bend to your will. From a library imposing late fees on tardy patrons to a parent sending an insolent child to their room, everyday life brims with the logic of coercion: obey me, or else. In their foreign policies, states often make grave economic or military threats to try to affect others' behavior rather than resort to costly war. It is little wonder, then, that states frequently choose coercion.

What is more surprising is how bad they are at it. Depending on how one counts, US threats, historically, have succeeded just 18 percent,[1] 29 percent,[2] or 31 percent[3] of the time.[4] More broadly, "stronger" coercers have achieved their compellent aims only 36 percent of the time.[5] Material power, it would seem, does not portend coercive success.

These striking figures fly in the face of how coercion is typically understood to work. A dominant paradigm explains coercive outcomes by pointing to the credibility and severity of threats. Targets will defy a coercive demand if they think the threat is a bluff. And even if a target believes that a threat is credible, it may still defy it if it thinks the expected pain is bearable. Threats must therefore be serious and severe.

This threat-centric paradigm is clear in theory and intuited by practitioners. But it is woefully incomplete. This book advances another paradigm, which points to the implicit logic of contingent action at the heart of all coercion: *coercive assurance.*[6] Threats must be perceived by their targets as *conditional* upon their behavior. "They'll have me whipp'd for speaking true; thou'lt have me whipp'd for lying; and sometimes I am whipp'd for holding my peace," laments King Lear's fool.[7] Far from being cowed, he finds freedom in his lot—jesting, boasting, and speaking truth to power. Pain sheds its coercive power when it cannot be avoided. Even credible and severe threats will fail if they are not perceived as sufficiently conditional.[8]

To develop the concept of coercive assurance in the study of international relations, this book pursues three questions. First, what is the relationship between threats and assurances in coercion? Second, why do coercers punish after receiving compliance? Third, why do targets of coercion fear unconditional pain? Addressing these questions involves investigating coercive assurance from the perspective of target states: how they receive coercive threats, how they evaluate their choices in light of coercion. But it also involves recognizing that coercers confront, are stymied by, and try to overcome a predicament inherent in cases of coercion: the *assurance dilemma*.

Argument in Brief

The assurance dilemma is a situation in which the actions coercers take to bolster the credibility of a threat undermine the credibility of their assurance not to punish. It is a trade-off that coercers must navigate to wrest concessions. Simply put, when leaders augment their threats, they do so at the expense of their necessary assurances, thereby unwittingly compromising their own coercive strategies.

Establishing the credibility of coercive assurance is challenging because coercers may end up punishing their targets unconditionally for several rational and nonrational reasons. First, targets of coercion typically face multiple coercive demands at once, creating the opportunity for coercers to continue threatening targets who have made concessions on some issues but not others. Second, targets often confront multiple coercers with different interests and independent capacities to punish. They therefore worry whether conceding to one coercer will actually avoid a punishment imposed by another. Third, when considering whether to concede to coercion, targets fear that they will reveal new information to their coercers through their concessions and only invite further threats.

From the perspective of targets, these sources of unconditional punishment are impediments to making concessions and avoiding pain. Yet coercers can mitigate all of these assurance challenges. From the perspective of coercers, this book demonstrates the effectiveness of three corresponding strategies of signaling coercive assurance. First, coercers can disentangle multiple demands from the same punishment such that partial concessions still avoid some pain. I call this "disentangling demands." Second, coercers can demonstrate control over potential spoilers to signal that they alone will decide whether to impose or relieve punishments. I call this "managing spoilers." Third, coercers can share with a target their knowledge of its misdeeds to communicate that its concessions will not reveal new information to the coercer. I call this "sharing knowledge."

Finally, assurances need not be perfectly credible to affect the outcome of coercion. Every concession includes a bet that punishment will be avoided. Targets cannot be truly certain that their coercer is sincere, but they accept bigger risks of unconditional harm to avoid severer punishments. Nevertheless, some coercive assurance is always necessary because targets do not make concessions to coercion if they conclude that they will be punished anyway. In a dynamic coercive bargaining process, targets look for assuring signals that their coercers will withhold the threatened pain. These powerful dynamics explain when and why targets of coercion concede or defy.

Improving Our Understanding of Coercion

Coercive assurance matters a great deal to the study of international politics because coercion is so prevalent. An international order underwritten by great powers that provide public goods to incentivize cooperation also relies heavily on coercive tools.[9] And much more of international competition is coercive than directly violent. States tend to issue threats before turning to force. But the consequences of failed coercion are grave: crises, tit-for-tat escalation, war.

More broadly, coercion is everywhere around us. Most of what we mean when we say "you can't park there" or "you must pay your taxes" is not really that you cannot or must not—it is that you would be punished if you did not comply. When we say, "I don't have a choice but to drive on the correct side of the road," we have it exactly backwards. Credibly conditional pain has presented us with a clear choice.

The necessity of coercive assurance has been underappreciated in the study and practice of coercion. In the coercion literature, it is an understudied type of commitment problem, and the relationship between credible commitments and credible threats has been undertheorized. This is in part because assurance is assumed to be automatic in the bargaining model of war, which the field extended to coercion. Punishments are costly to carry out, the logic goes. Coercers should not pay those costs if their target already backed down and they got what they wanted, so targets should not fear that they will be punished after they comply. In reality, targets can fear unavoidable pain and thus defy credible threats.

Threat-centric biases also inform how practitioners approach coercion. US National Security Strategy documents, which since 1987 have communicated signals of US interests and intent to allies, adversaries, and the public, eschew the logic of coercive assurance.[10] The documents contain an average of thirteen times more threats than coercive assurances (see figure 0.1).[11] Scholars have observed a similar rejection of coercion theory in general within the US military. "Military professionals are not entirely comfortable with violence as a bargaining process," writes Tami Biddle. "One does not, they believe, 'bargain' with one's enemies—one fights them."[12]

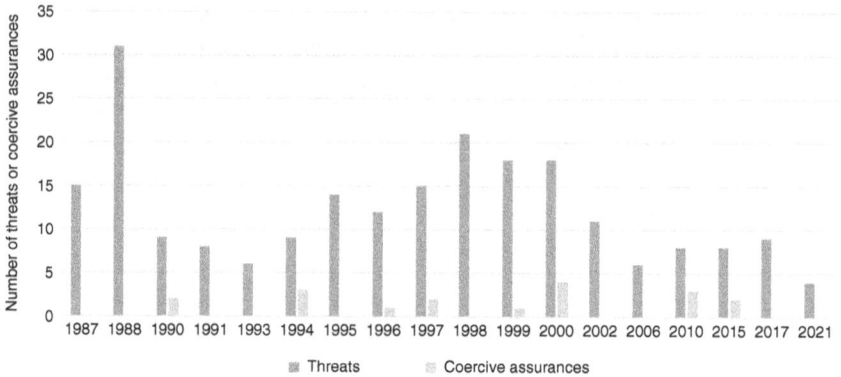

Figure 0.1. Frequency of threats and coercive assurances in US National Security Strategy documents.

A common analogy in statecraft to the game of chess also effectively scopes out the problem of coercive assurance. As Secretary of State John Foster Dulles explained in a 1957 National Security Council meeting on US nuclear strategy, "in a chess game you wouldn't normally ever go so far as to take your opponent's king; you checkmate the king and don't play out the rest."[13] In Dulles's view, effective nuclear counterforce was a checkmate that would lead to bargaining advantages. In the real world, cornered opponents can still defy or lash out.

The US government faces a particularly acute assurance dilemma. It has trouble coercing weak countries because of its strength, not in spite of it. In Pyongyang US threats are perceived as a ploy, in Tehran as a trap, in Caracas as a catch-22. Yet viewing the history of coercive diplomacy through the lens of coercive assurance reveals that even Washington's targets are more likely to concede when leaders come to acknowledge and address the assurance dilemma. The credibility of coercive assurance will matter a great deal to the achievement of important US foreign policy aims, from deterring a revanchist Russia, to restraining the North Korean nuclear arsenal, to avoiding a war with China over Taiwan.

This book, therefore, seeks to improve the study and practice of coercive diplomacy. When threats put targets in a "damned if you do, damned if you don't" position, we should expect defiance.

Studying Coercion in the History of Nuclear Nonproliferation

The spread of nuclear weapons is a consequential challenge of our time, one that many leaders have devoted significant energy and resources to combat. Proliferators, often motivated in their pursuit by security fears, are loath to give up acquisition of a security asset, especially when faced with coercive threats from the very enemies whose uncertain intentions they feared in the first place. Findings on which signals help to overcome the assurance dilemma in the high-stakes domain of counterproliferation are more likely to travel outside of it to coercive bargaining over other, lower stakes. The historical record also permits process tracing to reveal the intentions and perceptions of coercers and targets over time.

On at least twenty-one occasions, states have issued threats of sanctions or force to enforce the nonproliferation regime. This book delves into four cases of coercive bargaining between nonallies over nuclear weapons programs in South Africa, Iraq, Libya, and Iran. Exploiting within-case variation, I explain not only the occurrence but also the timing of nonproliferation bargains using primary documents from US government archives, the South African apartheid-era government archives, tape recordings of high-level meetings from Saddam Hussein's Iraq, and the International Atomic Energy Agency (IAEA) archives. I supplement these documents with the memoirs, recollections, and writings of target state policymakers, military leaders, and nuclear scientists. I also conducted interviews with policymakers who participated in the coercive bargaining processes.

In each chapter, the lens of the assurance dilemma reveals novel insights that revise conventional wisdom. Each case offers strong evidence that target perceptions of noncredible assurance hinder coercers, even when those targets perceive credible threats. Increases in the perception of assurance credibility, not threat credibility, are most proximately associated with acquiescence. Coercive assurance can tip the balance one way or another.

Plan of the Book

The book proceeds as follows. In chapter 1, I critique the threat-centric coercion paradigm and derive theory on the assurance dilemma as an impediment to successful coercion. I explain why targets fear that insincere coercers may choose to punish unconditionally and how even sincere coercers can lose control over the decision to apply or withhold punishment. The chapter concludes with case selection and a rationale of the book's methods and case studies.

Chapter 2 concerns South Africa, which succeeded in building a secret nuclear arsenal despite international pressure to sign the Nuclear Nonproliferation Treaty (NPT). Conventional explanations for this outcome point to South Africa's fears of Soviet domination and US indifference to anticommunist proliferation. Instead, internal regime documents show how counterproliferation pressure on South Africa failed in the 1970s and 1980s because of entangled demands. Owing to intense coercive demands to end its brutal practice of apartheid, Pretoria's leaders perceived that acquiescence on the nuclear issue would provide no relief from the pain of economic sanctions. The Ronald Reagan administration attempted to disentangle the issues in the mid-1980s until Congress passed comprehensive antiapartheid sanctions legislation. The assurance dilemma thus proves a powerful lens to explain the failure of coercion in South Africa. Later, South Africa's dismantlement of its nuclear arsenal is sufficiently explained by its racist motivation not to hand over nuclear weapons to a postapartheid Black-majority government. Primary documents reveal as well how from 1989 to 1993 South African leaders planned and executed a strategy to conceal their past weaponization from the IAEA.

Substantial documentary records of the South African nuclear weapons program are now available to scholars, and many South African policymakers and nuclear scientists have written firsthand accounts of their nuclear decision-making. The case is ripe for reexamination and theory testing. South Africa's nuclear journey was more interactive with external coercers than traditional accounts of its internal political machinations about nuclear weapons suggest.

Chapter 3 examines the case of Iraq, where a mercurial dictator in Baghdad sought nuclear weapons and came close to acquiring the capability. Saddam Hussein also came under intense counterproliferation pressure, up to and including noncoercive brute force. Conventional wisdom paints a tragedy of a duplicitous and quixotic dictator hiding his nuclear pursuits until exasperated great powers chose to invade. The reality is even more frustrating. After the Gulf War, Washington attempted to coerce Saddam into abandoning a weapons of mass destruction (WMD) program and at first to great success. Iraq destroyed its program and admitted inspectors, but it would not come totally clean. Its concessions consistently matched what it thought its coercers already knew about its past WMD programs. Yet it was never deemed enough. As the 1990s proceeded, Iraqi elites came to conclude that no amount of compliance would lift sanctions. In the midst of this coercive effort, Saddam framed his choices to his advisers: Iraq could either "have sanctions with inspectors or sanctions without inspectors."[14] He perceived no escape and so confidently defied.

Iraqi documents and recordings, captured and shipped out of the country by US forces after the 2003 invasion, offer a rare glimpse into the perspective of a target of coercion. In meetings with his advisers, Saddam evaluated his evolving position, the intentions of his enemies, and options available for compliance or defiance.

Chapter 4 explains how, in bargaining with Libya, the United States and Britain succeeded in coercing a rogue proliferator into abandoning its nuclear pursuits. The timing of the final bargain after the 2003 invasion Iraq has led to some shallow lessons drawn from the case about the importance of demonstrating highly credible threats—that is, invading another country in the region over similar stakes. The reality of the strategic interaction was far more consistent with the assurance dilemma. During negotiations, Muammar Qaddafi was continually suspicious that his coercers intended to disarm him and attack anyway. The invasion of Iraq and capture of Saddam Hussein fed these fears even more. Washington and London overcame this perception slowly, taking pains to assure Qaddafi. They froze out spoilers and privately shared with Libya intelligence gleaned from their penetration of the black-market A. Q. Khan network to assure him that his conceding would not reveal more than they already knew. Washington and London worked hard to convince Libya that it would not be the next Iraq. But eight years after striking a nonproliferation bargain, US and British airpower did help to topple Qaddafi. Despite reneging on their bargain, the evidence reveals that their signals of coercive assurance were critical to closing the 2003 deal and convincing Qaddafi to accept the risks of conceding.

Fewer primary records are available in the Libyan case. The fate of the official government archives after the 2011 civil war is unknown. Nevertheless, US and British participants have reflected on the case since and are willing to discuss the 2003 deal in writings and interviews because the Qaddafi government is gone. The case shows that even the most credible and severe threats alone cannot succeed without coercive assurance. Spikes in threat credibility—after the invasion of Iraq and the capture of Saddam—resulted not in acquiescence by Qaddafi but demands for assurance.

Chapter 5 examines Iran and its primary coercer, the United States. In 2015 Iran struck a bargain with the P5 + 1 coalition (the US, the UK, France, Russia, China, and Germany) to accept enhanced verification and limits on its nuclear program. It is puzzling why Iran was willing to strike a nonproliferation bargain so soon after the demise of Libya's Qaddafi. Conventional explanations for the Iran deal emphasize leadership changes and a window for bargaining—the elections of Barack Obama and Hassan Rouhani—as well as the inclusion of significant carrots in the deal for Iran. The lens of the assurance dilemma highlights instead Iran's fears of its coercers' duplicity and how the strategies of coercers changed to overcome these suspicions. For instance, another adversary, Israel, was not party to the negotiations and was a potential spoiler. I show that Tehran came to the table only after the window of a credible Israeli threat closed—a puzzle for threat-centric theory. The Obama administration also disentangled its demands and punishments to make clear that it was negotiating over Iran's nuclear program and not its missiles or foreign policy. Iran sought and acquired the specific separation of entangled sanctions designations during negotiations. Moreover, the Obama administration crafted domestic legislation to bound congressional oversight over sanctions relief. And documents from Iran's "atomic archive" compared with IAEA reports reveal how much coercers already knew about the "possible military dimensions" of Iran's past nuclear programs before the 2015 nuclear deal.

Earlier, in 2003, Iran had scaled back a nuclear weaponization program because of highly credible and severe military threats bolstered by the US invasion of Iraq. Iran curtailed its nuclear program in the absence of attempts to assure it. But Iran's concessions were only partial. The nuclear program transitioned underground and to more deniable pursuits. Iran's leaders then put out feelers for coercive assurance. The 2003 episode shows how assurance is necessary but that its credibility can vary with the severity of threatened punishments.

Research on the Iran case is important and possible because of the successful conclusion and subsequent US withdrawal from the 2015 Joint Comprehensive Plan of Action (JCPOA). Interviewees were motivated to speak to either defend or criticize the deal. Moreover, IAEA reports and a controversial tranche of Iranian documents stolen by Israeli intelligence in 2018 shed new light on technical aspects of the former Iranian nuclear weapons program.

The book concludes with lessons for theory and policy and examines extensions of the logic of coercive assurance outside of the nuclear domain—from the origins of the Pacific War to the Cuban missile crisis, ransomware, and beyond.

The Assurance Dilemma

Credible and Conditional Threats

Why do some coercive demands succeed while others fail? Why do targets of coercion defy credible threats? This chapter takes up these questions across four sections. First, I define "coercive assurance," a concept fundamental yet overlooked in coercive bargaining. Second, I situate the concept within existing explanations for the success and failure of coercion. Third, I present a theory of the relationship between threat and assurance credibility: the assurance dilemma. In doing so, I explain why targets fear unconditional punishment, why even earnest coercers struggle to navigate the dilemma, and what kinds of signals may bolster coercive assurance credibility. Finally, I explain how competing theories will be tested in the chapters to come.

Defining Coercive Assurance

Coercive assurance describes the conditional intentions communicated by one state to another in the process of coercive bargaining.[1] It is a pledge in the context of coercion not to punish once coercive demands are met: "If you comply, I will not carry out my threat."[2]

Coercive assurance is distinguished from, and occasionally confused with, two other types of assurance in international politics: ally reassurance and non-ally reassurance. Ally reassurance is a promise to come to the aid of an ally: "I will defend you." It is a positive assurance—a pledge to do something—and includes concepts such as security guarantees and extended deterrence commitments. Non-ally reassurance is an attempt to communicate: "I mean you no harm." It is a negative assurance—a pledge not to do something—and includes concepts such as promises of neutrality, nonintervention in sovereign affairs, and nonaggression pacts. These reassurances among nonallies fall outside of the realm of coercion and therefore this book.[3]

What makes assurance a unique dilemma in the context of coercion is the fact that the coercer intends to threaten the target. There is no connotation of "I mean you no harm" in coercive assurance; rather, "I am threatening you today, and I need you to believe that I mean it." The coercer is instead making conditional pledges. It wishes to send two seemingly conflicting signals: that its threats are both credible and contingent upon the target's behavior. The object is to present a choice, one that does not lead the target to believe they are "damned if they do, and damned if they don't."

States communicate coercive assurance only in the context of coercion.[4] To qualify as a case of interstate coercion, at least one coercer state must threaten at least one target state with the goal of affecting its behavior.[5] All coercive interactions have at least three components: a looming threatened punishment, at least one demand communicating what behavior the threat is contingent upon, and an assurance communicating that the punishment will not be carried out if the demands are met.

Coercive assurance is distinct from both threat-making (pledges to punish by inflicting a cost) and inducements (pledges to reward by providing a benefit).[6] It is neither stick nor carrot; it is the conditionality of the stick. The dichotomy between "sticks and carrots" often lumps coercive assurance together with "positive" inducements, such as bribes and side payments,[7] and papers over coercive assurance as a distinct concept. The removal of sanctions, for instance, tends to be subsumed into a broader category of positive inducements, instead of as the end of a punishment.[8] As a consequence, studies comparing different tools of coercion have been limited to conclusions affirming the complementarity of both negative and positive inducements without explanation of the conditions under which either are perceived as credibly conditional.[9]

Some more narrowly consider assurances to be explicit communications that leaders sometimes choose to offer.[10] But coercive assurance need not be explicit to exist, and treating it so unnecessarily omits much of the interesting variation in assurance credibility. In fact, any coercive threat always implies an assurance. Saying "I'm going to kill you" has no implied assurance because it is not a *coercive* threat; there is no demand made of the target and no conditionality—the pain is unavoidable except through self-defense. Statesmen do sometimes make threats or warnings of this noncoercive nature. At the time of the 2003 US invasion of Iraq, for instance, when asked what Washington wished Iran to learn from the war, a senior Bush administration official replied, "Take a number."[11] Whether credible or not, this was a threat that lacked coercive assurance. Whether any behavior on the part of Iran could have avoided the punishment remained opaque. Starting from Thomas Schelling's premise that one actually cannot communicate "stop or I'll shoot" without implying, credibly or not, that "if you comply, I won't shoot" opens up the possibility of studying types of more or less assuring threats, conditions, strategies, and contexts rather than explicit statements.[12]

An assurance is implied in all types of coercive threats—deterrent or compellent,[13] punishment or denial[14]—because all mean to communicate a conditional prospect and present a choice to their target. Nevertheless, the empirical chapters of this book focus on compellence. It is the more difficult of coercive interactions in which to communicate credible assurance. Findings about the effective communication of credible coercive assurance should be more likely to generalize beyond compellence. I return to deterrence in the conclusion.

Why Coercion Succeeds or Fails

Coercion succeeds if a target alters its behavior in accordance with the demands of a coercer. I call this compliance, concession, or acquiescence. A state that seeks a nuclear weapon but stops pursuing the bomb because it was threatened with punishment has just been the target of successful coercion. It is fundamentally a counterfactual exercise—the state would not have complied in the absence of being threatened. Alternatively, coercion fails if a target chooses not to alter its behavior in the face of explicit threats. I call this defiance or noncompliance. A state that pursues nuclear weapons and continues to do so even after a coercer threatens to punish it for pursuing the bomb has just been the target of failed coercion. It is the decision of the target that determines how the dependent variable is coded.

For the purposes of theorizing, a dichotomous distinction between coercive success and coercive failure is helpfully parsimonious. In reality, targets of coercion have more than two options. They might make partial concessions, change their behavior a bit but not entirely, or negotiate a coercive bargain to avoid pain.[15] While I account for such detail in my cases, this theory chapter considers partial concessions to be successful coercion. The target changed its behavior. Failed coercion also collapses into one outcome two types of defiance. Targets can defy coercive demands by ignoring them and continuing their behavior as planned, or they can defy by lashing out, escalating their undesirable behavior and otherwise confronting their coercers. Acquiring the bomb or going to war are two results of coercion failure in this book's chapters, but defiance comes in many forms. With their backs against the wall, victims take risks. Cornered dogs bite. Outlaws become recidivists, thinking "they can only hang me once." And many theories seek to explain the sticking points of failed coercive bargaining.

COERCIVE ASSURANCE AMONG EXISTING
EXPLANATIONS FOR COERCION OUTCOMES

This section distinguishes four explanations for coercion failure: threat credibility, traditional commitment problems, demand magnitude, and

Table 1.1 Explanations for coercion failure

	Threat credibility	Traditional commitment problems	Demand magnitude	Assurance credibility
Coercion will fail if . . .	threats are not perceived as credible or painful	concessions affect future relative power or reputation	demands are perceived as maximal	pain is perceived as unconditional

coercive assurance (see table 1.1). Each lens brings into focus different variables and therefore prescribes different solutions to improve the prospect of successful coercion.

Threat Credibility   Of all the reasons compellence can fail, one receives the most attention: insufficient threat credibility or severity. Consider figure 1.1 as a simple model of a coercive interaction. A coercer observes some behavior it does not like, and it chooses whether that stake is worth coercing over; if it is, the coercer issues a threat. The target then decides whether to defy or concede the stake. If the target concedes, there is peace. If it defies, the coercer may either carry out its threat or withhold punishment and back down, its bluff having been called.

Through this dominant lens, scholars and practitioners have for decades conceived of ways to bolster the credibility of threats. Coercers must first have the capability to inflict pain. A mugger without a gun plainly cannot credibly threaten to shoot. And even capable coercers must signal their interests over what is at stake to attempt to communicate their willingness to cause harm. A homeowner may be resolved to shoot trespassers on their own property but not on their neighbor's property. Hence the international relations literature suggests several possible strategies of costly signaling or demonstrating resolve:[16] when issuing threats leaders should try to tie their hands with strategies of commitment,[17] make public threats that are harder to back down from,[18] invoke their reputations in future crises,[19] mobilize military forces to create sunk costs,[20] or conduct military maneuvers to create risks in a contest of brinkmanship.[21] In a game of chicken, drivers can throw their steering wheel out the window, persuading their opponent to swerve. Military commanders have ordered their ships burned upon landing, signaling to both their own soldiers and the enemy's that they will conquer or die—there will be no retreat.[22]

A related proposition is that threatened punishments must be sufficiently severe to the target. Meager library fines may not compel some patrons to return their books. Rationally, for a target to comply, the cost of the punishment should outweigh the benefit of defiance.

Coercer

                                 Threat   No threat

Target   Defy   Concede

Coercer   Punish   Withhold

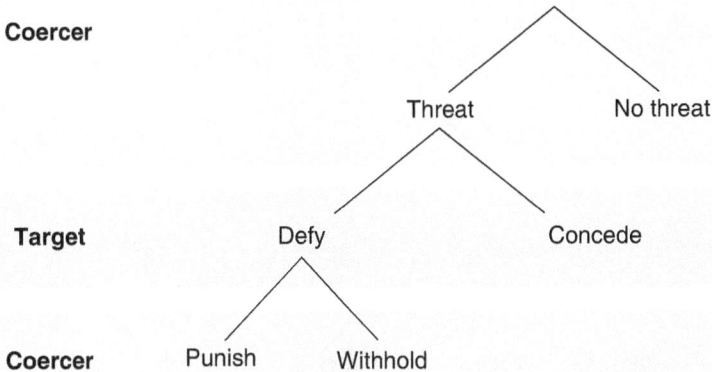

Figure 1.1. The threat credibility model of coercion.

Traditional Commitment Problems   A second approach iterates the simple model presented in figure 1.1 and blames coercion failures on the inability of states to commit to the terms of any bargain long into the future.[23] "Commitment problems" arise because coercers can return to the start of the decision tree in figure 1.1 and make new threats and new demands if something changes about the relationship between the coercer and target. The target's relative power may have diminished as a result of its concessions—for example, when Czechoslovakia ceded the Sudetenland to Germany in 1938, it also surrendered its border fortifications. Or the target's dependence on the coercer may have increased: after the Kingdom of Hawaii signed a trade agreement with the United States in 1876, its sugar cane industry became dependent upon American importers, and Washington used its new leverage in renewal negotiations to demand exclusive rights to Pearl Harbor.[24] Or the target may have acquired through its concession a reputation for being a pushover. Weak states have fought doomed wars against stronger neighbors to preserve their reputations for not being appeasers, as in the 1939 Russo-Finnish Winter War.[25]

Demand Magnitude   Third, some place the blame for coercion failure on the magnitude of coercer demands. For example, demands for regime change ask too much.[26] Targets do not commit suicide for fear of death. These are not commitment problems because defiance is not due to a lack of future certainty but to a lack of bargaining space. The target is unwilling to meet the coercer's demands, even to avoid punishment. The coercer is not merely perceived to have greater aims—it has actually pursued them by making maximal demands.[27]

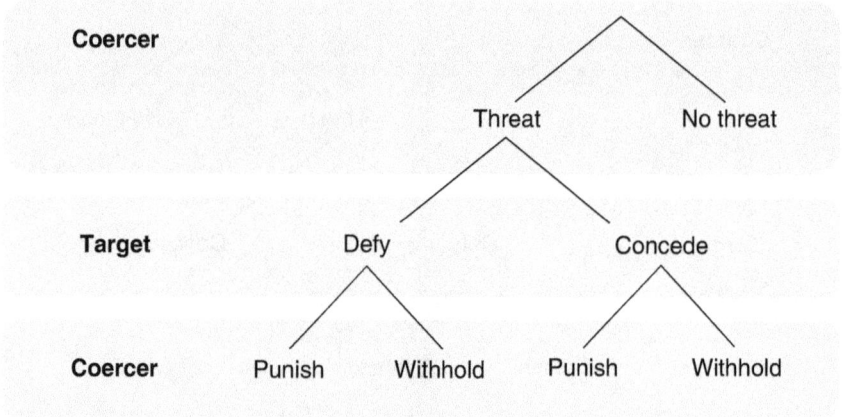

Figure 1.2. The coercion model with assurance.

Coercive Assurance Finally, adding coercive assurance to the simple model of coercion (see figure 1.2) makes explicit the implied aftermath of concession and therefore the prospect of unconditional punishment. If a target concedes, the coercer again faces a choice of whether to punish or withhold. This may include decisions about whether to carry out threats of imminent military action, impose threatened economic sanctions, stop ongoing coercive military operations, or lift economic sanctions. Most importantly, targets know this and factor their expectations about the coercer's behavior into their decision about whether to concede or defy in the first place. Compellence is a conditional relationship. The coercer and the target both have to understand that the coercer will only execute its threat if the target does not yield.

Hawkish policymakers sometimes imply a hypothesis about the sufficiency of credible threats to successful coercion: Applying "maximum pressure" can threaten the target so severely and credibly that it gives it no choice but to comply. You make it an offer it cannot refuse. In 1941 US oil sanctions wished to "slip a noose around Japan's neck and give it a jerk now and then."[28] When coercion fails, these leaders lament, If only our threats had been more credible, if only we had squeezed the adversary a little harder, for a little longer, surely then they would have given in, when we had them on the ropes.

The scholarly canon accepts the logic of coercive assurance. By definition, "to be coercive, violence has to be . . . avoidable by accommodation," Schelling wrote. "The pain and suffering have to appear *contingent* on his behavior; it is not alone the threat that is effective—the threat of pain or loss if he fails to comply—but the corresponding assurance, possibly an implicit one, that he can avoid the pain or loss if he does comply."[29]

Yet theories of coercion can overlook much of the interesting variation in assurance credibility by assuming that a unitary actor with stable preferences would not punish its target after receiving compliance.[30] Doing so would be gratuitous, many assume, since carrying out punishments is costly for the punisher too. It would follow that assurances are of uniform effect on the outcome of coercion. Thus, the credibility of threats is the critical variable in coercive bargaining—communicating more resolve should lead to more success.

That logic is flawed. Coercers are not fully in control of the dynamic process of coercive bargaining, and uncertainty about control makes targets unsure about whether to concede. Scholars cannot, therefore, assume that coercive assurance is constant across cases while correlating variation in the credibility of threats to their success or failure. Even highly credible threats can fail when assurance is not credible.

The distinction of assurance as a specific type of commitment problem in coercion is important because it captures immediate concerns. Coercive assurance is driven by direct fears of unconditional punishment, not second-order consequences of conceding. As such, it can take precedence for targets. What is the point of protecting for the future my reputation for fighting if preserving it means that I am sure to lose what I value today? A satisfying explanation for seemingly irrational defiance must account for these expectations of inevitable pain.

It is also important to distinguish because remedies will vary. Traditionally, proposed solutions to commitment problems aim to mitigate the consequences of relative power or reputational changes. Barbara Walter argues, for instance, that third-party interveners can end civil wars by guaranteeing the security of each side in a settlement.[31] In international politics, coercers do not have the luxury of escaping anarchy, yet in asymmetrical coercion even weaker actors sometimes make concessions to coercers who remain stronger into the future. Another solution that Todd Sechser prescribes for reputational sources of bargaining failure is that strong coercers offer side payments to weak targets.[32] But bribes (carrots) do not address the sources of suspicion.

All of these different lenses—threat credibility and severity, assurance, commitment problems, and demand magnitude—differ in their hypothesized sticking points of coercive bargaining. They prescribe different solutions to coercion impasses. But pulling the wrong lever can open the gates to unnecessary violence.

MOVING THE STUDY OF COERCION AWAY FROM THREATS

Scholars taking stock of the coercion literature, including Sechser, Kelly Greenhill, and Robert Art, have lamented that while assurance has been taken as axiomatic in coercion, there is a dearth of research on how assurance actually works—how it is interpreted or manipulated.[33] There are at least two reasons for this relative emphasis on threat credibility in the study of coercion. First, during the Cold War, nuclear threats understandably captivated policymakers and the academy. Stable nuclear deterrence required that both sides believed that each was willing to use nuclear weapons and even in defense of allies—a tough sell. By Schelling's own admission, his chapter "The Art of Commitment" in *Arms and Influence* focuses on threats alone. "This chapter is about the threats that are hard to make," writes Schelling, ". . . the ones that commit a country to an action that it might in somebody's judgment prefer not to take."[34] Work on hand-tying commitment-making, for Schelling and others he inspired, therefore focused on the pressing challenge of the day: reassuring allies of a US commitment to their defense.[35]

The second reason for the emphasis on threat-making in the study of coercion is that most foundational work studied deterrence, not compellence. Assurance is often a bigger challenge in compellence because the pain may have already started and one promises to stop, whereas in deterrence no action need yet have been taken by either side.[36] As Schelling himself observed while defining the concept of compellence, "the threat that compels rather than deters often requires that the punishment be administered *until* the other acts, rather than *if* he acts. This is because often the only way to become committed to an action is to initiate it."[37] Deterrent threats are therefore somewhat more assuring than compellent threats because the coercer has not yet undertaken any action. In compellence, it is the threatener who must promise to stop.[38]

This threat-centric coercion paradigm has improved over time, especially as Sechser factored the prospect of future punishment into coercive bargaining through the study of commitment problems, introduced above.[39] Matthew Cebul, Allan Dafoe, and Nuno Monteiro find in survey experiments that a reputation for reneging on past bargains can hinder one's assurances in future coercive diplomacy.[40] James Davis applies prospect theory to discover the suitability of assurances to negotiate with adversaries in the realm of losses.[41] Andrew Kydd and Roseanne McManus prescribe explicit assurances backed by audience costs in cases where war would result without them.[42] And Tristan Volpe explains how potential nuclear proliferators compel by acquiring just enough nuclear latency to credibly threaten to proliferate but not too much that it undermines their assurance to stop short of the bomb.[43] Still, this important work leaves big puzzles unanswered. Why would coercers punish unconditionally, and why do targets fear that they will?

The Assurance Dilemma

If assurance is a logical complement to threat-making, coercers should always attempt to provide assurance. But the reason assurance is so difficult to communicate in coercion is because of the inverse relationship between threat and assurance credibility. Demonstrating one's benign intentions is somewhat contrary to the enterprise of threat-making. By sending assuring signals, a coercer may be counterproductively communicating irresolution, fecklessness, or a tolerance for failure. Throwing the stick away, breaking the stick, or locking up the stick are all reasonable solutions to bolster an assurance that the stick will not be used, but how then will you still believe that I might use the stick?

This is the *assurance dilemma* in coercion. As states bolster the credibility of their threats, the credibility of their coercive assurance correspondingly diminishes. The relationship can be linear, as with relative power: the stronger the coercer, the more credible its threats but the less constrained it is from hurting the target even after the target complies. The trade-off can also occur at inflection points, such as when states take actions to bolster the credibility of their threats but lose control over the decision to apply or withhold punishment. It is a dilemma that has been underappreciated as the study of credible threats and credible commitments have diverged, obscuring their interactions and the relationship between signals of resolve and commitment.[44]

The assurance dilemma is an extension to the realm of coercion of the fears that drive the security dilemma in international politics.[45] To guard against the possibility of being suckered in a self-help world, international actors provide for their own defense and make worst-case assumptions about others' intentions. Yet the security dilemma canon explains peacetime relations and spirals of conflict, not the outcomes of coercion or the prospect of coercive assurance.[46]

Within the international relations canon, coercive assurance complements defensive and motivational realism, which argue that the pernicious effects of the security dilemma can be moderated.[47] The intensity of the security dilemma depends on a state's information about its adversary's motives. Signals aim to convey this crucial information credibly, especially to prevent conflict by communicating benign intent. But when states still disagree about the status quo and wish to resolve disputes short of war, they can use compellence. In so doing, they typically demonstrate that they are not status quo powers and must convey their resolve to change the status quo. The self-help fears of international anarchy are intensified between adversaries engaged in coercion. Coercers are not merely perceived to be threatening—they are actively menacing. And in this context of coercion, the need for reassurance of one's intent becomes conditional.

This section explains the sources of the assurance dilemma in coercion. It is always possible that a coercer is being insincere, and targets of coercion must guard against making concessions to an enemy bent on punishment. Yet even sincere coercers can sometimes apply unconditional punishments if they lose control.

EXPLAINING UNCONDITIONAL PUNISHMENT: INSINCERITY OR ENTANGLEMENT

The Benefits of Insincerity   For at least two reasons, targets can fear that coercers are being insincere when they make threats. First, targets may fear that threat-makers are bent on brute force but covering their prelude to war with the trappings of coercion. It is difficult, for instance, to ascertain whether a state mobilizing military force to another state's border is demonstrating resolve or preparing to invade. The window dressing of coercive diplomacy can disguise a mobilization and preserve operational surprise. Japan, for example, continued to send diplomats to negotiate with the United States in 1941 even after Tokyo had decided to go to war. Coercive diplomacy may also deflect blame in the eyes of third parties for ensuing violence—it was not me who was bent on aggression and caused the war but they who were intractable—or make violence appear more justified because it was a last resort after giving targets a chance to yield. Coercion is at least more acceptable as a tool for resolving disputes than warfare, and belligerents may wish to be seen attempting it. Targets must at minimum guard against duplicity and be wary of aggressors in coercer clothing.

Second, targets can fear that coercers will seek to predate. While it is costly to carry out unconditional punishments—both in terms of blood and treasure and to reputations as reliable assurers—coercers may perceive off-setting benefits. Attacking a target who has already made concessions will further weaken it, a potentially desirable goal among adversaries. Or a coercer may have in mind future adversaries who are observing today's interaction and wish to communicate to them that enemies do not go unpunished.[48] Henry Kissinger made such an argument during the 1975 crisis over the seizure of the SS *Mayaguez* when he called for air strikes even after securing the release of the forty crew members taken hostage by Cambodia. "I think it is essential in situations of this kind to make clear that it is we who define the hazards," he argued. "My recommendation is to do it [air strikes] ferociously." Later, he declared that "we should not give the impression that we will stop."[49] Punishment, he thought, would be an example to other would-be hostage-takers.

Multiple Demands and Issue Entanglement   A related, rational reason for targets to fear unconditional punishment is found in the complexity of

Entangled coercion

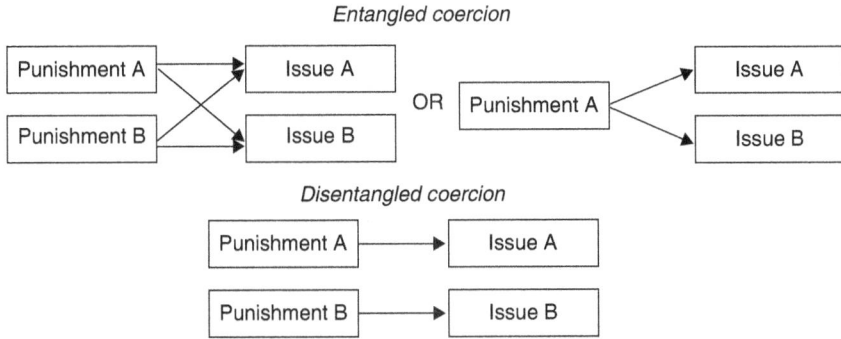

Disentangled coercion

Figure 1.3. Entangled versus disentangled coercion.

bargaining over multiple issues. Coercers may make multiple demands of their targets: for example, to both abandon a nuclear weapons program and cease human rights abuses. If the target considers conceding to one demand, it may fear that it will have to bear the pain of the threat anyway over the other issue that it has not conceded. These demands have become entangled. Schelling himself identified in a footnote this impediment to credible assurance by observing that his children defied his wrath if they saw that he was "mad already."[50]

Multiple issues are entangled if they are tied to the same threatened punishment(s). Disentangled issues are independently contingent on separable threatened punishments (see figure 1.3). Unless multiple demands are clear and kept disentangled, each with its own discrete punishment, a target lacks the coercive assurance to make one concession.[51] Applying separable punishments to each demand removes a practical impediment to coercive assurance; punishments may now be withheld individually. Moreover, disentangling demands sends a signal of a coercer's sincerity to strike a bargain. Disentanglement requires some change to existing policy, including the prioritization of demands, and duplicitous coercers are less likely to spend the political capital necessary.

A selection effect makes this even more of a challenge: coercion is applied most often against rivals with whom coercers have many bones to pick. Organized interest groups may pressure leaders not to disentangle from others their preferred demands of adversaries. Moreover, new issues may also crash onto the scene as the global context shifts. For instance, in August 2023 the United States and Iran reached an agreement to secure the release of five American detainees held in Iran. In exchange for their release, the United States would unfreeze $6 billion of Iranian oil revenue in South Korean bank accounts. The money would flow to Qatar, a third-party guarantor, who would oversee the release of the funds. In September the prisoners were released, and the money was transferred to Qatar. Before Iran accessed any of it, however, Hamas, the Iran-supported militant Palestinian organization in control of Gaza, launched a surprising and brutal rampage through southern Israel. A shocked Washington reversed course and leaned on Qatar to refreeze the money.

EXPLAINING UNCONDITIONAL PUNISHMENT: LOSING COERCIVE CONTROL

Another set of reasons why coercers might carry out their threats unconditionally I call "losing coercive control." Coercers do not always know their own future intentions, nor do they know the preferences of the actor(s) who in the future will be the ones deciding whether or not to punish their targets. And this is a difficult problem to overcome in the minds of targets. Even highly credible threats need to be paired with assurance that the coercer can control the decision over whether to punish or withhold punishment.

In the dynamic process of bringing pressure to bear on a target, coercers can lose control over two things: their coalitions (domestic or international) or themselves. As such, assurance credibility can diminish as coercers bolster the credibility of their threats and undermine their own ability to decide whether and when to punish. The wise coercer's goal is to convince their target that it is in control and will not lose control of the execution of its threats.

Losing Coalitional Control   Coercers have incentives to build coalitions, domestic or international, to augment the credibility and severity of their threats. Leaders may need to mobilize domestic opinion to back coercive strategies. They may logroll to aggregate the demands of multiple interest groups when writing sanctions legislation or authorizations to use military force. Or coercers may rally international coalitions to compel in concert, recruiting other states to join sanctions campaigns and choke off economic substitution, gathering votes in favor of multilateral resolutions, or preparing with allies for joint military action. In constructing these coalitions, coercers can lose control over the ability to withhold punishment on their own terms. Actors who oppose coercive bargaining with the target may also exist, absent efforts to mobilize them.

Targets will ask, In striking a bargain with *you*, will *they* punish me anyway? Some coalition members may have greater demands of the target and be potential spoilers who are less assuring—they may punish despite a target's compliance with other coercers' demands.[52] Those with smaller demands are partners who are more assuring—the costs of one actor reneging may be mitigated by the others not reneging. Consider this visually on a bargaining spectrum (see figure 1.4).[53]

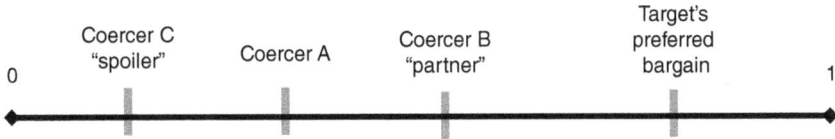

Figure 1.4. Spoilers and partners on a bargaining spectrum.

Coercer C's demands of the target are greater than Coercer A's demands. Coercer B's demands are smaller than Coercer A's demands. If the target concedes to the demands of Coercer A, Coercer B will go along with the agreement, but Coercer C may not. In fashioning coalitions of coercers, therefore, from the perspective of Coercer A, anyone to the right (closer to 1) is a "partner" while anyone to the left (closer to 0) is a potential "spoiler."

Domestically, multiple actors within a coercing state may be simultaneously empowered to impose punishments. In democracies multiple centers of power in a government may have authority over sanctions relief; legislatures can include or not include authorities for the executive to waive sanctions. The US Congress, for instance, restricted the president's ability to lift sanctions imposed on Russia for 2016 election interference as part of the 2017 Countering America's Adversaries Through Sanctions Act (CAATSA).[54] Or impending power transitions, such as elections, may raise the prospects of a new government reneging on a bargain. Scholars have often studied how domestic factors affect international signaling.[55] Yet these domestic factors have focused on explaining variation in threat credibility. For example, "two-level games,"[56] public approval for the use of force or casualty sensitivity,[57] and debates among political parties within democracies can all convey information about resolve.[58] This book highlights the domestic sources of coercive assurance credibility.[59]

Internationally, actors in a coalition have their own capabilities and interests.[60] Theories of international coalitional coercion also typically address how having multiple coercers can either bolster or diminish threat credibility and bargaining leverage.[61] This book helps to explain how fragmented coalitions can impede coercion.[62] The British suffered such a lesson at the 1757 surrender of Fort William Henry during the Seven Years' War. British commanding officers responsible for the twenty-three-hundred-man garrison reached terms of surrender with French general Louis-Joseph de Montcalm and readied a retreat to nearby Fort Edward. Outside of the walls, however, British columns were harassed by France's multitribal Native allies, resulting in dozens of casualties. The "massacre," thereafter embellished in British and then American lore,[63] was later used to justify vicious retaliations against First Nations. But rather than a coordinated deception, the bloody morning of August 10, 1757, had been the result of a chaotic disagreement between the French and their Native allies over the legitimacy of British surrender. Native warriors, who had canoed hundreds of miles to join the fight for no other compensation than the plunders of war, felt betrayed out of their earned spoils.[64] "They could not fathom French behavior in wasting their victory and protecting their enemies from their allies," writes the historian Ian Steele.[65] During the British retreat, a chaotic scuffle culminated in short-lived but brutal violence after someone let loose a "dreaded war whoop that was an intertribal signal to attack."[66] The French lost control.

Targets prefer to know that they are bargaining with the right coercer(s). An assuring coercer thus takes action to distinguish itself from potential spoilers. Observable communication among coercers within a coalition may serve such a signaling function to targets. As both Robert Jervis and Schelling appreciated, "messages in a strategic dialogue are often best conveyed not by speaking directly to the adversary, but rather by speaking seriously to some serious audience and let[ting] him overhear."[67] Removing veto players from coercive bargaining communicates to the target that its coercers are not seeking a pretext for punishment. A duplicitous coercer bent on punishment has less interest in managing spoilers whose interests overlap with its own and less desire to pay the costs to co-opt spoilers—for example, with bribery. Even if these spoilers are only temporarily sidelined until coercion succeeds—for instance, by being left out of secret bargaining—their influence over the outcome is diminished. Bargains are more easily prevented than undone.

Losing Control of Oneself   Another pathway to losing control is internal to a single actor. A coercer can lose control over its intention to withhold punishment if it learns new information from a target's concessions. The target fears not wanton predation per se but that its concession itself might enable or equip its coercer to predate. Målfrid Braut-Hegghammer invokes a version of this dynamic as the "cheater's dilemma," whereby coming clean about past wrongdoing, even if one might wish to do so, would only intensify a coercer's perception that one is hiding something.[68] Thus, it is better to defy and say nothing at all.

Scholars tend to think of coercive assurance as mostly a problem of private information: if only a coercer could convince a target that it intends to stick to its assurances, then the target would concede. Yet sometimes even coercers cannot know their own future preferences. They have private information from themselves. Coercers might learn from a concession about who the target is and what it is capable of, leading the coercer to conclude that it did not appropriately calibrate its initial demands. Information revealed through a target's concessions can cycle back into the previously discussed mechanisms, prompting coercers to make additional demands or empowering spoilers within a coercer coalition. Revelations from target concessions could also frustrate, enrage, or motivate the coercer, causing it to judge the target deceitful or the stake to be beyond a bargaining solution. Brute force, containment, or some other noncoercive solution could follow. If a target thinks that conceding will only increase the probability of its punishment and that compliance would be self-incrimination, it will defy.

To mitigate the prospect of a coercer's change of heart, a target may wish to be sure that its concessions will not reveal new material information to the coercer. Thus, the credibility of coercive assurance will be affected by the degree of shared knowledge between coercer and target—who already knows what about whom. Coercers can share how much they know already and how little the target's admission will alter their assessment of it. In an interrogation, for example, the guiding principle of a strategic subject is to only admit what the interrogators already know. But a criminal is more likely to bargain if investigators can prove that she will not be admitting to anything they do not already know. So, it is important for coercers to know what they are asking for. "We already know" is assuring for those who fear admitting guilt by conceding.

In sum, assurance is difficult because coercers may punish unconditionally for rational and nonrational reasons. Targets must guard against insincere coercers, yet even for sincere coercers there are constraints to assuring. They face a dilemma that trades off threat and assurance credibility. Coercers can make multiple entangled demands of their targets, and they can lose control of domestic and international coalitions with varying interests. They may also update their own will to punish upon learning new information about their target. Coercion theory, with its myopic focus on threat credibility, tends to overlook the fact that targets fear these impediments to credible coercive assurance.

TARGETS AND THE CONCESSION GAMBLE

Faced with threats, targets of coercion must make a choice about whether to concede. Accordingly, they evaluate several variables: the value of the stake and their interests in it, the credibility and value of any carrots promised, the credibility of the threats, the severity of the punishment for defiance, and, importantly, the probability that they will be punished anyway.

A target's coercive assurance fears can also vary in their time horizons—that is, it can have short- or long-term fears.[69] A chance of the coercer immediately reneging, whereby the coercer's punishments are imposed even after the target concedes, bears on whether the pain is avoidable at all. However, a chance of future reneging, whereby coercers later change their minds, bears on both the likelihood of a coercive bargain today and its durability. Consider the coercive tool of economic sanctions, for instance. Sanctioned governments that consider making concessions in exchange for economic relief must consider two possibilities. First, their coercer may not actually lift sanctions even after their concessions—a short-term commitment problem. Second, even coercers who lift sanctions upon receiving compliance can renege in the future and reimpose sanctions—a long-term commitment problem. Both matter to targets, yet the former is of primary concern. If the short-term problem is mitigated but not the long-term one, it still may be possible to reach a coercive bargain.[70] If the short-term fears are not mitigated, however, it does not matter whether the long-term assurance fears are addressed. The targets would have little incentive to acquiesce.

The assurance dilemma recognizes that there is always some probability that the coercer will renege and impose costs after compliance, but this chance must be low enough for the target to calculate that compliance is worth the risk.[71] Leaders of strong states cannot make perfectly credible commitments never to punish another state in the future. But sometimes target leaders do think them credible enough to take a concession gamble. As the severity of the threat increases, targets are willing to bear more risk to avoid it. But some coercive assurance is always necessary as targets do not make concessions if they believe that they will in fact be punished anyway.

Targets of coercion are primed to look for signals of coercive assurance. Too often coercion scholarship unnecessarily emphasizes the choices of the sender over the receiver. As Diego Gambetta writes, in a standard model the signaler chooses to send a signal, "but in a richer model the receiver herself when in doubt initiates the communicative exchange by probing and asking for further signals."[72] Costly signals may be preferred and can convey useful information if they are inconsistent with the expected behavior of a deceiver.[73] Yet even cheap signals can matter. While tying one's hands can make promises more believable, making promises without tying one's hands can still induce more cooperation than making no promises at all.[74] Targets are risk evaluators looking for a way out. Concession is a gamble. Some bets are better than others.

Nuclear Counterproliferation Cases

To investigate the assurance dilemma, I look to a universe of cases that is substantively important, in which adversaries make a range of compellent threats over similarly high stakes and in which there is sufficient available evidence to adjudicate my explanations versus alternatives. These criteria fit the tumultuous history of coercive bargaining over nuclear weapons programs.

There is important variation in the outcome of coercion over nuclear weapons programs. Many more states have pursued nuclear weapons than have acquired them, some ending their pursuit at an acceptable level of nuclear "latency" as a hedge to leave open future decisions. And while not all cases of nonproliferation success can be attributed to coercion, more can than scholars used to recognize. Nonproliferation is often, in fact, a process of coercive bargaining over how much nuclear capability coercers are willing to accept from potential proliferators. Sometimes target states accede to coercer demands in formal agreements. Other times they do so tacitly. Still other times they defy.

Each case study is really a two-stage investigation. The first stage is probing whether and when targets perceived coercive assurance to be credible and what coercer behavior affected those perceptions (or did not). The second is investigating the ultimate dependent variable—the success or failure of coercion—and whether coercive assurance was a necessary cause of success. In terms of external validity, coercive nonproliferation cases marginally privilege the first stage over the second. Confident in the logic of coercive assurance and while still tracing its necessity to coercive bargains, I seek to validate manipulable contributors to coercive assurance credibility and their relationship to threats within the assurance dilemma.

For many reasons, coercive assurance should be difficult to communicate credibly in episodes of coercive counterproliferation. Strategies that bolster their credibility are therefore more likely to generalize beyond the universe. First, the cases focus on compellence. Deterring a nuclear program from starting is easier than stopping one underway.[75] One reason is that compellence puts the initiative of action on the coercer, who must make the first move. The pain may have already begun and the coercer must pledge to stop it, whereas in deterrence no action has yet been taken by either side. Once an action has been taken, it is difficult to convince a target that it will stop.[76]

Second, these are generally cases in which coercers possess an asymmetrical advantage in relative power, which should impede the communication of credible assurance. Targets fear that stronger coercers will renege on their pledges not to punish because they can, and if they do, the weaker target may have little recourse. Threats between symmetrical powers should be more assuring because one party can punish the other for duplicity. In other words, their coercive bargains are mutually renegable. Assurance in asymmetrical coercion is more puzzling.

Third, each case of counterproliferation is of high stakes for the states involved. Targets care deeply about the outcome, mainly because it bears so greatly on their own security. If concessions affect the relative power between coercer and target, commitment problems are acute.[77] Credible coercive assurance should be more difficult to communicate if the target is being asked to renounce pursuit of a security asset, such as a nuclear weapons program. For the same reason, we might also expect this universe of cases to bias in favor of finding evidence that the magnitude of demands was a sticking point for coercive bargaining.

We should further expect that only the most determined proliferators select into the universe of cases because states calculate ahead of time that they are willing to run the risks of proliferating.[78] Coercers also decide to counter some programs and not others, thus we might expect coercers to attempt to compel only those targets whose compliance they deem to be possible. But because the consequences are so grave, there are few cases of proliferators who have not been challenged on their path to the bomb.[79] Moreover, the tool kit that coercers use to prevent proliferation is vast, and they devote significant resources to proliferation intelligence collection, offering data to calibrate their demands and threats.

Finally, the counterproliferation universe is useful for case studies and process tracing because there is ample evidence available. As better evidence emerges from archives, nuclear scholars have begun to show just how coercive and secretive enforcement of the nonproliferation regime has been historically—private threats, secret deals, winks and nods.[80] This follows a turn in the literature away from drivers of proliferation toward the process of proliferation[81]—decisions that states make along the way to the bomb[82]—and counterproliferation—why states attack nuclear programs,[83] when economic sanctions impede proliferation,[84] and how nuclear patrons coerce allies.[85] This book thus adds to our understanding of the strategic interactions of proliferators and counterproliferators,[86] including highlighting important dynamics of the coercive enforcement of the nonproliferation regime.[87]

For all the empirical progress on the dynamics and frequency of coercive counterproliferation, there remains a bigger and bigger puzzle in the study of nuclear politics: why is coercion ever successful in stemming nuclear proliferation? In a domain where violators are highly motivated by intense security fears and coercers are relatively strong (an impediment to coercion), it should be quite difficult to persuade a proliferator to abandon its pursuit of security via a nuclear ace. Yet, in reviewing this history, I estimate that compellent counterproliferation attempts have succeeded uncommonly often. This is in part due to the creativity coercers have shown in their strategies of coercive assurance.

Consider the full universe of proliferation cases ($n = 34$).[88] Of these proliferators, fourteen were targets of economic or military counterproliferation threats in a total of twenty-one attempts (see table 1.2).[89] (The same proliferator may account for multiple episodes of coercive counterproliferation if an earlier bargain broke down and renewed coercion began again or if multiple coercers attempted uncoordinated coercive efforts.) As table 1.2 shows, counterproliferators have successfully struck coercive bargains in fifteen out of twenty-one attempts.[90] Consistent with a strict but inclusive definition of "coercive success"—changing the behavior of a target to get it to do something it otherwise would not have done—I count any kind of concession. Examples may include closing and not replacing a facility, canceling a

Table 1.2 Coercive counterproliferation attempts

Counterproliferator(s)	Proliferator	Concession dates
US	Israel	None[a]
Egypt	Israel	None[b]
US	West Germany	1969–
US	Taiwan	1976–81
US	Taiwan	1988–
US	South Korea	1981–
Israel	Iraq	None[b]
US	Pakistan	None
USSR, US, France, UK	South Africa	1977
US	South Africa	1989–
US	Algeria	1992–
US, Russia	Kazakhstan	1992–
US, Russia	Belarus	1992–
US, UK, Russia	Ukraine	1994–
US	Iraq	1991–[b, c]
China, Russia, US, South Korea	North Korea	1994–2003
US, UK	Libya	2003–
EU3	Iran	2003–5
Six Party / US, South Korea	North Korea	None
P5+1, EU	Iran	2015–18
P5+1, EU	Iran	None yet

[a] Nuclear testing bargain not counted.

[b] Brute force used.

[c] Iraq conceded to coercion in 1991, but it was arguably not a true "bargain" because its primary coercer, the United States, did not accept that Iraq had actually made concessions. I do not consider in this table subsequent efforts to coerce compliance with inspectors and transparency from Iraq about its concessions. See chapter 3.

contract to purchase technology, surrendering equipment, or submitting to inspections. Some of these concessions may have proven to be temporary and others permanent, but all were nuclear concessions made during episodes of coercion. Moreover, proliferators who concede to coercive pressure may maintain some nuclear knowhow, even an intent to hedge for the future. Retreating from pursuit of a nuclear weapon to hedging with nuclear expertise or latency is still a concession. The proliferator has decided after all not to develop nuclear weapons today, and that is a behavioral change. I do not, however, count as a coercive bargain an effort to hide an ongoing nuclear weapons program in response to coercion. The proliferator's tactics may have changed while its policy has not.

The table shows a surprising 71 percent success rate. Counting cases of likely deterrent successes of just the prospect of economic sanctions (in Australia and Egypt) would put the figure even higher (74 percent).[91] And even including as "failures" cases where coercive confrontation was considered but rejected (Soviet Union, France, China, India) or cases met with covert brute force instead of coercion (Syria 2007), the success rate remains above 50 percent—well above the baseline of 35 percent average coercive success rates across other domains.[92] This success rate alone is not evidence for or against the assurance dilemma. I rely on the historical record only for case selection.

We also ought to consider an assurance selection effect in the historical record. It should be empirically rare to observe cases of reneged assurance after a coercive bargain is struck. Coercers that cannot credibly communicate coercive assurance will not successfully compel their targets to make concessions in the first place. Thus, unconditional punishments are feared by targets but uncommonly observed in practice. And yet we observe such examples in the nuclear space. Libya, Iran, Ukraine, and by some accounts Iraq have all been victims of reneged coercive assurances. Were these states wrong to believe that punishments would be lifted or prevented? Why did they believe it?

Moreover, cases of counterproliferation are not independent. New proliferators learn from the old; coercive enforcers can adapt their strategies. More broadly, therefore, why is coercion so common in the nonproliferation regime if there are such high-profile cases of reneging by coercers? Why are assurances ever believed? The nuclear literature has left many puzzles pertaining to the assurance dilemma.

CASE SELECTION WITHIN THE NONPROLIFERATION UNIVERSE

Given the small universe of cases and the need to parse alternative mechanisms, I turn to process tracing. This approach embraces what Elizabeth Saunders identifies in a review of the proliferation literature as "the continuing essential role of qualitative evidence . . . requir[ing] scholars to delve into leaders' beliefs and restricted domestic-political debates that are difficult to penetrate except through careful process tracing, often through primary documents or interviews."[93] The approach is also motivated by the foundational role of theory as a lens through which scholars can bring important aspects of historical cases into focus. John Mearsheimer calls theory a "powerful flashlight in a dark room" without which you would miss what is important to see.[94] In this book I use the assurance dilemma as a new lens to revisit cases and bring into focus new evidence that scholars may have overlooked with existing illumination techniques. As it turns out, coercers in the nonproliferation domain have demonstrated much innovation in their strategies of coercive assurance.

The ideal case study to test theory and mechanisms is one in which the proliferator had a concerted weapons program, was pressured to end it and permit inspections, and subsequently chose to come into compliance with the nonproliferation regime. At best, evidence should be available from the archives of the proliferator to reveal their intentions, perceptions, and assessments of coercion. A focus on targets is, borrowing John Lewis

Gaddis's parlance, an attempt to see "the hidden side of the moon" of coercive interactions that analysts so often only see from one perspective.[95] A lack of evidence on target perceptions has been identified as an all-too-common hindrance to the study of coercion.[96]

Coercive bargaining over the nuclear programs of South Africa, Iraq, Libya, and Iran meets these criteria. These are substantively important cases. South Africa is the only country known to have built and then dismantled a nuclear arsenal in its entirety. Iraq's Saddam Hussein frustrated his coercers by vacillating between compliance and defiance on nuclear matters. Muammar Qaddafi negotiated away Libya's nuclear program in 2003 only to be toppled in 2011 by rebels backed by the United States and its North Atlantic Treaty Organization (NATO) allies. Iran struck a coercive bargain to limit its nuclear program in 2015. But the deal unraveled in 2018 when the United States withdrew, leading to perpetual uncertainty about Iran's nuclear future. No definitive history of the Iran deal has yet been written.

These cases also complement each other in important ways that bolster the external validity of findings. First, Iraq, Libya, and Iran are enemies with their coercers, while South Africa was friendly with its coercer. Second, at least one primary coercer in each case is held constant (the United States), which is suitable given the substantive import of the United States as an international coercer and its core role in enforcing the nonproliferation regime.[97] Third, the tools of coercion also vary: sanctions against South Africa versus sanctions and threats of force against Iraq, Libya, and Iran. Fourth, the proliferator nuclear programs vary in their sophistication. Iran can produce large quantities of fissile material, while South Africa actually succeeded in assembling an arsenal. Libya's nuclear program was far less sophisticated and struggled to make technical breakthroughs. Existing coercion theories expect a proliferator with an advanced program to be harder to compel than a state struggling to produce fissile material or weapon designs.[98] We would want to know whether a proliferator with less to lose can be compelled into concessions without credible assurance.

WITHIN CASE VARIATION

These cases also capture variation on the dependent variable—success or failure of coercion—across and within cases. I emphasize in my analysis within-case variation to explain both the occurrence and, crucially, the timing of nonproliferation bargains.[99] Each case contains over time instances of coercive failure as well as instances of coercive success. Partial success is also possible when targets retreated in the face of pressure but did not actually abandon their nuclear programs.[100] These variations in outcomes provide greater confidence that in each case there was bargaining space, yet it took some determined coercive diplomacy to find it. Within each chapter,

I show that coercion failures usually did not merely reflect a lack of bargaining space.

The goals of this book are to estimate the effect of coercive assurance credibility on the outcome of coercion and interpret the causes of such credibility. Credibility is measured in the eye of the beholder. It is a perception. In cases of coercion, credibility is the target state's expectation about whether the coercer's deeds will match its words and signals. A threat is credible, regardless of the true intentions of the coercer, if the target expects the coercer to follow through on it under the specified circumstances. A threat is not credible if the target believes the threat to be empty. Likewise, coercive assurance is credible if the target expects that its concessions will reliably lead to no punishment. Coercive assurance is not credible if a target expects to be punished even if it concedes.

Thus, each case study traces the process of coercive bargaining, relying as much as possible on primary documents and interviews with policymaker participants. Some of my novel archival evidence comes from documents in the IAEA archives. As an international institution, the IAEA is a crucial interlocutor for coercive bargaining between the international community and potential proliferators. While the IAEA strives to maintain an apolitical stance, the information revealed through IAEA inspection is anything but apolitical.[101] Good evidence also comes from the archives of South Africa's apartheid government and the captured recordings of Saddam Hussein's meetings with his advisers in the Iraqi government. The writings and recollections of policymakers fill the gaps.

Measurements are best taken at key decision points in a target's internal decision-making about its nuclear program. Targets of compellence are not always consumed each and every day by the actions of their coercer; rather, they reevaluate their strategies in the face of compellence when there is new information to consider. At a moment when a target's leadership sat down to debate what to do in response to compellence, I endeavor to observe their perceptions of both threat and assurance credibility. If concessions come after the perception of credible threats alone, coercive assurance would be found to be a less necessary component of successful coercion. But if target perceptions of severe and credible threats are not associated with concessions, they are insufficient and something is missing from the formula for successful coercion. The necessity of credible assurance is affirmed by a change in the perception of credibly conditional threats preceding target concessions.

In each chapter, a table summarizes in given years the credibility of threats and coercive assurance. These are relative measures within each case. Credibility is a spectrum, but I code variation in three categories: low, medium, and high.[102] Speech evidence from primary sources about target perceptions is the preferred basis for coding, triangulated with changes in coercer strategy.[103]

The most important decision point is a moment when the target decided to concede to coercion. Acquiescence requires a target to adjust its behavior to conform to the demands of a coercer. When there is a moment of acquiescence, I am interested in target perceptions of credible threats, assurance, or both, and why. I am also interested in the counterfactual of how that target would have responded to coercion in the absence of credible assurance. I estimate this counterfactual by looking at key moments prior to decisions to concede. This approach exploits within-case variation. In other words, the counterfactual case that is "most similar" to a target that chooses to concede is, in fact, itself, at a moment before it chose to concede.[104]

Process tracing through the lens of the assurance dilemma illuminates new aspects of coercive nonproliferation cases. In each chapter I contrast my findings with conventional wisdoms and consider case-specific alternative explanations.

In this chapter I have defined the assurance dilemma in coercion and teed up the empirical chapters to come. Coercion cannot succeed without the contingent promise of withheld punishment: coercive assurance. But coercers face an assurance dilemma, whereby their efforts to bolster the credibility of their threats undermine the credibility of their coercive assurance. Targets have reason to fear that their coercers are being insincere and intend unconditional punishment. And even sincere coercers can be stymied by losing control over the application of punishment. Targets can be suspicious of entangled demands, spoilers, and revealing novel information through their concessions. Each of these potential assurance failings detailed in this chapter are logically distinct. However, they overlap in the real world and may interact in ways that magnify the problem of assurance. In practice the assurance dilemma is a difficult challenge. Three types of signals, tracked throughout this book, aim to bolster the credibility of coercive assurance: disentangling demands, managing spoilers, and sharing knowledge.

Chapters 2, 3, 4, and 5 present the cases of South Africa, Iraq, Libya, and Iran, respectively. Each case highlights how the lens of the assurance dilemma illuminates the most consequential strategic interactions of proliferators and counterproliferators. Leaders defied credible threats if they expected to be punished anyway. Perceptions of assurance could tip the outcome of coercion. Coercers who grappled with the hard problems of the assurance dilemma were more likely to strike coercive bargains.

"I at Least Want to Be Guilty"

Coercing South Africa into a Corner

This chapter explains the South African apartheid regime's decision-making about its nuclear program when it was subject to coercive pressure from the international community. From 1975 onward, the United States and others sought with varying intensity to compel South Africa to sign the NPT and submit all of its nuclear facilities to comprehensive safeguards. Save for Pretoria's decision to back down from a "cold" nuclear test in 1977, the effort failed. South Africa defied coercive demands and built six nuclear bombs. In 1989 the government dismantled its nuclear weapons ahead of the impending end of apartheid rule, and South Africa became the only country to have manufactured and fully destroyed a nuclear arsenal.

The assurance dilemma proves a powerful lens when passed over the South African case. South African leaders defied compellent demands because they perceived a lack of credible coercive assurance, not because they perceived compellent threats to be insufficiently credible or painful (see table 2.1). A short-lived bargain in 1977 came about through a strategy of sharing knowledge gathered through intelligence collection, but it was rapidly undermined by the perception of coercers' entanglement of nuclear and antiapartheid demands linked to economic sanctions. An opportunity to disentangle the two issues in Washington was thwarted by the US Congress acting as a spoiler. Coercers struggled with the assurance dilemma as South African leaders perceived coercive punishments to be credible and severe but chose to defy because they did not think that they could avoid pain by signing the NPT. I show this by examining three critical junctures in Pretoria's nuclear decision-making about how to respond to international pressure: in August and September 1977, September 1985, and 1986–88. Finally, examining South Africa's ultimate decision in 1989 to disarm ahead of the end of apartheid reveals the importance of information management to a target fearful of admitting its guilt. It does not, however, overturn

Table 2.1 South Africa

Date	Concessions	Threat credibility	Threat severity	Assurance credibility	Consistent with assurance dilemma?
1977	Partial	High	Low	Medium	✓
1985	No	High	High	Low	✓
1986–88	No	High	High	Low	✓
1989–93	Yes	High	High	High	~[a]

[a] While the assurance dilemma is not invalidated, South Africa gave up its nuclear arsenal and signed the NPT for reasons largely unrelated to coercive assurance.

conventional wisdom on the proximate cause of South Africa's nuclear disarmament: the end of apartheid.

This chapter relies on primary documents from the South African government and the IAEA to explain South African behavior. The IAEA was a crucial interlocutor for coercive bargaining between the international community and Pretoria. To give in to IAEA demands was often to give in to US demands. I supplement these documents with the recollections and writings of South African policymakers, military leaders, and nuclear scientists—Prime Minister John Vorster, Minister of Defense and later Prime Minister and then President P. W. Botha, Minister of Foreign Affairs R. F. "Pik" Botha, President F. W. de Klerk, and scientists and engineers such as Andre Buys, Nic von Wielligh, and Waldo Stumpf. It is essential to understand their own perceptions of the credibility of coercive threats and assurances, even with selective memory in their reporting.

Improving Existing Explanations

Established accounts provide good evidence for the security drivers of proliferation in South Africa and the end of apartheid as the cause of its nuclear dismantlement. Governed by a small circle of "securocrats" who were hypersensitive to the minority ruling class's internal and external security threats,[1] the former Dutch and British colony was acutely fearful of the Soviet Union and its regional proxies in Africa. Its fortunes in the war in Angola soured with the loss of Central Intelligence Agency (CIA) backing in 1975 and the sudden arrival of Cuban forces. Its regional security situation remained fraught throughout the 1980s.[2] With no security patron, Pretoria sought a nuclear insurance policy that saw it through the rest of the terrifying Cold War. These security drivers explain South Africa's nuclear acquisition.

Furthermore, at the end of the Cold War, South Africa disarmed because of a unique confluence of factors, chief among them the end of apartheid rule and a transition to democratic government. The December 1988 Brazzaville Protocol (a.k.a. the New York Accords) saw to the withdrawal of Cuban forces.[3] The subsequent collapse of the Soviet Union was a significant boon to South Africa's security and reduced its need for a nuclear deterrent. Most importantly, President De Klerk saw the writing on the wall for South Africa's apartheid government, the ire for which was only growing because of a transnational human rights campaign of naming and shaming.[4] In anticipation of a transition to democratic government and Black majority rule, racist South African leaders dismantled their nuclear arsenal rather than hand it over to the African National Congress (ANC) and Nelson Mandela.[5] Other factors included De Klerk's personal moral aversion to nuclear weapons and the disintegration of bureaucratic or technical-scientific consensus in support of an expensive nuclear program in the late 1980s.[6]

These established accounts emphasize the lens of threat credibility in the history of apartheid South Africa's defiance of coercive counterproliferation.[7] Its intense demand for nuclear protection made Pretoria resistant to external pressure, the argument goes, and that it was an anticommunist bulwark in Africa was enough to water down opposition to its nuclear proliferation. Neither of these factors is sufficient to answer the key questions of coercion at the heart of this case: Why did South Africa not give in to pressure to sign the NPT? Why did coercion fail for so long?

This chapter begins by reaching back to the origins of South Africa's nuclear program and motivation to acquire the bomb. It then describes the start of coercion against Pretoria and how it began to perceive the entanglement of two issues—nuclear proliferation and apartheid. The chapter subsequently examines the Kalahari crisis of 1977 and South Africa's construction of nuclear weapons, explains South Africa's decision-making when sanctions were hurting in the 1980s, and reviews its negotiations with the IAEA about safeguards. The chapter concludes with an explanation of South Africa's decision to dismantle the arsenal in 1989 and the tacit collusion that followed.

South Africa's Nuclear Program

NUCLEAR AMBITIONS

South Africa joined the ranks of capable nuclear states quickly.[8] Upon discovering abundant natural uranium deposits, it established an Atomic Energy Board (AEB) in 1948. The country developed into a major uranium producer after it signed purchasing agreements with the United States and the United Kingdom in 1950.[9] At the time the US and the UK thought uranium was scarce and that they needed to secure their access.

The United States and South Africa subsequently signed a nuclear cooperation agreement in 1957 as part of the Atoms for Peace program.[10] Under the deal, the United States supplied South Africa with a research reactor, Safari-1, safeguarded since 1965. The sharing arrangement did not set any coercive red lines on South African nuclear ambitions. Later, however, South Africa refused to sign the NPT, and the US nuclear fuel supply proved to be a source of leverage. Nuclear research also began at the Pelindaba Nuclear Research Center in 1961, overseen by South Africa's AEB.[11]

South Africa began a secret effort to develop an indigenous uranium-enrichment capacity in the 1960s. By 1967 South African scientists at the Pelindaba Nuclear Research Center had tested at laboratory scale a vortex-tube method for uranium enrichment.[12] The process was soon expanded to a pilot enrichment facility called the Y-plant. The first stage of the enrichment cascade was completed by the end of 1974, and the whole cascade was operational by March 1977.[13] Set up right next to Pelindaba, the Y-plant was built in a location aptly named Valindaba, a compound Sotho word meaning "we don't talk about this."[14]

For some time, the indigenous enrichment capability was merely motivated by economic factors—a desire to exploit the commercial potential of South Africa's abundant uranium deposits. Soon, the enrichment capacity became a clear hedge and then more.

Prime Minister John Vorster made the political decision to explore nuclear weapons technology in 1969 when he established through the AEB a committee to investigate the feasibility of building "peaceful nuclear explosives" (PNEs) for mining applications.[15] In March 1971 Carl de Wet, the minister of mines, approved the committee's recommendations to develop PNEs.[16] Then, in 1974 Vorster seamlessly shifted the objectives of this research from PNEs to a nuclear deterrent,[17] at the same time approving a plan to develop a nuclear test site in the Kalahari Desert.[18]

A DETERIORATING REGIONAL SECURITY SITUATION

What motivated South Africa to pursue nuclear weapons? In the mid-1970s South Africa faced a deteriorating regional security situation. Mozambique and Angola won independence from Portugal in 1975, and Pretoria watched as white colonists fled. The Soviet Union moved to fill the vacuum left by Portugal, and Black African nationalism expanded as minority rule ended in Southern Rhodesia (which became Zimbabwe) and put pressure on South African–controlled Namibia.

With the clandestine backing of the United States under President Gerald Ford, South Africa intervened against rebels in the Angolan Civil War in October 1975. When the secret US aid was exposed, however, the US, at the behest of Congress, withdrew its support.[19] Cuba took advantage and sent troops to Angola to support the rebels. (Cuban military advisers had already been involved in the conflict.) Soon Soviet weapons and logistical support followed. A lonely South Africa found itself with multiple enemies and few friends.[20] On March 27, 1975, P. W. Botha announced that the defense budget would increase by 36 percent, accounting for a total of 20 percent of the overall national budget.[21] Nuclear weapons took their place within this strategic picture.[22] During this time, South Africa also began to face the opprobrium of the international community.

Hydra-Headed Compellence over Apartheid and the NPT

White minority–ruled South Africa had institutionalized the separation of races after the surprise election of the National Party in 1948. Under the guise of equal development, the brutal policies of apartheid, meaning "apartness," required South Africans to register their ethnicities with the government, prohibited intermarriage and socialization, and forcibly removed "black," "colored," and "Indian" populations from white areas, among other iniquities. The descendants of European (mostly Dutch) settlers championed the racist policies as a method of preserving their Afrikaner identity.[23]

For a long time, the United States did not take action to oppose apartheid. It served US interests that South Africa's proapartheid National Party was fiercely anticommunist. When the government in Pretoria banned the ANC and the Pan Africanist Congress opposition parties from political participation in 1960 and imprisoned their leaders in 1963, the John F. Kennedy administration vetoed punitive United Nations (UN) resolutions and supported only a voluntary arms embargo against South Africa.[24]

Coercers came down harder in the 1970s. International coordination to condemn Pretoria for apartheid began in the UN. On October 24, 1970, the UN General Assembly (UNGA) passed Resolution 2627, calling apartheid "a crime against the conscience and dignity of mankind"; on October 5, 1973, it rejected the South African delegation's credentials; on November 28, 1973, Arab states imposed oil sanctions on South Africa; and on November 30, 1973, the UNGA ratified the International Convention on the Suppression and Punishment of the Crime of Apartheid in Resolution 3068.[25] An October 1974 motion to remove South Africa from the UN failed only because it was vetoed by the United States, France, and the United Kingdom, who while vetoing finally made clear their opposition to apartheid and expressed their desire that continued membership in the UN would result in changes to the state.[26]

At this time, too, coercers began to be warier of South Africa's nuclear intentions. Pretoria refused to sign the newly in force NPT and continued to make progress on enrichment technology. Observers feared that little could stop them from indigenously enriching uranium to weapons grade.

The United States began to engage in compellence against South Africa in 1975. There had been no mention of nuclear weapons or an end to US nuclear cooperation when the Kennedy administration took the half measure of supporting a voluntary arms embargo in 1963.[27] But in 1975 and 1976 the Ford administration imposed sanctions and discontinued the supply of fuel for the Safari-1 reactor, even refusing to reimburse South Africa its payments for the fuel.[28] These punishments were not yet severe but would grow over time. South Africa thus became the world's first target of US nonproliferation-related sanctions in 1975.[29]

Compellent demands to end apartheid also intensified in 1976 after a brutal state crackdown on the Soweto riots drew international public outrage.[30] The Jimmy Carter administration accelerated US compellent efforts. In a January 1977 meeting with Pik Botha, then the South African ambassador to the United States, US national security adviser Zbigniew Brzezinski warned that "the U.S. will never intervene in the conflict on the side of a white minority government, even if communists were involved."[31] Carter further labeled apartheid "a threat to international peace and security" in an October 25, 1977, speech and subsequently backed mandatory UN arms sanctions.[32] The UN Security Council (UNSC) voted in favor of this binding arms embargo on November 4.

South Africa was also voted off the IAEA board of governors in 1977.[33] On September 28, 1976, the IAEA general conference had formally requested that the board of governors consider the removal of South Africa from its seat on the board representing the region of Africa. And the IAEA board of governors took up the resolution at its meeting on June 16, 1977.[34] Jo-Ansie van Wyk, a scholar of South African–IAEA relations, writes that the IAEA's actions aimed "to persuade the South African government to terminate its nuclear weapons programme."[35] Nonetheless, the resolution cited "flagrant violations by the apartheid regime" of the UN Charter, asserting that "the apartheid regime of South Africa totally lacks any claim to be representative of the legitimate interests and aspirations of the area of Africa."[36] At the meeting, members, save South Africa itself, universally condemned the practice of apartheid, though some (including the US) sought to maintain South Africa's seat in accordance with the IAEA Statute. Article VI of the statute originally allotted thirteen seats on the board of governors to the member states "most advanced in the technology of atomic energy including the production of source materials" and included a provision to ensure representation from every geographic region.[37] South Africa was the obvious member to fill the African seat and had done so since 1957. Nevertheless, the board voted to remove South Africa and replace it with Egypt, a state with less advanced nuclear technology.[38] The compellent move was seen in Pretoria as humiliating.[39] South Africa began to perceive the two issues—nuclear and apartheid—as becoming linked.

The Kalahari Crisis of 1977

In August 1977 the United States and South Africa came head to head in a crisis over the latter's nuclear ambitions. South African leaders reflected on the Kalahari crisis as a "watershed moment" in South Africa's pursuit of nuclear weapons. In terms of testing theories of coercion, 1977 was a crucial moment at which Pretoria stared down Washington on nuclear proliferation and carefully considered whether to defy its compellent demands.

The assurance dilemma took center stage. During this episode, South Africa judged compellent threats to be credible. The threatened pain was also quite severe, though South Africa had not yet suffered the bulk of international sanctions that would later be placed upon it. Nonetheless, the primary driver of South African defiance was a perceived lack of coercive assurance.

THE KALAHARI CRISIS

As part of its clandestine pursuit of nuclear weapons technology South Africa dug two test shafts in the Kalahari Desert. They were hundreds of feet deep. With a flimsy cover story of drilling for water, the first shaft was completed in 1976 and the second in 1977. Local farmers referred to them as "the atom shafts," as "everybody knew there was no water in those parts."[40]

The secrecy did not hold long. In July 1977 two Soviet satellites photographed suspicious drilling equipment and boreholes in the Kalahari.[41] On August 6 the Soviets passed news of their discovery to the United States in a message from Soviet leader Leonid Brezhnev to President Jimmy Carter.[42] "According to incoming data on the South African Republic," Brezhnev wrote, the South Africans "are completing work on building nuclear weapons and on carrying out the first nuclear test. In the desert of Calabari [Kalahari] they have built a testing site which is practically ready."[43] US intelligence analysts verified the evidence and concluded that indeed "the Kalahari facility could have no military purpose other than nuclear testing."[44]

Only two days later, the Soviet Union announced publicly in a news item by TASS (the state-owned news agency Telegrafnoye agentstvo Sovetskogo Soyuza) that South Africa intended to test a nuclear weapon, without saying how or where.[45] The next day, another TASS announcement accused the West (NATO and Israel, in particular) of aiding South African nuclear weapons development.[46] Finally, on August 18 the Soviets slipped details about the Kalahari location into an additional news item.[47] The US embassy in Moscow cabled Washington with a quick translation.[48]

As the Soviets had wished, the United States and others brought coercive pressure to bear on Pretoria. Brezhnev's letter indeed specifically called out the United States' coercive leverage, saying that the Americans have "at their disposal the necessary channels and possibilities for the rendering of a direct restricting influence on this state."[49] UN ambassador Andrew Young, a Carter confidante, sent a cable to the president and the secretary of state warning that South Africa's intransigence regarding the NPT and safeguards "leaves us holding the bag before the international community on the question of South Africa's nuclear plans."[50] The US would have to confront Pretoria.

On August 18, the US ambassador to South Africa, William Bowdler, threatened South African foreign minister Pik Botha: "In light of the grave implications President Carter has instructed me to make clear that the detonation of a nuclear device . . . or any other further steps to acquire or develop a nuclear explosive capability would have the most serious consequences for all aspects of our relations and would be considered by us as a serious threat to peace."[51] Bowdler repeated the not-so-implicit sanctions threat by reiterating that Botha "should also be aware of the possibility that the issue may arise in the United Nations Security Council on short notice with unforeseeable results."[52] Other démarches came pouring in, threatening diplomatic rifts and sanctions, including a threat from France to cut off fuel it supplied for South Africa's Koeberg nuclear power station.[53]

Evidence from the coercive bargaining reveals the importance of shared knowledge to the South African target, which was loath to admit anything its coercers did not already know about its nuclear weapons program. Initially, Pik Botha and others reacted with outrage and denial, demanding evidence. Brand Fourie, the secretary of foreign affairs who later entered the meeting between Bowdler and Botha, issued further denials and asked for "proof of the assertion."[54] US secretary of state Cyrus Vance followed up and in an August 19, 1977, letter confronted the South Africans with evidence. "We are prepared to show you photographs," wrote Vance, who referred to specific coordinates in the desert of a drilling rig, lattice tower, power and communication lines, secured housing, an airstrip, and an outer patrol road—all consistent with a nuclear test site.[55] In an oral history, Pik Botha recalled the US ambassador placing on his desk "10–12 photographs" of "a drill in an arid region."[56]

The two sides shared knowledge of South Africa's plans, and both Pretoria and Washington knew it. Carter scrawled in the margins of a memo from Brzezinski: "Zbig—what we want is: no test. If they have to lie about what their plans were, let them do so—Let them save face. J. C."[57] And next to Brzezinski's recommendation that "our primary aim must be to get as much information about what the South Africans are really doing," Carter scrawled, "no—Assure no test."[58]

Botha took the information to Vorster, who agreed not to conduct a planned cold test.[59] After an exchange of diplomatic cables,[60] South Africa further agreed to make three pledges to end the crisis:[61] (1) that South Africa did not intend to develop nuclear explosive devices, (2) that the Kalahari test site was not designed for use to test nuclear explosives, and (3) that no nuclear explosive tests would be taken in South Africa.[62] President Carter announced the pledges at a press conference on August 23.[63] In a message to Vance, Botha further expressed South Africa's willingness to "enter into discussions with the United States on all aspects of South Africa's nuclear policy including the question of South Africa's accession to the Non-Proliferation Treaty."[64] Behind the scenes, South African leaders had no intention of honoring these pledges.

KALAHARI COMPELLENCE BACKFIRES

The Kalahari episode merely pushed the South African nuclear program underground. What a post hoc CIA assessment concluded was successful coercion had actually backfired.[65] South Africa interpreted the Kalahari testing fiasco as a "watershed" moment.[66] The United States had sought an end to South Africa's clandestine proliferation activities and to get Pretoria's signature of the NPT to prove it. But after 1977, in the words of Frank Pabian, the South African government believed that it had "no alternative but to develop a nuclear deterrent."[67] Pretoria doubled down on its nuclear ambitions.

The threat credibility lens struggles to explain this episode of coercion. Compellent threats from the United States and others were perceived as credible by South Africa. An August 31, 1977, dispatch from the South African embassy in Washington reported back to Pretoria that "the thesis that South Africa poses a threat to world peace is immensely reinforced and will be exploited in the UN"; thus, "the prospect of a chapter VII sanctions resolution is thus brought measurabl[y] nearer."[68] Furthermore, the pressure was great. An anonymous US official reported of the interactions, "We were pretty severe in private."[69] Speaking more broadly of foreign relations in the 1970s, Pik Botha recalled, "During the whole protracted period, there was severe pressure on us from Washington."[70]

But South Africa did not buckle under the pressure. Its leaders did not see abandonment of their nuclear weapons program as an option that would avoid punishment. Rather, they perceived inevitable pain. The embassy in Washington assessed that acquiescence to international pressure would not yield positive results. "United States policy vis-à-vis black Africa in general and vis-à-vis white ruled Southern Africa in particular," assessed the embassy, "has developed a momentum of its own to which it would now be difficult to apply a brake, even in the unlikely event of the Carter administration undergoing a change of heart."[71] Andre Buys, future chairman of the state-owned Armaments Corporation (Armscor) working group on nuclear strategy, later described the choice: "We must either terminate the program now, or we must go for nuclear weapons ourselves. If

I have to take the punishment, I at least want to be guilty."[72] Buys also referred to the Kalahari episode as a "watershed moment."[73] And a 1977 policy paper by Neil Barnard concluded that "the acquisition of nuclear weapons will not necessarily isolate South Africa any further."[74] This evidence is consistent with the absence of coercive assurance.

Despite the crisis abating, South African policymakers now expected an escalation of economic sanctions. The embassy assessed that the Carter administration was likely to use the moment to increase pressure on South Africa—the Kalahari episode being "further substantiation of the thesis of the Carter administration that pressure on South Africa is more productive" and that the latest crisis only provided "incentive to step up the pressures."[75] In this environment, they reasoned, South Africa should expect even less harbor from potential friends—"supporters (in Western Europe for example) will be able in future to offer less effective resistance to proposals for economic sanctions."[76] "South Africa is far more exposed than ever before," a cable concluded.[77] "Whether or not South Africa does in fact have the bomb"—it did not yet—"the overall effect . . . has been to make the international community believe that South Africa has manufactured a nuclear device. . . . Nothing can be the same again."[78]

Coercive assurance was undermined by Pretoria's perception that the world was "mad already" at South Africa. The two compellent demands of Pretoria—that it sign the NPT and end apartheid—merged in the minds of South Africans. Such an entangled web of compellent punishments and threats of more pain to come undermined the coercive assurance of either individual demand. According to the nuclear scientist Von Wielligh, "these events finally persuaded the South Africans that the sanctions against the country were of a political nature and that they had nothing to gain from joining the NPT."[79] Another lead scientist, Waldo Stumpf, also reports that at the end of the 1970s "these events convinced the South African government that the various sanctions were clearly politically inspired, and that Pretoria's accession to the NPT without fundamental political reform at home would not gain South Africa international acceptance."[80] Nuclear sanctions and demands to join the NPT lacked coercive assurance. Capitulation would not credibly make the punishment subside.

In this context, the leaders of the nuclear program decided that they faced a choice between giving in—remaining at the threshold of a bomb—or continuing to develop weapons in secrecy. When, in the wake of the Kalahari crisis, Andre Buys sought clarification from Minister of Defense P. W. Botha on the purpose of the nuclear program, he asked, "Do you have nuclear weapons in mind, or is just the ability to demonstrate that we have this knowledge sufficient?" He recalled, "The answer came back, firmly: nuclear weapons."[81]

COMPELLENCE CONTINUES

South Africa's coercers doubled down, exacerbating their assurance dilemma. In November 1977, after the Kalahari crisis, the UNSC issued its arms embargo in Resolution 418. It set a red line explicitly at nuclear weapons development, saying, "All states shall refrain from any cooperation with South Africa in the manufacture and development of nuclear weapons."[82] In the mind of Von Wielligh, "this offensive resolution brought home even more clearly to the South African government the fact that they were on their own." Armscor grew to indigenously fill an increased arms production demand.[83]

To their credit, US Department of State officials after Kalahari seemed to diagnose the correct problem with US strategy. The State Department internally debated what to do about the South African nuclear program after 1977 and lamented that Pretoria did not respond to US proposals for renewed cooperation and its signature of the NPT because Pretoria "considers us unreliable on fuel supply and on our commitment to veto UN sanctions; it regards the Administration and elements of the Congress as hostile."[84] Even more prophetic, they seemed aware of the entanglement of apartheid and nuclear issues but deemed them inseparable. "We cannot divorce the nuclear issue from political problems, but we should try to get it dealt with in a less highly charged framework than is now the case," Andrew Young wrote in a memo for the president and the secretary of state that was passed to Zbigniew Brzezinski.[85] Of course, US policy was not up to the State Department alone or even its branch of government.

In 1978 Congress passed the Nuclear Non-Proliferation Act (NNPA), which became the Carter administration's chief cudgel of compellence against South Africa. The full credible cutoff of any further nuclear cooperation with the United States was made clear with the passage of the NNPA, which outlawed US nuclear assistance to any country that had not signed the NPT and accepted full-scope safeguards. The NNPA did not mention apartheid, but congressional interest in reining in South Africa's human rights abuses was growing. As Peter Liberman writes, "anti-apartheid domestic sentiment would have made it difficult for a U.S. president to restore cooperation with South Africa even had it joined the NPT."[86]

Despite contracts to supply the fuel for South Africa's Koeberg nuclear facility, Carter refused to supply the fuel without Pretoria's signature of the NPT and continued the policy of denying reimbursement of the funds already paid for Safari-1 fuel.[87] South Africa was particularly upset by this means of US pressure because both Safari-1 and Koeberg were subject to IAEA safeguards.[88] In their eyes, these were their legitimate facilities, and even they were not free from US interference.

Pretoria further perceived the addition of insult to injury when the South African delegation was denied participation in the 1979 IAEA general conference in India. South Africa's nuclear program had become a standing item of concern on the IAEA general conference's agenda.

SOUTH AFRICA BUILDS ITS ARSENAL

Nothing its coercers did pushed South Africa off its path to the bomb after the Kalahari affair. In July 1977 Minister of Defense P. W. Botha had requested "national strategic guidelines" for the production of nuclear weapons and, after Kalahari, approved those plans on April 4, 1978. Botha then became prime minister in October 1978 and appointed the Witvlei Committee to guide the nuclear program. On July 4, 1979, Botha approved the committee's recommendations to building seven nuclear weapons and transferred responsibility to Armscor, which built a new facility dedicated to the production of nuclear weapons—the Kentron Circle facility (a.k.a. Advena), fifteen kilometers east of Pelindaba.[89] By November 1979 the Y-plant had produced enough highly enriched uranium (HEU) to arm a nuclear device with a fissile core.[90] South Africa's first device, code-named Melba, was completed by the end of 1979.[91] And its first aircraft-deliverable nuclear weapon, code-named Cabot, was completed in December 1982.[92] The rest of the weapons in South Africa's arsenal—all gun-type bombs with two spherical halves—were produced at the pace of HEU production.[93]

US intelligence struggled to follow the developments of South Africa's indigenous enrichment program after the 1977 Kalahari crisis. A 1978 CIA assessment acknowledged South Africa's ability to produce weapons-grade HEU but noted "we have little doubt about South Africa's ability to produce a device, but we have little evidence that they have yet developed a deployable weapon."[94] The more sobering conclusion: "We are still far from certain what the South Africans are up to. We do not know precisely what their capabilities are, or how they got there."[95] US intelligence agencies likewise suspected but could not prove that South Africa had built nuclear weapons in the early 1980s.[96] The CIA never did seem to know of the Kentron Circle facility, which housed the nuclear weapons in vaults.[97]

This ambiguity was central to South Africa's chosen nuclear posture. Pretoria's nuclear strategy was simple and relied only on the ability to detonate a nuclear device, not necessarily to deliver it. It planned to rattle its nuclear saber and even test a nuclear weapon openly to catalyze US support in a crisis.[98] In the words of President P. W. Botha, "Once we set this thing off, the Yanks will come running."[99] The nuclear strategy began with opacity. South Africa continued to refuse to sign the NPT.

Pretoria Confronts the Bite of Sanctions

During the next episode, South Africa judged compellent threats to be credible and even more painful. Sanctions were hurting the economy, and Pretoria wanted to end the pain. Nonetheless, South Africa remained opposed to signing the NPT because its leaders still perceived a lack of coercive assurance. They did not believe that signing the NPT would remove the compellent sanctions.

A LACK OF US COERCIVE CONTROL

In the 1980s the Ronald Reagan administration set out to pursue a more accommodating strategy with South Africa—a policy of "constructive engagement."[100] When President Reagan met with Minister of Foreign Affairs Pik Botha on May 15, 1981, he communicated for the first time a willingness to disentangle the two issues of nuclear weapons and apartheid. "The President, in welcoming the Minister, made it clear that he was no advocate of what he called 'one man, one vote once,'" read the meeting notes, "the inference clearly being that he had no illusions about democratic rule in Africa."[101] Reagan was in essence taking one demand off the table—fundamental political reform—that was complicating compellence over signing the NPT.

But Reagan also backed off on demands for a change in South African nuclear behavior. In the same meeting, Botha expressed South Africa's unwillingness to sign the NPT lest it "terminate the speculation about South Africa's possession of the bomb," which was a "deterrent of major psychological value."[102] Reagan was "particularly struck by this last argument which had not occurred to him before" and communicated his desire to break with the "previous administration's policy in this [nuclear] field."[103] In the May 1981 meeting, in exchange for Reagan supplying reactor fuel for Koeberg, Botha committed to "not execute an explosive test without first consulting the American Government."[104] The White House followed through.[105]

As the Reagan administration eased open US–South African relations, strong objections emerged from public interest groups and the antiapartheid faction of the US Congress. The small window of accommodation rapidly began to close. Sanctions legislation had been introduced in 1982, and by the end of 1984 comprehensive sanctions "appeared inevitable."[106] The window shut completely by 1985, as the US Senate overwhelmingly passed (80 to 12) a sanctions bill on July 11, totally banning nuclear commerce with South Africa.[107] The House had passed a sanctions bill earlier in June, so a conference committee set to work on writing compromise legislation.[108] To preempt an embarrassing policy defeat, Reagan signed an executive order on September 9, 1985, prohibiting the transfer of any materials or technologies that would support South Africa's nuclear enterprise.[109] But any hopes for exerting coercive control by managing spoilers departed when both houses of Congress passed the Comprehensive Anti-Apartheid Act (CAAA) in 1986, overriding the president's veto. The veto had lamented, in part, that the CAAA "discards our economic leverage, constricts our diplomatic freedom, and ties the hands of the President of the United States."[110] The CAAA came into effect on January 1, 1987.

At this point, the compellent demands of signing the NPT and abandoning apartheid were perceived by South Africa to be as entangled as ever. The CAAA now officially combined antiapartheid and nuclear demands in a single piece of legislation. Aimed primarily at compelling changes to apartheid, the act also outlawed any further nuclear cooperation with South Africa until it signed the NPT.[111] The "prohibitions on nuclear trade with South Africa" were listed as "measures by the United States to undermine apartheid."[112]

A lack of coercive control over domestic spoilers exacerbated the strategic problem. In a 1986 meeting with the US ambassador-at-large for nuclear affairs, Richard T. Kennedy, Pik Botha indicated some willingness to bargain over joining the NPT with "serious reservations." Kennedy rejected any conditional accession and "warned Botha that due to congressional pressure, relief from broader sanctions would be contingent on South Africa's progress on internal political reforms."[113] The coercive assurances of US compellent demands were undermined by the perception of entangled demands and domestic spoilers.

PRETORIA CONDUCTS A CRITICAL APPRAISAL

By the mid-1980s, sanctions were biting in South Africa. Creditors called in loans, and Pretoria resorted to capital controls to fight capital flight.[114] From 1975 to 1991, South Africa experienced about 1.6 percent annual GDP growth,[115] compared to a population growth rate of 3 percent and a recent historical experience of 5 percent annual growth.[116] A report on the effect of sanctions in South Africa found that financial sanctions had cost South Africa $15 billion to $27 billion.[117] Inflation was over 15 percent by the end of the decade.[118] The economy withered.[119]

In this context, the government held an ad hoc cabinet committee meeting on September 3, 1985. The purpose was to discuss South Africa's response to international compellence. Sanctions were hurting. According to Von Wielligh, "the committee had to reconsider the existing nuclear weapons programme and the additional materials and facilities that would have to be provided in future."[120] The meeting's participants were the president, the minister of defense, the minister of finance, the minister of foreign affairs, the minister of mineral and energy affairs, the director-general of mineral and energy affairs, the chairman of Armscor, and the chairman of the Atomic Energy Corporation (AEC).[121] This was a key decision moment for a target of coercion. The committee was "juggling a number of issues simultaneously and had to strike a balance between funding restrictions, international and American sanctions, the war in Angola, the internal state of emergency, and the scope and purpose of the nuclear weapons programme."[122]

Pretoria again chose to defy compellence. The ad hoc committee decided to keep the number of nuclear weapons limited to seven—consistent with the modest initial goals of the South African nuclear program. Enriched uranium and lithium-6 production would continue as required for the seven weapons, but plans to produce plutonium were scrapped.[123] The committee also agreed to upgrade the Kentron Circle facility and added a new facility—Advena Central Laboratories—for the total cost of R 36 million, about three to four times the annual budget of the weapons program in the early 1980s (R 10 million). Despite the cost-cutting pressure, the nuclear program budget also continued to increase; by the end of the 1980s the annual budget was R 20 million to R 25 million.[124] Missile research would also continue apace. And the catalytic nuclear strategy was reaffirmed. The ad hoc committee also chose to play for time on the question of IAEA inspections for a semicommercial enrichment plant (called the Z-plant), under construction at the time. At no point was the committee willing to consider signing the NPT.

Not by coincidence, Botha delivered his famous "Rubicon" speech just weeks earlier, on August 15, 1985. Widely anticipated to be an announcement of political reforms, including the release of Nelson Mandela, Botha instead recommitted Pretoria to the apartheid status quo to a live audience of two hundred million listeners.[125] "We have had to contend with escalating violence within South Africa, and pressure from abroad in the form of measures designed to coerce the government into giving in to various demands," argued Botha. "We have never given in to outside demands and we are not going to do so now." He declared, "We are today crossing the Rubicon. There can be no turning back."[126]

The nuclear program was no different. In the words of Waldo Stumpf, "in September 1985 the entire nuclear weapons effort was reviewed once again and President Botha reconfirmed that the program would be limited to seven fission devices."[127] The program remained as envisioned in 1979. Pretoria would not sign the NPT.

Negotiating Safeguards with the IAEA

Throughout the 1980s, South Africa also negotiated with the IAEA over accepting safeguards at all its nuclear facilities. The purpose of these meetings to Pretoria was cosmetic—a modest release valve for international pressure. Nevertheless, the records of these negotiations are an important window into the minds of the South African leadership. The IAEA was a significant interlocutor for coercive bargaining with South Africa over its nuclear program. While the IAEA had little coercive power of its own, it was a venue through which South Africa could communicate its positions and willingness or unwillingness to compromise. To defy the IAEA was to defy coercers. Accepting full-scope safeguards required working with the IAEA. Through communications with Pretoria and the deliberations of the IAEA board of governors, scholars can observe the tangled compellent demands of nuclear safeguards and apartheid and South African fears of concessions on inspections leading to greater punishment over its bad faith. South Africa judged compellent threats to be credible and costly. Yet South Africa continued to refuse to give in to compellence and sign the NPT because its leaders perceived a lack of coercive assurance.

The primary subject of communications was the safeguarding of the Z-plant. In August 1976 Pretoria had informed the IAEA of its intention to build a commercial uranium-enrichment plant and submit it for safeguarding. The IAEA responded with proposed text for such a safeguards agreement. In response, South Africa requested a delay until the plant's capacity and design were settled. Years went by until a January 1984 AEC press release included a reference to its willingness to restart Z-plant negotiations.[128] Rounds of talks were held in August 1984, February 1985, and April 1986.

As the historian Robin Möser shows, the South Africans had no intention of accepting full-scope safeguards in the mid-1980s.[129] The Witvlei Committee in the early 1980s had decided already that they would not accept full-scope safeguards and later that "negotiations with the IAEA should be delayed and dragged for as long as possible . . . [and, if feasible] . . . an attempt should be made to derail the negotiations at such a late stage and in such a way that South Africa suffers as little political damage as possible."[130] Allowing inspection of the semicommercial Z-plant would have revealed to the IAEA the extent of Pretoria's foreign technology procurement, leading to even more foreign restrictions. "Therefore, by 1985, leading figures in the nuclear-weapon program believed that the South African government was better off facing yet even more sanctions and a threat to their continued IAEA membership than it would have been after in-plant inspections by IAEA staff," concludes Möser. Indeed, "South Africans engaged in discussions with US nonproliferation officials and the IAEA Secretariat primarily to reduce international criticism and to limit the impact of additional sanctions, such as the blocking of IMF loans."[131]

To drag out negotiations, South Africa insisted on three special exceptions to safeguards: (1) to allow the diversion of fissile material for "military non-explosive purposes," (2) that the agreement would terminate if South African rights to participate in the IAEA were ever curtailed, suspended, or withdrawn (something very much debated at the agency), and (3) the right to terminate the agreement if it ever jeopardized the "supreme interests" of South Africa.[132] In a series of letters, IAEA director general Hans Blix repeatedly told South African representatives that the terms would not be acceptable to the IAEA. And Pretoria effectively called off the negotiations in a February 25, 1987, letter, in which it complained about a lack of credible coercive assurance.[133] Regarding the demand that it sign the NPT, the letter said, "The South African Government has also declared that it remains willing to consider accession to the NPT, provided its basic requirements could be met. Under the present international situation where punitive sanctions and boycotts are being imposed on South Africa by the international community, its basic requirements are certainly threatened." The letter further called for an end to negotiations with the IAEA "in view of the prevailing intransigent attitude towards South Africa."[134]

South African representatives were not wrong in their perception. As the nuclear program became a recurring item on the agenda of the IAEA board of governors and general conference, meeting records reveal a strong tangling of the nuclear issue with apartheid. In 1981 South Africa was removed from the IAEA's Committee on Assurance of Supply (the US abstaining in the vote). The resolution blended nuclear and apartheid issues, citing both that South Africa was a "racist regime" and that "the nuclear programme of the racist regime of South Africa constitutes a grave danger to international peace."[135] Many ambassadors in board of governors meetings, including from major powers, regularly referred to South Africa as a "racist regime" or prefaced their remarks with a reiteration of their country's abhorrence for apartheid when discussing the nuclear safeguards issue.[136] While members demanded that South Africa sign the NPT, they simultaneously condemned Pretoria for its bigoted domestic politics.[137] For example, it was a problem that "South Africa's nuclear programme was directed towards military ends and that its discriminatory and aggressive policies had aroused much concern," argued the ambassador from Cuba.[138] The Chinese ambassador lamented that "the South African regime continued to apply apartheid and to persecute the South African people and was expanding its nuclear capability," demanding that both practices end.[139] And the Indian ambassador concluded a lengthy diatribe against South Africa's "racist policies and present rulers" by saying that both "apartheid could not be reformed but had to be abolished . . . [and] the progressive building up of South Africa's nuclear capability posed a threat to peace."[140] Overall, it became nearly universal practice, including by the United States, to begin remarks about the South African issue with a statement of opposition to apartheid.[141]

This entanglement was even more prevalent in IAEA general conference discussions. The general conference indeed remained committed to compellence. On multiple occasions, it passed resolutions formally demanding that South Africa "submit all its nuclear installations and facilities to inspection by the Agency."[142] Nevertheless, its assurance was no more credible. The resolution adopted at the October 1986 general conference plenary meeting, ostensibly to condemn the South African nuclear program, contained multiple references to apartheid. One key sentence articulating the resolution's purpose reads, "acquisition of nuclear weapon capability by the racist regime constitutes a very grave danger to international peace and security."[143] The human rights and nuclear weapons issues were obviously linked.

CRACKS EMERGE IN PRETORIA

When the last round of safeguards negotiations collapsed in 1987, the IAEA moved to suspend South Africa's membership. The board of governors voted in favor of removal 22 to 12, with one abstention.[144] All that was left was for the general conference to concur. Pretoria showed real concern for such a punishment and averted it through a well-timed public announcement in September 1987: P. W. Botha declared that he was prepared to negotiate Pretoria's signature of the NPT. His ploy for a stay of execution worked. The following day, the Soviet and US delegations cited Pretoria's announcement as reason not to expel it from the body, and the board deferred its decision.[145]

Negotiations to join the NPT were now hung up on two issues. First, Pik Botha did not perceive that the IAEA actually wanted South Africa as a member, saying in August 1988 that he remained unconvinced that the NPT "would be applied to [South Africa] in a non-discriminatory manner" if Pretoria joined.[146] Second, those whose voices mattered most in Pretoria knew that South Africa still had a small nuclear arsenal hidden away. Signing the NPT presented South Africa with a problem of having to accept IAEA inspectors at all its nuclear facilities, where naturally they would find that it had produced nuclear weapons.

In the late 1980s South African obstinacy was showing signs of cracking internally. The South African Department of Foreign Affairs produced a memo on September 1, 1988, dissenting against AEC and Armscor positions on the South African catalytic nuclear strategy of calculated ambiguity and recommending the signature of the NPT. In addition to several other arguments, the department wrote that "foreign boycotts and sanctions and increasing political and physical isolation are evidence of the inappropriateness of reliance on a nuclear deterrent to secure our future." The authors questioned the benefits of possessing a nuclear arsenal. "The deterrence strategy has in fact led to increased pressure on SA and greater international condemnation of our nuclear policy."[147] But the department could not muster a winning coalition to wage this internal fight until months later. Others in Pretoria disagreed, remained committed to the nuclear program, and stuck by their weapons until late 1989.

By this point, Pretoria seemed eager for a way out of isolation yet continued to invest in its nuclear arsenal. Coming out of the September 1985 decision to maintain the nuclear weapons program, more research was required to miniaturize implosion warheads for missile delivery. South Africa followed through on funding the construction of two new facilities to conduct this research in 1988 and 1989.[148] It also built an additional warhead as late as 1989.

Dismantling the Arsenal

DE KLERK AND THE DECISION TO CONCEDE

Upon suffering a stroke, President P. W. Botha resigned as the leader of his party on February 2, 1989. After a general election on September 6, 1989, F. W. de Klerk assumed the presidency on September 20.[149] De Klerk managed to navigate these contentious internal party politics because of his reputation as a conservative committed to maintaining Afrikaner rule.[150] But he was about to break the mold.

De Klerk sought to end South Africa's international isolation by both ending apartheid and signing the NPT. He knew international sanctions were linked to both demands. Neither alone could bring economic relief.[151] Waldo Stumpf recalls that

> F. W. de Klerk's opening remarks to a few ministers and officials whom he convened in September 1989, shortly after he assumed office as the new state president, were: "In my term of office I am going to lead this country back to a position of an internationally respected member of the world community and this means two things: We are going to turn the political system round to a fully democratic system by unbanning the ANC and releasing Nelson Mandela, and secondly we are going to dismantle our nuclear arsenal and accede to the NPT." From this broad vision his instructions to me were to "garner the maximum amount of international credibility from our accession to the NPT."[152]

De Klerk perceived an opportunity to end the isolation of South Africa. At a cabinet retreat on December 3–5, 1989, responding to an economic briefing detailing how "sanctions were biting, oil was in short supply and the repayment of foreign debt was dragging the economy down," De Klerk said, "We can hold out for another ten or fifteen years, but there will be sanctions, sabotage and terror. Do we want that? We must avoid negotiating at a point where we have to yield under pressure. We must use this golden opportunity."[153] De Klerk indeed knew that he was already under coercive pressure but sought to avoid continued punishment. And at a meeting that same month with NPT depository states—the United States, the United Kingdom, and the Soviet Union—the South Africans found the NPT still entangled with apartheid. "With apartheid still in place, there was little they could offer" by way of access to international markets or technical exchanges or assistance, writes Möser.[154] De Klerk and his cabinet thus set out to acquiesce on both the nuclear and apartheid issues. The only question was how to do so in a manner that assured they would not be punished because of their concessions. They did not know how their coercers would react to an admission of having built a secret nuclear arsenal.

DOUBLE ACQUIESCENCE AND SANCTIONS RELIEF

The first step was to acquiesce to both demands at the same time, overcoming the hydra-headed compellence that had frustrated the coercive assurance perceived by earlier leaders unwilling to budge on domestic reform. De Klerk correctly concluded that both needed to be addressed to see any sanctions relief. Waldo Stumpf concurs that at the end of the 1980s, "as the progress of domestic political reform became better understood abroad, accession to the NPT assumed distinct advantages for South Africa internationally and especially on the African continent."[155] De Klerk announced on February 2, 1990, the steps his government would take to end apartheid: releasing Nelson Mandela, unbanning political parties, and negotiating a new democratic constitution.[156] The same month, South Africa secretly began to implement a nuclear dismantlement plan approved by De Klerk in November 1989.[157]

Sanctions relief followed, although not until the full extent of Pretoria's acquiesce was credibly communicated. In the wake of De Klerk's February 1990 speech announcing his intention to usher in a South African political system "in which every inhabitant will enjoy equal rights," sanctions were not immediately lifted.[158] In September 1990 De Klerk was invited to meet with President George H. W. Bush at the White House. The meeting was cordial. De Klerk complained that CAAA sanctions remained in place, but Bush noted that South Africa had to meet all five of the prerequisites for CAAA sanction relief to take effect: (1) the release of all political prisoners (including Mandela), (2) the end of the state of emergency, (3) the unbanning of political parties, (4) the repeal of the Group Areas Act and the Population Registration Act, and (5) the beginning of negotiations on true democratic governance. Conditions 1, 2, and 4 had not yet been fully met. De Klerk returned home and met the rest of the conditions by June 1991.[159] Pik Botha then signed the NPT on behalf of South Africa on July 8, 1991, and his signature was ratified on July 10. That same day, on July 10, 1991, President Bush signed an executive order lifting the CAAA sanctions. Washington was surprised by the rapid turnaround in South African policy.

On January 20, 1989, a CIA estimate titled "South Africa in the 1990s" had concluded that Pretoria "has weathered more than four years of unprecedented domestic and international pressure," with no changes imminent.[160]

Additional relief followed. The apartheid era ended on April 27, 1994, when Nelson Mandela won the presidency in the nation's first democratic elections. South Africa subsequently participated in the September 1994 IAEA general conference, rejoined the Committee on Assurance of Supply, and resumed its seat on the IAEA board of governors in September 1995.[161]

HESITATING TO REVEAL NEW INFORMATION TO COERCERS

Soon after his election, De Klerk had formed a committee to make recommendations about joining the NPT. According to Waldo Stumpf, an attendee of the first committee meeting, De Klerk said, "The nuclear devices would be a liability in South Africa gaining international acceptance in the process. . . . There was no debate about the decision but rather how it should be implemented."[162] At an ad hoc cabinet meeting in November 1989, De Klerk accepted the committee's recommendations and instructed the AEC and Armscor to terminate nuclear material production and dismantle the existing nuclear weapons.[163]

Pretoria hesitated, however, to reveal the extent of its nuclear weapons program out of fear that providing new information about its guilt to its coercers would only invite further pain. Here coercers' reputations also played a role, as recently observed US foreign policy undermined coercive assurance. "The heads of the AEC and Armscor were not sure whether the UN cowboys, who had unceremoniously blown up Saddam Hussein's facilities and physically destroyed all the enrichment equipment, might not arrive in South Africa with similar intentions," writes Von Wielligh.[164] Stumpf, concurred, writing that the South African government had been afraid of coming fully clean after witnessing "the confrontational verification process then unfolding between Iraq and the IAEA," which "convinced South Africa that it could easily have been branded as a second nuclear outlaw nation."[165] Years later Stumpf reiterated that "in 1991 when we signed the NPT, that would have been the right moment to say 'yes, there was such a program.' But the world was fighting Saddam in the first Gulf War, and although Saddam had signed the NPT, the general public would not have recognized the difference—it would have been 'another Iraq, another Saddam Hussein.' Obviously it wasn't the same, but newspapers wouldn't have recognised that."[166] They feared that concession would provide new information to justify further punishment.

Instead of coming clean, South Africa dismantled and destroyed evidence of its nuclear weapons program. A November 17, 1989, letter from Richard Carter (of the Department of Foreign Affairs) to Herbert Beukes (deputy director general of foreign affairs), summarizing an AEC meeting to discuss possible accession to the NPT, makes this plan plain. It highlights that "decontamination is a major problem."[167] Inspectors allowed into the Y-plant were certain to detect traces of weapons-grade uranium. "Even a major, 3 year decontamination program will be unlikely to completely eradicate all traces. . . . IAEA inspectors using sensitive equipment will be able to detect the prior existence of 95% enriched product."[168] Instead, the AEC suggested a cover-up. It advised that the uranium metal in nuclear weapon cores be "reduced to highly enriched [UF6] gas." South Africa could "'come clean' and admit that it has enriched uranium to weapons grade, but that it has not made weapons."[169] While "some records would have to be destroyed," the process could be completed in twelve to eighteen months. "If we came clean on the 95% enriched product," the memo further explained the deniability, "we would have to do very little arguing over safeguards. The 'secret' would be out. Manufacture of weapons however need never be admitted."[170] De Klerk accepted this strategy in November 1989. It was part and parcel of the decision to sign the NPT. Delaying accession to the NPT until July 1991 and the signing of a safeguards agreement with the IAEA until September 16 bought South Africa time to execute the plan.

Through these efforts, South Africa was navigating a concession strategy that permitted full transparency about its nuclear future while denying its nuclear past—admission of which it feared would provoke further punishment. The explicit "main objective" of the dismantlement effort, as described in the February 1990 official AEC document, was "to dismantle the present 5 [sic[171]] nuclear weapons devices together with half-completed devices, components and material in an orderly and controlled manner, melt down the highly enriched uranium they contain and store it safely and perform the necessary cleaning operations to attach credibility to the statement that the RSA did manufacture highly enriched uranium but did not undertake the final step of manufacturing nuclear weapons."[172] Under orders of President De Klerk, the AEC was thus not to admit the production of nuclear weapons.[173]

The weapons dismantlement process was "essentially completed" by the end of June 1991, and the last of the HEU from the weapons was returned to the AEC by September 1991.[174] Only after its dismantlement program was completed did South Africa conclude a comprehensive safeguards agreement with the IAEA.[175] The IAEA conducted twenty-two inspections missions from October 1991 to September 1993.[176]

The inspections process turned out to be nothing like Iraq's. Throughout, South Africa was allowed some leeway in admitting its past nuclear sins.[177] The IAEA focused on nuclear materials accountancy and did not force admissions from Pretoria that it had built a nuclear arsenal. For instance, in its initial report to the IAEA, Pretoria admitted that it had produced weapons-grade uranium. However, the report made no mention of nuclear weapons, the conversion of UF6 HEU into uranium metal, or the existence of facilities to do so.[178] At the first official meeting between the South African AEC and the IAEA inspections team, Von Wielligh writes that "the Initial Report remained lying on the table like the corpse with a dagger in its back but all eyes were averted and nobody asked the obvious question. It was stated on the first page that South Africa had declared a few hundred kilograms of weapons-grade uranium, but the IAEA team asked no questions and the AEC team volunteered no information."[179] As former AEC head Waldo Stumpf recalled, "They never asked us, so we never had to lie. . . . One of those funny things."[180]

Instead, the IAEA's primary task was to "ensure that no significant quantity was missing from the declared inventories" of fissile material.[181] Substantial work went into matching uranium input and output at each declared facility,[182] estimating ranges of enriched product produced, and checking against declared amounts. In the end, inspectors attributed any discrepancies to uncertainty of measurements used in the material accounting system, since "no formal measurement control programme had existed for the depleted uranium product which was a major component of the U-235 balance."[183] That is, the missing U-235 (the isotope uranium-235) was likely in waste drums, whose U-235 contents had been estimated with average ratios instead of cumbersomely measured individually. It was not until 2010 that the IAEA could confirm that there was no missing significant quantity in South Africa—reaching its "broader conclusion" that "all nuclear material remained in peaceful activities." It took a decades-long, painstaking process of opening, measuring, and categorizing the material in every single waste drum to prove this negative.[184]

After the inspections mission was complete, Demetrius Perricos and two IAEA colleagues explained their thinking:

> The inventory of HEU declared by South Africa in its initial report was substantial. The IAEA recognized that this material could have been taken to indicate that a significant component of the HEU inventory had been recovered from an abandoned nuclear weapons programme or, less likely, had been accumulated to supply a planned nuclear weapons programme which had been abandoned prior to its implementation. South Africa had no obligation to declare what had been the past purpose of this material. Equally, the primary task of the IAEA was to ascertain that all nuclear material had been declared and placed under safeguards; priority was given to this task during 1992.[185]

Only much later, on March 24, 1993, did De Klerk finally announce that South Africa had dismantled an arsenal of six nuclear weapons.[186] The venue was a speech to a joint session of Parliament, but he was really speaking to the whole world.[187] He explained that South Africa "did, indeed, develop a limited nuclear deterrent capability" but dismantled it because it was "an obstacle to the development of South Africa's international relations."[188] De Klerk emphasized that as it had joined the NPT as a nonnuclear weapons state, South Africa had technically not broken any rules. "We were not, in terms of the NPT itself, obliged to tell them," De Klerk asserted in a postspeech press conference.[189] After South Africa came fully clean about its nuclear weapons program, the IAEA mission, now supplemented with additional weaponization experts, expanded to confirming the arsenal's dismantlement and establishing measures to detect its reconstruction.[190]

Three IAEA inspectors visited the Kentron Circle / Advena facility on March 25, 1993. And inspectors witnessed the "rendering useless" of the Kalahari test shafts July 26–30, 1993.[191] Most importantly, the IAEA audited the records of material transfers between the AEC and Armscor and concluded that "HEU originally supplied to ARMSCOR/Circle had been returned to the AEC and was subject to Agency [IAEA] safeguards at the time of entry into force of the safeguards agreement."[192] It was all declared. The IAEA officially confirmed the dismantlement of South Africa's nuclear weapons on August 14, 1994.

The Assurance Dilemma in South Africa

The South African case yields clear evidence of an assurance dilemma that hindered effective coercion. The fear of unconditional punishment drove South African leaders to defy compellence from 1975 to 1989. Pressure on the regime to sign the NPT failed for so long not because threats were not credible or punishments were not painful but because South African leaders concluded that acquiescence on the nuclear issues would not end punishments that they perceived were also tied to their racist apartheid policies. Coercers, chiefly the United States, struggled to assure because they were unable or unwilling to disentangle punishments tied to both demands. In aggregating issues to bolster their threats and squeeze South Africa harder, they undermined their coercive assurance not to punish Pretoria if it signed the NPT.

South African leaders explicitly perceived external pressure through such a lens. Sanctions were imposed, escalating, and, in the 1980s, hurting. But still they defied. South African behavior and speech evidence corroborates the assurance dilemma, especially at three key decision points—1977, 1985, and 1986–88. South African policymakers justified not signing the NPT with assessments that punishments would be applied whether or not Pretoria signed.

A lack of coercive control also exacerbated the problem of entangled demands. When the Reagan administration attempted to disentangle US demands and reduce the severity of US economic pressure in the mid-1980s, Congress overrode the president's veto and imposed comprehensive sanctions. The administration did not manage spoilers domestically, and Reagan could not be bargained with. The US government overall was unwilling to accept the brutality of apartheid to get South Africa to sign the NPT. A similar dynamic played out within the IAEA, where feeble attempts failed to disentangle calls to sign the NPT and accept comprehensive safeguards from member state opposition to apartheid. The South African case also reveals how targets of compellence fear admitting to coercers new information about their misbehavior when complying. Pretoria tried to avoid coming clean about what its coercers did not know—that it had actually constructed a small nuclear arsenal.

Overall, the case is a convincing instance of how a lack of coercive assurance explains failed coercion in the 1970s and 1980s. But Pretoria had additional reasons for nuclear reversal in 1989—most clearly racist fears of handing over nuclear weapons to a Black-majority government and concern for nuclear command and control during a period of internal political upheaval.[193] The Soviet Union's collapse also improved South Africa's security situation. Deciding to give in to both demands—nuclear and apartheid—did not overcome the fundamental issue of entanglement of multiple demands. This ultimate compliance was due to domestic political changes within the target state, not a change in coercer strategy.

This chapter has chiefly validated the assurance dilemma in coercion. The following chapters build on it to offer more constructive solutions for mitigating the assurance dilemma and identifying when targets that face even more severe threats of military coercion are willing to gamble on concession.

"Sanctions with Inspectors"

Convincing Iraq to Come Clean

Iraq is a case of successful nonproliferation, yet the saga of Iraqi nonprolif-eration is an undoubted tragedy. The 1990–91 Gulf War interrupted a seri-ous Iraqi crash program to enrich uranium for a nuclear weapon. In its wake, Saddam Hussein made significant concessions by destroying his stocks of chemical and biological weapons, admitting UN inspectors, and accepting continuous monitoring. But Iraq's coercers never appreciated how successful their coercive nonproliferation policies had been and so squeezed Iraq ever more until its leadership disengaged. Saddam sought sanctions relief by publicly conceding only those aspects of his WMD pro-grams that coercers already knew about and secretly destroying the rest. Saddam and his advisers then made fewer concessions to coercion over time as they came to perceive that no amount of compliance would end sanctions (see table 3.1).

Scholarly breakthroughs in accounting for the Iraqi perspective have been possible since the 2003 US-led invasion of Iraq, when coalition forces captured many official records of the Saddam regime and shipped them to the United States. Saddam had made a habit of recording high-level delib-erations with his advisers. These archival records shed rare light on the perspectives of a direct target of coercive threats.

Improving Existing Explanations

The lens of the assurance dilemma revises several conventional wisdoms about Iraqi proliferation. First, common explanations for Saddam Hussein's defiance of coercion point to threat credibility and severity. Sanctions were not tight enough, especially during the Bill Clinton administration, some argue.[1] Saddam and corrupt elites were not hurting because they passed on the pain to regular Iraqis and hoarded wealth for themselves. The UN's

Table 3.1 Iraq

Date	Concessions	Threat credibility	Threat severity	Assurance credibility	Consistent with assurance dilemma?
1981	No	High	Low	Low	✓
1991	Yes	High	High	High	✓
1991–93	Yes	High	High	Medium	✓
1994	No	High	High	Low	✓
1995	Yes	High	Medium	Medium	✓
1996–98	No	High	Medium	Low	✓
2002	Yes[a]	Higher	High	Low	✗
2003	No	Higher	Higher	Lower	✓[b]

[a] Saddam readmitted inspectors, but there was no longer an actual program to concede.

[b] The magnitude of coercer demands was also an impediment to coercion after 1998.

Oil-for-Food Programme simply opened a loophole through which Saddam siphoned aid.[2] Others argue that Saddam perceived the United States to be casualty averse and therefore not credibly willing to use military force beyond occasional air strikes.[3] Or perhaps Saddam was willing to bear the costs of punishment in pursuit of an all-consuming goal of acquiring a nuclear weapon. These arguments contend that Iraqi behavior was driven by a fear of punishment. Coercion would have succeeded if only sanctions were tougher or the threat of force was more credible. Thus, speech evidence questioning the credibility or severity of compellent threats should accompany Iraqi defiance.

These explanations are unsatisfying against the empirical record—they are insufficient to explain the failures of coercion. Saddam and his coterie certainly insulated themselves from the harm that sanctions caused to the Iraqi people, but they did not think that the costs of sanctions were worth paying. They simply could not figure out how to have them removed. Coercive assurance provides a more compelling explanation. The assurance dilemma reveals in Iraqi documents perceptions of the unconditional nature of threats that accompanied defiance.

Second, some argue that Saddam was just irrational.[4] A mercurial dictator surrounded by sycophants and advisers too afraid to tell him the truth might make irrational choices. It would certainly seem crazy to declare victory after the Gulf War or to think that Iraq could defeat the United States in a ground war, as Saddam did.[5] But this view is also belied by the extensive documentary records available after the 2003 invasion and occupation. Saddam and his advisers did recognize the credibility and severity of imposed and threatened punishments, and they genuinely sought relief. Their behavior was affected by cost-benefit manipulations. A softer version of this irrationality argument in the literature has focused on misperceptions between Iraq and the United States, especially the failure of intelligence in seeing a WMD program where there was none.[6] These arguments are no doubt true as applied to the United States, but I find more rationality on the Iraqi side about signals between a coercer and target. Moreover, in contrast to arguments that see a commitment problem in Saddam's inability to commit to not developing WMDs in the future, I find a commitment problem on behalf of the United States not to punish Iraq regardless of its behavior.[7] The chief obstacle to full WMD transparency was convincing Baghdad that sanctions could ever in fact be lifted.

Third, some argue that the United States asked for too much. US demands to cooperate with inspectors were perceived to be aimed at undermining Saddam's rule.[8] Asking for lists of former WMD facilities was akin to asking for a targeting list for air strikes. And as the inspections progressed, they requested access to buildings and information that were part of Saddam's personal security apparatus. The magnitude of coercer demands was too great to comply. I find evidence in favor of this explanation later in the 1990s, especially after 1998. By then the Clinton administration made it known, even more than it had previously been signaled, that US policy was in fact aimed at the removal of Saddam and that sanctions would remain as long as he was in power. Prior to 1998, there was still hope or at least discussion within Saddam's inner circle about whether and how to get UN sanctions lifted. This explanation holds some weight through the lead-up to the 2003 war as well.

Fourth, an explanation that took hold after the 2003 invasion for the failure of Saddam to admit his actual dismantlement of a WMD program was that he sought to deter domestic uprisings or regional rivals—Iran and Israel—by maintaining the fiction that his capabilities were intact.[9] I find no new evidence for this explanation. Instead, I find that Iraqi officials did not wish to come clean out of a fear of greater punishment if they did reveal their misdeeds. Blaming piecemeal Iraqi admissions about its own disarmament on third-party audiences needlessly complicates the plain evidence that Iraq simply did not want to admit the extent of its past WMD programs to coercers themselves. After a short post–Gulf War period of hedging to preserve the option of reconstituting his destroyed WMD programs, Saddam changed his strategy to maximize, as he saw it, the likelihood of having sanctions lifted. Part of this plan involved destroying and hiding evidence of past proliferation to speed the UN's declaration of Iraq's clean bill of health. Every new admission, Iraqis feared, would anger, provoke, and sustain suspicious coercers while making sympathetic defenders at the UN more hesitant to speak up. Using the assurance dilemma as a lens, I trace a clear pattern of Iraqi leadership endeavoring to admit only that which they thought that their coercers already knew. And when confronted with new evidence or the defection of Saddam's son-in-law Hussein Kamil in 1995 that leaked substantial new evidence of past programs, Iraq made new admissions to try to satisfy coercers. Most of the time, information asymmetries between coercer and target exacerbated the assurance dilemma and kept the Iraqis from conceding new admissions. Ultimately, Saddam's fears of the consequences of making concessions that revealed new information to coercers were proven right. He was damned if he did and damned if he didn't.

Through this line of reasoning, this chapter builds on Målfrid Braut-Hegghammer's concept of the "cheater's dilemma," whereby the fragmented Iraqi bureaucracy struggled to coordinate compliance internally, as underlings feared that making new disclosures, even when authorized, would anger an unpredictable Saddam.[10] Braut-Hegghammer's story alone lays too much of the tragedy at the feet of internal Iraqi mismanagement when coercers themselves did not appreciate the assurance dilemma fears that kept Iraq from admitting the extent of its concessions before 1995 and could not see transparency for what it was after 1995. My argument builds on Braut-Hegghammer's to illuminate the ways in which the cheater's dilemma is also a problem of coercive assurance in a strategic interaction. In other words, it takes two.

This chapter offers a brief review of Iraq's nuclear program before describing the nature of international compellent demands directed at Baghdad. It shows that while Saddam and his advisers perceived many of these threats to be credible, they chose to defy when the threats were not perceived as conditional. I examine four phases of the case: the Israeli counterproliferation air strikes in 1981, the Gulf War, inspections throughout the 1990s, and the lead-up to the US invasion in 2003.

Iraq's Nuclear Program

After a 1958 coup, Iraq moved to secure enhanced nuclear assistance from the Soviet Union, eventually procuring a Soviet research reactor in 1959.[11] The reactor was constructed at Tuwaitha. Another coup in 1968 brought the Baath Party to power under the leadership of Ahmed Hassan al-Bakr and his deputy, Saddam Hussein. Some scientists at Tuwaitha began to discuss the option of a nuclear weapons program in the early 1970s, but no such order was given by Saddam until he came to power.[12]

Around 1973 Iraq developed an intent to hedge, as Saddam reorganized the Iraqi Atomic Energy Commission (IAEC) and told a group of scientists to explore the full nuclear fuel cycle. As part of this exploration, Iraq asked the Soviet Union for upgrades to the research reactor at Tuwaitha. Iraq also acquired a complex—dubbed Osirak—with two new types of research reactors from France, plus laboratory-scale reprocessing equipment. It initially asked to purchase a gas-cooled, graphite-moderated power reactor, which raised eyebrows for its weapons potential.[13] Iraq similarly asked Italy for proliferation-prone technologies, such as a reprocessing plant, but settled for radiochemical and uranium fuel laboratories.[14] The reactors were placed under IAEA safeguards.

In a 1978 speech, Saddam articulated his ambition to have a nuclear option, saying, "We should generate the unusual capabilities of the Arab nation, including the capability to have a bomb, and that is no longer monopolized science. The atom is widespread and thorough science, and any country can produce the atomic bomb."[15] The following month, Saddam complained in a meeting that Israel's monopoly on nuclear weapons in the region allowed Israel to draw "red lines" and coerce Arab states.[16] Once Saddam came to power in 1979, he finally gave the order to explore a nuclear weapons option.[17] At an IAEC meeting in late 1979, the director of the Nuclear Research Center at Tuwaitha communicated to Iraqi scientific leaders that Saddam wanted the program to take a more "strategic" direction. Braut-Hegghammer reports that the scientists understood this to mean nuclear weapons.[18]

Opponents Mix Brute Force and Coercion

ISRAELI BRUTE FORCE

Iraq's progress exploring the nuclear fuel cycle alarmed the Israelis, who began to covertly target Iraqi scientists and equipment for murder and sabotage.[19] Israel first detected Iraqi nuclear intentions in 1974. After a 1978 Israeli cabinet meeting, officials were instructed to "delay the Iraqi nuclear program by all possible means."[20] In 1979 Israeli saboteurs attacked the facilities in southern France that had produced the reactor cores shipped to Iraq. They also destroyed the offices of SNIA-Techint in Rome, where Iraq's separation plant originated.[21]

These efforts culminated in the 1981 overt bombing of the Osirak reactor.[22] Israel privately considered the use of force as early as 1977 but did not make any public threats before launching the 1981 attack.[23] Yet Saddam perceived coercion. In September 1980 he said, "The Arabs, the Zionists, and the Americans are going to work hard against us because they are afraid, which is a problem."[24] Moreover, Braut-Hegghammer writes that the Iraqi regime "feared that Israel would not allow an Arab state to acquire nuclear weapons and believed Tel Aviv was prepared to use force to prevent this from happening."[25] Iraq prepared to withstand both conventional and nuclear strikes from Israel. This was the perception of a credible threat, but it did not dampen Iraq's nuclear ambitions.

Israel bombed the Osirak reactor complex on June 7, 1981.[26] Israeli prime minister Menachem Begin held a press conference two days after the raid and drew a clear red line: Iraq would not be permitted to develop a nuclear weapon. After invoking the Holocaust, Begin said, "Tell your friend, tell anyone you meet, we shall defend our people with all means at our disposal. We shall not allow any enemy to develop weapons of mass destruction turned against us."[27] In a subsequent interview with CBS News, Begin reminded viewers that "this attack will be a precedent for every future government in Israel. . . . Every future prime minister will act, in similar circumstances, in the same way."[28]

SADDAM DEFIANT

Saddam was defiant after the Israeli attack. He concluded that the strike revealed that Iraq should devote even greater resources to the nuclear program.[29] Indeed, he claimed that he had "long expected" the strike and that future nuclear installations would be buried.[30] This translated as well into organizational action, as the scientists in charge sat down to develop concrete plans for nuclear weapons development.[31] The real effect was of pushing the program underground.[32] For example, Saddam instructed his scientific team after the raid to avoid sensitive foreign assistance that could tip off intelligence agencies.

Avoiding foreign procurement foreclosed the plutonium route to the bomb as well as large-scale centrifuge uranium enrichment. Iraq pursued multiple enrichment pathways, including electromagnetic isotope separation (EMIS), laser isotope separation, gaseous diffusion, and centrifuge enrichment. The IAEC was reorganized around this new effort in January 1982.[33] The EMIS path made the most progress, and in January 1986 Iraq successfully separated uranium isotopes.[34]

At a meeting between Saddam and senior IAEC members in April 1985, Vice Chairman Humam Abdul Khaliq made a promise: the nuclear program would fulfill its objectives by 1990. He did this apparently without consulting the other IAEC leaders.[35] By 1987 a special organization was formed at Tuwaitha—Group 4—dedicated to building a bomb.[36] Then Saddam made an ill-timed decision: in August 1990 he invaded Kuwait. The war came at the wrong time for a nuclear program that was making significant progress, successfully hidden. As a last-ditch effort, Hussein Kamil ordered a "crash" nuclear weapons effort after Saddam invaded Kuwait. The goal was to build a bomb in six months.[37]

THE GULF WAR

Despite a massive military buildup in the region and crippling sanctions, multilateral efforts could not compel Saddam to leave Kuwait. Though this effort was not aimed at nonproliferation coercion and therefore falls just outside of the scope of this chapter, its parallel exposure of the assurance dilemma is worthy of note. As Paul Avey concludes, "Saddam and his lieutenants believed that even if they withdrew from Kuwait, the American military threat would remain."[38] On October 6 Saddam described his think-ing to a Soviet interlocutor: withdrawal or no withdrawal, "you cannot bring an end to the American siege of Iraq."[39] "If America decided on war it will go to war whether I withdraw from Kuwait or not," he concluded.[40] And up to the last moment before hostilities began, on January 14, 1991, Saddam told Yemeni officials, "We have no guarantees if we withdraw. . . . Why should we surrender at the last moment?"[41] US air strikes began on January 17, and ground forces entered Kuwait and Iraq on February 24.

Saddam's invasion of Kuwait proved to be a strategic blunder. US brute force set back his nuclear program that had been on the verge of scaling up successful uranium enrichment.[42] While the counterfactual is impossible to know with confidence, Braut-Hegghammer and Gudrun Harrer both con-clude that Iraq would likely have acquired nuclear weapons in the 1990s had Saddam not invaded Kuwait.[43] Iraq's reconstituted nuclear infrastruc-ture, including the Tuwaitha facility, was destroyed by the United States during the Gulf War. Indeed, one of the US war aims was to degrade Iraq's ability to build nuclear weapons.

The United States was surprised to discover the extent of the Iraqi nuclear program after Operation Desert Storm.[44] Nor did Israeli intelligence know about Iraq's nuclear progress in the 1980s, only first beginning to hear about the clandestine enrichment program in 1989.[45] Reflecting later on the IAEA's failure to detect violations in Iraq, Director General Mohamed ElBaradei described his organization as "a beat cop with a blindfold."[46] The IAEA and coercers had been deceived.

Inspections and Coercion throughout the 1990s

After the Gulf War, the United States and Iraq engaged in nearly a decade of frustrating coercive diplomacy. UNSC Resolution 687 established UNSCOM—the UN Special Commission—and tasked with it verifying the dismantlement of the Iraqi chemical, biological, and missile programs. The IAEA, through its newly established Iraq Action Team, oversaw dismantle-ment of its nuclear program.[47] Resolution 687 prohibited Iraq from possess-ing any nuclear, chemical, or biological weapons or missiles above a range of 150 kilometers or facilities for their production.

Severe threats backed up these dismantlement demands, and the Iraqi government knew the stakes of not cooperating. Legally, WMD disarma-ment was a criterion for the Gulf War cease-fire, so a breach of Resolution 687 would void the cease-fire and default back to a state of war—a clear military threat. Painful economic sanctions also supported the coercive strategy. Iraq's $180 billion gross domestic product in 1990 tumbled to below half a billion in 1991 and recovered to just $20 billion by 1998.[48] Prior to its invasion of Kuwait, Iraq had relied on imports for 70 percent of its food, medicine, and agricultural chemicals.[49] UNSC Resolution 661, passed on the day of Saddam's invasion of Kuwait, had imposed comprehensive multilateral sanctions and frozen all of Iraq's foreign assets. After the war ended, the sanctions remained. Resolution 687, passed on April 3, 1991, tied the sanctions to Iraqi cooperation with WMD inspectors.

Saddam's Iraq wrestled in private with how to respond throughout the 1990s. Four periods stand out. First, after displaying short-lived instincts to defy, Saddam ordered the destruction of all WMD stocks and from 1991 to 1993 attempted to hide the existence of such programs. Inspections then began to show a pattern of revealing only that which Iraq believed that its coercers already knew of its past program, Saddam fearing that revealing new information would only make his coercers seek to punish him more. Second, when his concessions did not result in sanctions relief, he lashed out in 1994 and attempted to manufacture a crisis on the Kuwait border aimed at breaking the coalition of sanctions supporters. Third, in 1995 the defection of Hussein Kamil was an inflection point in Iraqi strategy. Saddam came clean about the full extent of programs that he feared Kamil had now divulged to his coercers. Finally, from 1996 to 1998 Saddam became increasingly convinced that sanctions would never be lifted. He ultimately kicked out inspectors, believing that their presence, no matter his cooperation, could never relieve pressure on his regime. Throughout, the assurance dilemma was the primary driver of Saddam's behavior.

1991–93: DESTRUCTION AND HIDING

In the immediate aftermath of the Gulf War, Saddam was initially inclined to resume the nuclear project. "Perhaps emboldened by the vague terms of the cease-fire, Saddam ordered an immediate resumption of the centrifuge program," recalled the nuclear scientist Mahdi Obeidi, who ran Iraq's centrifuge research program. "Hussein Kamel [sic] became furious as I've ever seen him, urging us to redouble our efforts to produce enough enriched uranium for a nuclear weapon as soon as possible."[50] Equipment was brought out of hiding.

Coercion quickly changed Saddam's mind. Resolution 687 threatened renewed force, which Saddam wished to avoid. He then chose not to reconstitute old programs and instead allow inspectors into the country. But first he issued a broad order to destroy and cover up past WMD work,[51] which he and his advisers expected would make verification a relatively simple and short affair. In doing so, he followed the advice of Hussein Kamil, who, in Braut-Hegghammer's words, successfully argued that "Iraq should declare only what the UN and the IAEA already knew about."[52] In the spring of 1991, Kamil told Jafar D. Jafar, who was preparing the disclosure to the IAEA, "Don't write about anything except the activities that are known already."[53] Admitting to proscribed weapons would, in the view of

Minister of Foreign Affairs and Deputy Prime Minister Tariq Aziz, grant the United States a pretext to attack Iraq.[54] A 2004 CIA assessment agreed in retrospect that "Iraq initially tried to end sanctions without fully revealing WMD programs. . . . Iraqi leaders were optimistic that inspections and sanctions would end quickly. Their approach to inspections was to make sure that nothing was found to contradict their initial false declarations while they destroyed contradictory evidence" and thus "make its inaccurate assertions of no programs correct in a legalistic sense."[55] Compliance, in other words, included hope for relief from pressure—sanctions and looming war.

Iraq's strategy was informed by its perception of UNSCOM. The CIA described Iraqis as "shocked by the unexpected aggressiveness."[56] They feared handing over new evidence of their WMD programs that would enrage or empower the United States to make the case of further punishment and cause sympathetic UNSC member states to balk in their defense of Iraq. Saddam himself articulated his intuition on the assurance dilemma in a recorded meeting with advisers in August 1991. It was a feeling that would only grow deeper over the decade:

> SADDAM: One of the mistakes some people make is that when the enemy has decided to hurt you, you believe there is a chance to decrease the harm by acting in a certain way, but it won't. The harm won't be less.
> MALE 1: The enemy is determined; he has a plan he is following.
> SADDAM: And he is determined to follow his plan. . . . What did the Americans show us as a possible sign for partially decreasing their harm? We didn't see anything coming from them. I have given them everything. I mean, I have given them everything: the missiles, and the chemical, biological and nuclear weapons. They didn't give you anything in exchange, not even a piece of bread. They didn't give us anything in exchange, well, they have become worse.[57]

Saddam appears to be referring to his dismantlement of his WMD programs. In 2004 the CIA undertook a series of intelligence assessments called the "Iraq WMD Retrospective Series," which aimed in part to understand "how the Iraqis perceived and reacted to the international inspection process."[58] Among its key findings, the CIA's Office of Iraq Analysis assessed that "in 1991, Iraq secretly destroyed or dismantled most undeclared items and records that could have been used to validate the unilateral destruction, leaving Baghdad unable to provide convincing proof when it later tried to demonstrate compliance."[59]

Iraq's strategy of hiding its past proliferation involved a difficult balancing act between admitting what it thought coercers already knew and covering up what they did not. The Iraqis navigated it ham-handedly. At times, the hiding goal resulted in belligerence with inspectors. UNSCOM inspectors were blocked from multiple site visits, including the infamous "parking lot incident" in September 1991, when Iraqis attempted to prevent inspectors from leaving a facility with sensitive documents containing details of Iraq's nuclear weapons efforts.[60] Suspicious facilities and documents also proved relatively easy to come by. UNSCOM's first conclusion in mid-1991 was that Iraq had not come fully clean in its declaration to the UN of WMD facilities.

True to a pattern exhibited throughout the Iraq WMD saga, Saddam continued to admit that which coercers could show that they knew already. For instance, in 1991 Iraq's Oversight Committee admitted its plans for a centrifuge facility at Al-Furat. Obeidi recalls that it did so "faced with evidence presented by inspectors."[61] The disclosure revealed Saddam's ambitions for large-scale centrifuge enrichment. That same year the Oversight Committee again responded to "evidence provided by inspectors" by revealing the Al-Atheer facility in Murayyib, where Iraq had conducted nuclear weaponization research.[62] When David Kay and his inspections team presented a choice between providing "better answers" on the past purpose of the facility or the destruction of the eight buildings at Al-Atheer, "rather than concede his intentions to produce nuclear weapons, [Saddam] granted permission to destroy al-Atheer," recalls Obeidi.[63]

When Saddam and advisers were reasonably confident that their secrets were safe, they did not admit past wrongdoing. In an example from Iraq's proscribed missile program, the CIA after 2003 discovered that he "hid documentation related to the consumption and unilateral destruction of Scud propellant because it would show that Iraq had produced its own oxidizer for its Scud-type ballistic missiles before 1991."[64] Obeidi was also tasked with the cover-up of the past purpose of the Engineering Design Center at Rashdiya (Iraq's centrifuge laboratory), which involved the extraordinary task of tearing it down to studs, removing topsoil, and constructing "an exact replica of the facility" without detectable traces of enriched uranium.[65] While his initial understanding for the cover-ups after the Gulf War was that Saddam sought to reconstitute the nuclear program at a later date, Obeidi concluded by 1993 that "as the inspectors had effectively denuded Iraq's machinery for building nuclear weapons, the deceptions had become less of a measure to preserve the program and more of a reaction against foreign pressure."[66]

These pendular cover-ups and revelations were a pattern that US officials labeled "cheat and retreat."[67] Indeed, they were interpreted by coercers as signs of Iraqi intransigence and duplicity. Yet the assurance dilemma suggests that this is the role of information in coercion. When targets think that revelations will cause coercers to lose control and punish unconditionally, they defy. When coercers share knowledge with their targets, we are more likely to see concessions.

As ad hoc as their admissions were, Iraqi leadership truly thought, in the assessment of the CIA, that it took "steps during this period that the regime thought would alleviate Iraq's isolation."[68] Saddam did perceive the potential for sanctions relief. As another example, in November 1993, after objecting to it for two years as a breach of sovereignty, Iraq complied with UNSC Resolution 715 and accepted long-term UN monitoring of key facilities. In the CIA's retrospective assessment, Baghdad "hope[d] that this step would lead to the immediate lifting of sanctions."[69] It did not. Soon Saddam grew frustrated and grasped for other means of acquiring sanctions relief.

1994: LASHING OUT

Saddam lashed out in 1994 by trying to manufacture a crisis on the Kuwait border. He did so despite the pain of continued economic sanctions and despite the credibility of US threats of military force.[70] He hatched his plan after the September UNSCOM report disappointed hopes for sanctions relief. The idea was to move ground forces to the border and compel his coercers to lift sanctions in exchange for his backing down from a reinvasion. Saddam felt that there was some hope of success because of cracks that were emerging between the permanent members of the UNSC. The United States and the United Kingdom remained steadfast in their belief that paragraph 22 of Resolution 687, which provided for the lifting of sanctions on the approval of the UNSC, would be invoked upon verification of Iraq's complete disarmament.[71] France and Russia, however, supported lifting sanctions a little at a time to reward partial compliance.[72] It was this daylight that Saddam sought to exploit. In a recorded October 1994 meeting with political advisers, Saddam described his plan:

We have moved two divisions. One of them is a Republican Guard division to Basra, and we have followed that with a third. This third division we have moved is what has made the Americans place its army on alert, because this means there are four Republican Guard divisions close to each other. . . . Together with the presence of army capabilities in depth, it became apparent to them [the Americans] that such a capability can carry out a serious action, I mean, this action will move the situation. . . . There is no idea that could serve the action of lifting the sanctions that the mind could come up with, without placing it in its correct context. . . . I have spoken about mobilization and I believe that mobilization must continue because the sanctions continue, and because the alternatives we could choose if we found out that the mean—or other means—are incapable of achieving the objective, our clear objective in this phase, which is the lifting of the sanction phase.[73]

Saddam hoped that UNSC members more willing to work with Iraq—France, China, and Russia—could help to turn the provoked crisis into sanctions relief. The United States resisted and managed to hold together the sanctions regime. Saddam backed down.

In the aftermath, Saddam's meeting with his advisers displayed even more skepticism consistent with the assurance dilemma. In early 1995, for instance, when Tariq Aziz briefed Saddam on questions from UNSCOM director Rolf Ekéus and the inspectors about procurement for the missile program, Saddam interrupted, frustrated with entangled demands: "Here we go again, we are going back to the missile issue? . . . When we close this file, then start looking for its key, then this means that it was not closed!"[74] He thought that his coercers were reneging on their implied coercive assurance. Later in the meeting when the biological weapons facility inspections came up for discussion as well, an incredulous Saddam bemoaned, "I am concerned that all of this is nothing but excuses." Aziz, while optimistic that the missile issue could be resolved, was similarly skeptical about US willingness to lift sanctions and replied that "when the technical and legal excuses are removed from America, then America will play a political role and say, 'I will not suggest lifting the sanctions against Iraq for political reasons,' ha, for reasons neither related to Ekéus nor to [inaudible]."[75] In a meeting the following June, Saddam and his advisers continued to feel that ongoing inspections became merely "a cover to extend the blockade [sanctions]."[76] In a meeting with Saddam, science adviser and later Iraq's liaison with UN weapons inspectors Amir Hamudi Hassan Al-Sa'adi compared sanctions to the harrowing Iran-Iraq War of 1980–88: "Even with the war going on between Iraq and Iran, it was not foreseen that the war would take so long. It was like lifting sanctions. Every year, we'd think it's coming this year. So every year, from even the moment it started, the Iraq-Iran war was going to finish this year, this year, and so on."[77] Saddam considered himself to be bereft of favorable options in the face of compellence.

Saddam and his advisers also questioned the likelihood of sanctions relief because of the role the United States as spoiler to the partial relief preferred by some members of the UNSC. Saddam assessed Rolf Ekéus's intentions:

> In this period, Ekeus is also interested in sending messages that would reassure us of their intentions, because when he speaks with non-aligned nations, he knows that we will hear about such discussions. . . . When he speaks with the Russians, he knows that we will hear about such discussions one way or another. He is afraid that April will come and Iraq has not received anything yet. At that time, Iraq will stand up and say, "Look we have accomplished all these achievements, but we did not receive anything in return, we do not have anything. Then we will review all of our previous positions."[78]

But Washington lingered as a spoiler: "The Americans are pressuring him more than he can stand," Tariq Aziz assessed.[79] When April came around, Saddam was indeed disappointed in the new UNSCOM report that among other gaps included suspicions that Iraq was hiding a biological weapons program.

1995: SHARED KNOWLEDGE AND HUSSEIN KAMIL'S DEFECTION

Records of meetings among Saddam Hussein's inner circle are especially valuable evidence at inflection points that affect a variable associated with coercive control and the assurance dilemma. The defection of Hussein Kamil in August 1995 can perform one such test of theory. Kamil's sudden treachery leveled the information gap between Iraq and inspectors. Saddam much more freely made concessions that he no longer thought revealed new information to his coercers.

In the spring and summer of 1995, prior to Kamil's defection, Saddam had grown more defiant of and angrier about lingering issues in UNSCOM reporting. He was not inclined to make more concessions, nor did the threat environment suggest that he would. In April 1995 the UNSC, under pressure from China, Russia, and France to avert the humanitarian suffering of the Iraqi people living under sanctions, approved the Oil-for-Food Programme. Iraq could access up to $1 billion every ninety days to purchase food and medicine. The credibility of severe economic coercion against Iraq was declining. The CIA assessed that "by the summer of 1995, international will to sustain sanctions and inspections was dwindling."[80] Yet Saddam declined the lifeline. In July he responded daringly with his own threat to cut off cooperation with UN inspections if sanctions were not lifted completely.[81]

Before the defection of Hussein Kamil, what coercers knew of Iraq's WMD programs was discussed intently at a May 1995 meeting between Saddam and high-ranking officials. His advisers recommended admitting what coercers knew, without sharing new details. Tariq Aziz was not confident that Iraq could please the Americans with transparency, but he felt that Iraq could admit enough to satisfy members of the UNSC who were more sympathetic to relieving sanctions in part. Especially, he advised admitting that Iraq had had a past biological weapons program.[82] "Yesterday's [UNSCOM] file frustrated Russia and France because they saw a large gap they could not fight," Aziz argued. "Therefore, I have stated that if we solve the biological program problem . . . the French and the Russians will lay their plans on the table, and the Americans would discuss their plans, of course. They would then say, 'there is a point here and a point there,' at which point the serious discussion would start." Hussein Kamil also suggested some revelations but cautioned against too much sunlight:

Sir, I will repeat, is it better for us to announce it or stay secretive? . . . Sir, about the nuclear program, we say that we have revealed everything. In addition, we have an unannounced problem with the nuclear program, and

I think they know about it because there are working teams that are working and some of these teams are not known to anyone. . . . Truthfully, Sir, we have to be honest so that when the Resolution is issued, it will not only be based on the biological program because if it were, it would [include] the missiles tomorrow, and the nuclear program would be the day after, and so on.[83]

But Kamil went on about biological weaponization: "If we continue to be silent about the issue at hand, I must say that it is in our best interest not to reveal it." He advised seeking a workaround to account for the seventeen tons of biological agents that Iraq had already destroyed without admitting their sophistication or that they had been armed in warheads. He suggested, "Instead of us admitting to the biological programs, Sir, we should ask the specialists: 'How can we close [the issue of] the 17 tons? We do this and that and these are all the details that we have. How can we know when this file will be closed?'"[84] In July 1995 Iraq duly acknowledged a biological weapons program consistent with the evidence presented by UNSCOM but denied that agents had in fact been weaponized.

Everything changed on August 7, 1995, when Hussein Kamil fled to Jordan. In a matter of days, he was spilling the beans in interviews with UN inspectors and US intelligence. His revelations included the biological weaponization program that had produced warheads for Scud missiles in 1990, the crash program to obtain a nuclear weapon prior to the Gulf War, and details of an illicit procurement network in Europe.[85] A list of his revelations is included in an UNSCOM report from October 1995.[86] Baghdad scrambled to assess the damage. "Even the highest levels of leadership were unsure what Kamil could reveal," the CIA assessed.[87] Saddam put his internal security apparatus to work, and on August 14 Husam Muhammad Amin al-Yasin, the director of the National Monitoring Directorate, produced a report detailing the weapons programs of which Kamil had knowledge and that had or had not been declared to inspectors.[88] Iraq came clean about all of them. Obeidi recounts the manner of the admissions that Iraq attempted to pin on Kamil alone:

Knowing that the game was up, the Oversight Committee moved to preempt the anticipated inquiries from the inspectors. They collected many documents from the WMD programs, along with remaining scattered materials such as a few tons of maraging steel and centrifuge jackets. They packed wooden and metal boxes full of microfiches, computer diskettes, videotapes, and photographs that had been kept hidden from inspectors throughout the early 1990s. Then they drove them to a chicken farm owned by Hussein Kamel in the Baghdad suburb of Haidar and locked all of the boxes in a henhouse. On August 18, an SSO [Special Security Organization] operative hinted to inspectors that they should investigate Hussein Kamel's chicken farm.[89]

According to the CIA retrospective in 2004, Kamil's defection was "the key turning point in Iraq's decision to cooperate more with inspections."[90] With the benefit of postwar clarity, the agency recognized "that the movement of documents to Husayn Kamil's chicken farm and their turnover to the UN represented a genuine attempt to come clean on programs albeit while saving face. . . . Captured documentary evidence and interviews support the idea that major concealment operations ended in 1995."[91] The Iraqi leadership had (correctly) "feared that Kamil . . . would reveal additional undisclosed information," and orders now came down to "release information to the UN without restrictions."[92] In sober meetings with Saddam in the fall after Kamil's defection, advisers demonstrated concern about admitting what had been proven already—for example, "concerning the biological weapons program." Tariq Aziz briefed Saddam in November: "It has been proven that we produced 200 bombs, and we must prove that they have been destroyed."[93] Iraq in November also finally felt the need to accept the Oil-for-Food Programme.

Yet Iraq's fears, driven by the assurance dilemma, came true in the wake of Saddam's new concessions to inspectors. Coercers did lose control of themselves. "Some of the information revealed in 1995, such as a more extensive weaponization effort for BW [biological warfare] aerial bombs, missile warheads, and spray tanks, was not previously suspected and surprised the UN, provoking deep suspicion of future Iraqi behaviors and declarations," the CIA assessed.[94] New information revealed through concessions "strengthened the West's perception of Iraq as a successful and efficient deceiver"[95] and "reinforced the prevailing analytical paradigm that the Iraqis had been successful in hiding evidence of significant WMD programs, proved that they had not intended to cooperate with the UN, and would only reveal or dismantle programs after being caught in a lie."[96] This was the wrong conclusion. Not only were the Iraqis attempting to come clean in 1995, but they were also continuing a pattern, consistent with the assurance dilemma: the Iraqis would reveal what coercers knew of their past behavior. By 1992 they had already destroyed their program. Yet they saw a path to sanctions relief through hiding their guilt from coercers who could use new evidence against them. Shared knowledge consistently led to concessions in Iraq.

Bush administration officials also learned the wrong lessons from episodes like the defection of Hussein Kamil and the chicken farm revelations. Vice President Dick Cheney claimed that the events "should serve as a reminder to all that we often learn more as a result of defections than we learned from the inspection regime itself."[97] And Secretary of Defense Donald Rumsfeld similarly said in December 2002 that "things have been found [in Iraq] not by discovery but through defectors."[98] These are misinterpretations of the case. Yes, defectors revealed information, but the Saddam regime followed up on these revelations with new concessions and admissions. The target responded to the knowledge of its coercers. It was the assurance dilemma at work.

1996–98: KICKING OUT INSPECTORS

By the end of 1995, Iraqi elites had gleaned the lesson of the previous half-decade: compliance would not beget sanctions relief.[99] The assurance dilemma hardened. UNSCOM responded to the Kamil revelations with a new probe into the "concealment mechanisms" of the Iraqi regime, which included more requests to visit military facilities and Saddam's palaces. The Iraqis, according to the CIA, interpreted this "new investigation as proof that WMD was being used as a pretense to bring about regime change"[100] and "deepened their belief that inspections were politically motivated and would not lead to the end of sanctions."[101] Saddam on multiple occasions framed to his advisers the choice he faced: Iraq could either "have sanctions with inspectors or sanctions without inspectors."[102]

These sentiments were shared in meetings with advisers from November 1995 to January 1996. Some blamed inspectors' refusal to resolve technical issues on their personal greediness and desire to keep receiving high UN salaries.[103] Others perceived hostile domestic politics in the United States that would have hindered their coercers from providing relief anyway. Vice President Taha Ma'ruf, speaking at a meeting with Saddam, reported that he sensed "the issue of implementing paragraph 22 [on sanctions relief] is no longer a technical or legal issue . . . rather a mere political issue, subject to the procedures and maneuvers of America in the next year. No matter how much we offer and cooperate and committees that come and go those people keep coming back. . . . They say something different every time or come up with a new way and so on."[104] Another of Iraq's three vice presidents, Taha Yassin Ramadan, concurred but assessed that US domestic politics would impede sanctions relief: "We are certain that in the political atmosphere now, America, and the elections, paragraph 22 cannot be imposed."[105]

The White House indeed would have faced domestic opposition to any sanctions relief. As Lee Feinstein, the director of policy planning at the State Department, recalled, "We had a hostile Congress that would have leapt down our throats had we drastically loosened the sanctions."[106] Rolf Ekéus, in retrospect, concurred that "the biggest problem UNSCOM faced was selling cooperation to the Iraqis. . . . [Our strategy] would only work if sanctions could be credibly removed after Iraq was decreed free of WMD. However, lifting sanctions was politically untenable for the American leadership."[107] Still, these domestic impediments to coercive assurance were quickly overshadowed by an explicit evolution of US strategy from coercion toward brute force.

In its second term, the Clinton administration began to make more obvious its desire for regime change in Iraq—a problem of demand magnitude.

Secretary of State Madeleine Albright infamously called in March 1997 for "a change in Iraq's government" and a "successor regime" to Saddam's, whose "intentions will never be peaceful."[108] The problem of coercive assurance remained, too, as Albright reminded, "We do not agree with nations who argue that if Iraq complies with its obligations concerning weapons of mass destruction, sanctions should be lifted."[109] The Clinton administration dubbed the policy "keeping Saddam in his box." Moreover, in October 1998 Congress passed the Iraq Liberation Act, which declared that it was now the policy of the United States to overthrow the government of Saddam Hussein. Speaking at the signing ceremony, President Clinton declared that "the United States looks forward to a democratically supported regime that would permit us to enter into a dialogue leading to the reintegration of Iraq into normal international life."[110] There is no evidence that the Clinton administration thereafter grappled with the assurance dilemma. David Palkki and Shane Smith, in their assessment of the recordings of internal Iraqi decision-making, find that "Saddam and his advisors were perfectly aware of American leaders' statements indicating that the sanctions would remain as long as Saddam was in power, and suspected that no amount of Iraqi compliance would satisfy the United States."[111] The CIA retrospective agreed in 2004 that "passage of the Iraq Liberation Act by the US Congress enhanced Iraqi suspicions."[112]

On August 5, 1998, Iraq announced that it would cease cooperation with UNSCOM and the IAEA. It said that it would restart cooperation on November 14 after US and UK threats to attack but reversed itself again, and inspectors left the country on December 16 ahead of Operation Desert Fox. On December 17–20 US and UK air strikes targeted suspected nuclear sites in Iraq.[113]

The assurance dilemma best explains why Iraq kicked out inspectors, despite the obvious military consequences it would face. As the CIA in 2004 concluded, the belief "that Iraq would never get a clean bill of health from the UN . . . was one factor that prompted them to cease cooperation with the UN in August 1998."[114] The records of Saddam's meetings at the time demonstrate such frustrations. In a meeting one week before kicking out UNSCOM inspectors and precipitating the Operation Desert Fox bombings, Saddam complained of the sincerity of his coercers' demands: "Iraq implemented 95 percent of the resolutions. Isn't that what Ekeus said? As for the five percent, it might take another ten years without getting results. We hardly accomplished 95 percent in three years. So, where are we going to end up if we pursue the five percent? . . . I am afraid, comrades, after all I said that you might think we still have hidden chemical weapons, missiles and so forth. We have nothing; not even one screw."[115]

In a brief discussion of the credibility of US threats at the same meeting, Taha Ma'ruf argued that the United States would not invade because "the American reputation is fading now in Somalia and other places. The last attack on Iraq raised a torrent of criticism even by their close allies." Saddam concurred that "a comprehensive war" against Iraq was unlikely, but he did perceive that bombing was likely in the absence of negotiation. Saddam came down in the end on the importance of the more specific US reputation in its dealings with Iraq: "Based on our experience, I would say the worst possibility is more likely to happen and therefore, you have to be prepared for the worst possibility."[116] Saddam chose the punishment over more compliance. Soon US missiles were flying as part of Operation Desert Fox.

When the dust settled, Iraq was no more willing to comply with coercion. In the perceptions of Mahdi Obeidi, "Operation Desert Fox was intended to force Iraq's full cooperation with the UN inspections. But it had the opposite result" inside Baghdad.[117] Saddam refused any more inspections. In the aftermath, Tariq Aziz echoed Saddam's assessment of coercive assurance in his justification for keeping inspectors out: "It was enough to have sanctions. To have inspectors as well had been too much."[118] Coercion fails if its target expects to be punished regardless of its behavior.

The 2003 Invasion

The pattern repeated itself one final time in the lead-up to the 2003 invasion of Iraq. The George W. Bush administration once more aimed to coerce Saddam. "Maybe if he thinks we'll overthrow him, he'll change," President Bush hypothesized in his office at Camp David in February 2002.[119] National security adviser and political scientist Condoleezza Rice told him that academics would call it "coercive diplomacy." She recalls that the president "loved the term."[120] Its implementation was the rub.

The United States relied on sticks alone, primarily through the mobilization of military power, and did little to appreciate or mitigate the assurance dilemma as it did so. Rumsfeld recalled of the strategy, "President Bush believed that the key to successful diplomacy with Saddam was a credible threat of military action. We hoped that the process of moving an increasing number of American forces into a position where they could attack Iraq might convince the Iraqis to end their defiance."[121] But it did not. In his study of the lead-up the Iraq War, the historian Melvyn Leffler aptly observed that the Bush administration's strategy of coercive diplomacy "was adopted without resolving its priority—regime change or WMD elimination, without a careful assessment of the diplomatic tactics and political inducements that might be necessary to make it a success, and without a thorough examination of its consequences should it not work."[122] "Coercive diplomacy had the air of a cynical exercise," Steve Coll similarly concluded in a thorough history of the period, "a test designed for Saddam to fail."[123]

The assurance dilemma does not explain why Saddam readmitted inspectors after the UNSC passed Resolution 1441 in November 2002.[124] The head of the UN Monitoring, Verification and Inspection Commission (UNMOVIC), Hans Blix, recalls an "almost frantic" effort to seek evidence and provide interviewees to UNSCOM's successors in UNMOVIC.[125] This is a test this book's theory fails. But Saddam had little to show, having already disarmed. Inspectors concerned themselves with dismantling Al-Fatah and Al-Samoud II missiles that exceeded the permissible range by just thirty kilometers. The evidence suggests that there was indeed nothing that Saddam could have done to avoid a US invasion.

Internally, President Bush seemed less committed to sincere coercion. In March 2002 he reportedly "waved his hand dismissively" to summarize his Iraq policy to a group of senators: "Fuck Saddam, we're taking him out."[126] In April 2002 Bush said in a press interview, "I have made up my mind that Saddam needs to go."[127] And US diplomat Richard Haass recalls a conversation about Iraq with Condoleezza Rice in July 2002 in which Rice interrupted him to say, "You can save your breath, Richard. The President has already made up his mind on Iraq," which Haass interpreted as though "the way she said it made clear [Bush] had decided to go to war."[128]

Still, on the war's doorstep, the president's advisers blamed the failure of coercive diplomacy on inadequate threats. "There is still hope," Deputy Secretary of Defense Paul Wolfowitz assessed in a speech to the Council on Foreign Relations in January 2003, "if Saddam is faced with a serious enough threat."[129] Years later, President Bush would reflect on his thinking on the eve of war, still puzzled. "If Saddam doesn't actually have WMD, why on earth would he subject himself to a war he will almost certainly lose?"[130] They did not appreciate how unconditional their threats were perceived to be.

As Saddam continued to defy, two sources of momentum also seemed to push the United States toward war. First, arguments about preserving a US reputation for making credible threats began to trickle into decision-making. In early January 2003 Bush said to Rice, "We're not winning. We're probably going to have to go to war." "You have to follow through on your threat," concurred Rice. "If you're going to carry out coercive diplomacy, you have to live with that decision."[131] Second, mobilized military power began to introduce into the dynamic bargaining process incentives to employ it. Having mobilized tens of thousands of troops in support of compellence, the Pentagon communicated to the White House in early 2003 that they could not stay forward-deployed and at a high level of readiness for the duration of the hot summer. If the United States was to go to war against Saddam, it would be better if that order came in the spring, so that fighting did not have to contend with the heat.[132]

Washington abandoned coercive diplomacy and went to war in March. Puzzlingly, the White House issued a final ultimatum forty-eight hours before US forces began the invasion of Iraq.[133] The last concession the US demanded was indeed for Saddam himself to step down and leave the country. He had no incentive to comply and did not. In March 2003 Bush privately held that "if Saddam Hussein leaves, we'll go in anyway."[134] Although the Bush administration did not rush to war, it was bound to be frustrated by a strategy of all threats and no coercive assurance.[135]

Iraqi elites indeed perceived US military mobilization through the lens of the assurance dilemma. Obeidi recalls that the head of the Military Indus-trialization Commission (MIC), Abdul Tawab, spoke at a security meeting of the MIC in February 2003 to say, "There is much talk about the ultima-tums of President Bush and the United Nations weapons inspectors. They are creating a pretext for war, and they want to use our honorable scientists as tools for their hostile intentions."[136] Obeidi himself in February "sensed that an American invasion was inevitable. The U.S. troop buildup neared completion in northern Kuwait, with too many supplies and soldiers amassed to allow for a face-saving retreat."[137] And during a February 2003 dinner in Baghdad, IAEA director general Mohamed ElBaradei reported that his last attempts alongside Blix to implore the Iraqis to be more forth-coming about their past nuclear weapons program fell on deaf and defeated ears. The credible threat of US military force held little sway anymore. Husam Muhammad Amin al-Yasin, one of the Iraqi officials present, said to Blix, "You cannot help us, because this war is going to happen, and nothing you or we can do will stop it. We both know that. Whatever we do, it is a done deal." Amir Hamudi Hasan al-Sa'adi, Saddam's chief scientific adviser, nodded along next to Husam.[138] After the war, according to the CIA, Iraqi scientists who were captured and debriefed by US intelligence services "expressed surprise when a former US inspector came into the room to try to resolve old material balance issues because they felt it had been a ruse for US policy goals and not a legitimate concern."[139]

The Assurance Dilemma in Iraq

After his nuclear, chemical, and biological weapons infrastructure was wrecked in the Gulf War, Saddam destroyed his stocks of illicit weapons and submitted to what he thought would be a short inspections process. He did so to avoid another military attack and in the hopes of having crippling sanctions lifted; coercion pressured him into taking the concession gamble. But Saddam was soon disappointed. Punishing sanctions and occasional air strikes remained. As he authorized disclosures of past weapons pro-grams according to the evidence in the possession of his coercers, he and his advisers came to conclude that nothing they could do would end the coercive punishments Iraq faced. Defiance became preferable. Saddam ceased cooperation with inspectors in 1998.

Iraq's coercers made little effort to communicate the contingency of their punishments. They did not demonstrate coercive control over themselves or their coalition, contributing to the failure of coercion. They also acquired a reputation for noncredible assurance in the eyes of Baghdad, built up over eight years of jockeying for sanctions relief only to see no end to punishment. Only shared knowledge, especially caused by the defection of Hussein Kamil, encouraged Iraq to be more forthcoming for a time.

The assurance dilemma lens is strongest in the period from 1993 to 1998, after Saddam abandoned his hedge to reconstitute WMD programs and before the passage of the Iraq Liberation Act that signaled that the United States sought regime change. From 1998 to 2003, it is possible that Washington no longer intended for sanctions against Iraq to be coercive. In service of a brute force goal, perhaps sanctions intended to starve Iraq of resources and keep Saddam conventionally weak. President H. W. Bush's national security adviser, Brent Scowcroft, certainly implied as much when looking back in 2003 he claimed that sanctions on Iraq "worked in the sense that [Saddam] was never able to rebuild his conventional army."[140] If the strangulation is the point, the punishment is not coercive because it does not demand a change in the target's behavior.

"They Will Laugh at Us"

Coaxing Libya to Confess

This chapter explains Libya's decision-making about its nuclear program when it faced compellence from the United States and the United Kingdom. From 1980 onward, the US and others sought to compel Tripoli to abide by its NPT commitments. Until 2003 Libya defied coercive demands and made consistent efforts to build a weapon. It was coerced by the very states whose threats had motivated its clandestine nuclear program. Libya's compliance with their demands in 2003 warrants explanation.

I find that from 1998 to 2003 Libya defied compellent demands over its WMD program because it perceived a lack of credible coercive assurance, not because it perceived compellent threats to be insufficiently credible or painful. Efforts to overcome the assurance dilemma finally led to Libya's ultimate concession. The 1998 disentangling of UN and US sanctions to apply to different demands—Lockerbie and WMDs, respectively—allowed Libya to concede one issue at a time. The secrecy of talks in 2003 kept spoilers, such as hawkish US advisers and Israeli leaders, out of the bargaining process. And Tripoli held on to information that it thought would incriminate it and anger its coercers until US and British spies shared the extent of their knowledge of Libya's WMD programs. New Libyan admissions consistently followed this pattern of confessing only what coercers knew already. The assurance dilemma lens helps to explain Libya's acquiescence in 2003 as well as the failure of coercion for years before (see table 4.1).

Prior to 1998, however, the assurance dilemma receives less support because it is not a sufficient explanation for Libyan defiance. At the time, the United States' main goal in its relations with Libya was the destruction of the Muammar Qaddafi regime. From 1986 to 1998, therefore, Libya defied coercion because of its correct perception of US intent. As discussed in chapter one, a coercer may undermine its own coercive strategy by making maximalist demands of a target. This is a problem of demand

Table 4.1 Libya

Date	Concessions	Threat credibility	Threat severity	Assurance credibility	Consistent with assurance dilemma?
1980	No	Low	Low	–	–
1986	No	High	High	Low	✓[a]
1995	No	High	High	Low	✓[a]
1998	No[b]	High	Medium	Low	✓
2001	No	Higher	High	Low	✓
Mar. 2003	No	Higher	Higher	Lower	✓
Dec. 2003	Yes	Higher	Higher	High	✓

[a] While the assurance dilemma is not invalidated, the magnitude of coercer demands is a better explanation for the failure of coercion until 1998.

[b] This table only considers nuclear-related concessions, not Libyan support for terrorism.

magnitude. Target defiance is not due to a lack of coercive assurance but to a lack of bargaining space. The United States therefore had to change its goals, not its strategy. Only after the US dropped its goal of regime change did it confront the assurance dilemma, and Washington had to communicate that it no longer sought to use force against Libya unconditionally.

My research relies as much as possible on Libyan perspectives of US and British coercion. Statements from Qaddafi himself are the most salient evidence, supplemented by the statements of top officials such as Musa Kusa, Abdul Rahman Shalgham, and Qaddafi's son Seif al Islam Qaddafi, his father's counsel and likely heir. For similar reasons, I place particular emphasis on Målfrid Braut-Hegghammer's accounts of the Libyan nuclear program—her access to interview Libyan officials prior to the toppling of the Qaddafi regime contributed to her comprehensive history of Libya's nuclear investments and bureaucratic organization.[1] I add to this history a focus on interaction between Libya and the international community putting pressure on the regime and explain variation in its efficacy over time. Libyan perceptions are also often filtered through interlocutors. For example, I use primary documents from the IAEA, which became involved in the Libya nuclear issue after the secret nuclear program was revealed publicly in 2003. I supplement these documents with secondary accounts. I do not rely on US documents as few are yet available to scholars. US records are also unlikely to provide ample details on the case since the matter was handled with such secrecy in the US government. Negotiators did not receive formal orders: "No national security decision directives, no Presidential Finding, no State Department cable with negotiating instructions," recalls William Tobey, a member of George W. Bush's National Security Council (NSC) staff.[2] Moreover, the fate of Libyan government records after the 2011 civil war and military intervention is unknown.[3]

Improving Existing Explanations

The conventional wisdom of the Libyan case myopically focuses on threat credibility. After the invasion of Iraq and toppling of Saddam Hussein in 2003, the story goes, another mercurial dictator in the Arab world with WMD ambitions feared that he was next on the US invasion list. After years of insufficiently credible threats of severe punishment, US threats of military force were so highly credible in 2003 that Muammar Qaddafi finally gave in. The lesson: flex your muscle to scare your enemies into submission.

This narrative that the Iraq War cowed Qaddafi into concessions was later exaggerated.[4] It was a legacy of the war nurtured by the Bush administration itself. Running for reelection in the context of emerging revelations about intelligence failure in Iraq and a gathering insurgency, President George W. Bush especially sought to connect the Iraq War to successful Libyan disarmament during the 2004 presidential election campaign. In the first presidential debate against Senator John Kerry, Bush highlighted the victory: "I hope to never have to use force. But by speaking clearly and sending messages that we mean what we say, we've affected the world in a positive way. Look at Libya. Libya was a threat. Libya is now peacefully dismantling its weapons programs. Libya understood that America and others will enforce doctrine."[5] Vice President Dick Cheney, in his debate, similarly called the Libya deal "one of the great by-products . . . of what we did in Iraq and Afghanistan."[6] He often referred in his campaign stump speech to the mere "five days" between Saddam's capture and Libya's announcement. "Moammar Ghadafi, in Libya," Cheney asserted, "watched what we did in Afghanistan, watched what we did in Iraq, and five days after we dug Saddam out of his hole, north of Baghdad, Ghadafi went public and announced he wanted to give up all of his WMD—all of his weapons of mass destruction, get out of the nuclear business."[7] Tough US threats and bold action had cowed Qaddafi. The implication is that until 2003 coercion failed because threats were not credible or severe enough.

As I show in this chapter, the invasion of Iraq increased the credibility of US threats, but that alone was insufficient. The assurance dilemma remained, and Qaddafi still defied these spikes in threat credibility until he received assuring signals that concession was worth the gamble. The most extreme version of the connection between Iraq and Libya is the folklore that Saddam's capture led days later to the Qaddafi deal, but the record of secret bargaining suggests that Qaddafi was ready to concede his nuclear program prior to Saddam's capture, and, in fact, seeing Saddam pulled from a hole on television caused Qaddafi to balk at disarmament. He only came around after another phone call with his coercers.

Some standard histories also argue that Qaddafi had no real nuclear program and traded away nuclear "junk" for carrots. Braut-Hegghammer writes that due to insufficient indigenous expertise, "the Libyan nuclear weapons project is better described as a plan than a program."[8] Hymans agrees that despite its "dalliance" with the A. Q. Khan network, Libya was "defeated by the fine print on his purchases, which read 'some assembly required.'"[9] Supply-side disruptions certainly impeded Libyan progress on nuclear weapons. Owing to proliferation concerns, many nuclear suppliers refused to conduct business with Libya. The Soviet Union, for example, canceled plans to sell Tripoli a 440-megawatt pressurized water reactor in 1986 at least in part because of Mikhail Gorbachev's concern about Libyan proliferation.[10] Indeed, IAEA reports do reveal how much Libyan scientists struggled to master nuclear technology and develop expertise. A lot of what Libya received from the black market were useless, first-generation centrifuges that Pakistan could not get to work.[11]

Yet the available evidence of Libyan perceptions of coercion shows few signs of such thinking. Qaddafi thought the program was real, valuable, and advancing. He held genuine ambitions to possess the bomb. Although it made halting technical progress, Libya continued to throw money at its nuclear program. Despite purchasing some nuclear junk, other black-market shipments were serious, especially later in the decade and into the early 2000s, including Chinese warhead designs, some second-generation centrifuges, and converted uranium hexafluoride (UF6) to feed into them. Libya's ambitions are clear in its investments. Tripoli spent hundreds of millions of dollars to try to solve its technical problems. Early on it sought to buy a bomb outright from Pakistan or China. As late as 2002 it purchased weapons designs and a turnkey uranium-enrichment facility from A. Q. Khan. In 2003 Libyan leaders believed they were just a few years away from building a nuclear weapon. Indeed, in the aftermath some experts realized that the Libyan program had been more advanced than they appreciated.[12] Libya might never have figured out how to build a bomb. We cannot know now. But the underlying policy and investments pursued right up until the end of 2003 were consistent: pursuit of the bomb. Libya indeed had to be compelled out of its nuclear ambitions. The evidence is much stronger that Qaddafi was coerced and, critically, assured.

This chapter begins by reviewing the origins of Libya's nuclear program and interest in the bomb. It then describes the nature of international compellent demands directed at Tripoli and shows that while Libya's leaders perceived coercive threats to be credible after 1986, they chose to defy because of the perception that the United States sought nothing less than regime change. The chapter subsequently examines Libya's decision-making in the late 1990s and early 2000s, zooming in especially on the critical bargaining over WMDs in 2003. The evidence reveals how scaling back its demands still resulted in US failure to compel nuclear concessions from the Libyans because leaders in Tripoli perceived that concessions would not preclude punishment. In 2003, finally, a US and British coercive strategy aimed at signaling coercive control to surmount the assurance dilemma convinced Tripoli to give up its nuclear ambitions and seek an end to compellent punishments.

Libya's Nuclear Program

Muammar Qaddafi came to power in a 1969 coup. The following year, he began Libya's nuclear weapons program. Initially, the ambitions were motivated by pan-Arab nationalist prestige and a desire for regional status as a leader of the Arab world, as well as the hope of achieving "strategic parity" to nullify the Israeli nuclear deterrent and open a window for further Arab conventional aggression against Israel.[13] Libya was not threatened by Israel per se, only in the sense that it identified with the anti-Israel Arab cause and supported pro-Palestinian groups. In 2004 Qaddafi claimed of the program, "In 1969 and early 1970s we did not reflect on where or against whom we could use the nuclear bomb. Such issues were not considered. All that was important was to build the bomb."[14]

In the early 1970s Qaddafi irritated the United States and many European countries by nationalizing foreign assets, including oil fields.[15] A resulting surplus of oil revenue—aided by a surge in oil prices—allowed Qaddafi to finance his nuclear ambitions. The initial strategy was twofold: attempts to directly purchase a nuclear warhead and financing foreign nuclear programs. Libyan representatives approached China (1970),[16] Pakistan (1977), and India (1978) about buying a bomb outright. None agreed. Qaddafi also sought to fund an Egyptian nuclear weapons program. His discussions with Egyptian president Gamal Abdel Nasser were ongoing when Nasser died, and his successor, Anwar Sadat, killed the prospects of such cooperation when he came to power. Libya did, however, contribute funds to the Pakistani nuclear program. From about 1973 until about 1979, Libya contributed $100 million to $500 million to the Pakistani nuclear program in exchange for "full access" to it.[17] Instead of "full access," Libya seems to have only received scientific training for some personnel.[18]

The strategy was supplemented with attempts to cover a clandestine nuclear weapons effort with a civilian nuclear power program. Libya asked the IAEA for early-stage nuclear assistance in the early 1970s—uranium exploration and mining, research, and exploring a nuclear energy program.[19] From 1978 to 1981, Libya also imported 2,263 metric tons of yellowcake uranium ore from French mines in Niger (much more than required for any foreseeable uses), declaring only one thousand tons to the IAEA.[20]

Libya shopped around for a reactor supplier in the 1970s, ultimately finding the Soviet Union to be the most receptive. On the heels of signing a major conventional arms deal with the Soviets in 1974,[21] a sign of an expanding security relationship, Libya purchased in 1975 a Soviet ten-megawatt IRT-1 research reactor. It became operational at Tajoura in November 1983.[22] Under pressure from the Soviet Union, applied as a condition to its supply of the research reactor, Libya ratified the NPT in 1975.[23] Safeguards came into force in July 1980.

Further reactor deals ultimately fell through. Libya was turned down by the United States in 1975, France canceled a prospective deal in 1976, and China turned it down in 1978.[24] Libya then sent a delegation to Moscow to request a heavy-water reactor, a heavy-water plant, and a spent-fuel reprocessing facility. "According to one senior Soviet official," Braut-Hegghammer writes, "it was obvious to both parties that this was intended to be a military program."[25]

At the end of the 1970s, Libya's nuclear weapons program was flailing, spending a lot of money in many strategic directions. An IAEA expert assistance mission to Libya, meant to help the Libyans develop their peaceful nuclear science and technology, noted how the Libyan civil program was lavishly funded but lacked scientific experts. The report noted the "very ambitious plans for the development of nuclear sciences in Libya" but a "severe shortage of trained personnel."[26] The vast scope of the investments had been made "without a clear idea of the type of investigation to be performed and the results to be expected" as "equipment is installed, but is idling because of the shortage of personnel."[27] In sum, its investments clearly indicated Libya's weaponization ambitions, but scientists in the nuclear program struggled to make progress toward the bomb.

Compellence Begins

Libyan relations with the United States soured in the late 1970s, and the 1980s saw a series of tit-for-tat escalations. Tensions erupted with US air strikes on Libya in 1986 and the Lockerbie bombing in 1988. The nuclear weapons program continued throughout. This section assesses the evolution of coercive pressure against Libya in this period and how it was perceived by the regime. Until 1986 Tripoli did not perceive US threats to use military force to be credible. Thereafter, the goal of US coercion was the end of the Qaddafi regime—a demand too extreme to succeed whether or not it was paired with credible threats.

1980: NONCREDIBLE THREATS BEGIN, LIBYA DEFIES

The 1980–86 period is no real mystery for theories of coercion. Libya simply did not perceive compellent threats over its nuclear program to either exist or to be credible. The United States had initially tried to get along with the Qaddafi regime. Libya was a source of crude oil for the US market, and the US provided access to technology and other goods. The US even shared

CIA estimates with Qaddafi about internal threats.[28] But within a few years of his taking power, his anti-Israel policy and support for international terrorism had caused a rift. In 1977 the Carter administration foiled a Libyan plot to assassinate the US ambassador in Egypt over his role in the Camp David peace talks.[29] President Carter imposed partial sanctions ("trade restrictions") and put Libya on its list of state sponsors of terrorism, the first such list, in 1979. He also closed the US embassy in Tripoli in 1980 (the building having been burned in an anti-American protest in 1979).[30] Sanctions, however, were not linked explicitly to nuclear issues.[31]

I code 1980 as the beginning of Libya's perception of a red line on nuclear weapons development, when nuclear safeguards came into force. IAEA inspectors monitored Libya's nuclear facilities to ensure they were used for peaceful purposes only. Nonetheless, there is some evidence to suggest that Libya did not perceive any credible threat of punishment in the early 1980s. To begin with, Tripoli believed that it could obtain fissile material for nuclear weapons from nuclear reactors purchased from the Soviet Union. This would have been a poor proliferation strategy, as any diversion of nuclear material from a safeguarded facility was liable to be caught. Libya did not seem to appreciate that risk.[32] More importantly, Qaddafi placed faith in the backing of the Soviet Union. The Soviet Union had indeed been a friend to Libya. In 1981 Tripoli and Moscow inked an extensive agreement that included, Braut-Hegghammer writes, "contracts for conventional arms, technology transfers—including nuclear technology—and a promise of Soviet support if Libya were subjected to foreign aggression."[33] Thus, relying on its Soviet patron, Libya had less to fear from its coercers.

Libyan leaders accordingly plowed ahead with the nuclear program. Beginning in the 1980s Libya tried to get serious about the gas centrifuge path to uranium enrichment. Throughout the 1980s Libya sought gas centrifuge technology, a modular uranium-conversion facility, and two mass spectrometers (to help build centrifuges) and engaged in uranium-conversion experiments. From 1981 to 1983 Libya sought assistance from Romania in constructing a heavy-water nuclear reactor. Romania was tempted by the money, but the deal never closed.[34] In January 1984 the Libyans sought assistance from A. Q. Khan for the first time, but Khan declined this first offer because they did not have the capability to scale up their efforts.[35] In 1984 they conducted plutonium-separation experiments at the IRT-1 research reactor using imported natural uranium (violating safeguards). Libya sought to purchase a "hot cell" facility for plutonium reprocessing from Argentina; US pressure killed this deal. Libya also sought a uranium-conversion facility with help from a Belgian firm from 1981 to 1984; US pressure killed this deal as well. But in 1984 Libya and Japan signed a deal for the supply of a modular uranium-conversion facility.[36] Components arrived in 1986 without instructions for assembly. (Suffering from a lack of expertise, the facility remained unassembled until 1998. Some of the equipment was supposedly used in "cold tests" [i.e., without uranium] in 2002.[37]) Finally, in 1985 Libya sent some of its imported yellowcake uranium to "an undisclosed nuclear weapons state" where it was processed into UF6 and other compounds and sent back to Libya in the same year.[38]

Simultaneously, Libyan and US forces engaged in a series of provocations and punishments as the Reagan administration began to direct more of its attention to Qaddafi. In September 1980 Libyan jets fired at US reconnaissance aircraft over the Gulf of Sirte, asserting their extended claim of territorial waters. In August 1981 Libyan jets again fired on US aircraft in the Gulf of Sirte, and US F-14s shot down two Libyan jets in response, killing one Libyan pilot. And in March 1986 Libya fired six missiles at US aircraft in the Gulf of Sirte. In response, the US sank one Libyan vessel and destroyed a coastal SA-5 missile site.

While the issue at stake in these early 1980s military clashes was ostensibly freedom of navigation in international waters, a litany of disputes drove Washington's ire with Tripoli. Qaddafi had nationalized the oil industry and kicked out American businesses, become cozy with Moscow, and promoted anti-American riots.

In parallel to its military posture, the United States imposed economic pressure. It instituted an embargo on Libyan crude oil in 1982 and extended it in 1985 to include refined petroleum products. Libyan citizens were banned from studying nuclear science in the United States, and in January 1986 the Reagan administration froze all Libyan assets in the US and imposed additional unilateral sanctions. What had been a piecemeal effort at economic coercion coalesced as comprehensive sanctions with Reagan's January 1986 executive order.[39] The sanctions later expanded in 1992 and 1996.[40]

This time, Qaddafi's response came in the form of terrorism. On April 5, 1986, Libyan-backed terrorists bombed a West Berlin nightclub frequented by US military personnel. Three people died, including two Americans, and two hundred were injured, including seventy-nine Americans.

1986: CREDIBLE THREATS BEGIN, LIBYA CONTINUES TO DEFY

The Libyan perception of US military threats changed in 1986. On April 15 the United States conducted air strikes on terrorist camps and military facilities in Libya. The strikes hit one of Qaddafi's homes and allegedly killed one of his children. Such deep US air strikes revealed to Libya that it could not rely on the Soviet Union for protection. This was in addition to the already underway souring of Soviet-Libyan relations, including the demise of prospective reactor-purchasing deals. US threats to use military force on Libyan territory were now more credible.

The threat credibility lens would predict a corresponding greater willingness to make concessions. But Qaddafi still defied. The nuclear program and clandestine research at Tajoura continued apace and went further underground.[41] Just after the raids, components for the uranium-conversion facility began to arrive clandestinely in 1986, and Libya stored them in hidden facilities around Tripoli.[42]

Libya's continued defiance of compellence no longer stemmed from non-credible threats but from the magnitude of its coercer's demands. Targeting Qaddafi outright in 1986 signaled that the Reagan administration was in pursuit of regime change rather than coercion to change Qaddafi's behavior. A demand to commit suicide allows for no bargaining space. US intelligence assessments from the time corroborate this perception of US intentions. A 1984 CIA assessment doubted that Qaddafi could be compelled and concluded that "no course of action short of stimulating Qaddafi's fall will bring any significant and enduring change in Libyan policies."[43]

Additionally, Libya's motivation for its nuclear program shifted after 1986 in a way that suggested a fear of regime change. The Libyan nuclear program became motivated by a desire to deter US aggression. After the 1986 strikes, Qaddafi said, "The Arabs must possess the atomic bomb to defend themselves." He further explicated this thinking in 1990, saying, "If we possessed a deterrent—missiles that could reach New York . . . [the US] and others [would] no longer think about attack. . . . We should have a nuclear bomb."[44] Braut-Hegghammer writes that "the new focus on national security following the American air strikes in 1986 strengthened the Libyan regime's commitment to its nuclear project," citing an interview with a senior Libyan official.[45]

Across the board, Qaddafi was not cowed by direct US punishments. He continued to pursue nuclear weapons, claim extended sovereignty in the Mediterranean Sea, and support terrorism. He planned and executed the Lockerbie airplane bombing on December 21, 1988, and the bombing of a French airliner over Niger on September 19, 1989, which killed 259 and 171 people, respectively.

1988: LOCKERBIE INTRODUCES MORE IMPEDIMENTS TO COERCION

The Lockerbie bombing cast a pall over all US-Libya relations for a decade and became an impediment to counterproliferation coercion by causing the United States to cling to its goal of regime change in Tripoli. Of the 259 people killed in the Lockerbie bombing, 189 were US citizens— many college students returning home for Christmas vacation. The American public rallied behind the Lockerbie victims, empowering a lobby of grieving families. Washington's position could not soften in public.

When the US and the UK indicted two Libyan intelligence agents in November 1991 for plotting the Lockerbie bombing, they made five demands of Libya: (1) surrender the suspects for trial, (2) accept responsibility for the suspects' actions, (3) disclose everything you know about the bombing, allowing access to witnesses, (4) compensate the victims' families, and (5) cease all support for terrorism.[46] The UNSC imposed multilateral sanctions in 1992, having given Libya three months to comply with the demands. Sanctions further tightened in November 1993.

Tripoli's perception of maximal demands prevented this additional pressure from contributing to a bargain between Libya and its coercers. Lockerbie had introduced a powerful new interest group in American domestic politics that sought justice. After the January 1992 UNSC vote to impose sanctions,[47] for instance, the Bush administration rebuffed a Libyan outreach for dialogue due to pressure from the Lockerbie victims' families.[48] Sanctions could not be lifted or weakened unless the Lockerbie issue was fully resolved and compensation paid. Congressional passage of the Iran-Libya Sanctions Act in 1996 was a direct result of the lobbying of victims' families.[49] Lockerbie had to be settled before the demand for regime change could be scaled back and bargaining space could reemerge.

1990S: LIBYA "REINVIGORATES" ITS NUCLEAR PROGRAM

At the end of the 1980s and in the early 1990s, Libya began to amend its proliferation strategy. Its economy was stagnant.[50] Qaddafi experienced an unsuccessful military coup attempt in 1993. Sanctions were hurting, and Tripoli wanted relief, but it did not want to go all in for rapprochement with Washington and give up its nuclear program. Qaddafi gave his advisers leeway to probe the possibility of opening up the country economically. He understood WMDs to be an impediment to such liberalization, and he appeared willing to negotiate them away. Yet he also feared unconditional punishments. Qaddafi therefore pursued a dual-track approach: probe for the possibility of rapprochement but build nuclear weapons in case of failure.[51]

In 1989 the Libyan nuclear program was reorganized under the leadership of Matuq M. Matuq, a nonscientist regime insider whom Qaddafi trusted. Matuq embraced the black market for nuclear procurement, continuing to focus on the gas centrifuge uranium-enrichment path to the bomb.[52] Taking note of the 1981 Israeli strike on the Iraqi Osirak reactor, Libya sought to keep its illicit procurement activities quiet and keep enrichment sites secret and mobile. Matuq reconnected with A. Q. Khan and purchased P-1 centrifuges in early 1991. Soon Libya had a disagreement with the Khan network and refused to pay because the P-1 centrifuges were outdated.[53]

In 1995 Libya decided to "reinvigorate its nuclear activities" and turned again to Khan.[54] In 1997 it ordered twenty complete L-1 (P-1) gas centrifuges and most of the components for another two hundred centrifuges. By

1998 Libya had assembled its uranium-conversion facility. In late 1999 or early 2000 Libya acquired two new mass spectrometers and in September 2000 acquired two L-2 (P-2) advanced centrifuges.

Why did Libya double down on its nuclear program just as it was coming under greater pressure from its coercers? A threat credibility lens would predict a greater willingness to make concessions. The evidence instead suggests that Libya continued to defy because of the magnitude of US demands. Libya was quite clearly stung by its experience feeling out the Bush administration in 1992. The imposition of UN sanctions convinced Libyan officials that their coercers would never relent. "It is now known that Libya attempted to offer giving up the nuclear weapons programme to the US before United Nations (UN) sanctions were imposed in 1992. However, the cool reception these attempts were met with suggested that no rewards would be given for abandoning the nuclear proliferation efforts," writes Braut-Hegghammer, citing an interview with a senior official in the Libyan General People's Congress.[55] And another senior official learned the following lesson: "After Libya was accused of the Lockerbie attack in 1992, officials began to fear that Washington and its allies would attempt to overthrow the regime. Libya would not benefit from giving up its nuclear weapons project in this context, and potentially had a lot to lose in light of the entrenched conflict with the West," Braut-Hegghammer writes, citing an interview with a formerly central figure in the Revolutionary Committee system.[56] This was an accurate reading of US intentions. Washington would not take yes for an answer with Qaddafi in power.

Direct Coercive Bargaining between the US, UK, and Libya, 1998–2003

In the late 1990s and early 2000s Libya began to speak directly with its coercers. When in 1998 the United States and Libya began to resolve the issue of Lockerbie, Washington scaled back its demand for regime change in Libya. This reduction in the magnitude of its demands opened the possibility of a coercive bargain over the nuclear issue. Nevertheless, Libya continued to defy. Once the US goal changed, it encountered the assurance dilemma. While Libya sought to remove the punishment of painful sanctions, insufficient coercive assurance that Qaddafi would not be punished anyway impeded bargaining. Moreover, the record shows that the United States sought to overcome the assurance dilemma—by disentangling demands, managing spoilers, and sharing knowledge—before Libya agreed to concede its nuclear ambitions. I walk through each of these signals in turn, including how each was implemented by coercers and perceived by the Libyan leadership. The analysis focuses especially heavily on 2003, when secret talks over the nuclear issue were deepest and led to a breakthrough.

DISENTANGLING LOCKERBIE AND WMDS

By the late 1990s, two major issues impeded sanctions relief for Libya and better relations with the United States: Lockerbie and WMD proliferation. Libyan support for terrorism had subsided in the 1990s, but the issue was still very much on the table in the form of accountability for the Lockerbie bombing. Ron Suskind reports that the Clinton administration handled Libya discussions with "utmost secrecy" because "families of the Lockerbie victims had long since organized into a fierce, somewhat unruly advocacy group, lobbying for arrests, sanctions, and anything else that would amount to a facsimile of justice. Notice of a dialogue with the monsters from Tripoli would have summoned a righteous explosion."[57] It was politically costly to even negotiate with Libya. William Burns, assistant secretary of state for Near Eastern affairs, recalls that during a session at the State Department with Lockerbie families, "one furious mother" told him, "Go to hell with your Libyan friends."[58]

Libya's coercers effectively disentangled the issues by tying Lockerbie concessions to UN sanctions relief and WMD concessions to US sanctions relief. In August 1998 the US and UK offered through the UNSC that UN sanctions would be lifted if Libya surrendered its two Lockerbie suspects for trial in The Hague. But US sanctions would remain tied to the WMD program.[59] And US officials communicated this to Libya.[60] At the time, Washington saw this as a practical solution. It was moving to resolve the Lockerbie compensation issue before the multilateral sanctions regime fractured; Russia, China, the Arab League, and the Organization of African Unity had been insisting that the United States accept Libya's Lockerbie compromise offer.

Libya complied in April 1999, handing over the two suspects, and UN sanctions were suspended.[61] As the assurance dilemma predicts, when coerced over multiple entangled issues, targets like Libya lack the necessary coercive assurance to concede on any individual issue. The demands had to be disentangled by being tied to separate punishments.

The resolution of the Lockerbie issue did allow the United States to scale back its demands on Libya. Regime change was no longer the end goal of coercion. Washington was free to pursue a coercive bargain with Qaddafi still in power. Crucially, while the United States eliminated its demand for regime change, it maintained its threat of regime change if Libya did not comply with other demands. Convincing Libya that it had in fact abandoned its goal of regime change was now the impediment to coercion.

Secret US-UK-Libya talks then began in May 1999,[62] in which Qaddafi was feeling out the possibility of a deal to give up his nuclear program, but he remained skeptical. During direct talks with their US and British counterparts, according Braut-Hegghammer, Libyan officials "had to balance their efforts to strike a deal . . . against the risk that Gaddafi could pull back from their proposed agreement."[63] Qaddafi was not yet committed to concessions, even though he felt the pain of economic sanctions.[64]

SUSPENDED TALKS AND 9/11

Direct talks continued in fits and starts. Negotiations were suspended by the US for fear of leaks during the 2000 presidential election, and then the terrorist attacks of September 11, 2001, reoriented US foreign policy. This episode is important to examine as it refocused US policy on the threats of terrorism and WMDs. In this context, compellent threats to Libya over these issues would have theoretically increased in their credibility.

After 9/11 Qaddafi did perceive a spike in the credibility of US threats, yet he expanded his nuclear program—evidence inconsistent with the threat credibility lens and consistent with the assurance dilemma. Bush administration officials assessed that "Qaddafi understood what Saddam didn't: that 9/11 changed everything."[65] Libya's foreign minister, Abdul Rahman Shalgham, recalled that in 2001 President Bush used the Algerian president as an intermediary to communicate that "either you get rid of your weapons of mass destruction or he will personally destroy them and destroy everything with no discussion."[66] Qaddafi supposedly asked "every Arab leader in his rolodex" to help him convince Washington that Libya was opposed to terrorism. He also offered to help the United States with counterterrorism intelligence.[67]

But the nuclear program continued and grew. Qaddafi did not perceive credible enough assurance to dispose of his insurance policy in the face of compellence. In late 2001 or early 2002, Matuq paid A. Q. Khan $100 million to $200 million for a turnkey gas centrifuge plant with ten thousand P-2 centrifuges. The plant was supposed to be completed by June 2003.[68] The Khan offer included blueprints for a Chinese warhead design, UF6 feed material, installation, and training. Libya did receive the designs, technology, and "several cylinders" of UF6 in 2001 (shipped on a Pakistani airplane).[69] Libya further imported through Khan approximately sixteen kilograms of other uranium compounds in 2002. By then Libya had one nine-centrifuge cascade operational, and two other nineteen- and sixty-four-centrifuge cascades were partially completed.[70] From May to December 2002, Libya conducted two successful tests of its centrifuges but without UF6 inside.

Meanwhile, after 9/11 the Bush administration had picked up secret talks again with the Libyans in October 2001. William Burns was in charge of the negotiations and recalls that he was "careful to reiterate the main lines of the positions conveyed earlier by [Assistant Secretary of State Martin] Indyk" that "the lifting of U.S. national sanctions, built up since the Reagan-era conflicts with Qaddafi, would depend upon Libya giving up its nuclear and chemical weapons programs."[71] The talks bore fruit on counterterrorism cooperation, as Tripoli had already abandoned its support for terrorism.[72] They also reached further agreement on compensation for Lockerbie victims' families.[73] But in the fall of 2001 Burns still found his Libyan negotiating counterparts—Musa Kusa, Abdelati Obeidi, and Adbul Rahman Shalgham—to be reticent on the nuclear issue and "nervous about hidden agendas from us."[74] He felt the need to emphasize "that there was no ulterior motive in this—we had no interest in regime change."[75] Then in October 2002 UK prime minister Tony Blair wrote to Qaddafi about opening negotiations on Libya's WMD program.[76] He waited for a reply.

BARGAINING OVER WMDS IN 2003

Seif al Islam Qaddafi broke the silence in early 2003 by reaching out to British intelligence (MI6), asking it to intercede with Washington. Tripoli was, he said, interested in "clearing the air" on WMDs.[77] Director of Central Intelligence George Tenet and his counterpart from MI6 briefed Prime Minister Tony Blair and President Bush on the overture from Libya.[78] Blair then convinced Bush at a March Camp David meeting on Iraq to be willing to negotiate with Libya on WMDs. As Lockerbie and terrorism concerns subsided as major impediments to rapprochement, the US, the UK, and Libya were poised for a breakthrough.

Its coercers were credibly and severely threatening Libya. Decades of sanctions prevented Libya from expanding its oil production and left existing oil infrastructure rusting.[79] William Burns describes how "the energy sector was starved for investment, and the country's infrastructure was in shambles."[80] As a result, Libya produced half as much oil in 2003 as it had at its peak in the 1970s.[81] Economic punishment was indeed painful. Inflation reached 50 percent in 1994. In 2003 unemployment was 25 percent.

Negotiations began in March 2003—before the US invasion of Iraq.[82] The first trilateral meeting was held in April. Yet Qaddafi began to be scared that negotiations were a trap. Seif al Islam Qaddafi recalled to *Time* magazine that his father "'suspected an ambush' by the West: getting him to give up his only deterrent but withholding diplomatic rehabilitation."[83] "When Bush has finished with Iraq, we'll quickly have a clear idea of where he's going," he told *Le Figaro* in March. "It won't take long to find out if Iran, Saudi Arabia, or Libya will be targets as well. . . . Bush isn't logical. You can't tell what he's going to do. So you have to be ready for anything. Today, nobody can say: 'I will or won't be a target.'"[84] Braut-Hegghammer reports, citing an interview with Seif al-Islam Qaddafi, that "as talks intensified in early 2003 the Libyan leader feared that it could be a trap, and that there was a hidden agenda at play aiming for the overthrow of his regime."[85] Libya's coercers had just invaded another "rogue" state, Iraq, under the banner of counterproliferation. Graffiti in Tripoli read: "Today, Saddam. Tomorrow, Qaddafi."[86] The war certainly got the Brother Leader's attention. But speaking with his foreign minister, Shalgham, Qaddafi said in response, "They will laugh at us and document that we have WMD. They implicated Saddam Hussein and they want to implicate us too."[87]

It was, rather, the assurance dilemma that proved to be the difficult impediment throughout direct bargaining. Over the course of 2003, the United States and the United Kingdom came around slowly to offering coercive assurance signals. Early in the clandestine talks, Bush administration officials did not seem to grasp the need for coercive assurance. "The Libyans asked for non-aggression pacts and other security guarantees," Gordon Corera writes. But the US and UK responded that Libya had to give up its WMDs "before anything would be guaranteed."[88] Later they were more assuring. Table 4.2 lists the meetings that took place. The following sections review these efforts to communicate coercive assurance.

Table 4.2 Meetings with Libyan officials

Date	Location	Participants	Notes
Mid-Apr. 2003	Geneva	Kappes, Allen / Kusa, unknown Libyan diplomat	First meeting; near miss with Israelis; not much progress
Late May 2003	Europe	Kappes, Allen / Kusa, Seif	Not much progress
Aug. 2003	Europe	Kappes, Allen / Kusa, Seif	Not much progress; invitation to meet Qaddafi directly
Early Sept. 2003	Tripoli	Kappes, Allen / Qaddafi	First meeting with Qaddafi
Oct. 7, 2003	Tripoli	Allen / Kusa, unknown Libyans	Sharing of *BBC China* intercept
Oct. 19–29, 2003	Libya	Technical experts	"Technical visit" #1
Nov. 20, 2003	Bay Tree Hotel, Cotswolds, UK	Kappes, Allen / unknown Libyans	Sharing of A. Q. Khan recording; letter from President G. W. Bush
Dec. 1–12, 2003	Libya	Technical experts	"Technical visit" #2
Dec. 16, 2003	Travelers Club, London	Joseph, Kappes, Allen, William Ehrman and David Landsman (UK Foreign Office) / Kusa, Abdul al-Obeidi (Libyan ambassador to Rome), Mohammed Azwai (Libyan ambassador to London), three other unknown Libyans	Discussing content of the statement
December 18, 2003	Phone call	Blair / Qaddafi	After Saddam's capture

MANAGING SPOILERS

As theorized, targets of coercion as a practical matter need to know that they are bargaining with the right coercer(s) and that either domestic or international spoilers with independent abilities to inflict pain are not likely to punish them after they comply. Isolating spoilers from the bargaining process also has the benefit of signaling the sincerity of a coercer's willingness to strike a coercive bargain short of regime change. If regime change were the goal, spoilers would be more useful to include.

The Libyans first expressed their fears of bargaining with the wrong coercers in 2003 when they observed that secret communication channels did not reflect a unified willingness to strike a deal within its coercers' governments. When the Libyans, according to Corera, "insisted that they meet with someone who was not an undercover intelligence officer and of sufficient authority to show that the UK government as a whole was committed,"[89] the British arranged for a senior diplomat to deliver Qaddafi a pledge of good faith. Tony Blair sent a letter with "a high-ranking subordinate" to Tripoli and promised a "positive response" from the Washington and London if Libya disarmed. The Libyans appreciated the gesture.

Later in negotiations, the United States sent a similar signal. When Libyan concessions seemed within reach in December 2003, the highest-ranking US delegation yet, traveled to meet the Libyans. Stephen Kappes and Robert Joseph circumvented official travel procedures to secretly travel to London and work with their Libyan partners on language for Libya's concession statement. According to Bush administration official William Tobey, Joseph's attendance was meant to "signal to the Libyans that President Bush himself endorsed the effort."[90]

Secrecy, too, helped to keep the right actors in the know and spoilers at bay until the parties struck a coercive bargain. While well-positioned spoilers can also undo agreements after they are reached, they can more readily impede them before coercion succeeds. Managing spoilers until coercion succeeds is still valuable for communicating coercive assurance. President Bush gave the Libyan negotiation portfolio to CIA director George Tenet to ensure secrecy. Not even Donald Rumsfeld or Colin Powell were to be told about it.[91] Tenet delegated to Kappes, the deputy director of operations at the agency.[92] As this choice was explained by Tobey, "it is easier to keep the secret domestically if the CIA is in charge. The State Department is not good at deep secrecy."[93]

One Bush administration official known, including to the Libyans, for his uncompromising attitude was the then undersecretary of state for arms control and international security affairs, John Bolton. Bolton had wanted President Bush to name Libya as a member of the "axis of evil" in his January 2002 State of the Union address, but UK foreign secretary Jack Straw and David Manning, later the British ambassador to the United States, convinced Condoleezza Rice and Colin Powell to keep Libya out. Bolton also pushed for greater sway over Libyan relations but was kept out of the loop on purpose. Senior British officials reportedly pressed for Bolton's sidelining.[94] IAEA director general Mohammed ElBaradei similarly reports that he learned after the Libya deal was concluded that the "reason for the extreme secrecy governing the Libyan negotiations was to protect the talks from U.S. hard-liners. The fear, I was told, was that they might have tried to torpedo a peaceful resolution of the Libyan case. So they were informed only when the deal was done."[95] The White House, "uncharacteristically, sidelined the administration's neoconservative wing" from the Libya portfolio, according to Flynt Leverett, a member of the Bush administration's NSC.[96] Bolton knew nothing of the Libya deal until after the December 19, 2003, Libyan agreement was announced.[97]

Indeed, the US and UK governments were remarkably quiet about coercive bargaining with Libya.[98] When in January 2003 the CIA and British counterparts briefed George W. Bush and Tony Blair on the activities of the A. Q. Khan black-market network and Libya, it had been roughly a year since US and British intelligence identified Libya as a Khan customer. Until that point, the CIA publicly reported to Congress rumblings of nuclear activity in Libya but nothing more.[99] In the crucial year of 2003, US leaders and intelligence agencies made no public mention of its discoveries about Libya's cooperation with the Khan network. In its semiannual report to Congress in June 2003, the CIA wrote only cryptically that Libya "continued to develop its nuclear infrastructure" during the previous six-month period. It referenced only innocuous developments, namely cooperation between Libya and Russia at a known nuclear research center and "various technical exchanges through which [Libya] could have tried to obtain dual-use equipment."[100] The CIA said nothing publicly about Khan and Libya, despite the extensive intelligence it had amassed on that link. Neither did US officials mention the matter or hint at ongoing dialogue. Only after the fact, the CIA tacitly admitted that it had withheld certain information from the public about Libyan activities. In January 2004, after Libya made its concessions, the CIA issued an update on Libya that revealed the hidden bargaining.[101] The CIA report also referenced Khan for the first time.[102]

A similar dynamic played out internationally to keep the Israelis from learning about secret US-UK-Libyan talks and acting as a spoiler. Israeli participation, insistence on humiliating terms, or, worse, air strikes had the potential to doom coercive bargaining. An Israeli military strike would have been difficult but possible. A 1985 air strike against a PLO headquarters near Tunis had demonstrated the long reach of the Israeli air force in North Africa. Over a decade earlier, in September 1973, Ariel Sharon had bragged in the Knesset that Israel could hit "any target in the Arab world including Libya."[103]

Tobey recounts an awkward encounter in a Geneva hotel just prior to the first trilateral meeting in April 2003. As Kappes and his British counterpart sat waiting for the Libyans to arrive, former Israeli prime minister Ehud Barack entered the breakfast room. "While Kappes watched the Israelis apprehensively, his British colleague raced to head off the Libyans and direct them to another room on the hotel's top floor," writes Tobey.[104] Israel was in the dark about the Libyan nuclear program. Israeli intelligence completely missed Khan's smuggling network until the US shared intelligence to about it and not until 2002. Still, the United States insulated one of its closest allies from what it learned about Libya's activities specifically. After Libya disarmed, the scope of Libya's activities came as a shocking surprise to Israeli intelligence.[105] Indeed, after the fact, Israeli leaders angrily demanded of Washington an explanation for why Tel Aviv had been left out of the loop. An Israeli Knesset committee report condemned its intelligence community for its ignorance but also the United States for its actions:

> Israel was surprised to discover that Libya, under Muammar Qaddafi, has been intensively engaged in the development of a military nuclear capability. . . . The intelligence services of the USA (and of Britain) did not share with their colleagues in Israel in real time their recent and significant exposures of the Libyan nuclear program, and even concealed from the State of Israel the steps taken vis-à-vis the Libyan regime in the apparently successful attempt to bring about the liquidation of its nuclear industry.[106]

The United States (and Britain) declined to let Israel—even a select group of elite officials—in on its information.[107] Washington prioritized coercive assurance vis-à-vis Libya. This isolation of the bargaining process mattered both for its practical elimination of potential spoilers and for the signal it sent about the coercers' serious intent to strike a deal.

SHARED KNOWLEDGE

Specific knowledge of Libya's nuclear program also afforded the United States the opportunity to assuage the Libyans' concerns about revealing new information through their concessions. As Corera put it, "the Libyans were nervous about revealing what they had procured (even though it was far from operational), because they feared that their opponents could simply walk away from secret negotiations and use the information as a pretext to attack."[108] In the early 2000s, US and British intelligence officials began to penetrate Khan's global black-market network. They identified Libya as a Khan customer seeking centrifuges and weapon designs.[109] The CIA circulated classified estimates inside the US government regarding Libya's weapon activities. In late 2001 the CIA moved up the date by which Libya might be able to "produce enough weapons grade uranium for a nuclear warhead."[110] In February 2002 US intelligence intercepted a conversation between Khan and Matuq, the Libyan official in charge of the secret nuclear program. The two men discussed importing centrifuges to Libya and their plans for uranium enrichment.

As early as 2001 and 2002, William Burns hinted as part of broader negotiations with Musa Kusa, Libya's intelligence chief, that the United States was aware of a secret Libyan proliferation. "I made clear that we had solid evidence [that Libya had active WMD programs]," Burns recalls.[111] Yet, without specifics, denial was the watchword for a long time. Prior to WMD negotiations beginning in March 2003, Libya's foreign minister had publicly denied having a nuclear weapons program in January, calling such concerns "CIA propaganda."[112] The same denials echoed at Kappes and his British colleague's first meeting with Qaddafi in Tripoli. To show that security from US aggression was on his mind, a Bush administration official hypothesized, Qaddafi picked as the location for the meeting the very office where US bombers had targeted him in 1986.[113] After a fifteen-minute diatribe about the West, Qaddafi expressed a desire to "clean the file."[114] When Kappes asked about Libya's WMD program, however, Qaddafi "angrily denied having such weapons."

Six months into secret talks, Libya's coercers caught Tripoli red-handed. According to several accounts, the CIA used its sources inside the Khan network to identify a shipment of centrifuge equipment from Malaysia aboard MV *BBC China*, bound for Libya.[115] In October 2003, in conjunction with the Proliferation Security Initiative, an informal network of states that cooperate to disrupt the illicit transfer of nuclear technology, the CIA and MI6 intercepted the ship in the Italian port of Taranto. As expected, they found five forty-foot shipping containers containing centrifuge equipment, labeled on the German-owned ship's manifest as "used machine parts."[116] The United States and the United Kingdom removed the offending shipping containers and then sent the *BBC China* back on its way to Libya.

The question now was how to play this ace. It could have been used as a hammer, to come down hard on the Libyans and prove to the world that they were up to no good. This is certainly what some in the Bush administration preferred. Aware of the interception but unaware of the talks, John Bolton planned to hold a press conference hailing the seizure of the *BBC China*. But those who knew about ongoing negotiations thought better of it. Robert Joseph, the NSC's senior director for counterproliferation strategy, argued that the intercept should be kept secret to use as leverage in the negotiations. NSC adviser Stephen Hadley concurred. "Bush and Blair determined that the *BBC China* intelligence would advance the negotiations if we kept it secret and conveyed it privately to the Libyans," recalls William Tobey.[117] Tenet explained, "We were reluctant to make too big a deal of it at the time, hoping that we could use the incident to drive home to the Libyans that we knew all about their plans and to give them greater incentive to renounce all their WMD."[118] Tenet effectively gagged Bolton.

Four days after the secret interception, the British acted to assure Qaddafi. They dispatched Mark Allen, the senior British intelligence officer involved in the secret talks, to make Qaddafi aware of the seizure. Allen contacted Musa Kusa and sought an urgent meeting to discuss the nuclear program that Libyan officials had continued to deny existed. Kusa accepted. On October 7, Allen and Kappes flew to Libya and shared with Kusa their proof of Libya's centrifuge program.[119] Kappes reportedly told Kusa, "You are the drowning man and I am the lifeguard."[120]

The strategy worked. Libya perceived the *BBC China* interception as pressure with credible coercive assurance. Seif al Islam Qaddafi later reported (as written by Tobey) that "the firm, but discreet way in which the U.S. and Britain handled the incident had reassured his father that London and Washington were acting in good faith, rather than creating a pretext for military action."[121] The fact that the intelligence was not made public assured the Libyans. To *Time*, Muammar Qaddafi's son recalled that while the seizure added pressure on Libya to come clean, the lack of bullying by MI6 and the CIA reassured his father. "We realized that we were dealing with friends and sincere people," he said.[122] Members of a US congressional commission wrote that the seizure of the *BBC China*, which constituted "definitive proof" of Libya's wrongdoing, "served as a critical factor in Tripoli's decision to open up its weapons programs to international scrutiny."[123] A British parliamentary report investigating British intelligence performance regarding WMDs drew the same conclusion: "The discoveries made enabled the UK and US Governments to confront Libyan officials with this evidence of their nuclear-related procurement at a time when Libya was still considering whether to proceed to full admission of its programmes."[124]

Libya relented on inspections ("technical visits"), and a secret team flew to Libya within two weeks. Sharing intelligence had made the Libyans more willing to admit their guilt. But their caution remained. At the visit, which lasted ten days (October 19–29, 2003),[125] the Libyans "provided additional information about their missile and chemical weapons programs" but continued to dissemble about much of their nuclear program. They argued that they only sought nuclear power. The inspectors concluded, according to Tobey's account, that their Libyan counterparts "had not been instructed to speak freely or 'come clean.'"[126] Additionally, at this first technical visit, Tenet writes that during a personal encounter with Kappes, Muammar Qaddafi asked "if the United States would really fulfill its commitments if he renounced his WMD programs." "'Yes sir, the president is a man of his word,'" Kappes replied. "'But if he feels his word has been dishonored . . . well, he is a very serious-minded man.'"[127]

After the *BBC China* incident, Tenet recalled, "we repeatedly surprised them [Libya] with the depth of our knowledge. . . . US and British intelligence officers secretly traveled to Libya and asked to inspect Libya's ballistic missile programs. Libyan officials at first failed to declare key facilities, but our intelligence convinced them to disclose several dozen facilities, including their deployed Scud B sites and their secret North Korean–assisted Scud C production line."[128]

That US and British intelligence officials shared their secret knowledge in these ways is made more interesting by the risks such sharing posed to ongoing intelligence-gathering missions. For instance, the CIA's plan to intercept the *BBC China* and catch Libya red-handed risked its most prized informants. US and British policymakers accepted that the interdiction would likely cause key sources to lose access to further information about the Khan network. Before the seizure, the CIA warned its informant inside the Khan network, Urs Tinner, and other sources that Khan would likely suspect that a mole was in his network if the United States intercepted the *BBC China*.[129] But the United States and Britain apprehended the components on the ship anyway.

The pattern of shared knowledge leading to concessions repeated itself. On November 20, 2003, US and UK negotiators confronted the Libyans with additional intelligence. At a "tense meeting" in a small Cotswolds hotel, the CIA presented its recording of a bugged conversation from February 2002 between Khan and Matuq in Casablanca.[130] Tenet writes that Kappes and his British counterpart communicated, "Look, we know you guys purchased a centrifuge facility."[131] After the fall of the Qaddafi regime, British journalists uncovered a Libyan transcript (in Arabic) of this meeting. According to the document, Kappes first told Musa Kusa that the United States and the UK knew of Libya's uranium-enrichment program, including "everything that was talked about—the amount of uranium, 10 tons, and the centrifuge equipment."[132] Kappes then handed Kusa a CD with the recording that he said proved Libya's nuclear program was for "military and not peaceful purposes."[133] The Libyan account, quoted by journalists, further captures that Kappes went on: "Maybe in other circumstances and in other times, this information [on Libya's nuclear plans] could be used adversely. . . . Maybe Powell could talk about it in the UN," referencing the Bush administration's public campaign to justify the forthcoming invasion of Iraq.[134] The *Times* of London emphasizes that Kappes "quickly reverted to focusing on how the goal was to restore relations with the Tripoli regime."[135]

Kappes then delivered a message to Qaddafi direct from President Bush conveying his "personal desire for friendship." In the meeting, Kappes stressed Bush's sincerity. "The President has not sent any letters lately so it is a very important decision for him to write," Kappes said, "This is the strongest sign for the President to be personally involved."[136] Libyan negotiators agreed to a second on-site technical visit.

The second technical visit took place on December 1–12, 2003.[137] The Libyans were much more forthcoming. They admitted to having nuclear weapons ambitions, revealed the UF6 cylinders acquired from Khan, and surrendered their designs for a nuclear warhead. These admissions satisfied the CIA and MI6. True to a pattern of this case, these technical visits were kept secret from the IAEA.[138]

Shared knowledge consistently convinced the Libyans that concessions would not reveal substantially more than their coercers already knew. More acquiescence followed each disclosure.

THE END GAME

At this point in coercive bargaining, the parties were inches from concluding a deal, but fate sent one more curveball. On December 14, 2003, US troops in Iraq pulled Saddam Hussein out of a hiding hole. The manhunt for the toppled dictator had ended at a farm near his hometown of Tikrit. Cameras recorded his capture.

The signal was strong, and Qaddafi received it. But the capture of Saddam had the counterproductive effect of exacerbating the assurance dilemma with Qaddafi and making him rethink gambling on concession. Libya again balked, suggesting a postponement of the upcoming concession announcement and asking for assurances that the US would not pursue regime change. Qaddafi feared once more that the US would be after him next, personally, WMDs or no WMDs.

Blair decided to place a personal phone call to Qaddafi on December 17.[139] As Tobey recalls the end game, "Bush and Blair wanted to know how to push Qaddafi over the hump and reassure him. The call was intended to push Qaddafi over the hump."[140] He recounts the call as follows:

> To improve their chances, Tony Blair called Qaddafi at midday, London time. Qaddafi expressed two concerns, perhaps inadvertently revealing his underlying motivation for abandoning his banned weapons programs. First, he said he did not wish to appear to have capitulated to Washington's demands. In light of Saddam's capture only days earlier, comparisons between Iraq and Libya would be inevitable, he complained. Second, he feared that the United States would attack Libya if it acknowledged possessing proscribed weapons—paradoxically, the reverse of Washington's view of the matter. Qaddafi added that because he disliked the wording of the draft statement, he wanted his foreign minister to make the announcement.[141]

Blair responded with an explicit assurance. If Qaddafi was "clear and explicit about Libya's possession of the WMD programs and his determination to eliminate them," Blair told him, "the United States and Britain would respond positively in return."[142] The call lasted thirty minutes.

Afterward, Blair called Bush. Both leaders agreed that after hearing Qaddafi himself come clean and pledge to dismantle his WMD program, each would make reassuring statements welcoming the decision and looking forward to better relations.[143]

Finally, after last-minute back-and-forth over the precise language, on December 19, 2003, Libya announced that it would abandon its nuclear weapons program, destroy its chemical weapons stockpile, declare activities to the IAEA and allow inspections, destroy missiles with ranges over three hundred kilometers and payload over five hundred kilograms, and join the Chemical Weapons Convention. "Libya has decided, with its own free will, to get rid of these substances, equipment and programmes and to be free from all internationally banned weapons," Foreign Minister Shalgham said on radio.[144] Qaddafi endorsed the statement afterward with a single written sentence.[145] "Qaddafi's 'endorsement' was satisfactory," Tobey said. "Sometimes you don't get everything you want, but we were generally satisfied."[146]

President Bush and Prime Minister Blair made complementary statements. Blair "applauded" Qaddafi's "courageous decision" and noted that "Libya's actions entitle it to rejoin the international community."[147] Bush's remarks communicated both the threats and assurances that yielded Libyan compliance, saying, the United States had "sent an unmistakable message to regimes that would seek or possess weapons of mass destruction. Those weapons do not bring influence or prestige. They bring isolation and otherwise unwelcome consequences"—a threat. Bush continued, "And another message should be equally clear: Leaders who abandon the pursuit of chemical, biological, and nuclear weapons, and the means to deliver them, will find an open path to better relations with the United States and other free nations"—a coercive assurance.[148] The United States had, in Bush's words, "clarified the choices left to potential adversaries."

Aftermath

By September 2004 all materials acquired from the A. Q. Khan network had been shipped out of Libya.[149] President Bush lifted most US sanctions on April 23, 2005. The United States restored full diplomatic relations with Libya on May 15, 2006. By the end of June, Libya was officially removed from the list of states designated as sponsors of terrorism. Libya was elected to a term on the UNSC in October 2007.

Bush and Blair had a vested interest in cultivating the legacy of the "Libya model." According to Tobey, "they talked about this explicitly at Camp David. They had an interest in convincing others that Libya's was a good path to follow."[150] Robert Joseph concurs that US and UK leaders wished to "send the powerful message that, if these countries also were to

abandon WMD programs, explicitly and verifiably, there would be benefits."[151] In other words, they wanted the Libya case to help mitigate the
assurance dilemma in coercion against future proliferators. William Burns's
overall reflection on the case is consistent with such a view:

> Afghanistan was evidence enough of our determination and capabilities
> after 9/11. Moreover, the track record we built up with the Libyans, on the
> foundation of what the previous administration had pursued, underscored
> that we were focused on changing behavior, not the Qaddafi regime, and
> that however difficult the choices and the pathway for the Libyans, our
> word could be trusted. Sanctions had taken a long-term toll. Qaddafi's
> political isolation in the international community was tightly sealed. He
> needed a way out, and we gave him a tough but defensible one.[152]

Yet this goal of shaping a constructive legacy—a Libya model—was
undermined in the years to come. First, Bush administration officials themselves seemed to be unable to agree on the right lessons. "There was a lively
debate within the Bush Administration about why Qaddafi had acted,"
Burns further recalls, "with Vice President Cheney and other hawks drawing a direct connection to Iraq and the demonstration effect of Saddam's
removal."[153] As an insurgency intensified and no evidence of a WMD program could be found in Iraq, it became quite tempting to connect the Libya
success to the Iraq intervention. The story helped rescue the Iraq adventure
from ignominy, even if it did by sleight-of-hand distort the original justification for the war.

Second, the meaning of the Libya model changed dramatically when
only eight years later the Obama administration reneged on the 2003 bargain and intervened in Libya's civil war. While the United States had not
put a formal security assurance in writing, the United Kingdom did. Building their new relationship, Libya and the UK signed a "Joint Letter on Peace
and Security" on June 26, 2006. The letter specified that each country "will
refrain in their international relations from the threat or use of force against
the territorial integrity or political independence of either state" and committed to "settlement of their mutual differences through dialogue and
direct negotiation and peaceful and friendly means."[154] In 2011 the UK
reneged on these codified commitments. Through the lens of the assurance
dilemma, the United States also reneged on a coercive assurance in 2011
when it ultimately helped to topple Qaddafi.

The key question for a study of the assurance dilemma is why the Obama
administration felt it wise to renege on the United States' assurance. What
arguments were made in the White House? Fascinatingly, rather than
debating whether or not to renege on a 2003 nuclear bargain, the issue
seems to have come up negligibly during the Obama administration's
deliberations about Libyan intervention in 2011. Instead, the immediate

humanitarian crisis crowded out the issue. Many advisers argued that the dictator was about to massacre his own people and the US and NATO had a responsibility to intervene. *New York Times* coverage of the 2011 decision reports that "no one in the Situation Room debated what message the decision to turn on Colonel Qaddafi might send to other countries that the United States was trying to persuade to relinquish their weapons, according to interviews conducted later with more than a half-dozen people engaged in the discussion."[155] More research will be needed as official documents become available, but for now we have several corroborating memoir accounts of the series of meetings between President Obama and his national security staff debating the intervention—including by Hillary Clinton, Susan Rice, Samantha Power, Ben Rhodes, William Burns, and President Obama himself.[156] These accounts point to one conclusion: the 2003 bargain was a nonfactor in 2011 decision-making. As the president went around the table at a crucial meeting, listening to principals argue for and against intervention—Robert Gates, Joe Biden, Thomas Donilon, and William Daley against; Clinton, Rice, Power, Rhodes, and Antony Blinken for—none appear to have raised the 2003 context or nuclear nonproliferation at all. Only once President Obama polled the backbenchers in the room did the nuclear issue enter the discussion (though even NSC staffers present reportedly also favored intervention[157]). Still, they did not argue about the assurance dilemma or that conditions were different or that the deal was moot—they simply prioritized other issues over it, such as atrocity prevention and support for democracy in the Middle East. Only three accounts of the deliberations—Burns's, Powers's, and the president's himself—even mention nonproliferation. "A few younger staffers expressed concerns that a military action against Libya might have the unintended consequence of convincing countries like Iran that they needed nuclear weapons as a hedge against future U.S. attack," writes Obama without further discussion.[158] The conversation pivoted instead to the benefits of supporting regional protests for democracy. Rather than recall the 2003 bargain, many accounts express frustration that Qaddafi in 2011 remained a mercurial and brutal dictator. Burns's memoir credits Qaddafi with sticking "to his part of our deal on terrorism and the nuclear issue" but laments that he "continued to rule with weirdness and repression."[159] "This was not a man who was going to meet our demands," Rhodes writes ambiguously.[160] He had to go.[161]

Prior to the first bombs falling, President Obama publicly offered Qaddafi "one last chance" to pull back his forces and respect Libyan protestors. Unsurprisingly, Qaddafi was unbowed. The intervention was at this point foregone, and any final ultimatums lacked assurance. "The Pentagon was prepared and awaiting my order to begin airstrikes," writes Obama.[162] Qaddafi did not last much longer.

The Assurance Dilemma in Libya

Libya's coercers succeeded in concluding an agreement to verifiably elimi-nate Tripoli's nuclear weapons program in December 2003. During the negotiations, Qaddafi was continually concerned that the US and the UK intended to disarm him and attack. Indeed, 9/11 and the Iraq War caused Qaddafi to hold fast to his nuclear ambitions because they underlined the credibility of threats without supporting complementary coercive assur-ances. As secret negotiations dragged on, however, the US came around to understanding that it faced an assurance dilemma and needed to assuage Libyan fears. Indeed, negotiations were deadlocked until credible threats were paired with coercive assurance that convinced Qaddafi to make concessions.

For a long time, however, regime change was the US goal. From 1986 to 1998 Libya defied coercion because of its accurate perception of US maxi-malism. Demands of such great magnitude undermine coercion by elimi-nating bargaining space. Only after the United States dropped its goal of regime change did US-Libya relations encounter a coercive assurance prob-lem, during which time Washington took pains to signal that it no longer sought regime change. Earlier, from 1980 to 1986, Libya defied coercion because it did not perceive that US threats to use military force were credi-ble. It believed that the Soviet Union would protect it against Western aggression.

"Qaddafi only came around to conceding to pressure incrementally," recalls William Tobey. "He needed to be brought along."[163] Libya's coercers did so by disentangling demands, managing spoilers, and sharing their knowledge of Qaddafi's guilt. First, Lockerbie accountability was resolved and taken off the table before Libya agreed to WMD concessions. This had two key effects: allowing the United States to scale back its demands of regime change (resolving the problem of demand magnitude) and disen-tangling UN and US sanctions over the two issues of Lockerbie and WMDs, which had resulted in Libyan concessions on neither stake. Applying each punishment to a different demand in 1998, however, contributed to Libya's decision to concede one issue at a time, as one stake did not impede the other. Moreover, even in 2003 the Bush administration had to consider how to disentangle stakes to provide sanctions relief. As Tobey recalls, "WMD, terrorism, and human rights sanctions were all interwoven. The Bush administration debated how to decouple these sanctions and provide some relief on the WMD issue after the announcement."[164] It helped that Bush and Blair wanted to provide relief as a means of upholding the Libya model as a path worthy of emulation by other isolated states.

Second, Libya's coercers managed spoilers both internationally and domestically, keeping veto players in the dark who could act independently to prevent a coercive bargain. Internationally, the United States maintained coercive control by freezing Israel out of the coercive bargaining process. Domestically, the United States relied on the secrecy of negotiations with Libya to keep hard-line opponents out of the process. Bargaining with Libya was unacceptable to some members of the Bush administration and members of Congress backed by the lobby for victims of the Lockerbie bombing.

The UK was a partner to the United States in negotiations and not a potential spoiler. It would accept bargains acceptable to Washington. Between the two coercers, the United States dominated Britain in terms of leverage. US sanctions mattered most to Libyan revival. As W. Q. Bowen writes, "while the British government certainly fulfilled a pivotal role in the secret negotiations, and provided the Libyans with a bridge to the Americans, only the United States had in its gift what the Libyans most sought: an end to American sanctions and reengagement with Washington."[165]

Although these efforts by coercers to signal coercive control are clear, we have less direct evidence that these signals were received in Tripoli. Perhaps the best indication that the Libyan leaders were concerned with coercive control was when they asked for signs that they were bargaining with the right members of the US and UK governments. Both the United States and the United Kingdom, at different times, responded by sending messages from their heads of state and sending high-level representatives to assure the Libyans of sincerity.

Third, the Libyan case affirms the utility of shared knowledge to overcoming the assurance dilemma. "Qaddafi genuinely feared that if he admitted to his WMD program we would use force against him," recalls Tobey.[166] The United States and Britain therefore chose to share intelligence with Libya—chiefly that related to the seizure of the *BBC China* and recordings of conversations with A. Q. Khan.

The Libya case also provides a good test of the relationship between the credibility of threats and assurance. The fact that Libya perceived credible threats and severe punishments but did not concede until coercers bolstered their assurance affirms the necessity of assurance in coercion. Moreover, when perceptions of threat credibility spiked, the target's demand for coercive assurance remained. Two instances in the Libya chronology allow us to see this relationship: the invasion of Iraq and the capture of Saddam Hussein. At these two moments, the military threat from the United States increased rapidly, and Tripoli's leadership responded by demanding credible assurance that Libya would not suffer the same fate. Qaddafi was indeed afraid, and he was more willing to take a concession gamble. But he was not immediately compelled into concessions. Libya continued to import black-market nuclear infrastructure until late 2003. Qaddafi saw the US and UK make the case for war against Iraq based on WMD proliferation, and he feared that coming clean about his own program would only hand over the case for war against him. Later, the capture of Saddam increased the severity of the threatened punishment to Qaddafi personally.[167] But again the timing of this spike in threat severity suggests that it was on balance counterproductive for coercion. Qaddafi was indeed fearful, but after Saddam's capture he balked one last time on a deal that was virtually completed. The Libyans had fully revealed the most secretive elements of their nuclear program in early December—before the United States captured Saddam. Blair spent another thirty minutes on the phone with Qaddafi, assuring him that his fate would not be the same.[168] Of course, neither knew that Qaddafi's fate in just eight years would actually be worse.

"We Knew That They Knew We Knew"

Compelling Iran to Concede

This chapter explains the Iranian response to coercion over its nuclear program during critical years when it was the target of compellence. In 2003 Iran made concessions both publicly and secretly to rein in its nuclear weapons pursuit. The bargain fell apart in 2005. A subsequent decade of coercive bargaining resulted in the 2015 Joint Comprehensive Plan of Action, in which Iran agreed to enhanced verification and limits on its nuclear program in exchange for sanctions relief. In 2018 the Donald Trump administration reneged on the deal and resurrected sanctions to exert "maximum pressure" on Tehran to make more concessions. Iran did not comply (see table 5.1).

The assurance dilemma explains the timing of Iran's 2015 concessions. In bargaining leading up to the JCPOA, signals of coercive assurance mitigated the assurance dilemma and made coercion more likely to succeed. First, Iran's coercers hived off the nuclear issue alone and separated nuclear- from non-nuclear-related sanctions in negotiations. Iran sought and acquired the specific separation of entangled sanctions designations during bargaining. Second, Washington partnered with the P5+1 and the European Union (EU) while restraining international and domestic spoilers—publicly discouraging Israeli air strikes and legislatively bounding congressional oversight over sanctions relief. Tehran came to the table only after the window of a credible Israeli threat closed—a puzzle for the threat credibility lens. Third, documents from Iran's "atomic archive," as the Israeli government called it—Iranian documents stolen by an Israeli intelligence operation in 2018—compared with IAEA reports expose how much coercers already knew about the "possible military dimensions" (PMD) of Iran's past nuclear programs. The lens of the assurance dilemma highlights Iran's rational fears of its coercers' duplicity and how the strategies of coercers changed to overcome these suspicions. It is especially puzzling why Iran was willing to strike a nonproliferation bargain so soon after the

Table 5.1 Iran

Date	Concessions	Threat credibility	Threat severity	Assurance credibility	Consistent with assurance dilemma?
1990s	No	Low	Low	–	–
2003–5	Partial	High	High	Low	✗
2006	No	Medium	Medium	Low	✓
2009–11	No	Medium	Medium	Low	✓
2012–15	Yes	High	High	High	✓
2017–18	No	High	High	Low	✓
2018–	No	High	High	Lower	✓

demise of Libya's Qaddafi in 2011. Iran's supreme leader indeed complained about an American reputation for "backpedaling on its commitments."[1] But Iran struck a bargain anyway. Iran was coerced and assured.

Merely three years later, the United States abrogated the 2015 deal and reimposed sanctions to wrest greater concessions from Iran. The strategy failed due to a lack of effort to overcome the assurance dilemma. When Iran defied compellent demands, it did so primarily because it perceived a lack of credible coercive assurance, not because it perceived compellent threats to be insufficiently credible or painful.

Nevertheless, fifteen years earlier, Iran had made partial concessions in the absence of efforts to provide coercive assurance. Extreme threat credibility in the wake of the 2003 US invasion of Iraq did convince Tehran to take a concession gamble. Iran scaled back what had been a concerted effort to build atomic weapons and divvied its nuclear program into more deniable pursuits while it negotiated with European governments. It hid, rather than halted, its nuclear ambitions but in so doing slowed down its quest for the bomb. This 2003 episode is largely inconsistent with the theory of the assurance dilemma.

Documentary evidence for the Iran case is difficult to obtain. I use some primary evidence from the IAEA archives. I also conducted interviews with US and Israeli policymakers who participated in the coercive bargaining process with Iran. Their perceptions of Iranian perceptions provide indirect evidence to test theory. The exodus of many Democratic policymakers from the US government after the election of a Republican administration in 2016 gave scholars good access to former officials willing to speak on the record about coercive bargaining with Iran. Of course, this evidence came with a validity trade-off: officials were willing to speak in order to defend the record of their policy choices. Indeed, I interviewed officials both before and after the Trump administration withdrew from the JCPOA and reimposed sanctions. Prior to that decision, interviewees were inclined to defend the deal in the hopes of saving it; afterward, they were more inclined to cast blame. Neither is biased in favor of or against the assurance dilemma. Subjects may have even been more inclined to tout the efficacy of their threats, consistent with a common bias in US policymaking. Interviews and memoirs are also naturally self-serving and selective accounts. This kind of evidence often lacks important substance. Indeed, some interviewees expressly admitted that they could not share some details of the Iran negotiations, especially about the role of the intelligence community. Nonetheless, compiling this evidence yields a valuable first draft of history. Some cases are important enough not to wait until records are declassified.

I am also able to observe critical aspects of the case related to the former Iranian nuclear weapons program and coercers' knowledge thereof by comparing IAEA documents to a tranche of documents stolen from Iran in a 2018 Israeli intelligence operation. These documents have been filtered through a state intelligence service en route to scholars and are heavily biased sources. The Israeli sources had a clear agenda: the demise of the JCPOA and unyielding containment of the Iranian regime. I therefore use the partial and filtered atomic archive in ways that bias against finding evidence in favor of the mechanism of shared knowledge.

Improving Existing Explanations

Common explanations for Iranian behavior focus on the credibility of its coercers' threats. First, perhaps Iran was so terrified in the aftermath of the US invasion of Iraq that it made concessions and came to the negotiating table in 2003. As discussed, I find evidence in favor of this explanation. The assurance dilemma cannot explain why Iran scaled back its nuclear program in 2003. But it can help to explain why Iran continued more deniable nuclear weapons research after 2003.

Second, some scholarship finds variation in the severity of economic sanctions to be a sufficient explanation for Iranian decision-making.[2] Perhaps sanctions against Iran were not painful enough, until gradually, around 2013, Iran realized that its nuclear program was not worth the suffering. I find evidence against this interpretation. Severe sanctions were a necessary but insufficient cause of Iranian acquiescence to the JCPOA. And when sanctions became just as painful after the United States reneged on the bargain and reimposed sanctions in 2018, Iran remained defiant.

Other conventional explanations for the timing of Iran's concessions in 2015 look beyond threats or assurance to the role of individual leaders as well as inducements offered by Iran's coercers.[3] I consider these alternatives in the chapter. They are not invalid—just insufficient as explanations for the success of coercive bargaining. The assurance dilemma complements them.

The chapter begins with an overview of the origins of Iran's nuclear program, the country's interest in the bomb, and the attention it began to attract from foreign observers. It then considers Iran's partial concessions in 2003 and the failure of coercive diplomacy thereafter. Following sections explain the initial failures and eventual successes of the Obama administration's coercive diplomacy leading to the 2015 JCPOA. Finally, the chapter considers the consequences of US withdrawal from the JCPOA in 2018.

Iran's Nuclear Program

Motivations for a bomb program in Iran changed over time. In the days of Shah Mohammed Reza Pahlavi, Iran sought to hedge. The shah signed the NPT in 1968 (ratified in 1970) and an IAEA safeguards agreement in 1974,[4] but thereafter he explored nuclear weapons.[5] In the words of Akbar Etemad, director of the Atomic Energy Organization of Iran (AEOI) in the 1970s, the shah wanted "the option of assembling the bomb should his regional competitors move in that direction."[6] The first pressure brought to bear on Iran over its nuclear ambitions came from its then patron, the United States. When Henry Kissinger met with the shah in Tehran in August 1976, he "raised the potential of an aid cutoff or limits on arms sales if Iran were to acquire [plutonium-] reprocessing facilities." But he also, according to Nicholas Miller, "reassured Iran of America's commitment."[7] The shah complied and did not pursue plutonium reprocessing any further.

Student-led antimonarchy demonstrations in 1978 thrust Iran into political turmoil. The shah fled in January 1979, never to return. In April Iran formed an Islamic republic, and by December Ayatollah Ruhollah Khomeini had become supreme leader of the world's newest theocracy. Iranian nuclear efforts paused during and after the revolution, from 1979 to 1983, as Khomeini thought nuclear weapons incompatible with Shia teachings.[8]

Saddam Hussein's invasion of Iran in 1980 and his cruel but effective employment of chemical weapons on the battlefield changed this new status quo. Security motivations during the Iran-Iraq War led to a new compromise between the secular and religious bureaucracies, which agreed that the bomb was worth pursuing but only to serve as a deterrent.[9] Covert efforts to build a uranium-enrichment capacity began in 1985.[10] In 1987 Iran made contact with A. Q. Khan and purchased centrifuge designs and parts as well as information about uranium metal casting and weapons designs.[11] Having signed nuclear cooperation agreements with Pakistan (1987), the Soviet Union (1989, then Russia in 1992), and China (1990),[12] Iran expanded its covert weaponization efforts in the 1990s. Iran began to build a uranium-enrichment facility at Natanz and a heavy-water reactor at Arak. It made contact with Khan again in 1994.[13] China agreed to supply a uranium-conversion facility at Isfahan in 1995 but withdrew in 1997, leaving Iran to complete the project by itself.[14] Russia agreed in 1995 to complete construction of a reactor at Bushehr.[15] Iran separated its first plutonium in 1988,[16] imported UF6 in 1991, and started to enrich small amounts of uranium with laser-enrichment technology.[17] It tested its gas centrifuges for the first time in 1998.[18] A military front company began a uranium mine and milling project at Gchine in 2000.[19]

Even after the fall of the government of archrival Saddam in Iraq in 2003, security imperatives for Iran's nuclear program remained motivated by the threat from the United States, which maintained forces on Iran's eastern and western doorsteps.[20] From the outset of its nuclear interest, Iran seemed determined to master the full fuel cycle. Scholars also find a consistent narrative of technological self-reliance at the core of these nuclear pursuits.[21]

US COMPELLENCE

In the wake of the Iranian Revolution and the Iran hostage crisis of 1979–81, the United States imposed sanctions and seized billions in Iranian assets.[22] It targeted the Iranian oil and military sectors, support for terrorism, trafficking, and money laundering.[23] Sanctions prevented Iran from upgrading its oil infrastructure with American technology.[24]

The United States also sought to impede Iranian proliferation through suppliers, convincing potential nuclear suppliers—including Germany, Argentina, and Russia—to curtail some agreements with Iran.[25] The US continued to monitor Iranian progress, including sharing intelligence with the IAEA that led to inspections of suspicious buildings in November 1993.[26]

Sanctions tied explicitly to WMDs began in the 1990s.[27] US compellence against Iran especially increased after US and Israeli intelligence estimated in January 1995 that it could be five years away from acquiring the bomb.[28] Iran's support for terrorism grew more deadly as well—the 1996 Khobar Towers bombing killed nineteen US service members with Iranian backing. The Iran-Libya Sanctions Act of 1996 threatened financial penalties against any firm that invested more than $20 million in the Iranian oil sector.[29] President Clinton's Executive Order 12959 banned all US trade and investment in Iran.[30]

In August 2002 Iran was caught red-handed. Satellite images revealed publicly that it was concealing an enrichment facility at Natanz and a possible heavy-water production plant at Arak.[31] The revelation spurred an IAEA investigation, and in early 2003 Iran admitted to these facilities as well as a centrifuge-production facility in Tehran. So began the decades of the Iranian nuclear crisis.

Successful Compellence, 2003

Iran's concessions in 2003 yield mixed evidence for the importance of threat credibility and Iran's willingness to take a concession gamble. The assurance dilemma cannot explain Iran's acquiescence to coercion in this period. The US invasion of Iraq compelled Iran to make some significant concessions, yet Iran hedged, preserving its nuclear weapons research programs and made known its desire for assurance.

Iran's approach to the newly public nuclear crisis in 2003 was conciliatory. The Mohammad Khatami government in Tehran agreed to participate in talks with France, Germany, and the United Kingdom (known collectively as the E3) to avoid being referred to the UN Security Council.[32] In October 2003 Iran suspended uranium-enrichment and plutonium-reprocessing activities and pledged to behave in accordance with the enhanced inspection requirements of the IAEA's Additional Protocol.[33] Furthermore, in secret, Iran halted and hid a clandestine nuclear weapons project.

After making contact with A. Q. Khan in 1987, Iran had institutionalized a nuclear weapons program through the offices of the Physics Research Center overseen by the Defense Industries Education Research Institute within the Ministry of Defense Armed Forces Logistics.[34] These efforts were consolidated into the "AMAD Plan" in 1999 or early 2000, with a budget of $100 million to build five ten-kiloton nuclear warheads.[35] Concurrent with this reorganization, senior Iranian leaders made a political decision to acquire and test a nuclear device by 2003.[36]

In a November 2007 national intelligence estimate (NIE) on Iran's nuclear intentions and capabilities, the US National Intelligence Council (NIC) judged with "high confidence" that in the fall of 2003 Tehran had "halted" its "nuclear weapon design and weaponization work and covert uranium conversion-related and uranium enrichment-related work."[37] This "halt" order came from high up in the Iranian government. Iran had dissolved the official organizational structure of the AMAD Plan and abandoned plans to construct and test a nuclear device by the end of 2003. It also ceased construction of a tunnel complex under Parchin intended to house metallurgy equipment to make nuclear cores. Together, these significant concessions represented a very real slowdown in the Iranian pursuit of a nuclear weapon.

Iran's behavior in 2003 is the most consistent in this book so far with the threat credibility lens. Iran made these concessions out of fear. The United States had invaded its neighbor, Iraq, and brought hundreds of thousands of military personnel to the region. With US troops on its eastern border in Afghanistan as well, Iran saw threats on two fronts. US ground forces had routed Iraqi units in combat—essentially two divisions conquered the country in just three weeks. Washington had also justified its war with Iraq on the basis of a (nonexistent) WMD program. Iran's *real* nuclear weapons program was by comparison a more than sufficient causus belli, and Tehran, now under greater scrutiny and a named member of the "axis of evil," did not know how much A. Q. Khan's network, now penetrated, was telling the US intelligence community. One indication in 2003 of how seriously Iran took US threats was Tehran's increased military spending.[38] Even the liberal *Banyon* newspaper called for "preventive plans and measures that would render any possible aggression of the United States to be irrelevant."[39] And Iran braced itself for asymmetrical warfare.[40] Short of military conflict, Iran sought to avoid referral to the UNSC, which could act to impose more painful multilateral sanctions.

The threat of punishment was so credible and severe in 2003 that Iran scrambled to avoid potentially imminent costs. It did so even in the absence of US efforts to signal coercive assurance. The George W. Bush administration's aggressive rhetoric communicated no limits to US policy on Iran.

Yet Tehran's concessions were partial. It conceded what it perceived as enough to provide more apparent transparency to the IAEA and avoid an invasion, while maintaining progress toward building nuclear weapons in the future. Iranian policymakers gathered with Supreme Leader Khamenei for this crucial decision point at a meeting in the fall of 2003. One side argued in favor of concessions, while another advocated racing for a weapons option. Khamenei chose a middle strategy.[41]

With the benefit of IAEA reports and Iranian files stolen by Israel, scholars can now more accurately understand Iran's choice.[42] Iran's concessions in 2003 were significant; however, they were not an end to the Iranian nuclear weapons programs. The 2003 "halt" order was also a "hide" order, aimed at a slower but consistent and hidden ambition to acquire nuclear weapons. Iranian documents show that Iran's 2003 decision did not stop all nuclear weapons work.[43] Iran divided its research programs into overt and covert parts.[44] Research with civilian applications continued in the open.[45] IAEA documents corroborate this characterization of the 2003 decision to hide the program.[46]

Tehran further probed the possibility of making more concessions in 2003 if its coercers could provide sufficient coercive assurance, but none was forthcoming. Iran reportedly offered to discuss a "grand bargain" with the United States in a letter that was passed through Switzerland as well as delivered to the Bush administration via Mohamed ElBaradei, director general of the IAEA. ElBaradei said the letter was given to him by Hassan Rouhani, secretary of the Supreme National Security Council and later president.[47] In it Iran expressed a willingness to negotiate over its nuclear program as well as regional security issues. If the letter was sincere, it is a notable sign of insufficient coercive assurance that Iran's first request to the United States would have been to "refrain from supporting change of the

[Iranian] political system by direct interference from outside."[48] Washington did not respond.[49]

Iran's behavior in 2003 provides faint evidence in favor of the assurance dilemma. Iran took a concession gamble because of threat credibility. Still, it did not abandon its nuclear pursuits or accept intrusive verification of its intentions. The E3 took the lead in subsequent talks with Iran. Critically, the Bush administration did not participate.

Failed Compellence, 2003–8

After its 2003 concessions, Iran defied further compellence because it perceived that it would endure punishments regardless of its behavior. Consistent with the assurance dilemma, the 2003–5 E3 talks failed, in part because Iran's coercers lacked coercive control—the United States, a potential spoiler, did not participate. In 2006 the IAEA referred Iran to the UNSC for noncompliance with its nonproliferation obligations. Iran continued to defy, restarting enrichment once paused. As sanctions tightened and the Bush administration even floated a carrot of maintaining a limited enrichment capacity, Tehran still defied. Coercive diplomacy with big sticks and little carrots failed to break the impasse. Assurance was lacking.

THE AMERICAN ELEPHANT IN THE ROOM

Iran's coercers were split on their strategies of coercion in 2003. The United States sought immediate referral to the UNSC by the IAEA board of governors. The EU, on the other hand, preferred to use trade incentives as carrots, holding the referral as a threat in abeyance.[50] To pursue this linkage of trade carrots to the nuclear issue, the EU suspended trade negotiations with Iran in June 2003, the same month the IAEA reported that Iran had indeed concealed the Natanz facility.[51] The IAEA put its weight behind the EU plan. It did not refer Iran to the UNSC and called on Iran to come clean and cooperate with full verification by end of October 2003.

In the fall of 2003, Iran provided to the IAEA an incomplete declaration of its nuclear program. Talks sputtered on.[52] As a confidence-building measure, the E3 and Iran reached the Paris Agreement on November 15, 2004. Iran agreed to temporarily suspend all enrichment and reprocessing activities and abide by, but not ratify, the Additional Protocol while talks continued.[53] However, the sides could reach no further agreements.

This coercive diplomacy lacked coercive assurance for a number of reasons but most grievously because it left out the United States. As Ariane Tabatabai writes, "even though the United States was not directly involved in the talks, it nonetheless played a role. President George W. Bush advocated a zero-enrichment standard that Iran was unwilling to accept."[54] Iran had no reason to believe that any deal struck with the E3 would be followed by US restraint.

Iranians voiced their frustrations about a lack of coercive assurance at IAEA board of governors meetings. Iran's representative to the IAEA, Ali Salehi, often complained of "obvious political motivation"[55] behind its coercers' demands and an "existing hostile environment,"[56] and he hoped that in short order "the underlying political motivations would be dispelled."[57] Claiming that Iran's coercers meant it harm regardless of Tehran's behavior, Salehi declared that threats were "futile" because, "despite its unprecedented cooperation, Iran had received only increased pressure from a few influential Member States."[58] The United States merely meant to "set the stage for confrontation."[59] IAEA director general ElBaradei sympathetically writes of Iran's quandary that "any revelation of past involvement in a military nuclear program, however minor or distant, coming during a moment of confrontation, would be seen as vindication of the view that Iran was not to be trusted. But if they refrained from giving a full account, they were perpetuating the original sin of concealment"[60]—a classic "cheater's dilemma."[61]

The relative power of their coercers, especially the United States, was forefront in Iranians' minds. Noting the power asymmetry, Salehi observed that "when powerful countries took the attitude that might makes right, they assumed the roles of both judge and prosecutor" and that "some countries seemed not to want the problem to be solved, but rather to exploit it for their own ends."[62] He was clearly skeptical of US intentions. Further, three months later he argued that "the United States . . . might even wield its massive power to crush the perceived culprit. Nothing could quench its thirst for vengeance short of confrontation and war. It was no secret that influential groups in the current United States administration were toying with the idea of invading yet another country as part of a plan to reshape the Middle East region."[63]

In the spring of 2005, talks stalled in anticipation of the Iranian presidential elections. Iran was dissatisfied with elusory trade carrots. Hard-liner Mahmoud Ahmadinejad used US opposition on the nuclear issue as part of his platform to assume the presidency on August 3.[64] Tehran rejected the E3's final offer in August 2005. Shortly thereafter Iran restarted uranium-conversion and -enrichment activities.[65]

The assurance dilemma contributed to the failure of E3 negotiations in 2003–5. The episode is a weaker test of theory, however, because the credibility of US military threats decreased during this period. The peak of military coercion came in 2003, when an imminent invasion of Iran was plausible. US ground forces in the region to support the invasion of Iraq initially were highly lethal and maneuverable armored units. As the United States adapted its theater mission to counterinsurgency, its type of ground forces became less of a threat to Iran. The appetite in Washington for another war in the Middle East also declined. Still, Iran was vulnerable to US airpower and, most importantly, feared an escalation of economic coercion in the form of referral to the UNSC, which soon followed.

UNSC REFERRAL

By January 2006 Iran had resumed enrichment and ceased compliance with the Additional Protocol.[66] After a brief delay to give Iran one more chance,[67] on February 4, 2006, the IAEA board of governors voted to refer it to the UNSC for noncompliance with its safeguards obligations.[68] The referral made the threat of painful multilateral sanctions against Iran more credible, but the UNSC did not immediately act on the Iran portfolio. In July 2006 the United States entered the formal fray to offer with the E3+3 (France, Germany, and the UK, plus China, Russia, and the US) a new package of incentives to Iran.[69] This coercive diplomacy again failed.

Despite its new seat at the table, the Bush administration did not prioritize offering coercive assurance. The E3+3 offer to Iran made in 2006 maintained US preconditions, including the suspension of enrichment. Moreover, US officials explicitly did not include an assurance of nonintervention. And when asked about nonintervention, the United States refused to discuss it. "Security assurances are not on the table," said Condoleezza Rice.[70] While "security assurances" are not synonymous with coercive assurance, I consider an unwillingness to discuss security assurances to be an indicator of noncredible coercive assurance. Moreover, when Russian foreign minister Sergey Lavrov said that the P5+1 ought to be prepared to "give Iran security guarantees," Washington responded the same day through White House deputy press secretary Gordon Johndroe saying, "Security guarantees are not something we are looking at [at] the moment."[71] Iranian officials continued to question the Bush administration's intentions. The secretary of the Supreme National Security Council, Ali Larijani, said on June 25 that Washington was still intent on "overthrowing Iran's government."[72] To be clear, there is little evidence to suggest that Washington had any serious intention to overthrow the regime in Tehran. If it did, we should observe a host of accompanying phenomena, such as military planning for an occupation or a strike that would decapitate the regime. We do not. Instead, Washington pursued a coercive strategy that emphasized threats without assurance.

Even the discussion of crucial carrots could not budge the Iranians. While "the United States and the other parties have opposed any Iranian domestic centrifuge facilities," a summary of an E3+3 offer on June 6, 2006, states, "They have now agreed that a final agreement would include a provision for reviewing the program's suspension and permitting Iran to have a uranium-enrichment facility on its own territory."[73] The US representative at the IAEA board of governors meeting in February 2006 also spoke about needing to "find a way" to allow Iran to have peaceful nuclear energy without proliferation risk.[74] Without specifics, the outline of a final agreement that left Iran with some residual enrichment capacity was clear to all parties by 2006. It was other impediments that remained.

Following Iranian defiance of Resolution 1696 of July 2006, in which the UNSC threatened sanctions unless Iran "suspended all enrichment-related or reprocessing activities," the UNSC finally acted and imposed its first Iran sanctions in December 2006 (Resolution 1737).[75] Thus began multilateral efforts to economically squeeze Iran into compliance. Long fearing UNSC referral and multilateral economic coercion, Iran braced for punishment. Condoleezza Rice predicted in private conversation with the IAEA that Iran would "buckle under pressure."[76]

TIGHTENING SANCTIONS

Initial UN sanctions in 2006, while not sufficiently painful on their own, represented the opening salvo of a renewed campaign of economic coercion. UN sanctions only targeted at first trade and financial elements related to the nuclear program, but their strength grew over time. Resolution 1747, though still watered down by Russia and China, was passed in March 2007. And the United States capitalized on IAEA frustration over Iranian delays and deflections to galvanize more UNSC action.[77] The US cut off Iranian banks from even indirect access to the US financial system and froze the assets of individuals suspected of ties to the nuclear program.[78] These targeted sanctions, coupled with matching efforts by the UK and Australia, were estimated by Hassan Rouhani, later president of Iran, to have increased the costs of Iranian imports by 10 to 30 percent.[79] The E3+3 offered Iran another inducements package. Iran rejected it.

Throughout this period, Iranian officials often came back to the language of coercive assurance. "The more Iran had cooperated with the Agency [IAEA] since 2003, the harsher the response it had been faced with and the tougher the resolutions proposed by certain countries," complained Ali Asghar Soltanieh, Iran's IAEA representative, to the board of governors.[80] Expressing further frustration over the role of the United States as spoiler, he protested that despite Iranian compliance, the E3 "probably owing to political pressure from the United States, had responded by proposing a tougher resolution against Iran." "Consequently, the Government of Iran had come to the conclusion that, no matter how many concessions it made, the intention was to keep the Iranian nuclear issue on the Board's agenda because there was in fact a hidden agenda, namely to pave the way for the issue to be referred to the Security Council in order to impose sanctions and further punitive measures," he argued.[81] Iran consistently questioned the intentions of coercion. Iran's persistent place on the IAEA's agenda was "merely a pretext to cover the hidden agenda of the United States and other countries, such as France and the United Kingdom."[82] The United States was supposedly an unrelenting coercer. The vexing Iran portfolio passed to the Obama administration in January 2009.

President Obama's Failed Compellence, 2009–11

A period of unrequited outreach from 2009 to 2011 shows that it was not accommodation that brought Iran to the table ready to make concessions. The Obama administration initially took a softer line on Iran, in essence turning away from threats. Iran rejected this outreach both because the pain of sanctions was not yet dire and because the conditions were not yet conducive to complementary assurance.

President Obama came into office offering to return to negotiations with Iran without preconditions. He recorded a Nowruz holiday message in March 2009.[83] Deputy Assistant to the President and National Security Adviser to the Vice President Colin Kahl described the idea behind the signal: "The regime was extraordinarily skeptical of U.S. intentions. We began by trying to change Iranian perceptions that we were after regime change. Obama tried to engage on common interests and mutual respect. Obama's Nowruz message was not just for the people, but for the Iranian leaders."[84] The White House put building further sanctions pressure on hold, instead opting for a period of outreach. Obama also sent two letters to the supreme leader in 2009, one proposing direct talks.[85] Khamenei replied to the first letter but did not respond to the request for talks.[86]

The outreach yielded little. Iran remained skeptical. "The international community was well aware that the United States sought an excuse for pursuing its hegemonic and aggressive policy in the Middle East," Iranian officials said at IAEA board of governors meetings. New American statements were "reminiscent of those made under the preceding administration."[87] Iranian president Ahmadinejad was also reelected in a disputed election in June 2009, followed by political unrest and a government crackdown. He then rejected a P5+1 offer to exchange uranium for fuel for the Tehran Research Reactor—Iran would have received 20-percent-enriched LEU nuclear fuel for the five-megawatt reactor in exchange for sending a large portion of its 3–5 percent enriched uranium to Russia for fuel fabrication. Ahmadinejad had been interested in the swap, but he balked in the face of domestic criticism that he was weak and willing to accommodate enemies.[88]

Recognizing temporary failure, the Obama administration decided to escalate financial pressure. The president issued an ultimatum: Iran had until the end of the year to comply with the IAEA's demands and end enrichment, otherwise he would pursue tighter sanctions.[89] Iran defied. At the IAEA board of governors meeting when the resolution was passed,

Iran's representative took it as evidence that Iran "was justified in not believing that the United States was truly extending its hand in cooperation."[90] Concurrently, in late 2009 the Stuxnet cyberattack began to damage Iranian centrifuges.[91] The stage was set for the next round of compellence. With the public revelation in September 2009 that Iran had been hiding another secret uranium-enrichment facility—the Fordow Fuel Enrichment Plant—the US rallied the UNSC to ratchet up sanctions.[92]

Successful Compellence, 2012–15

Iran struck a bargain with its coercers in July 2015: the JCPOA. Negotiations that led to that agreement show that Iran was successfully compelled because it was credibly threatened and coercively assured.

BUILDING PRESSURE

UN Resolution 1929, passed in June 2010, had begun a renewed and concentrated effort of strict and painful sanctions to compel Iran to make nuclear concessions.[93] Up to 2009, sanctions had been effective but bearable. GDP growth fell from 5.7 percent to 4.1 percent.[94] Now, new sanctions targets included the Central Bank of Iran (CBI) and the Islamic Revolutionary Guard Corps (IRGC) and sectors including nuclear, energy, banking, shipping, and insurance. Resolution 1929 included a ban on conventional arms sales and, for the first time, mandatory financial restrictions. Most importantly, the language in Resolution 1929 that connected Iran's oil revenue to its proliferation activities allowed the EU to impose an oil embargo in 2012.[95] And in March 2012 the EU cut off access to the SWIFT banking communication system and froze European assets of the CBI.[96]

Washington complemented these multilateral efforts with targeted and secondary sanctions. The Comprehensive Iran Sanctions, Accountability, and Divestment Act (CISADA) signed into law in July 2010 articulated that any bank doing business with the CBI could not also do business in the United States. The Iran Threat Reduction and Syria Human Rights Act (August 2012) locked oil revenue in escrow accounts. And the Iran Freedom and Counterproliferation Act (January 2013) targeted shipping and shipping insurance.[97] And blacklisting the IRGC, the United States sanctioned part of another state's armed forces for the first time.[98] The Treasury Department ramped up its enforcement efforts, more actively seeking out front companies and punishing violators.[99] Israeli intelligence also aided with the enforcement effort by passing along to the US Treasury information about shell companies for Iranian nuclear procurement and financing.[100]

These punishments hurt. Iran's GDP contracted by 9 percent from 2012 to 2014.[101] Analysts estimated in 2015 that given the pre-2012 growth trajectory, the Iranian economy was 10–15 percent smaller in 2015 than it would have been without sanctions.[102] The value of its currency (the rial) fell by 56 percent from 2012 to 2014, causing inflation to reach 40 percent.[103] Iran's total exports fell from $145 billion in 2011–12 to $98 billion in 2012–13 and continued to fall thereafter. Crude oil exports fell by 50 percent from 2011 to 2013.[104] While a 2012–15 loss of $160 billion in revenue for the oil sector was painful,[105] the prospect of even more pain was intense, as oil was trading over $100 a barrel through the fall of 2014—any volatility and the pain would be felt even more. While there were many reasons for Iranian economic malaise,[106] sanctions clearly had an effect. In his campaign for the presidency, Hassan Rouhani acknowledged the harsh pain caused by nuclear sanctions, "All of our problems stem from this [mismanagement of the nuclear program]. It's good to have centrifuges running, provided people's lives and sustenance are also spinning," he said. Economic mismanagement also exacerbated these effects and impeded coping.

The US military force posture in the Persian Gulf also became highly visible and prepared for air strikes on short notice.[107] Procurement and deployment of the GBU-57 Massive Ordnance Penetrator (MOP) "bunker buster" bomb signaled that Washington could put the deeply buried Fordow centrifuge facility at risk. The Pentagon tailored war plans and exercised them regularly. Washington's somewhat arbitrary choice of "one year of breakout time" as the key measurement of Iranian nuclear capability during the negotiations reflected this logic of military action. One year was considered long enough to detect and destroy a clandestine Iranian weaponization effort.

US force posture changes were explicitly coercive. "We carried out a very aggressive deployment of aerial and supporting assets to multiple countries in the region, and in a conspicuous way so that Iran could see that we could pursue a military strike if we wanted," recalled Jake Sullivan, then national security adviser to the vice president. "It had also emerged publicly that we had the capability to hold Fordow at risk." Second, the Obama administration's rhetoric about using force changed toward the end of 2012. "It went from 'all options on the table' to specifics from Obama himself about American resolve and willingness to strike. And the Iranians saw this," said Sullivan.[108] Iranians perceived these threats clearly, he believes. In negotiations, "the Iranians sought negative security assurances from the United States—that we would not attack—and even, I believe, some kind of language that would include Israel as well."[109]

In April 2012 the Obama administration gave Iran a "last chance" to negotiate concessions, cease enrichment at Fordow, and ship out 20-percent-enriched uranium.[110] Everything began to peak. In November 2011 the IAEA had released its most comprehensive report on Iranian weaponization suspicions, showing starkly what Iran had to answer for.[111] Soltanieh was defiant at the spring 2012 board of governors meeting, assessing that "while sanctions had been in place since the victory of the Islamic revolution, the nuclear issue was a recent phenomenon and so the Supreme Leader had concluded that the West's real problem with Iran was that it was a nation that had decided to be independent."[112] Iran's coercers, in his view, would never relent. The coercive campaign was reaching an inflection point. Would it break in favor of war or peace?

BREAKTHROUGH

The breakthrough began in the summer of 2012 when the United States and Iran opened a secret diplomatic channel, which remained secret through eight rounds of negotiation.[113] In June Director of Policy Planning Jake Sullivan and Special Assistant to the President and NSC Senior Director for Iraq, Iran, and the Gulf States Puneet Talwar traveled to Oman to meet with an Iranian delegation led by Secretary of the Supreme National Security Council Saeed Jalili.[114] The sides were feeling each other out. Deputy Secretary of State William Burns made another trip to Oman in March 2013. Rouhani was then elected the new Iranian president in June 2013 on a platform that included seeking sanctions relief. Talks continued when he came into office. In August 2013 the United States then returned to the enrichment carrot, offering "to entertain the possibility of very limited uranium enrichment, if it could be tightly monitored and verified."[115] Under Secretary of State for Political Affairs Wendy Sherman, lead negotiator of the JCPOA, returned from a subsequent meeting in Oman in October 2013 with the draft text of an interim agreement.[116]

The two sides took the talks public and unveiled the interim Joint Plan of Action (JPOA) in November 2013. The JPOA provided for limited sanctions relief, allowing Iran to gain access to $7 billion in frozen assets from January to November 2014. In exchange, Iran agreed not to enrich uranium beyond 5 percent, dilute the concentration of its 20-percent-enriched uranium, and not install new centrifuges. Initially providing six months for negotiations, the parties extended the window for continued talks in July 2014 and again in November 2014. The P5 + 1 and Iran came to a framework agreement in Lausanne in March 2015. And the final JCPOA was concluded in Vienna on July 14, 2015.

Broadly, the terms of the JCPOA lifted nuclear-related sanctions in exchange for Iran uninstalling two-thirds of its centrifuges, limiting enrichment to 3.67 percent, shipping out nearly all its enriched uranium, and changing the design of its Arak reactor core. Intrusive inspections, including novel monitoring of the nuclear supply chain and uranium mills, would verify Iranian compliance with these limitations. These were major concessions. Why did Iran make them?

The question is all the more puzzling given that the supreme leader himself made many statements about an American reputation for noncredible coercive assurance. He commonly referred to the United States as "obstinate, unreliable, dishonest and into backstabbing"[117] and "known for backpedaling on its commitments."[118] He believed that the US would seek to sanction Iran regardless of its behavior or the contents of a deal.[119] In April 2015, in his first speech after the unveiling of a framework agreement, Khamenei warned, "I have told the officials to not trust the opposing side, to not be fooled by their smiles, to not trust their promises because when they have achieved their objectives they will laugh at you."[120]

There is some evidence that Obama administration officials were aware of these Iranian perceptions and therefore knew that they had to coercively assure Iran. Wendy Sherman reflected that the White House was sensitive to the "long, bitter history" between Iran and the United States; overcoming this meant "operating not solely from a position of overwhelming power but treating Iran as a party who could bargain credibly."[121] Sherman further acknowledged that "power can be a burden. . . . Negotiations rarely come down to a simple calculation of who has more of it."[122] The following sections evaluate how three strategies—disentangling demands, managing spoilers, and shared knowledge—augmented the credibility of the P5 + 1's coercive assurance and proved important complements to coercive threats.

Mitigating the Assurance Dilemma in JCPOA Negotiations

Iran had three reasons to question the credibility of US coercive assurance: (1) Tehran feared that nuclear-related sanctions might easily be relabeled missile-related or terrorism-related and in practice remain in effect; (2) domestic and international opponents—Congress and Israel, respectively—were not party to the negotiations and were therefore potential spoilers even if Iran acquiesced; and (3) Iranian leaders feared that concessions would reveal more about their guilt than their enemies already knew. Washington sought to overcome each of these impediments and mitigate the assurance dilemma.

DISENTANGLING DEMANDS

Iranian negotiators were skeptical that striking a bargain would actually result in the end of severe sanctions. US officials were aware of this concern. In opening the secret channel, President Obama had been explicit that talks should focus on the nuclear issue alone.[123] "Iranian negotiators were very worried about whether they would get sanctions relief or whether there would be some kind of bait and switch to keep existing sanctions," recalled Jake Sullivan.[124]

The prospect of lifting sanctions was far from straightforward. As the United States and others had constructed their sanctions regime, they had built what Ali Vaez aptly describes as a spider web, "mutated over three decades . . . imposed by a variety of actors and aimed at a wide range of objectives."[125] These objectives (or coercive demands) included curtailing nuclear proliferation, ballistic missile development, support for terrorism, and human rights violations.[126] This was the assurance dilemma in practice—the process of building pressure undermined the assurance to remove that pressure. Indeed, in its original construction of Iran sanctions, the United States seems not to have considered the problem of assurance or at most assumed it was axiomatic. Robert Einhorn, former State Department special adviser for nonproliferation and arms control and an architect of the Iran sanctions regime, recollected that "our message to partners was that sanctions pressure was necessary to give us leverage to get meaningful limits on Iran's nuclear program. That they would be lifted in the event of a deal was implicit in that message."[127] As former White House coordinator for arms control and weapons of mass destruction Gary Samore reflected, "There was no mastermind of the sanctions regime. We had been 'thicketing' the campaign of sanctions since 1979."[128] Entangled sanctions made the problem of coercive assurance more difficult.

Only "nuclear-related" sanctions were to be lifted under the JCPOA. Indeed, negotiating over the discrete nuclear issue alone, disentangling it from other issues of concern to Iran's coercers, helps to explain why Iran came to the table at all. Nonetheless, Iran needed to know from its coercers which nuclear-related sanctions would be lifted and which nonnuclear ones would not. As Ambassador Sherman reflected, sanctions were a "very tangled mess, and we just had to make judgments about which sanctions would continue and which sanctions were nuclear-related and would be lifted . . . to give them enough of a benefit to make it worthwhile."[129] Samore concurred that judgments had to be made to disentangle. "The fact that sanctions were tangled was an impediment to negotiations," he reflected, "so there was a little bit of latitude on how to define 'nuclear-related' for relief."[130]

Two key disentanglement efforts helped to assure Iran of the lifting of sanctions against the CBI and of the lifting of UN sanctions. First, Iran's central bank was subjected to US and EU sanctions that essentially severed it from international financial markets. In taking such action, the US and the EU had "emphasized the central bank's role in money laundering—helping other evade sanctions."[131] As one former Obama administration official observed prior to the conclusion of the JCPOA, this action was "not strictly 'nuclear-related,'" yet Iran was unlikely to agree to any deal that left the CBI disconnected from the global financial system.[132] Samore more explicitly admitted of the CBI's money-laundering designation that "of course it was aimed at the nuclear issue. We used the tools we had available."[133] In the end, the two sides split the difference, keeping the CBI designated as a money-laundering concern yet unfreezing its foreign assets and reconnecting it to the SWIFT communication system.[134] Where possible, the definition of what was nuclear-related was essentially relaxed.

Second, UN resolutions meant to coerce Iran entangled sanctions for both nuclear proliferation and ballistic missile development. Sanctions could not simply be rescinded, therefore, as only nuclear-related punishments were to be lifted under any deal. Iran and its coercers overcame entanglement by negotiating a wholly new UNSC resolution that endorsed the JCPOA and lifted prior sanctions but maintained ballistic missile authorities. Iran refused to agree to any concessions without this disentanglement. In fact, this UN resolution language was the very last piece of the puzzle to fall into place before Iran agreed to the deal.[135]

The terms of the JCPOA itself reflect Iranian fears. The text spells out that it would be a violation of the bargain to reimpose the same sanctions with other justifications (e.g., replacing nuclear sanctions with terrorism sanctions).[136] "Iran was very concerned about this," recalled Jon Wolfsthal, who served as the NSC's senior director for arms control and nonproliferation.[137] Robert Einhorn concurred.[138] Tabatabai cites senior Iranian officials who complained during negotiations about the lack of clarity on sanctions relief. One senior official described it as insufficient "reassurance" that "the sanctions that needed to be lifted would indeed be lifted."[139] Iranian minister of foreign affairs and nuclear negotiator Javad Zarif observed during negotiations that "the United States is obsessed with sanctions," perhaps pursuing them for their own sake.[140] Iranian and US officials both reported a disagreement over terminology. Americans preferred to call it "suspension" of sanctions, while the Iranians preferred "termination."[141] "In the delicacy of negotiations," Sherman writes, both sides landed on the word "lifted."[142]

Coercers in part allayed Iran's concerns with specifics. Of the negotiating process, Jake Sullivan recalls that "Iran's main interest was in making sure that the deal included annexes on the specifics of entities that would experience relief—on whom and what sanctions would be lifted. And then they wanted to walk through in detail how exactly sanctions relief would work."[143] Even after the deal, President Obama instructed his communications staff to "make sure we frame this as a nuclear issue. We don't want to let the critics muddy the nuclear issue with the other issues."[144]

After the conclusion of the JCPOA, the Obama administration experienced a lesson in the assurance dilemma and the structural difficulties of turning off financial sanctions. To be sure, the Iranian economy did see benefits from the JCPOA. Iran's GDP expanded by 13.4 percent in 2016, due in large part to the unleashing of the oil and gas sector.[145] Yet Iranians claimed to be in a purgatory of sorts, having received sanctions relief yet still waiting to see the effects of punishment to subside.[146] In the words of Ayatollah Khamenei, "Today, all across Western countries and those who are under their impact, our banking restrictions are still facing problems and repatria-tion of our assets are facing problems. . . . The United States is severely working not to allow the deal's results to become beneficial for the Islamic Republic. . . . They have threatened us through other sanctions."[147] "We haven't had much experience unraveling sanctions," admitted Einhorn after the deal. "These sanctions [on Iran] were so interrelated that it is hard to unwind them."[148] As Gary Samore assessed prior to the conclusion of the JCPOA, "many international corporations, stung by billions of dollars of fines meted out by the U.S. government, will not be eagerly re-establishing relationships with Iran."[149] The Obama administration attempted further outreach to the private sector to explain the terms of the JCPOA and smooth legitimate business with Iran. The administration's intention to conduct such private-sector outreach was in fact communicated to the Iranians dur-ing the negotiations.[150]

Some US policymakers reported learning an important lesson about the assurance dilemma in the aftermath of the deal: relief should be considered in the construction of sanctions regimes. For instance, Richard Nephew, for-mer principal deputy coordinator for sanctions policy at the Department of State, regretted that in the process of imposing and enforcing sanctions, the United States had intentionally fostered the myth of omnipresent IRGC fin-gerprints throughout the Iranian economy. As Nephew writes, "the intent of the US strategy was to make the IRGC and Iran inseparable concepts with the aim of chilling even still legal forms of business."[151] Under the JCPOA, the IRGC remained a sanctioned entity for nonnuclear issues; the belief in its tentacles was sticky.[152] On balance, Nephew assessed that this strategy to bolster the severity of sanctions may not have been worth it.[153] After the JCPOA, he believed that the United States, and the Treasury Department in particular, was "learning to be more discrete with sanctions over specific issues. No more omnibus sanctions against entire countries," and "being specific about what an entity is designated for."[154]

MANAGING DOMESTIC SPOILERS

Even more important to Iran's prospect of sanctions relief was the ques-tion of who would be doing the lifting. The sanctions facing the biggest impediment to removal were American. European sanctions are imposed and lifted by a unanimous decision of the European Council.[155] These are easier to lift and harder to reimpose. Most US sanctions, however, were enshrined in legislation and could only be repealed by Congress.[156] As a Republican majority controlled the legislature, observers rightly concluded at the time that "permanently terminating US sanctions in the short term is nearly impossible."[157] There were simply not enough votes in the Senate to ratify a coercive bargain as a treaty.[158] Instead, the White House pursued an executive agreement, and sanctions would have to be suspended through presidential waiver, an executive authority provided for in the original sanctions legislation. Allowable waivers varied in length (thirty days up to a year) but were renewable.[159]

Tehran perceived these US domestic impediments to sanctions relief. According to Nephew, "the Iranians specifically asked us: 'What if a Republican takes over? What will you do?'"[160] Congressional opposition also inserted itself into the process in such a way that the Iranians could not have missed. On March 9, 2015, forty-seven Republican senators sent an open letter addressed to the leaders of Iran.[161] Explaining the US Constitution, the letter warned Iran that treaties required ratification by two-thirds of the Senate and that executive agreements could be undone by "the stroke of a pen." White House officials were livid.

Obama officials first tried to assure Iran by pointing out historic consistency in US foreign policy. "Historically there has been inertia to agreements," recalled Nephew, "so we said, 'There is more space here than you think.' We also told them that if a future administration backed out, it would be criticized by the rest of the world, and they understood this could be to their advantage."[162] But more needed to be done to assert the White House's coercive control—that it alone would impose or relieve punishments. Even if a deal would not be a treaty, Congress could still spoil an agreement on sanctions relief by passing new ones.[163] To rein in this potential spoiler, the administration negotiated a new piece of legislation: the Iran Nuclear Agreement Review Act (INARA).

In parallel with the formal negotiations abroad, the Obama administration negotiated with a Republican Congress to bound congressional oversight of any sanctions waivers.[164] Opponents originally conceived of legislation as a poison pill to a nuclear deal, attempting to require the president to certify Iran's lack of support for terrorism at regular intervals—a provision that would have reentangled nuclear and nonnuclear demands.[165] However, with interlocutors Ben Cardin and Bob Corker, the ranking member and the chairman of the Senate Foreign Relations Committee, respectively, the executive and legislative branches pursued a creative compromise along the following terms: Congress could act to disapprove a deal and presidential sanctions waivers by a certain deadline (eventually decided to be September 17, 2015), but if it did not disapprove, the deal would stand. "This gave members the option of a 'pocket' approval," writes Sherman, "in which nobody had to go on the record with a vote at all."[166] Additionally, if opposition to the deal did force a vote and a majority disapproved, the White House could veto the legislation to preserve the deal. Thus, only a two-thirds majority in each chamber could upend a coercive bargain with Iran.

Rallying senators to this compromise was a feat. "Many members of the Senate and House were reluctant to give up sanctions because they had been so successful in getting Iran to the table," recalled Sherman, expressing frustration at poor instincts about coercive assurance. "We tried to explain to these opponents that the sanctions were a tool."[167] The White House's full-court press needed to work to communicate coercive assurance. Kahl recalled, "Initially we were trying to avoid an INARA, and then we shifted to just getting INARA right. If INARA had required ratification, Iran would have said that that was never going to happen."[168] In other words, instead of opposing congressional review, the White House sought to constrain it. Kahl continued: "We said to the Iranians, 'We wrote the legislation to be able to have the votes.'"[169] Iran was watching carefully to see what happened.

INARA was passed by the Senate (98 to 1[170]) on May 7 and then the House (400 to 25) on May 14, 2015—two months to the day before the JCPOA was finalized. INARA formalized the White House's position that any deal would be considered an "executive agreement," not a "treaty" that required Senate ratification. President Obama would therefore be free to waive by executive order many nuclear-related sanctions.[171] "Had INARA failed, we could not have signed [the JCPOA]. But INARA came together in a complementary way before the final agreement was signed," said Jon Wolfsthal.[172] And Robert Einhorn assessed that "the Iranians were confident that Obama could waive sanctions. INARA provided for very weak oversight. INARA's passage essentially guaranteed that the JCPOA would enter into force."[173] The timing of INARA's passage before finalization of the JCPOA affirmed the importance of demonstrating coercive control by managing spoilers to mitigate the assurance dilemma.

P5 + 1 PARTNERS AND MULTILATERAL ASSURANCE OF SANCTIONS RELIEF

The United States was the indispensable negotiating partner in the JCPOA, and its participation was necessary to demonstrate coercive control. Earlier coercive diplomacy with Iran and European states had failed in large part because Washington was on the sidelines. As Sherman writes, "there was more than a little truth to the idea that the nuclear talks were fundamentally between the United States and Iran. . . . If a deal escaped us, it would be up to the United States to take military action to stop Iran from gaining the bomb. . . . The deal was ours to make, even if we couldn't make it alone."[174] Iran appreciated this necessity as well. In the words of the head of the AEOI, Ali Salehi, "If we hadn't negotiated with the US, the reality was, we wouldn't have reached a deal with the P5 + 1. . . . We couldn't have moved forward with the others."[175]

At the same time, the presence of multiple coercing partners assured Iran that sanctions relief would be forthcoming after it struck a deal. One party's reneging on sanctions relief would be both more costly to the reneger and less costly to Iran. According to Colin Kahl, Iran "believed that other actors—the UNSC, the EU, and other countries—would constrain the United States. They believed that if the US reneged, they would be the ones isolated and not Iran."[176] Wendy Sherman agreed that "the genius of the deal was that it gave Iran nowhere to turn to evade its provisions. By the same token, it made it harder for any one nation to unravel the agreement."[177] This view proved too optimistic as the Trump administration's later deployment of secondary sanctions made unilateral reneging more effective than negotiators had anticipated.

MANAGING ISRAEL AS A POTENTIAL SPOILER

Internationally, the United States also sought to demonstrate control over the coercive threat of military force and manage a potential spoiler in Israel. Before a deal could be struck, it thus tried to communicate that Israel, a state not officially party to the bargaining process, would nonetheless be bound by an agreement. If anyone were to carry out an air strike on Iranian nuclear facilities, it would be the US and not Israel alone. It is suggestive evidence in favor of the assurance dilemma and against a threat credibility lens that Tehran came to the table after the window for an Israeli strike closed. Other theorists have difficulty explaining this puzzling timing of Iran's concessions. As Miller writes, "while it is possible that Iran restrained its nuclear program partly in order to avoid preventive attack on its nuclear facilities, it is unclear why Iran would make this decision only in the 2013–2015 period."[178] Israel's shifting role helps to explain it.

The White House took this signaling effort seriously. "There was genuine concern that the Israeli government might launch such a strike," said former deputy secretary of state William Burns in an interview.[179] Jon Wolfsthal concurred: "There was some recognition that the Israelis were another party, like Congress, with whom we had to contend."[180] And according to Colin Kahl, the Americans "were not confident that the Iranians would even be able to tell if they were struck whether it had been the US or the Israelis. It would just look like fighter aircraft anyway, and we owned Iraqi airspace [on Iran's western border] at the time."[181]

The Israeli Debate   Ever since discovering secret enrichment facilities at Natanz in 2002, Israel had considered striking Iran. At the time, instead of attacking, Prime Minister Ariel Sharon decided to sound the alarm by leaking the discovery to an Iranian dissident group.[182] It thereafter concentrated on improving its own capability to strike Iran. As Prime Minister Ehud Olmert's defense minister (2007–9), Ehud Barak directed Lt. Gen. Gaby Ashkenazi, chief of staff of the Israel Defense Forces (IDF), "to develop a plan for a surgical strike to destroy the most important facilities in the Iranians' nuclear network." Barak soon learned that Israel lacked the necessary penetrating munitions and aerial refueling capacity to strike

Iranian nuclear facilities effectively.[183] His subsequent requests for more heavy munitions and to lease American tankers were rebuffed in Washington. Secretary of Defense Robert Gates recalled that he recommended denying Israeli requests for certain military items. The United States should not be "handing over the initiative," he thought.[184] Barak further recalled a meeting with President Bush in June 2008, in which the president made clear "that he knew what we were up to." After a dinner, over whiskey and cigars, Barak recalls, "the president looked straight at me, and said to Olmert, 'This guy scares the living shit out of me when he tells me what you want.'"[185]

Despite his efforts, Barak assessed that Israel still did not have the capability to strike Iran when he became defense minister to the Benjamin Netanyahu government in May 2009.[186] His aim was to acquire the capability to strike before Iran's nuclear program entered a "zone of immunity," which he defined as a point at which damage from an Israeli strike would be "too negligible to be worth the operational, political, and diplomatic risks."[187] What followed were several critical months of military preparations and debates about whether to strike, which in Barak's words was "both an internal debate among Israel's political and military leadership and discussions with the Obama administration."[188]

Internally, Israeli policymakers debated a strike on Iran at the highest levels of government and mostly within the Group of Eight (or Octet)—an informal security cabinet made up of senior ministers of the Israeli prime minister's governing coalition.[189] Despite the need for secrecy in this small forum, there was no shortage of leaks and vote counting in public about who did and who did not support a strike.[190] Barak was believed by Israel analysts to be the leading proponent of a strike.[191] Yet two other members of the Octet, Dan Meridor and Benny Begin, were opposed to a strike from the start.[192] In Barak's telling, "ministers who opposed a strike argued that we should rely on American economic and political pressure to deal with the threat. And if that failed, on *American* military action."[193] In other words, they were satisfied by US control of the tools of coercion.

The assessments of Israel's military and intelligence leadership—the head of Mossad and the chief of staff of the IDF especially—also matter greatly to the outcome of Group of Eight decisions. These establishment voices were the most consistently opposed to a strike. For instance, when Israel came closest to striking Iran in 2010, the Group of Eight met at a Mossad facility near Tel Aviv in November for a briefing on an attack plan.[194] The group agreed at that meeting that the chief of staff "and ideally the heads of military intelligence and Mossad" would have to sign off on the plan before it could be executed. To the hawks' dismay, General Ashkenazi did not approve the plan, saying that Israel had not yet "crossed the threshold of operational capability."[195] Consensus eluded the Group. No strike occurred.

Mossad chief Meir Dagan and General Ashkenazi were two of the more opinionated voices against a strike.[196] Both men were removed—Dagan in early 2011 and Ashkenazi in February 2011—in a likely effort by Netanyahu to eliminate obstacles to a strike. But their successors held the line. Tamir Pardo replaced Dagan as head of Mossad and testified to the Knesset in 2011 that he did not think an Iranian nuclear weapon was an "existential" threat.[197] Ashkenazi's replacement, Lt. Gen. Benny Gantz, was also hesitant to support a strike.[198] Opposition then seemed to increase.[199]

Overall, many sources concur that Israel's national security chiefs consistently opposed a strike on Iran.[200] US counterparts perceived the Israeli debate similarly. In the assessment of Colin Kahl, "the Israelis pushing back most against Netanyahu and Barak were the military and intelligence professionals. These professionals didn't believe that we wouldn't come to their aid. They likely thought that we would, but they rightly perceived a threat to strategic long-term US-Israeli relations."[201] The climax of Israeli strike deliberations occurred in late 2011 and early 2012. By the fall of 2012, public reports of imminent Israeli strikes had waned.

US Influence The Obama administration weighed in heavily on Israel's deliberations.[202] "We had a civilized intellectual discussion with Israel about the merits of a strike," recalled Samore. "Every couple of months, Donilon would meet with his counterpart, Amidror, to argue about the pros and cons of a strike."[203] First, the United States attempted to influence the Israeli debate about its own capabilities. It did so by withholding critical assistance (tankers, heavy munitions) for the Iran mission while bolstering US capabilities to carry out the mission and sharing military plans with Israel.

To fly the thousand miles to their targets and back,[204] Israeli jets would have to refuel once or twice, depending on the availability of tanker support, which was insufficient at the time.[205] An even more challenging military problem would have been the weaponeering to destroy the hardened targets of Natanz and Fordow: Natanz is underground and covered by steel-reinforced concrete, while Fordow is dug into the side of a mountain 220 feet deep.[206] In 2012 Israeli ordnance might have been able to penetrate Natanz but no more than the entrances to Fordow.[207] In a January 2012 report, Pentagon officials stated explicitly that the United States was working to improve its thirty-thousand-pound MOP bomb in an effort to "ensure the weapon would be more effective against the deepest bunkers, including Iran's Fordow enrichment plant facility."[208] Secretary of Defense Leon Panetta said directly in an interview that the bunker-buster munition was meant to reassure and rein in the Israelis.[209] "They can't do it right without us," an anonymous former Obama adviser said tersely.[210]

Colin Kahl described Washington's strategy to restrain Israel as a policy of "big hugs, little punches." "The Israeli threat to strike was highest in

2010–12," said Kahl, during which time "the hugs were shared intelligence, generous military aid, emphasizing that the US goal was 'prevention and not containment' (Obama said this explicitly at an AIPAC event as a message to the Israelis[211]), insight into our military planning, sharing details on the MOPs—which Israel could not deliver, and they knew we could. The little punches were we've got this, not you; don't strike; if you do, Americans could die, and we won't help you."[212] A military aid package announced a few months after the conclusion of the JCPOA totaled $38 billion over ten years, a more than 25 percent increase. Tankers and advanced penetrating munitions were still withheld.

Israeli policymakers received American signals. In their eyes, what changed over time was their perception of the degree of concerted US operational planning for a strike. "During the first couple of years that Israel worked on acquiring the capability for a military strike against Iran," wrote Ehud Barak, "the Americans had been no more ready than we were. They had tanker aircraft and heavy bombs, but their *plan* was so obviously prone to lead to a wider conflict that it would never have received the go-ahead." However, Barak continued, "by the time I met the president in 2012, that had changed. . . . The Americans now had high precision heavy munitions we couldn't dream of, and stealth air-attack capabilities we also lacked."[213] His final assessment was that the United States "had the operational capability to launch an attack that, within a period of hours, could push the Iranian nuclear program back by years, and that, even if the Iranians knew the strike was coming, they'd be powerless to stop."[214] Israeli national security adviser retired major general Yaakov Amidror recalled that "the Obama administration was the first administration to take seriously military planning for a strike on Iran. Before Obama, no president asked for an Iran military solution plan. The Obama administration came up with a military plan and exercised it. Israel was satisfied by the plan."[215]

Second, the Obama administration tried to undermine the legitimacy of any unilateral Israeli strike. It made no secret of the fact that it opposed unilateral Israeli action, hoping to dispel any notion of even tacit support for independent action. It attempted to amplify the voices of Israeli leaders who opposed a strike.[216] In June 2012 President Obama awarded Shimon Peres the Presidential Medal of Freedom. Shortly thereafter, Peres publicly opposed a unilateral attack and said that he was "convinced . . . after having had talks with him [Obama]" that "we are not alone."[217] US intelligence monitored Israeli military bases and airwaves for signs of mobilization, watching extra close on tactically advantageous moonless nights.[218]

High-level visits to Israel also helped the United States to force delays. It would be even more of a thumb in the eye of Washington to conduct an uncoordinated strike while a senior member of the US government was visiting and in harm's way for Iranian retaliation. In 2012 Chairman of the Joint Chiefs of Staff Martin Dempsey, Secretary of State Hillary Clinton,

Secretary of Defense Leon Panetta, and National Security Adviser Tom Donilon all visited Israel.[219] The administration "figured that Israel couldn't launch an attack when the vice president was on his way, or Tom Donilon was on his way, or Gen. Dempsey was on his way," recalled Gary Samore; visits were "a very conscious, deliberate strategy to stop the Israelis from attacking."[220] He elaborated: "At one point we had a new American official visiting Israel every week to constrain the Israelis from attacking. . . . It would have been too much of an embarrassment to strike while an official was there."[221]

Finally, the Obama administration sought to coordinate details of its coercive diplomacy with Israel. By some accounts, Israeli security chiefs were "talking to their U.S. counterparts 'on a daily basis.'"[222] Israeli intelligence especially found productive partners in the Treasury Department, where Israeli intelligence helped to enforce and tighten sanctions. Keeping the coercive diplomacy route open removed the imperative of an immediate strike in the minds of some Israelis, especially since a strike would eliminate the prospect of a negotiated solution.[223] "We're trying to persuade them [the Israelis] that a strike that just drives the program more underground isn't a solution; it's a bigger problem," said a former Obama adviser anonymously.[224]

The Window Closes In the end Israel closed the door to acting independently before Iran came the negotiating table. Israeli deliberation over whether to strike had subsided by mid-2012. In November 2011 Ehud Barak began assessing that Iran would reach a "zone of immunity" within a year, "probably three-quarters."[225] And a "very senior Israeli" told a reporter in January 2012 that Iran would reach the zone of immunity within six to nine months.[226] Secretary of Defense Panetta assessed in February 2012 that there was a "strong likelihood that Israel would strike Iran in April, May, or June."[227] Facing what Barak called a "final decision" on whether to strike, Israel rescheduled a joint military exercise with the United States in April 2012.[228] The chairman of the Joint Chiefs was sent to Israel almost immediately. Barak also took this time to consult with US leaders—Panetta, Donilon, Clinton, and Obama—who all attempted to dissuade him from striking.[229] Benjamin Netanyahu also met with President Obama in the White House on March 5, 2012.

The flurry of activity ended not with a bang but a whimper. Barak and Netanyahu still had not secured the support of the Group of Eight and Security Cabinet.[230] Ultimately, there was no culminating moment. The plan fizzled out.

Crucially, the United States recognized that the ultimate receivers of its signals to Israel were in Tehran. Indeed, there is evidence of US efforts to make these signals of coercive control unmistakable. Tom Donilon and Susan Rice, national security advisers to President Obama, established a

US-Israeli consultation group that met on a regular basis to discuss the Iran portfolio. As JCPOA negotiations deepened, the US also welcomed Israeli technical experts to consult on the details. Washington then publicized its consultations with Israelis. In the words of retired brigadier general Yaacov Nagel, a national security adviser to Benjamin Netanyahu, "Israel and Washington could keep the consultations secret, but the US decided not to do so. Maybe the US did it in order to 'hug' Israel publicly so that they could claim Israel was part of the deal."[231] To the Iranians, US-Israeli coordination was meant to communicate that Israel was unlikely to act independently as a spoiler. The P5 + 1 demonstrated coercive control, and afterward Iran came to the table willing to make concessions. For their part, Obama administration officials believe that their strategy succeeded. "Iranians made no distinction between the US and Israel," said Colin Kahl. "They assumed that if Israel attacked, it would be with American permission."[232] It also likely helped for the perception of control that Tehran tends to see American puppeteering behind every Israeli action. As Jake Sullivan diagnosed, "Israel is perceived by many, entirely incorrectly, to be a pawn of the United States. In terms of our ability to conduct coercive diplomacy, I think we actually benefited from this perception in the Iran case."[233]

CONCLUDING THE JCPOA WITH SHARED KNOWLEDGE

This next section establishes with some confidence that in the conclusion of the JCPOA, the United States and its partners did know already that which Iran had to admit and that they consciously did not push Tehran to reveal more than they knew already about its past nuclear weapons program. In other words, the two sides shared knowledge even if there is no declassified record yet that the coercer directly shared evidence of this knowledge with the target.

The analysis requires careful consideration of source biases. I rely on interviews with Obama administration officials to understand US strategy in negotiations with Iran. However, I do not rely on interviews to establish what coercers knew and when about Iran's nuclear program. Instead, to establish a baseline of pre-JCPOA knowledge, I rely on declassified US intelligence reporting and IAEA inspections reports. These sources are biased against finding deep knowledge on the part of coercers. By revealing what the United States (and other coercers) knew publicly about Iran's nuclear program, they are a proxy for what coercers knew privately. Evidence in IAEA records has passed through two filters: what information intelligence agencies were willing to share with the IAEA and what the IAEA was willing to make public. I make an assumption that private knowledge was at least as great, and likely greater, than public knowledge.

I then compare this pre-JCPOA baseline to the post-JCPOA evidence from the so-called atomic archive.[234] I was granted access to some of these files passed from Israeli intelligence officials to Harvard University researchers, and I rely on their independent analysis of the records. Several documents have also been published by journalists and analysts.[235] These stolen Iranian documents are heavily biased sources, but they are biased against finding shared knowledge. The evidence has passed through an Israeli intelligence filter, which has held back much material.[236] Israel had an agenda to push in its publicity of these documents. It focused on publishing the most alarming findings first, hoping to turn policymakers toward disapproval of the JCPOA. If the most touted revelations about the Iranian nuclear program are still shown to be consistent with what intelligence organizations knew before the conclusion of the JCPOA, we can be more confident that Washington shared knowledge of Iran's misdeeds before it conceded.

What Coercers Knew   The IAEA opened a file on the PMD of the Iranian nuclear program in 2003. After years of inspections, demands, stonewalling, and breakthroughs, the IAEA summarized its consistent suspicions in a thorough report in November 2011. Evidence in the report came from three sources: the United States, which provided the "alleged studies documentation";[237] intelligence provided by at least ten other member states;[238] and IAEA inspections themselves. These corroborated sources allowed the IAEA to assess the contents of its report to be, "overall, credible."[239]

The 2011 report contained a wealth of knowledge about Iran's weaponization activities. It expressed concern about procurement of nuclear-related and dual-use equipment by the Iranian military, the development of undeclared pathways for the production of fissile material, and the acquisition and indigenous refinement of nuclear warhead designs.[240] The IAEA had knowledge that these activities had taken place as part of "a structured programme" prior to the end of 2003.[241] It mentions the AMAD Plan specifically, directed by Mohsen Fakhrizadeh and with other "senior Iranian figures featured within this command structure."[242] And even after 2003 the IAEA knew that work had continued in more covert or deniable ways.[243] For specific research and development of concern, the IAEA (citing the "alleged studies documentation") pointed to Iranian activity related to detonators (bridge wires for exact timing), high explosives, hydrodynamic tests, neutron initiators, fusing for air and ground bursts, indicators of preparation for a nuclear test,[244] and other projects relevant to weaponization. Research on projects such as neutron initiators allegedly continued beyond 2004.[245] The report references Project 110 on the design of a payload, although without details.[246] And Project 111 worked to fit a "new payload into the re-entry vehicle of the Shahab-3 missile."[247] The report also zeroed in on the military facilities at Parchin, specifically construction of a "large explosives containment vessel in which to conduct hydrodynamic experiments."[248]

One other source that can shed light on coercer governments' knowledge is the November 2007 NIE on Iran's nuclear intentions and capabilities.[249] The NIC judged with "high confidence that in fall 2003, Tehran halted its nuclear weapons program," defined as its "nuclear weapon design and weaponization work and covert uranium conversion-related and uranium enrichment-related work." The NIC also assessed with "moderate-to-high confidence" that Tehran "at a minimum is keeping open the option to develop nuclear weapons."[250]

What did Iran's coercers do with this detailed knowledge? In its final report, the IAEA concluded what it had long known: that "activities relevant to the development of a nuclear explosive device were conducted in Iran prior to the end of 2003 as a coordinated effort, and some activities took place after 2003" and, signaling its focus on future verification, that it had found "no credible indications of the diversion of nuclear material."[251] Iran had had a nuclear weapons program.[252]

Iran made just two admissions. First, it did not deny its well-known contacts with the A. Q. Khan network.[253] Second, it agreed to environmental sampling at the Parchin facility.[254] While not an explicit admission, the sampling tacitly communicated Iran's guilt and confirmed IAEA suspicions. Two IAEA visits to Parchin in 2005 had not uncovered conclusive proof of Iran's weaponization research, as inspectors were not provided access to the building allegedly housing the containment vessel for explosives testing. Satellite imagery showed that the facility had since been renovated.[255] When the IAEA visited Parchin on September 20, 2015, they indeed observed "recent signs of internal refurbishment," and the explosive testing chamber was no longer visible.[256] The IAEA's last word was only that environmental samples had disputed the Iranian assertion that the building had been used for "long-term storage of chemicals for explosives."[257] None of this was surprising to Iran's coercers.

Laid bare, the final compromise on the PMD of Iran's nuclear program was an agreed-upon fiction. As long as Tehran conceded to accepting new limits and verification of its nuclear program spelled out in the JCPOA, it did not have to admit anything that its coercers did not already know. The statements of US policymakers make this strategy plain. "We know what they did. We have no doubt. We have absolute knowledge with respect to the certain military activities they were engaged in," said Secretary of State John Kerry in a June 2015 speech. "What we're concerned about is going forward. It's critical to us to know that going forward, those activities have been stopped, and that we can account for that in a legitimate way."[258] Other administration officials described the strategy similarly. "It was never an issue for the United States about whether there were possible military dimensions. We knew there were," said lead negotiator of the JCPOA, Amb. Wendy Sherman. "We cared about [PMD] tremendously, not because we didn't know what the judgment was but because we knew politically we had to resolve this issue."[259] Jake Sullivan recalled, "We knew Iran had been conducting weaponization activities. The whole point of us having these negotiations to begin with was that they were doing this."[260]

Intelligence collection enabled this US strategy. In 2007, at the insistence of a frustrated President Bush, the CIA established an Iranian Operations Division to improve intelligence collection on Iranian nuclear intentions.[261] The efforts appear to have borne fruit. As Jon Wolfsthal reflected, "On PMD we said, look, we don't want to do anything to prevent the IAEA from doing their work well. But we already knew everything we needed to know about the past military dimensions of Iran's nuclear program from our intelligence agencies. So, we decided there was not much to be gained by pushing PMD. What could have been lost was the deal itself. If there had been insufficient intelligence, then we might have pushed it."[262] Washington sensed the game and played its strong hand strategically. In Jake Sullivan's telling, "the Iranians asserted from start to finish that all of this was a bunch of bunk—that they had never attempted to weaponize. But we knew, and they knew that we knew, and we knew that they knew we knew."[263]

Comparing Pre-JCPOA Coercer Knowledge to Post-JCPOA Iranian Records
On January 31, 2018, Mossad conducted a raid on a nondescript warehouse on the outskirts of Tehran. Working through the night, they torched open safes and stole about fifty-five thousand pages and 163 CDs of documents and videos—by their estimate about 20 percent of the files in storage. All pertained to the Iranian nuclear weapons program. Benjamin Netanyahu did not announce the theft until April 2018, when he delivered a press conference excoriating Iran's duplicity and demanding an end to the JCPOA. These Iranian documents provide scholars the rare opportunity to compare documentary evidence with the public record of coercive bargaining to evaluate a modern instance of shared knowledge between coercer and target—what coercers knew or what Iran simply got away with.

I compare revelations of the Iranian atomic archive to the previously established baseline of what coercers knew about the sophistication of the weapons program in 2003 and about how the late 2003 "halt" order was also a "hide" order to continue clandestine work after 2003. The analysis, summarized in table 5.2, establishes that coercers shared a great deal of knowledge about Iran's nuclear weapons research.

First, atomic archive documents show that in 1999 or early 2000 very senior Iranian leaders made a political decision to acquire and test a nuclear device by 2003.[264] The effort, the AMAD Plan, was overseen by the Supreme Council for Advanced Technologies, which consisted of President

Table 5.2 Evidence of shared knowledge about Iran's nuclear weapons program

Category of comparison	Item	IAEA records (before JCPOA)	Iran's "atomic archive"
Sophistication of nuclear weapons program	Explosives • Detonators (bridgewires for precise timing) • Hydrodynamic testing • Test chamber at Parchin	Yes	Yes
	Neutron initiators	Yes	Yes
	Fusing for air and ground bursts	Yes	Yes
	Preparation for a nuclear test	Yes	Yes
	Project 110 (payload design) • Uranium metallurgy facility	Vaguely referenced	Metallurgy tunnel complex at Parchin under construction
	Project 111 (preparations to mate a payload with the Shahab-3 missile)	Yes	Yes
	Warhead design • Implosion computer modeling • Manufacture of simulated components	Yes	More foreign weapons designs than known
	Foreign assistance	Yes	More substantial than known
Nature of 2003 halt/ hide order	AMAD Plan • Existence • Leadership and organization	Yes	Yes
	Work continuing after 2003 • Staff remained in place • Neutron-initiator research beyond 2004 • Computer modeling until 2009 • Research known to have continued until 2009 • Some procurement until 2007	Yes	Yes

Mohammad Khatami, Supreme National Security Council Secretary General Hassan Rouhani (later president), Minister of Defense Ali Shamkhani, and the head of the AEOI, Gholamreza Aghazadeh.[265] The council approved a budget of $100 million (in 1999 dollars)[266] to build five nuclear warheads of ten kilotons each.[267] The scale of foreign assistance was large—over a dozen foreign experts and four foreign bomb designs (from which the Iranians innovated their own design). And the program was intended to have a "parallel fuel cycle to produce HEU for nuclear weapons," including use of the Fordow enrichment plant.[268] Additionally, the documents describe a tunnel complex underneath Parchin intended to house metallurgy equipment for uranium casting of a nuclear core (Project 110 of the AMAD Plan).[269] Construction of the tunnel complex was nearly completed in 2003, but the halt order came down before equipment was installed.

This evidence from the atomic archive is consistent with the IAEA's 2011 report. Iran's planning to carry out an underground nuclear test,[270] while much more specific in the stolen Iranian files, is consistent with language in the 2011 report that "in 2002–2003 Iran may have planned and undertaken preparatory experimentation relevant to testing a nuclear explosive device," including preparing explosive bridge wiring to reliably detonate "a test device located down a deep shaft."[271] As early as 2006, experts had been writing publicly about Iran's "sophisticated drawings of a 400-meter-deep subterranean shaft with remote-controlled sensors to measure pressure and heat," more than suggestive of preparations for a test.[272] The IAEA did not mention Iranian activities in uranium metallurgy in the 2011 report. It did, however, mention knowledge of Project 110, which aimed to produce nuclear cores. Curiously, the report does not mention any specifics on Project 110 after disclosing knowledge of it. Israeli intelligence officials say that both Israeli and US intelligence agencies knew about the site during its construction but were not aware of its connection to the AMAD Plan.[273] This is not so surprising, given that the tunnel complex was empty at the time of the 2003 halt order.[274] None of the uranium metallurgy equipment had been moved in. It is plausible that US or Israeli intelligence agencies would have detected uranium metallurgy activity if the facility had ever been completed.

Second, stolen Iranian documents also illuminate the nature of Tehran's high-level 2003 decision to halt its nuclear weapons program. The late 2003 order, described as a "halt" by the 2007 NIE, "did not stop all the work."[275] Instead, it divided the research program into overt and clandestine parts intended to "fill in technical gaps."[276] Overt research continued "openly under civilian rationales"—for example, on neutron generator development.[277] Secret, dual-use work was believed to be deniable.

Some analysts assert that this information shows that the 2007 NIE assessment was incorrect.[278] On the contrary, a "hide and preserve" order would be consistent with the 2007 NIE's "moderate-to-high confidence" assessment that "Tehran at a minimum is keeping open the option to develop nuclear weapons."[279] In addition, the IAEA reported that it was aware that even after the halt order in 2003, "staff remained in place to record and document the achievements of their respective projects,"[280] while "equipment and work places were either cleaned or disposed of so that there would be little to identify the sensitive nature of the work which had been undertaken." Moreover, the IAEA remained interested in Fakhrizadeh as he moved to university settings and knew that "some activities previously carried out under the AMAD Plan were resumed later."[281] The IAEA's 2015 PMD report specifies that from 2005 to 2009, Iran continued "computer modelling of a nuclear explosive device."[282] It also documents that Iran continued procurement of items relevant "to the development of a nuclear explosive device" until 2007.[283] Obama administration officials additionally told reporters in 2010 that "in contrast to the 2007 NIE finding," they and US key allies believed Iran's nuclear weapons design work was "continuing on a smaller scale."[284]

Overall, when compared to what coercers knew about the Iranian nuclear weapons program before the JCPOA, the post-JCPOA stolen Iranian files reveal little that is new. Instead, they add detail to categories of activities previously known.[285] This knowledge of Iran's nuclear weapons activities is indeed important. It shows publicly the sophistication of the Iranian program and its scalability into building an arsenal should Iran break out and race for the bomb. Yet the purloined records also confirm the quality of earlier intelligence once debated by experts.[286] Indeed, the fact that we now have access to these stolen documents at all provides suggestive evidence that the Iranian nuclear program was heavily penetrated by foreign intelligence.[287] Most importantly, the records show that in 2015 the P5 + 1 and Iran shared detailed knowledge of Tehran's nuclear sins, providing some additional coercive assurance that Iran's concessions would not reveal truly new information. When documents become available, it would be no surprise to find that the United States privately shared evidence of what it knew with Iranian negotiators to alleviate some assurance concerns.

Alternative Explanations for the JCPOA

Alternative explanations for the Iran deal emphasize the elections of Obama and Rouhani opening a window for bargaining as well as the inclusion of significant carrots in the deal for Iran. These were indeed important factors. However, they are distinguished from the importance of coercive assurance and do not negate its necessity in this case of coercion.[288]

First, moderate candidate Hassan Rouhani won the Iranian presidential election in 2013, and thus the window opened for a possible deal with the Obama administration.[289] This confluence of leadership was no doubt helpful to the eventual success of coercive bargaining, but as a common narrative of the case it overlooks an important detail: the secret US-Iran diplomatic channel via Oman had already been opened the year before. Rouhani's election naturally accelerated progress in negotiations, but the Ahmadinejad administration had already approached coercers seeking sanctions relief. Thus, while Rouhani opened the window wider, the Iranian government still sought coercive assurance that punishment was truly avoidable.

Second, perhaps inducements (carrots) in the form of the Obama administration's willingness to allow Iran to keep a limited enrichment capacity explain Iran's acquiescence in 2015.[290] Although within-case variation in the success and failure of coercion across many years with Iran offers confidence that there was a bargain to be had, it took some determined coercive diplomacy to find it. Coercion failures did not merely reflect a lack of bargaining space; there were in fact commitment problems to overcome, chiefly the assurance dilemma. Indeed, as early as 2006 it was clear that any bargain with Iran would have to maintain some indigenous nuclear capability.[291] But other impediments to any coercive bargain remained, including threat and assurance credibility. Obama administration officials recalled the same understanding as they considered their own negotiation strategies years later. "Iran pocketed that they were going to have an enrichment program long before the JCPOA negotiations," reflected Richard Nephew, "so the Obama enrichment offer was less of a big deal inside of Iran than we think. In 2008 we said that the resolution would result in Iran being treated as any other NPT state (thus a right to enrichment). It didn't change things for five years. So, it was not as big a deal to offer enrichment [in 2013] as we think."[292] William Burns similarly writes of the enrichment carrot that "there had been considerable internal back-and-forth on this issue, beneath the president's level, less over whether to play this card then when."[293] And the scholar Nicholas Miller agrees that inducements had less of a role to play in Iran's decision to sign the JCPOA "unless we define the lifting of sanctions as an inducement, a definition which would make it very difficult to distinguish the effect of sanctions versus rewards in changing state behavior."[294] As this book shows, the lifting of sanctions is best understood as a coercive assurance, not an inducement.

After the JCPOA, the Trump and Biden Administrations

After a stark political transition, the United States reneged on its coercive bargain with Iran. President Donald Trump assumed office in January 2017, having pledged to tear up the "worst deal ever." Initially, however, he did not withdraw. The White House recertified Iranian compliance and sanctions waivers as required by the INARA legislation. The president reportedly did so reluctantly, bowing to the consensus recommendation of his advisers and granting them time to recommend a new strategy for Iran.[295]

For a time that strategy was one of threatening to withdraw from the JCPOA in order to compel Tehran to renegotiate.[296] Yet this coercive strategy lacked assurance for two reasons.[297] First, the president himself, in public and through reporting on his deliberations, had made clear that he wished to withdraw from the JCPOA regardless of Iran's behavior.[298] Second, with the imposition of new demands on Iran, especially in the form of new sanctions for human rights violations and ballistic missile development, the Trump administration reentangled demands that the Obama administration had sought to disentangle.[299] The magnitude of US demands appeared to also increase, as Secretary of State Rex Tillerson testified before Congress that the United States sought a "peaceful transition" of the Iranian government, which many heard as a call for regime change,[300] including the supreme leader himself.[301] And in April 2018 President Trump hired as national security adviser John Bolton, who only three months earlier had penned an op-ed advising that "America's declared policy should be ending Iran's 1979 Islamic Revolution before its 40th anniversary."[302]

In May 2018 the Trump administration finally announced its decision to withdraw from the JCPOA and reimpose nuclear sanctions on Iran. Other members of the P5+1 refused to support the new strategy, but the White House staunched their impact by threatening secondary sanctions against foreign firms that continued to conduct business with Iranian entities. The president's Iran Action Group, led by Special Representative for Iran Brian Hook, formally reentangled demands by pursuing "the entire range of Iran's threats," listing twelve demands.[303] Invoking many previously disentangled demands, John Bolton complained that the JCPOA "didn't end [Iran's] nuclear ambitions, missile tests, support for terrorism or regional expansionism."[304]

The United States escalated its coercive strategy again in May 2019 when it refused to extend any waivers for countries importing Iranian oil. This policy provides a natural quasi-experiment. When Iran made concessions in 2013–15, its oil exports had fallen at their trough to just over one million barrels per day.[305] That was the previous level of pain under which Tehran felt it was worth negotiating concessions. Under renewed sanctions, Iran's oil exports hit the same level in mid-2018 and kept falling. Its oil exports plunged below half a million barrels per day in 2020.[306] The value of the rial plummeted as well, and its currency reserves dwindled from $122.5 billion in 2018 to $4 billion in 2020. Administration officials stressed the pain of sanctions as a measure of their efficacy.[307] Yet, this time, in response to renewed and severe coercion, Iran gradually reduced its compliance with JCPOA nuclear limits. It ceased its sale of excess enriched uranium and heavy water, stopped blending down LEU, increased its pace of enrichment, gradually began enriching above the 3.75 percent JCPOA limit (first to approximately 4.5 percent, then to 20 percent, and then 60 percent), reinvested in research and development, and restarted uranium enrichment at the Fordow centrifuge facility. It also began to produce uranium metal. These reversible steps seemed designed to generate counterpressure; nonetheless, they were significant violations of the deal and reduced Iran's breakout time if it ever sprinted for a bomb. Tehran also lashed out militarily, deniably striking a Saudi oil facility, harassing ships in the Persian Gulf, and supporting proxy attacks on US personnel in Iraq. Washington escalated again in January 2020 by killing Quds Force commander Maj. Gen. Qasem Soleimani. Channeling Iranian outrage, President Rouhani reiterated that Tehran would not reengage in negotiations with the US while the "maximum pressure" campaign remained, including that "it makes no difference who will be the next [US] administration."[308] Earlier, Supreme Leader Khamenei had already decreed, "We will not negotiate with America, because negotiation has no benefit and carries harm."[309]

Iran's behavior confirms that targets of coercion without assurance defy or lash out. "I couldn't care less if they negotiate," admitted Trump in January 2020.[310] The same day, four months after leaving his White House post as national security adviser, John Bolton revealed his true preferences in a tweet: "The Khamenei regime has never been under more stress. Regime change is in the air. The people of Iran can see it. America, Europe and France should not try to prop it up or negotiate with its illegitimate representatives."[311] The waning weeks of the Trump administration's attention to the Iran portfolio were spent on purposely reentangling demands to construct a so-called sanctions wall that would be difficult for a successor to lift.[312]

Where the Trump administration failed, in 2021 the Biden administration attempted to pick up the pieces. Its efforts were stymied far more than its policymakers seemed to be prepared for. Negotiations recommenced with the Rouhani government, albeit indirectly, with other P5 + 1 states passing messages between US and Iranian negotiators. In Vienna the US delegation had to stay in a hotel across the street. Early reports were optimistic about JCPOA revival, underestimating the problem of assurance.[313] Behind the scenes, the IAEA had to extend and reextend a monitoring agreement to keep the intrusive JCPOA safeguards in place while the parties negotiated.[314] By the sixth round of indirect negotiations, most issues of technical compliance, inspections, and sanctions relief had been solved. Indeed, they had reportedly been solved for a while. What remained was an assurance problem. "We are closer than ever to an agreement but there are still essential issues under negotiations," Iranian deputy foreign minister Abbas Araqchi told Al Jazeera. "We want to make sure that what happened when Trump pulled out of the deal will not be repeated by any other American president in the future."[315] According to the *New York Times*, Iran was asking for a "written commitment that no future American government could scrap the deal as Mr. Trump did."[316] The issue troubled Ayatollah Khamenei as well. "They once violated the nuclear deal at no cost by exiting it," Khamenei said. "Now they explicitly say that they cannot give guarantees that it would not happen again."[317]

Talks broke off in June 2021. Khamenei's handpicked conservative candidate, Ebrahim Raisi, assumed the Iranian presidency in August, and Khamenei took the opportunity to criticize the departing Rouhani administration: "In this government, it was shown up that trust in the West does not work."[318] He implied that the Raisi government would learn from it.

Some were pessimistic that the United States could ever provide credible coercive assurance. A senior US official called Iran's requested guarantee "a reasonable-sounding demand that no real democracy can make."[319] US Special Envoy for Iran Rob Malley bemoaned that "there is no such thing as a guarantee; that's not in the nature of diplomacy."[320] Yet in the framework of this book, coercers can bolster the credibility of their coercive assurance by disentangling multiple demands, managing spoilers, and sharing knowledge. The ultimate question is: How credible does that assurance need to be? If the pain of sanctions is severe enough, even a little coercive assurance can aid successful coercion. But the bar in this instance may have been too high. The Biden administration could not overcome the raw US reputation for so recently reneging on sanctions relief. Iran was left on the threshold of a nuclear weapons capability.

The Assurance Dilemma in Iran

The long saga of coercing Iran over its nuclear weapons program reveals mixed results for the assurance dilemma. A credible threat of extreme pain in the wake of the 2003 US invasion of Iraq caused Iran to make partial concessions absent assuring signals. The assurance dilemma fails this test. Tehran took a concession gamble, but it also hedged significantly. The assurance dilemma does a better job of explaining why the 2006 referral of Iran to the UNSC did not yield more concessions but rather was associated with greater demand for coercive assurance. And when Tehran finally agreed to verifiable limits on its nuclear program as part of the 2015 JCPOA, it did so both because it faced credible and painful punishments and because it perceived that concessions offered an opportunity to avoid that pain. It was coercively assured.

Iran's 2015 concessions were more substantial than those made in 2003. In 2003 Iran tacitly conceded to coercion by secretly scaling back a weaponization effort that had already settled on a nuclear warhead design and prepared testing equipment. At the time, however, Iran lacked the fissile material for a weapon and accepted no additional verification while some overt and covert research programs continued. In 2015 Iran acceded to coercion in a formal agreement and scaled back an advanced fissile material production capability, redesigned the core of a reactor, and accepted an intrusive verification regime to enforce research and production limits and detect violations. Moreover, considering cumulatively to its knowledge of nuclear weapons production, Iran was closer to the bomb in 2015 than in 2003.

Iran's primary coercer, the United States, offered assuring signals from 2012 to 2015 in three ways. First, Washington disentangled its nuclear demands from demands over ballistic missiles, terrorism, and human rights. In the trenches of negotiating over sanctions relief, entanglement proved a sticking point as the parties devised specific compromises to suspend only nuclear-related punishments while offering relief. Second, Washington demonstrated coercive control by managing spoilers domestically and internationally, attempting to communicate that the White House, not Congress or Israel, would get to decide when to impose or withhold punishments. Third, Washington and Tehran shared substantial knowledge of Iran's past nuclear research, which reduced the chances that concessions would reveal new information about Iran's capabilities or intent. JCPOA negotiations, the longest sustained international deliberations of their kind, included several attempts to creatively communicate coercive assurance.[321]

Overall, the case highlights the limits of sticks and carrots alone. During back-channel talks in Oman, William Burns recalls that a member of the Iranian delegation once "objected to American references over the years to the use of 'carrots and sticks' against Iran. Raising his voice, he exclaimed, 'Iranians are not donkeys!'"[322] The analogy is indeed poor and needlessly constrictive of the coercer's tool kit.

Conclusion

The True Sources of Coercive Leverage

Successful coercion requires credible coercive assurance that pain is conditional upon the behavior of the target. Coercers must make both credible threats and assurances at once. Threats of punishment should be contingent on noncompliance; assurances of withheld punishment should be contingent on compliance. Effective threats do not make targets think that they are "damned if they do and damned if they don't."

This book has explained why coercers struggle to make credibly conditional threats. Coercers confront an assurance dilemma, whereby the actions they take to bolster the credibility and severity of their threats undermine their corresponding assurance. Threats are not truly avoidable if insincere coercers pursue brute force policies under the guise of coercion. But even sincere coercers can wind up applying unconditional punishments.

First, coercers can entangle multiple demands and punishments, such that concessions to one demand do not relieve pain. Multiple issues are entangled if they are tied to the same threatened punishment(s); disentangled issues are independently contingent on separable threatened punishments. If the issues are entangled, a target may rationally calculate that it cannot avoid punishment by conceding to one demand while the other demand remains unsated. Second, coercers can lose control over international or domestic coalitions, within which spoilers with greater demands and an independent capacity to punish can take it upon themselves to carry out threats. Targets will not concede to *you* if *others* are going to punish them anyway. Third, coercers may stand to lose control over themselves when they learn new information from their target's concessions that expands their demands. A target that thinks that conceding will only self-incriminate and enable or encourage the coercer to punish will defy. Targets of coercion therefore fear unconditional punishment and look for signals that their coercers are being sincere and retain control over the choice to punish. They take bigger risks to avoid more severe pain, but some assurance must always remain. Variation in the credibility of coercive assurance thus affects whether coercion succeeds or fails.

Three corresponding signal types stand out in theory and empirics to mitigate the assurance dilemma. First, coercers can disentangle multiple demands of targets and tie each to separable punishments that can be independently lifted. Disentangling demands can also take the form in practice of abandoning a maximalist demand, such as for regime change. In such cases coercion is again made more likely to succeed but not because of coercive assurance. Another body of theory describes how the magnitude of demands can impede coercion; this alternative explanation for coercion failure finds some support in this book as well. Second, coercers can manage spoilers to try to convince targets that they are bargaining with the right coercer who will be able to control whether and when any punishment is carried out. Demonstrating coercive control can take the form of co-opting, compensating, or freezing out potential spoilers. Third, coercers can share knowledge to communicate how much they already know about a target's misdeeds to assure them that concessions will not reveal novel information. It helps to know what you are asking for.

Overall, the assurance dilemma helps to explain why targets defy coercive demands backed by credible and severe threats and therefore elucidates broader patterns of coercion success and failure in international politics. To concede, targets must believe they face a real choice and that their own behavior will determine their fate.

Nuclear Proliferation Cases

The history of coercive counterproliferation of nuclear weapons programs bears out these ideas. In coercing South Africa, Iraq, Libya, and Iran, assurance was more often the sticking point of coercive bargaining than threat credibility. Before proliferators made concessions, coercers tended to have to communicate which punishments applied to which demands, manage potential spoilers, and share what they already knew of the target's clandestine misdeeds. Sometimes these signals even overcame reputations for past duplicity.

Primary evidence from South African leaders and archives unveils how Pretoria refused to sign the NPT in the 1970s and 1980s because it perceived that its coercers had entangled nuclear demands with demands to abandon the brutal practice of apartheid. Acquiescence on the nuclear issue, they believed, would provide no relief from the pain of economic sanctions.

Recordings of meetings between Saddam Hussein and his advisers also reveal how Iraq made concessions in the 1990s with an eye toward never revealing more than what they thought their coercers already knew about their WMD programs. And as the decade proceeded, the concessions ceased when Saddam concluded that no amount of compliance would lift sanctions. He perceived no escape, so he defied.

Signals of coercive assurance were also critical to closing a 2003 coercive bargain with Libya. While the US invasion of Iraq had primed Muammar Qaddafi to explore taking a concession gamble, he was still suspicious that his coercers intended to disarm him and attack anyway. Washington and London overcame this perception over many months by freezing out spoilers and privately sharing intelligence already gleaned from their penetration of the A. Q. Khan proliferation network. Both the Iraq and Libya cases show how targets of coercion are loath to make concessions that would reveal capabilities or intentions they believe to be secret. That both Saddam and Qaddafi acquiesced after updating their beliefs about how much their coercers already knew of their secret capabilities shows that their concerns stemmed less from reputational anxieties about being known as coercible leaders and more from assurance fears that concessions would convey new information to their coercers and make them more inclined to punish.

Finally, Iran accepted limits on its nuclear program in 2015 after the Obama administration disentangled nuclear demands and punishments from those tied to missiles and foreign policy, after legislation bounded congressional oversight over sanctions relief, and after Israel decided at the time against independent air strikes. Documents from Iran's "atomic archive" matched to IAEA reports also reveal how much coercers already knew about Iran's past nuclear weapons program.

These findings make no judgments about which tools of statecraft are best to check proliferation—sanctions, military threats, security guarantees, sabotage, or brute force—only that if enforcers select coercion, they must consider the credibility of their coercive assurances. Increases in the perception of assurance credibility, not just threat credibility, are most proximately associated with acquiescence.

This book also sheds light beyond proliferation cases and should elevate assurances in the minds of policymakers as they engage in coercion over any issue in international politics. Conceiving of the coercer's tool kit only in terms of "carrots and sticks" needlessly narrows and papers over the important role of coercive assurance. The key to coercive leverage is in making any tool credibly conditional upon the behavior of the target.

Extensions beyond the Nuclear Domain

For as long as there have been humans, there has been coercion. Scholars are fond of saying that the first deterrent threat failed when Eve ate the apple.[1] If so, that biblical story is swiftly followed by the first compellent demand: Moses's "Let my people go!" The pharaoh's stubbornness makes him the target of God's graduated compellent punishments in the form of the ten plagues. This first case of compellence has a mixed record. While the pharaoh complies after the final plague, freeing the enslaved Israelites after his firstborn son is killed, soon he changes his mind and pursues them to the Red Sea, where his army must be crushed by brute force. And there is a hint of an assurance dilemma in the text of Exodus: the pharaoh refuses for the eighth time, saying, "Clearly you are bent on evil."[2]

The preceding chapters have shown that the assurance dilemma is pronounced in coercive counterproliferation. Nevertheless, nuclear weapons are a high-stakes issue, a heavily monitored technology, and an ambition that most proliferators pursue in secrecy.[3] Here I explore how the concept of coercive assurance travels to other domains of coercion and show that when coercers make threats of many kinds their targets look for coercive assurance.

RANSOMWARE AND CYBER COERCION

In May 2017 cyber criminals linked to North Korea unleashed a global ransomware attack targeting 230,000 computers running the Microsoft Windows operating system in 150 countries. The hackers used an aptly named WannaCry virus to encrypt users' files and demanded ransom payments of $300 to $600 for their safe return. It was classic compellence: a ransom note of "Pay me or else." Yet, in making their threat, the hackers issued no complementary coercive assurance to their victims. How would a victim know that their files would be decrypted safely and intact? Would the cyber thieves care for your data? Would the hackers even provide the decryption key upon payment? In the words of one victim in Shanghai, "Even if you do pay, you won't necessarily be able to open the files that are hit. There is no solution to it."[4] Many victims made similar calculations, and these instincts were correct; the hackers made little effort to restore access to encrypted files. A week into the attack, only three hundred victims had paid the ransom, netting the hackers a mere $95,000 worldwide—a coercive success rate of just over 0.1 percent.[5] Another cyberattack in Ukraine in June 2017, dubbed NotPetya, targeted more than 12,500 machines and spread online to sixty-four other countries.[6] Similar to WannaCry, the virus "spread wider and faster than previous forms of known ransomware," yet "combined, they barely banked $100,000."[7] Cybersecurity analysts concluded that even if victims paid the ransom, the code lacked a decryption key that would "unscramble the noise of the computer's contents."[8] "They are just being destructive," said one expert.[9] Moreover, when the city of Baltimore was hit with a ransomware attack in May 2019, the mayor refused to pay the $76,000 ransom "in part because there was no guarantee the files would be unlocked."[10] Overall, victims tend to be more likely to pay ransoms with the hope of decrypting their files if the cost is relatively inexpensive,[11] if they face high consequences for not accessing data immediately (e.g., they are a hospital), or if they have cyber insurance to cover the cost.[12] But few pay if they are not coercively assured.

CRIMINAL JUSTICE

Similar logics play out in the criminal justice system. Scholars of crime and punishment find that if there is a deterrent effect to capital punishment for single murders, there is demonstrably no deterrent effect to multiple murders. This is because "the marginal cost of murders after the first is approximately zero."[13] By then there is little assurance of nonpunishment. For the same reason, raising the severity of the penalty for petty crimes can backfire. If, say, robbers faced the death penalty, rather than a decline in theft we might observe a rise in thieves murdering their victims.[14]

International legal institutions have benefited from learning these lessons as well. Despite its inability to enforce indictments and convict perpetrators, the International Criminal Court (ICC) has actually reduced attacks on civilians by groups affiliated with indictees.[15] The cause of this puzzling effectiveness is credible coercive assurance—the violators' belief that their punishment will be easily lifted or "beaten" in exchange for improved behavior. Yet war criminals also respond if coercers renege. While ICC "indictments lead to a substantial initial decline in attacks against civilians by armed groups affiliated with indictees," Andrew Miller writes, "the attacks return to pre-indictment levels when the indictments are not lifted."[16]

THE CUBAN MISSILE CRISIS

Not only does coercive assurance help to explain the outcomes of a lot of coercion—it also helps to explain big, important cases. A brief look at one of the most consequential coercion successes of the twentieth century and coercion theory's most iconic case—the Cuban missile crisis—makes plain the relative importance of assurances and threats as coercive tools. In October 1962 blindsided US leaders implemented a coercive strategy aimed at the removal of recently delivered Soviet intermediate-range missiles from the island of Cuba. They eventually succeeded.

Washington's principal threat was to invade Cuba and destroy the missiles directly, risking nuclear escalation and a general war with the Soviet Union. Indeed, the Joint Chiefs of Staff infamously pressured President John F. Kennedy to attack without delay. For years afterward, at the encouragement of US policymakers, the history of the crisis was told as a war of nerve.[17] In the words of Secretary of State Dean Rusk, Kennedy and Soviet premier Nikita Khrushchev were "eyeball to eyeball, and I think the other fellow just blinked."[18]

For twenty-five years Kennedy administration officials refused to acknowledge that the United States had also deployed a second tool—a carrot—when it secretly offered to trade the removal of US Jupiter missiles in Turkey for the Soviet ballistic missiles in Cuba.[19] Robert Kennedy had secured the backroom deal with Soviet ambassador Anatoly Dobrynin at the height of the crisis and insisted on secrecy. Six months later, Washington dutifully withdrew the Jupiters.

A sticks-and-carrots lens is satisfied with these explanations. To this day, it is underappreciated that during the Cuban missile crisis the Kennedy administration employed a third tool—a coercive assurance—in the form of a noninvasion pledge.[20] The assurance not to invade Cuba was not just another carrot—it was a distinct and meaningful tool of coercive bargaining. Indeed, the assurance was more important than the carrot. Behind the curtain of Soviet decision-making during the crisis, Aleksandr Fursenko and Timothy Naftali discovered in Russian archives that "Khrushchev was preparing to ask the Presidium to support him in accepting Kennedy's letter of October 27 [without the missile trade]."[21] The lens of the assurance dilemma affirms a minority view of the Cuban missile crisis held by scholars such as Robert Jervis that "Khrushchev would have withdrawn the missiles in return for the no-invasion pledge; the sweetener of the Jupiters arrangement was not needed."[22] Coercive assurance won the day.[23]

THE PACIFIC WAR

Consider one of the most consequential coercion failures of the twentieth century: the outbreak of the Pacific War in 1941. In the 1930s the Empire of Japan swallowed up neighbors in a bid for autarky and regional hegemony. Washington looked to protect its interests in Southeast Asia, including British garrisons, and prevent Japanese dominance of the Pacific. The key coercive tool at its disposal was squeezing oil exports to Japan, which accounted for about 80 percent of Tokyo's supply. Yet the US oil embargo failed to compel Japan. How could Washington, with its preponderance of power, not only fail to coerce Japan but also convince it to fight so hopeless a war?

Perhaps Tokyo was just irrational. Indeed, no theory of coercion alone can fully explain the causes of the Pacific War begun by a fanatical and militaristic government in Japan. Yet the American coercive failure is far too interesting to dismiss as just a symptom of Tokyo's unpredictability. In the face of coercion, Japanese leaders ended up believing that they were in a "damned if you do, damned if you don't" position. First, as Dale Copeland observes, Washington attempted to keep Japan "uncertain" about its oil policy, "create confusion," and "keep the Japanese guessing."[24] President Franklin Roosevelt wished to impose graduated punishments on Japan in the form of escalating oil sanctions, and while in the summer of 1941 he was "unwilling to draw the noose tight,"[25] he did wish to "slip a noose around Japan's neck, and give it a jerk now and then."[26] He did not seem to appreciate that his target might not want to live with a noose around its neck, unsure of when the next jerk might come.

Second, Roosevelt undermined his coercive assurance when Tokyo displayed a willingness to make concessions to Washington's coercion. After the oil sanctions began, when diplomatic negotiations recommenced between Secretary of State Cordell Hull and the Japanese delegation led by Amb. Kichisaburō Nomura, Japan was more conciliatory. On August 28 Nomura offered significant concessions to the US negotiating position—including adopting language about nonaggression toward its East Asian neighbors similar to that which the Americans had asked for in April talks. On September 3 Roosevelt responded by adding two more conditions—"deal killers, as Roosevelt certainly understood," Copeland writes.[27] The next day, after consulting Tokyo, Nomura offered more concessions in a memo to Hull, worded as the Americans had requested.[28] Again, the United States refused to accept them and ended negotiations.

The reaction in Tokyo was predictable from the perspective of the assurance dilemma. At an imperial conference on September 6, clear-eyed about the overwhelming might of America, Prime Minister Fumimaro Konoe stressed that Japan could not stomach the status quo. A permanent oil embargo would mean "the gradual weakening of our national defense" and "inevitable" imperial decline.[29] Japan resolved now to pursue what diplomatic paths remained while simultaneously preparing for war. By mid-November Washington knew it had Japan on the ropes. A November 13 report assessed that Tokyo could not "withstand the present strain very much longer" and that it "must accept the inevitable or fight."[30] Roosevelt reopened negotiations on November 17 one final time and prepared to accept a prostrate Japan's best offer. Nomura was prepared to comply. But then, on November 26, Roosevelt lost a chance for a deal by making an additional ten demands of Japan.[31]

Far short of acquiescing, Tokyo lashed out. In the minds of Japan's leadership, Roosevelt and Hull had reneged on near bargains in September and November.[32] The United States would never remove its noose from Japan's neck, Tokyo assessed. The coercive oil embargo was not contingent on Japan's behavior. War was its choice. "In the eyes of the Tokyo decision-makers," Scott Sagan writes, "the decision to attack the United States was compared, not to an act of suicide, but rather to a desperate but necessary operation given to a man with a terminal disease . . . a desperate operation offered the only hope of saving his life."[33] Sagan further laments that the "belief that the Japanese must have been irrational to attack the United States [in 1941] continues to plague our understanding of the origins of the Pacific War."[34] Indeed, it plagues our understanding of all coercive international politics. Leaders make these mistakes to this day.

Implications for Theory and Future Scholarship

EXPANDING THE STUDY OF COERCION BEYOND THREATS

This book has encouraged a shift in the study of coercion away from threat credibility. It is more common in scholarship on military coercion to focus on ever more reasons why strong states' threats lack credibility—for example, the casualty-sensitivity of the public,[35] why disproportional nuclear threats are not credible,[36] and how unremarkable and inexpensive military operations, especially signals sent with aircraft, demonstrate little resolve.[37] In the literature on economic coercion as well, the credibility and severity of sanctions was for a long time the only explanation for their success or failure. Sanctions would be more effective against vulnerable democracies[38] and economically dependent allies and partners[39] if multilateral coalitions could staunch leaks in a sanctions regime,[40] if pain could be more targeted against leaders and elites,[41] and when the United States weaponized the interdependence of the global financial system.[42] These approaches overlook coercive assurance.[43] And while this book has focused on compellence, assurance is integral to and must be investigated in cases of deterrence as well.[44]

Coercive assurance is important enough to merit a new paradigm in coercion studies. To properly reckon with the assurance dilemma in the study of international relations, scholars can no longer explain the dependent variable of coercion success and failure without controlling for the credibility of coercive assurance. Appreciating the assurance dilemma makes it less surprising that strong states are poor coercers. But we could go even further. The field of international relations should measure power differently if our measures capture only the capacity to hurt. Strategy matters to the utility of power.

Scholarship on costly signaling could do an even better job of accounting for the assurance dilemma. A vast literature proposes that leaders use words and deeds to signal foreign policy interests and communicate resolve. More work must apply these strategies of commitment to pledges *not* to carry out threats and investigate how signals of resolve affect coercive assurance. We ought to know when sunk cost signals, such as positioning an aircraft carrier off a coastline, communicate more of an intent to use it than to not or when burning the bridge behind you to tie your hands impacts on the credibility of your assurances in addition to your threats. This book illuminates the downsides of resolve concepts, such as saber rattling, the madman theory, and two-level games.

Scholarship on how leaders suffer "audience costs" for backing down should also not revolve around their impact on threats. Existing debates focus on questions asked through a threat credibility lens: Do domestic audiences really punish leaders for backing down?[45] Do targets perceive that they do?[46] Are democracies therefore better coercers?[47] Or do autocracies have their own audience costs?[48] Instead, evidence of a democratic coercion deficit should prompt us to examine how regular elections, multiple domestic power centers, or norms of transparent diplomacy impede the communication of credible coercive assurance. Perhaps even a proportion of the intended audience invoked by audience costs theory may prefer punishment not contingent upon a target's actions.

The study of reputation is also chiefly concerned with threats—bluffing,[49] empty threats,[50] and resolve in the eyes of allies or adversaries.[51] An emergent consensus in the study of coercive assurance is that a reputation for reneging on past bargains can hinder one's assurances in future coercive diplomacy. This book has shown that targets of coercion consider their coercers' reputations for reneging on coercive assurances but that other tools of assurance can overcome them. For instance, Iran was willing to strike a nonproliferation bargain with the United States after the public demise of Libya's Qaddafi. Nonetheless, I have not fully investigated when coercers can develop positive reputations for upholding past coercive assurances. Nor have I delved into the debate about whether conceding states acquire reputations for backing down and therefore become more likely targets for future predation or when these reputational incentives alter strategies.[52]

The assurance dilemma lens should also prompt a deeper appreciation that the concept of "credibility" is fundamentally a probabilistic risk calculation. Actors themselves can be neither credible nor incredible. Any coercive interaction is liable to include myriad causes of threat or assurance credibility or incredibility. In choosing whether to concede, targets of coercion are calculating the probability that they will be punished anyway. When we ask whether a threat or assurance "is credible or not," we really mean "How credible is it?" and "What risk are you willing to take that they are lying?" It is the net effect of signaling that matters in the end and the relationship between threat credibility, severity, and the confidence in the assurance that a target requires.

Further research should also consider individual-level variation in the appreciation of coercive assurance as a component of successful coercion. The cases in this book suggest that coercers either tend not to recognize the assurance dilemma or else grow to understand it as their coercive strategies struggle to achieve results. But some leaders never seem to appreciate the importance of coercive assurance. Why do coercive intuitions differ, where do they come from, and how do they change?

Future scholarship might also further consider the principal-agent problems of coercive assurance. For instance, military coercers have lost control over the ability to withhold punishment through organizational failure, miscommunications, or delays. This can have disastrous consequences in the extreme, as in 1940 when the city of Rotterdam was bombed despite surrendering. Surrounding the city, the local German commander threatened to raze it by aerial bombardment, and he ordered preparation for such a raid to make his threat more credible. During multiple rounds of communication with the surrendering city, however, his order to stay the execution arrived late to the air base. Just as he acquired the city's surrender, German bombers appeared in the sky and unloaded sixty tons of ordnance anyway.[53]

PROBING VARIATION IN THE ASSURANCE DILEMMA

This book has focused on identifying the assurance dilemma and its rational mechanisms—insincerity and multiple demands—as well as non-rational mechanisms—losing control. Nevertheless, each could be affected by broader geopolitical or domestic factors, suggesting a larger research agenda on variations in the acuteness of the assurance dilemma. When it is acute, the trade-offs between threat and assurance credibility will be more stark; when it is mild, they will trade off less.

Consider the following possibilities. First, asymmetrically powerful coercers have more trouble convincing targets that they will not wield their power. Yet the polarity of the international system could impact these perceptions if one pole checks another pole's capacity for predation. The assurance dilemma may be more acute under unipolarity.

Second, regime type is another clear factor as democratic politics and especially large swings in partisan preferences can exacerbate fears of spoilers. Democracies may also be more likely to conduct multilateral coercive diplomacy. And in a more populist world, such coalitions may be more fractious, if they are formed at all. Leaders of democracies may face more acute assurance dilemmas.

Third, the concept of trust could matter more than I give it credit for and moderate the acuteness of the assurance dilemma. A trusting relationship between coercer and target may be a boon to coercive assurance. A loving parent has no inherent desire to punish their child for the sake of it.[54] Yet a coercer in a trusting relationship with its target will also struggle to make credible threats, complicating their ability to bargain.

Fourth, the characteristics of particular coercive tools or certain stakes of a bargaining process could provide important context for the evaluation of assurance credibility. If threats can be automatically defanged upon compliance, the assurance dilemma would be mitigated—for instance, if retreat could put one outside the range of harm's way.

An ideally assuring threat is one that loses its teeth upon the target's compliance. Kenneth Oye once invoked the logic of such an interaction in a study of "linkage" in trade negotiations—side payments uncommonly understood as applicable to coercive punishment.[55] Oye drew a distinction between three types of contingent action: exchange, extortion, and explanation.[56] Exchangers (using carrots) and extortionists (using threats) "are seeking to construct a connection between issues," wrote Oye. "Do X and I'll do Y," or "Do X or else I'll do Y," respectively. But explainers point to an "already existing connection between issues": "If you do X, it will be in my interests to do Y," or "If you do X, I'll have no need to do Y." While Oye did not put it in these terms, credible assurance is what makes explanation work. Of course, whether a linker is perceived as exchanging, extorting, or explaining depends on the target's perceptions of the linker's interests.[57] Most of the examples in this book concern what Oye calls extortion (threats to carry out punishments). Even so, highly assuring contexts have in some coercive interactions made threateners appear as explainers.

Some punishments once imposed by a coercer can still be avoided by the actions of the target. As part of a strategy in 1890 of squeezing the Hawaiian Islands into submitting to annexation, the McKinley Tariff imposed duties on the importation of Hawaiian sugar. The policy quickly caused a local depression. As a result, Alfred Castle explains, "many businessmen and planters formerly opposed to annexation to the United States now believed that annexation, which would give planters access to the domestic subsidy, was the only solution to permanent instability."[58] Concession, which would no longer classify Hawaii as a foreign market, would eliminate the punishment automatically.

Similarly, some concessions themselves defang threats. In 2016 Turkey successfully extorted the European Union into providing billions of euros in aid to handle the Syrian refugee crisis. To do so, Turkish president Recep Tayyip Erdoğan threatened to send migrants into Europe.[59] "We can open the doors to Greece and Bulgaria anytime and we can put the refugees on buses," Erdoğan told Jean-Claude Juncker of the European Commission and Donald Tusk of the European Council.[60] In this context, conceding to Erdoğan's demand to house, feed, and secure Syrian refugees in facilities on Turkish soil would drain the threat of its potency. Compliance would in fact help to ensure that Ankara did not put the refugees on buses. The frequency of such coercive contexts with more mild assurance dilemmas is a question for future research.

The cases in this book varied in terms of the acuteness of the assurance dilemma. All targets were bargaining over pursuit of a security asset and faced asymmetrically powerful coercers, who were mostly democracies. In all cases, coercion at some point confronted spoilers and multiple demands. These factors suggest that the assurance dilemma was acute. Yet South Africa faced economic coercion only, and while it was not an ally of the United States, they shared an adversary in the Soviet Union. The assurance dilemma may have been milder in this case. Iraq, Libya, and Iran faced both economic and military coercion, including from their chief adversaries, whom they had little basis to trust. These cases likely contained more acute assurance dilemmas. Moreover, the information environment varied.

In the cases of South Africa and Iraq, coercers had poor intelligence about the state of the targets' nuclear programs. In the cases of Libya and Iran, coercers collected better intelligence upon which to base policy decisions.

This book has parsimoniously considered together both economic and military coercion. Scholars would do well to further consider the assurance dynamics of each tool. Both sanctions and force may be employed in a graduated fashion to compel a target to concede once the pain becomes unbearable. Yet, in terms of coercive assurance, imposed sanctions are "on" at the time of negotiation, so coercers must commit to take action and lift them. Force is often "off" during negotiation, so coercers must commit not to take action after a bargain. (Although the two get closer together once a state mobilizes military force, delegates authority for its use, or engages in limited force as a threat of more to come.) Moreover, in terms of their severity, comprehensive sanctions can be imposed during a coercive effort, while comprehensive force is not used unless coercion fails and the coercer opts to impose its will by brute force. Relieving sanctions should be more difficult to credibly communicate.[61]

Implications for Policy

When coercion fails, states can turn to even more violent means to resolve disputes. It is therefore important that scholars identify levers that policymakers might pull to bolster coercive assurance. By exploring the reasons why targets perceive inevitable pain, this book offered some productive policy lessons. Much existing theory on coercion assumes that targets will understand the incentive structures of their coercers, or at most it prescribes that leaders should explain their own incentives to targets—for example, their own interests, resolve, alliance politics, domestic constraints, and liberal values. The thinking is that if they understand us, they will know we are serious. This book instead advises coercers to understand their targets—their incentives, their fears, their perceptions. Indeed, the enterprise in which the coercer is engaged is explicitly one of manipulating those incentives and fears. Coercers need some empathy—coercive empathy but empathy all the same.

Before leaders make threats, they should be honest with themselves about their sincerity. When brute force is the more appropriate policy, it should not come in trappings of coercion. In the aftermath of 9/11, for example, the Bush administration issued an ultimatum to the Taliban government of Afghanistan to hand over Osama bin Laden and other al-Qaeda terrorists or "share in their fate."[62] Bush later explained that "exposing their [Taliban] defiance to the world would firm up our justification for a military strike."[63] The target was never going to avoid retribution. President Obama made a similar error in 2014 attempting to coerce the Islamic State of Iraq and the Levant (ISIL). Following a deadly terrorist attack in Paris, the president threatened, "We're sending a message," Obama declared. "If you target Americans, you will have no safe haven."[64] Yet the US military was already engaged in a military campaign to degrade and destroy the ISIL organization. Indeed, just moments earlier in his statement, the president himself had articulated how "Special Operations Forces are hard at work" and "hitting ISIL harder than ever in Syria and Iraq . . . taking out their leaders."[65] The threat was already being carried out.

Coercive assurances, explicit and implicit, have also been publicly violated by coercers. When Russia annexed Crimea in 2014 and invaded the rest of Ukraine in 2022, observers decried the violation of coercive assurance offered to Kyiv while compelling the removal of former Soviet nuclear weapons at the end of the Cold War.[66] In toppling the Qaddafi regime in 2011, the United States and Britain similarly reneged on a coercive assurance made to Libya in 2003 bargaining over its weapons programs.[67] And in 2018 the Trump administration reimposed economic sanctions waived under the terms of the 2015 Iran nuclear deal.

All of these choices are puzzling from the perspective of rational coercion theory. Even the most hawkish coercers should desire a reputation for making credible assurances. The ability to assure is power, just as the ability to threaten is power. A state that cannot assure is a weaker state, no matter how much it can threaten. When states elect to coerce, they should do so sincerely by being willing to let the target choose to avoid punishment. Insincere coercion should be avoided.

Leaders should also be careful not to become so committed to their threats that they do not take yes for an answer if it finally comes. Sometimes we see last-minute concessions on the brink of war, a sign of targets taking concession gambles. Yet we also see a failure to accept concessions at the last minute. Windows for bargaining can open at the precipice—as with Iraq in 2002 and Iran in 2003—if only the momentum of punishment does not carry you over the cliff.

DIVERSIFY THE COERCION TOOL KIT

Policymakers need to similarly look beyond threats alone to improve their prospects of coercive success. To policymakers steeped in the logic of threat credibility, it is usually too soon to deem coercion a failure. Concessions are always just around the corner. More pressure is the best path forward. And when coercion fails, these leaders lament: If only our threats had been more credible, if only we had squeezed the adversary a little harder, for a little longer, surely then they would have given in when we had them on the ropes. But this myopic lens ignores the sources of leverage and the prospects of success if leaders attempt to bolster the conditionality of their threats.

There is a limit to the utility of credible threats. As a mobilized Pentagon awaited final orders to begin bombing, the final ultimatums to Iraq in 2003 and Libya in 2011 were fruitless. Targets stood fast, resigned to inevitable war. In 2003, days before the US invasion, with troops deployed to the region, Iraqi elites concluded grimly to IAEA visitors that "this war is going to happen, and nothing you or we can do will stop it."[68] Echoes of that sense of inevitability pervaded William Burns's phone call with his old Libyan negotiating partner, Musa Kusa, in 2011, in which he attempted to dissuade the Qaddafi regime from violent repression. Burns warned Kusa that "this would not end well," to which Kusa "sighed heavily" and replied, "I know."[69]

Targets of coercion must believe that it is their own behavior that will determine their fate. Yet too often policymakers' instincts in the face of defiance tell them just to threaten more. In an attempt to bolster the credibility and severity of their threats, coercers can place their targets in a "damned if you do, damned if you don't" position. Targets are loath to live at the whim of another's punishment. Roosevelt's oil sanctions wished to "slip a noose around Japan's neck" but provoked the opposite of acquiescence.[70] Iran hawks have also called coercive economic measures a "sanctions noose."[71] Protestors in Hong Kong braved Chinese authoritarians because they saw themselves "like a frog in a beaker of water that is being boiled. . . . If we die, well, we were going to die anyway."[72] And we should expect comparably desperate reactions to omnipresent prospects of punishment, such as how drone warfare aims to put its targets in a "constant state of ambush."[73] Without assurance, threats are less effective and can provoke targets to lash out. What would you do with a knife to your neck?

COERCIVE PROSPECTS FOR NORTH KOREA

The contemporary case of coercion most similar to the cases covered in this book is that of coercive bargaining over North Korea's nuclear weapons program. As of this writing, North Korea has conducted six nuclear tests, including one with a thermonuclear device in September 2017. It has also tested ballistic missiles with intercontinental range. Its Hwasong-14 and Hwasong-15 missile tests demonstrated the ability to reach the continental United States. The Trump administration called its strategy to confront North Korea "maximum pressure"—a mixture of economic sanctions, diplomatic isolation, and threats of military force. It was a strategy driven by the logic of the threat credibility. Matched with summit diplomacy, the goal was North Korean "denuclearization." And North Korean leader Kim Jong-un met with South Korean president Moon Jae-in at five inter-Korean summits and President Trump at two US–North Korean summits (Singapore in June 2018 and Hanoi in February 2019) without progress.[74] While it did far less to act on it, the Biden administration did not change US policy to denuclearize North Korea.

The lens of the assurance dilemma yields pessimistic conclusions for coercion on the peninsula.[75] Washington's demands are entangled. Pyongyang wonders whether nuclear sanctions will not just be relabeled missile, chemical weapons, biological weapons, or human rights sanctions after any bargain. When nonnuclear issues have come to the fore, North Korea has bristled. For example, when the UN Human Rights Committee passed a resolution in November 2018 condemning North Korea's gross violations of human rights, Pyongyang accused the United States of weaponizing the issue to "justify their racket for sanctions and pressure."[76] A Foreign Ministry statement said that it would be the "greatest miscalculation" if Washington believed it could compel nuclear concessions from Pyongyang by ratcheting up the "human rights racket to an unprecedented level." Rather, the Foreign Ministry warned, such a strategy "will block the path to denuclearization on the Korean Peninsula forever."[77]

Many spoilers also lurk with independent capacity to punish North Korea economically. Domestically, any US president faces meager odds of getting Congress to provide sanctions relief to the North under any foreseeable circumstances. In September 2018 Foreign Minister Ri Yong-ho blamed "U.S. domestic politics" for pessimism about the implementation of the US–North Korean joint statement at the Singapore summit the previous June.[78] As in the past, any sanctions relief or economic carrots that are part of a coercive bargain with North Korea would have to come from countries in the region, such as South Korea, Japan, China, or Russia.[79]

Another domestic reason to question the Trump administration's signals of coercive control was the conspicuous division of the White House against itself.[80] Reacting in 2017 to a contradiction between the President Trump's hawkish tweets, one of which described the United States as "locked and loaded," and a softer op-ed coauthored by two US cabinet officials that expressed "no interest in regime change or accelerated reunification of Korea,"[81] a North Korean official described the United States as "a divided country." He "could not understand how the two Cabinet members could so clearly contradict the President."[82]

Perhaps no example was more emblematic of the confused signaling of a divided White House than National Security Adviser John Bolton's invocation of the "Libya model" in May 2018 in his first television interview since assuming his post. North Korean state media responded with a statement describing how the United States had "coaxed" Libya to "disarm itself and then swallowed it up by force."[83] North Korea's vice foreign minister, Choe Son-hui, further emphasized the point: "In order not to follow in Libya's footstep, we paid a heavy price to build up our powerful and reliable strength that can defend ourselves."[84] And, for an internal audience, a May 2018 editorial in *Rodong Sinmun*, the official newspaper of the Workers' Party of Korea, commented on a US reputation for duplicity: "Yielding to imperialists and choosing to make compromises with them is essentially a death sentence. . . . Libya continued down the path to make concessions to the U.S., not knowing that it would have to strip all the way down to its underwear. These concessions led to misery."[85]

The North is a state whose gross domestic product is a fraction of the annual US defense budget. Pyongyang knows and fears US power. Yet it defies Washington's coercive demands over its nuclear program. US threats are not complemented by coercive assurance. These serious impediments to successful coercion suggest that the United States should abandon denuclearization as a realistic goal anytime soon and adopt new strategic aims, such as arms control and risk-reduction initiatives to keep the North Korean nuclear arsenal in check and posturing US and South Korean military forces for stable deterrence instead of compellence. But if compellence remains the US strategy of choice, policymakers in Washington should recognize that their threats of sanctions and military force are not yet perceived in Pyongyang as contingent upon North Korean behavior. Assurance credibility, not threat credibility, ought to be the focus of further efforts.

IMPROVING US SANCTIONS

Foreign policy scholars and practitioners are now awaking to the absurdity of imposing coercive economic sanctions without being able to lift them.[86] Yet sanctions, especially American financial sanctions, continue to be a primary tool of statecraft.[87] The Threat and Imposition of Sanctions dataset records that the United States imposed 191 sanctions on 74 countries from 1946 to 1990; in the far fewer years since the end of the Cold War, it has imposed 252 sanctions on 101 states.[88] That trend masks even larger growth in the number of entities sanctioned by the Treasury Department's Office of Foreign Assets Control (OFAC), which has ballooned by 933 percent since 2000.[89] And the imposition of sanctions has far outpaced their reprieve. From 2009 to 2019 OFAC designated twice as many "individuals, entities, vessels, and aircrafts" than it delisted—twice as much punishment as relief.[90] The Trump administration's annual delisting rate was one quarter of the Obama administration's average delisting rate.

This book suggests a few ideas for how to signal a capability and willingness to relieve economic pain in exchange for concessions. First, the Treasury Department could separate the mission of sanctions imposition and enforcement from the mission of sanctions relief. A separate office tasked with sanctions relief—ensuring sanctions are tied to specific and separable demands, explaining the scope of relief to private actors, and monitoring whether economic engagement has indeed recommenced—would be beneficial to the coercive prospects of economic sanctions. It might be called the "Office of Coercive Leverage" and should be well staffed.

Second, the larger and more complex a sanctions regime, the harder it will be to unravel and thus the harder to assure the target that it will be unraveled.[91] Treasury may be learning this lesson today by seeking to avoid omnibus sanctions packages and being more specific in the designation of sanctioned entities.[92] But the logrolling mechanics of congressional agreement will push in the direction of less credible coercive assurance. Congressional leaders should be wary of undermining US foreign policy strategies as they seek to impose severe punishments on adversaries.

Third, sanctions could be imposed with time limits, so-called sunsets. Sanctions relief is too readily framed as a "reward" in public discourse. Automatic termination might avoid the politically unpalatable option of appearing to reward a sanctions target, typically an adversary. Sunsets would be the practical equivalent of the congressional pocket approval of sanctions waivers that the INARA legislation secured in 2015. The UNSC has indeed imposed sanctions with sunset provisions in the past.[93]

Fourth, Congress should recognize the value of keeping presidential waiver provisions in legislative sanctions. While in 2015 INARA removed Congress as a domestic spoiler to sanctions relief and established a policy precedent for sanctions waivers by executive order, congressional action to impose sanctions on Russia for 2016 election interference (part of CAATSA) overturned that precedent. For domestic political reasons, those sanctions tried to limit the White House's ability to lift them. To waive sanctions pertaining to Russian cyberattacks, for instance, the president would have had to "provide evidence that Russia had tried to reduce such intrusions . . . and Congress would have at least 30 days to vote on any changes he sought."[94] And waiving CAATSA sanctions required a two-thirds vote in Congress—a high bar. Even some European allies opposed these legislative sanctions, in part because they were harder to lift.[95] After Russia's invasion of Ukraine in 2022, the United States and its European allies concentrated on leveling unprecedented sanctions on Russia, including on its central bank and oil exports, to punish Vladmir Putin. Under what conditions these sanctions could ever be lifted was left for later discussion. If these coercive measures were to result in leverage over Putin's behavior, some signal that they could be lifted in exchange for a Russian withdrawal would need to be credible. The assurance dilemma is pernicious in the case of Russia.[96]

There have already been calls to reform the institutions that implement US economic coercion,[97] and the Treasury Department considered some of them in a review of sanctions policy.[98] In this regard, the field of international political economy is ahead of the security field in its appreciation of the assurance dilemma.

DETERRING A WAR OVER TAIWAN

Perhaps the most catastrophic foreign policy pitfall on the horizon for the United States would be to blunder into a war with the People's Republic of China. That there is a clear tinderbox for such a conflict—Taiwan—rightly gives many pause. The status of Taiwan has been intentionally ambiguous since 1972, when the United States recognized China diplomatically and gained a major partner to balance against the Soviet Union. As part of that bargain, the "one China policy" allowed Beijing, Taipei, and Washington to disagree over the standing of Taiwan and yet accept the status quo. The 1972 Shanghai Communiqué reads: "The United States acknowledges that all Chinese on either side of the Taiwan Strait maintain there is but one China and that Taiwan is a part of China. The United States Government does not challenge that position."[99] And this remains the status quo.

The fear is that a rising China will finally be strong enough relative to the United States, at least in the Western Pacific, to change the status quo over Taiwan, either by coercion or brute force. As it has increased its military capacity, Beijing has flexed its muscle in the region, from the construction of artificial islands in the South China Sea to carrying out military exercises in the air and waters around Taiwan. Its preparations for military contingencies are clear. Yet a war over this democratic island of twenty-four million people is by no means inevitable. China should be dissuaded from ever attempting to conquer it.

A war over Taiwan can be deterred. But it will take more than credible threats to deter it. In addition to arming the Taiwanese with advanced weapons and signaling its willingness to Beijing to fight for Taiwan, Washington must communicate its acceptance of the status quo. Washington should make it abundantly clear that it will not accept changes to the status quo from any party—not from Beijing or from Taipei or in its own policy. US leaders should not refer to Taiwan as a country, as independent, or a formal ally.[100] US lawmakers need not visit as part of partisan outbidding to show resolve. Washington should prevent Beijing from ever concluding that it seeks a formal alliance or diplomatic relationship with Taiwan. Attempting otherwise could be perceived as a fait accompli to change the status quo across the Taiwan Strait.

Beijing and Taipei should be sending similar signals that they are willing to accept the status quo provided no one else changes it. China's aggressive behavior in the Taiwan Strait—intercepting surveillance aircraft, flying beyond the median line, encircling the island with drones, or conducting exercises farther and farther around Taiwan[101]—has not effectively communicated status quo ambitions and have not been stabilizing for deterrence. Rather it communicates the need to be deterred.

That deterrence must come in the form of both credible threats to defend Taiwan, or at least deny China a military victory at acceptable cost, and coercive assurances that complement those threats. Leaders must not equate assurance over Taiwan as a carrot for or appeasement of Beijing. It is just the opposite: a logic of conditional pain—pain that China could avoid.

It would be a mistake, however, to think that Beijing will understand implicitly that governments in Washington or Taipei have no designs to hurt China. Multiple demands of China—for instance, to cease unfair trade practices, cyber espionage, or human rights abuses—could become entangled with red lines in the Taiwan Strait or the South China Sea. There are spoilers within Taiwan and the United States who seek to out-hawk each other on China policy. Some might even argue in favor of preemptively altering the status quo over Taiwan before China does so. This book advises caution and careful attention to how coercive assurance can be undermined.

Assuring signals need not come at the expense of improving the credibility of US or Taiwanese threats. As the scholars Bonnie Glaser, Jessica Chen Weiss, and Thomas Christensen appreciated, "it is precisely because the United States should bolster and diversify its military presence in the region and help strengthen Taiwan's defenses that it must also provide clearer and more persistently conveyed assurances."[102] This is the assurance dilemma at work. As the United States aims to augment the credibility of its threats, it risks undermining its corresponding assurances and must focus as much on shoring them up as it does the defense of Taiwan's beaches. A war over Taiwan is avoidable but not with credible threats alone.

I began this book with the puzzle of high-leverage coercion. Washington often fails to coerce despite power asymmetry. Confrontations with Panama, Serbia, Afghanistan, and Iraq all ended in conflict despite attempts at coercion by the United States. But it is not just a US problem. Many powerful actors are frustrated in their coercive aims. Even highly credible threats can fail because they are perceived as insufficiently conditional. If targets expect punishments to be applied anyway, defiance runs little or no additional risk, and compliance is fruitless. Yet, given the duplicity of statesmen and the uncertainty of the international system, it is a wonder that states can ever communicate credible coercive assurance. Through such a lens, the puzzle of this book is not why the strong have trouble coercing the weak but why the strong can ever coerce the weak. The United States predates at will, an argument goes, so why should any weaker state ever be so naive as to strike a coercive bargain?

From either perspective, the message of this book is the same. Coercive assurance is a necessary component of coercion. But coercers face an assurance dilemma: efforts to bolster the credibility of threats can undermine the credibility of assurance. In any coercive interaction there are factors that pull toward credible assurance and factors that push against it. Targets make a choice based on this information they glean from their coercers, and they wish to know that their coercers will remain in control of the application of punishment. Will I be punished anyway? What is the likelihood? How much am I willing to risk? Smart coercers do not ignore these questions. They answer them.

Notes

Introduction

1. Blechman and Kaplan 1978, 92.
2. George and Simons 1994, 270.
3. Art 2003, 376–78, 385–87.
4. Downes (2018) finds on average across major studies a 35 percent coercion success rate.
5. "Stronger" measured by higher military expenditures (Sechser 2011, 389).
6. I borrow the phrase "logic of contingent action" from Oye 1992, 43–45. I use the words "conditional" and "contingent" interchangeably.
7. William Shakespeare, *King Lear*, act 1, scene 4.
8. See also Pauly 2024.
9. As Colgan observes, to "describe international order as 'Pareto optimal' impl[ies] that it relies purely on voluntary consent." Instead, much compliance is coerced (Colgan 2021, ch. 1; see also Miller 2014; Farrell and Newman 2023).
10. Office of the Secretary of Defense, National Security Strategies, https://history.defense.gov/Historical-Sources/National-Security-Strategy/. Figure 0.1 only includes years when a new National Security Strategy was published.
11. US National Security Strategies also contain over nine times more reassurances to allies than coercive assurances. Similarly, in a collection of explicit US presidential statements about the Soviet Union from 1950 to 1989, Kydd and McManus (2017) found nearly twenty times more threats than assurances.
12. Biddle 2020.
13. Trachtenberg 1999, 181. I thank Tim McDonnell for this example.
14. *Comprehensive Report of the Special Advisor to the DCI on Iraq's WMD* (Duelfer Report), vol. 1 (Washington, DC: Central Intelligence Agency, 2004), 61, https://www.govinfo.gov/app/details/GPO-DUELFERREPORT.

1. The Assurance Dilemma

1. This is how Thomas Schelling (1966, 4) uses the term "assurance" in *Arms and Influence*. The concept was also included but not explicitly called "assurance" in Schelling 1960, 6–7 (see also Schelling 1989, 113–18). For more conceptual brush-clearing, see Knopf 2012b.

2. In his personal notes, Schelling called it an "assurance promise," which communicates that "I won't double cross you" (handwritten loose-leaf notes in "Altruism, Meanness, and Other Strategic Behaviors, 1976–1978, 1994," folder 1, box 13, Thomas C. Schelling Collection, Hauser RAND Archives, Santa Monica, CA).

3. Non-ally reassurances are studied in scholarship on how states can mitigate the security dilemma (Lebow and Stein 1987; Lebow 2001; Stein 1991), yet scoping out coercion explicitly, Stein (1991, 31) defines reassurance as "a set of strategies that adversaries can use to reduce the likelihood of resort to the threat or use of force." Lebow and Stein's theorizing echoes Charles Osgood's (1962) proposed system of Graduated Reciprocation in Tension-reduction (GRIT) to defuse the Cold War.

4. I consider the context of coercion only, not the related conduct or termination of war (see Weisiger 2013; Fortna 2004; Mastro 2019). Several scholars extend the bargaining theory of war onset to wartime itself, especially to understand war termination (Wagner 2000; Powell 2004; Goemens 2000).

5. Coercion may consist of only threats, but Alexander George coined the term "coercive diplomacy" to expand the concept to include threats and inducements (sticks and carrots) (George and Simons 1994, 7–8).

6. This is generally accepted in the literature on coercion theory. "Assurance, or what some call 'reassurance,' is not to be confused with inducements [i.e. carrots]. . . . If assurances are akin to contracts, inducements are akin to side payments" (Art and Greenhill 2018, 23).

7. Jervis 2013; Davis 2000.

8. See, e.g., Solingen 2012; Miller 2018.

9. Haass and O'Sullivan 2000; Dorussen 2001; Knopf 2012a; Petrovics 2019. If a "carrot" works through the mechanism of assurance, it does so by signaling that the offerer is not bent on harm.

10. See Kydd and McManus 2017; Davis 2000.

11. Sonni Efron, "Looking Past Baghdad to the Next Challenge," *Los Angeles Times*, April 6, 2003, http://articles.latimes.com/2003/apr/06/news/war-whatnext6.

12. Paraphrased from Schelling 1966, 74.

13. Deterrence aims to maintain the status quo, while compellence seeks to change it. Following Schelling (1966), I use the term "coercion" to encompass to both deterrence and compellence.

14. Deterrence by punishment aims to dissuade its target from action through the fear of retaliation, while deterrence by denial aims to dissuade the target from action by denying it the ability to achieve its objectives (Snyder 1961, 14–16).

15. Sechser (2011) codes "partial concessions" as an outcome of coercion.

16. On costly signaling, see Fearon 1994, 1997 (see also Spence 1973). The faith that intent and credibility can be "signaled" and shape international politics beyond the dictates of relative power stems back to Schelling 1960 and 1966 and Jervis 1970.

17. Fearon 1994, 1997; Schultz 2001; Ramsay 2004.

18. Fearon 1994; Weeks 2008.

19. Sartori 2005. Rationalist theory on the causes of war also assumes that states acquire reputations for reneging on commitments (Powell 2006, 1999; see also Lupton 2020).

20. Slantchev 2005. Saber-rattling and swaggering (e.g., parading military equipment at public rallies) are related concepts. See also arguments about how the United States is a poor coercer because it sends cheap signals (Chamberlain 2016).

21. Schelling 1966.

22. Most famously, Schelling uses the story of Xenophon. In retreat and pursued by the Persians, his army runs into an impassable ravine. As his generals begin to panic, Xenophon turns and confidently recognizes that the tables have turned, saying, "I should like the enemy to think it easy going in every direction for him to retreat; but . . . that there is no safety for us except in victory" (Schelling 2006, 1). Hernán Cortés also burned his ships upon landing at Veracruz in 1519.

23. Sechser 2018, 2010 (see also Fearon 1995; Powell 2006; Posen 1996). Power transition theory is also premised on a fundamental commitment problem between rising and declining powers (Gilpin 1981; Copeland 2000).

24. Carnegie 2015, 1.

25. Sechser 2010.

26. Haun 2015; Drezner 2022. A coercer's relative power advantage may also produce excessive demands (Sechser 2018). On regime type preferences in interstate bargaining, see also Fearon 2011.

27. A related problem is issue indivisibility, if asking for a part of a stake is akin to asking for its whole (Fearon 1995).

28. Sagan 1988.

29. Schelling 1966, 2–4. See also chapter 2 of Schelling 1960 (especially pages 43–46), based on Schelling 1956. Schelling (1966, 74–75) asserts that assurances, like threats, may be made more credible by putting reputations on the line. Schelling also developed ideas on the reassurance value of communications between the superpowers in crisis—e.g., via the Washington-Moscow hotline (Schelling 1984).

30. Fearon 1995 (see, e.g., Bas and Coe 2018, 608).

31. Walter 1997.

32. Sechser 2010. On helping adversaries save face and avoid reputation costs, see Nutt and Pauly 2021; Pauly 2021.

33. See Art and Greenhill 2018, 24; Sechser 2018. Noncredible assurance has been blamed for the inefficacy of the "madman strategy," terrorist violence, and deterrence of chemical weapons use (McManus 2021; Pauly and McDermott 2023; Abrahms 2013; Bowen, Knopf, and Moran 2020; see also Miller 2022).

34. Schelling 1966, 36.

35. Note that as a signal of commitment, reassuring allies is theoretically akin to threatening adversaries; both are commitments to do something (carry out a threat or provide security assistance). Committing to do something that you would rather not do is harder than to commit to not doing something that you would rather not do. Thus, allies are very difficult to reassure. As the UK defense minister Denis Healey quipped during the Cold War, "it takes only five percent credibility of American retaliation to deter the Russians, but ninety-five percent credibility to reassure the Europeans" (Healey 1989, 243). Both "credibilities" refer to the believability of US threats in the eyes of different audiences. (On ally reassurance credibility, see Fearon 1997; Fuhrmann and Sechser 2014.) To this day, in policy debates too, ally reassurance is commonly the only understood meaning of the terms "assurance" or "reassurance" (see, e.g., Department of Defense, "Nuclear Posture Review," February 2018, https://media. defense.gov/2018/Feb/02/2001872886/-1/-1/1/2018-NUCLEAR-POSTURE-REVIEW-FINAL-REPORT.PDF; Howard 1982; Mara Karlin 2017; "You Get Deterrence, and You Get Deterrence, Everybody Gets Deterrence!," War on the Rocks, May 5, 2017, https://waron-therocks.com/2017/05/you-get-deterrence-and-you-get-deterrence-everybody-gets-deterrence/).

36. Deterrence theory first began deductively, as scholars theorized how to raise the prospect of costs in the minds of a rational adversary and how deterrers could credibly commit to punish aggression (Brodie 1959; Kahn 1960; Kaufmann 1954; Schelling 1960, 1966; Snyder 1961; Wohlstetter 1959). A second wave of deterrence theory emerged inductively, as scholars tested the rationalist theories of deterrence against historical empirics (Russett 1963; George and Smoke 1974; Mearsheimer 1983; Huth and Russett 1984, 1988). This new deterrence school critiqued the validity of rigid deterrence models in the real world of imperfect decision-making and psychological biases (Lebow and Stein 1990, 1989). Empirical deterrence scholars then confronted the specter of selection effects (Morrow 1989; Fearon 2002).

37. Schelling 1966, 70.

38. I consider threats to stop an ongoing action to be compellent. On the challenges of compellence, see Schelling 1966, 75.

39. Sechser 2018, 2010.

40. Cebul, Dafoe, and Monteiro 2021.

41. Davis 2000.

42. Kydd and McManus 2017.

43. Volpe 2017, 2023. For an application of the concept of coercive assurance to the study of civil conflict, see Lessing 2018.

44. The assurance dilemma is unsatisfied by prescriptions that there is always a "Goldilocks principle" for bargaining, whereby coercers can back off of their threats in order to be more assuring. The challenge for coercers is to address targets' fears of unconditional punishment without undermining the credibility or severity of their threats. Works that assume a linear threat-assurance trade-off include Cebul, Dafoe, and Monteiro 2021; Kydd and McManus 2017; Sechser 2010, 627; Volpe 2017; Nephew 2018b, 124; Bowen, Knopf, and Moran 2021, 321.

45. The security dilemma is a structural tragedy exacerbated by the psychological biases that cause leaders to see others as aggressive. Wasteful arms races or distasteful alliances of convenience can be the result (Jervis 1968, 1976, 1978; Waltz 1979). Scholars have previously leveraged its logic to explain state behavior in new empirical domains. For instance, Barry R. Posen (1991, 12–13) was the first to apply security dilemma logic to the realm of limited war.

46. At first glance, the assurance dilemma in coercion smacks of spiral properties—unintended consequences of threats. But the threat credibility and the assurance dilemma lenses do not map neatly onto the deterrence and spiral models. The spiral model prescribes conciliation or accommodation, not contingent punishments; in fact, it advises against threats. If the deterrence model prescribes sticks and the spiral model prescribes carrots, assurance is missing (see Jervis 1976). Jervis was interested primarily in explaining the downside of appearing too threatening, not the contingency of one's actual threats. Jervis did offer hypotheses on when threats are apt to work, including some that invoke the assurance dilemma, such as when "the actor making the threat refrains from . . . inflicting gratuitous punishment." Nevertheless, Jervis wrote that "to discuss these hypotheses in detail would take us away from the theme of this book" (Jervis 1976, 100–101).

47. See Glaser 2010.

48. See also Butt 2019, which argues that the hegemonic United States invaded Iraq in 2003 to demonstrate its strength to others and reinforce general deterrence.

49. "Minutes of National Security Council Meeting," Washington, May 14, 1975, 3:52 p.m.–5:42 p.m., box 1, folder "NSC Meeting, 5/14/1975," p. 21, National Security Adviser's NSC Meeting File, Gerald R. Ford Presidential Library, https://www.fordlibrarymuseum.gov/library/document/0312/1552389.pdf.

50. "In personal life," wrote Schelling, "I have sometimes relied, like King Lear, on the vague threat that my wrath will be aroused (with who knows what awful consequences) if good behavior is not forthcoming, making a tentative impression on one child, only to have the threat utterly nullified by another's pointing out that 'Daddy's mad already'" (Schelling 1966, 74n18).

51. Classic literature on cooperation also shows the benefits of breaking up issues into smaller pieces to guard against duplicity by the prospect of mutual reneging (Jervis 1978, 181; Keohane 2005; Axelrod 1984).

52. Tsebelis (2002) points to a parallel phenomenon in institutions whereby increasing the number of veto players reduces agreements.

53. In reality these are ranges, but I visualize them as bargaining positions.

54. Peter Baker and Andrew Higgins, "White House Signals Acceptance of Russia Sanctions Bill," New York Times, June 23, 2017, https://www.nytimes.com/2017/07/23/us/politics/trump-russia-sanctions.html.

55. On domestic cohesion and international cooperation, see Milner 1997 (see also Jervis 1970, 14).

56. Putnam 1988.

57. Byman and Waxman 2002, 130–51.

58. Schultz 1998.

59. See also Milner 1997; Schultz 2017; Myrick 2021.

60. See also Thompson 2009.

61. Byman and Waxman 2002, 152–74; Martin 1992.

62. This builds on Christensen 2011, 260.

63. Cooper 1826.

64. Steele 1990, 82, 113. This example is revealing as to how fragmented coalitions can lose control. To impede coercion, such fragmentation must be observable to or anticipated by targets.

65. Steele 1990, 113.
66. Steele 1990, 117.
67. Schelling 1965, 10; Jervis 1970, 44.
68. Braut-Hegghammer 2020.
69. On time horizons in international politics, see Edelstein 2017.
70. For weak targets confronted by strong coercers, the shadow of the future is quite short. They must concern themselves with survival today before planning for prosperity tomorrow.
71. I see the concession gamble as operating distinctly from prospect theory, which tells us that when leaders perceive themselves in the realm of losses, they are more risk-acceptant. As Stein (2012, 40) explains, prospect theory is about biased perceptions of reality, in which "estimates depart systematically from what objective probability calculations would dictate." A concession gamble requires no such departure. On prospect theory, see Davis 2000; McDermott 1998; Levy 2003; Mercer 2005.
72. Gambetta 2011, 183.
73. A signal can effectively communicate honesty if it would be relatively more costly for a liar to send the same signal. Gambetta (2011, 181) reminds, "A frequent mistake is to think that only signals that are costly for the honest signaler are informative. . . . Drinking from a nonpoisoned chalice [to demonstrate that it is safe] has no cost for the nonpoisoner."
74. Lab experiments on the game theoretic thought experiment of "the prisoner's dilemma" confirm that "enforceable promises" (in which the subject loses compensation for breaking a commitment) improve cooperative behavior, whereas "unenforceable promises" yield less cooperation but still more cooperation than when no promises were made (Evans 1964; see also Gahagan and Tedeschi 1968).
75. Lanoszka 2018.
76. Kydd and McManus 2017, 326.
77. Powell 2006. As Art and Greenhill (2018, 18) acknowledge, "giving way once can weaken the target enough militarily that it is harder to stand up to the compeller if it comes back for more concessions."
78. Miller 2014.
79. Pre-NPT acquirers were not seriously challenged coercively (US, Soviet Union, UK, France, China).
80. Carnegie and Carson 2018; Rabinowitz 2014; Miller and Rabinowitz 2015; Miller 2014 (see also Carnegie and Carson 2019).
81. On demand drivers of proliferation, see Sagan 1996; Katzenstein 1996; Singh and Way 2004; Monteiro and Debs 2014. On supply, see Jo and Gartzke 2007; Fuhrmann 2009; Kroenig 2010; Kemp 2014.
82. See work on nuclear rollback, reversal, and the political and technical processes of proliferation: Levite 2002/2003; Narang 2016/2017; Hymans 2012; Braut-Hegghammer 2016; Koch 2023.
83. Fuhrmann and Kreps 2010; Whitlark 2021.
84. Miller 2014; Fuhrmann and Kreps 2010; Solingen 2007.
85. Gerzhoy 2015; Gavin 2015; Miller 2014. On cooperation over policing proliferation within spheres of influence, see Coe and Vaynman 2015.
86. Mehta 2020; Saunders 2019; Debs and Monteiro 2017a; Solingen 2012; Georghe 2019; Gibbons 2022.
87. Two works of particular note have drawn the nuclear proliferation literature toward the study of the assurance dilemma: Knopf 2012a and Volpe 2023.
88. Bleek 2017.
89. A country counts as a potential "proliferator" if it had any interest in hedging or ever possessed nuclear weapons (a low bar for inclusion). Cases do not count if policymakers discussed but rejected the option of coercing (e.g., in the cases of Soviet, French, or Chinese proliferation). Some cases lack sufficient evidence of coercion (e.g., US pressure on Sweden, Italy, Japan, and Australia lacked express threats). Some episodes included brute force, which can be the result of bargaining failure. Consistent with the literature, military coercion does not require an explicit threat; the use of limited force can be a threat of more punishment to come (see Pape 1996, 12). However, I exclude cases of purely covert brute force (e.g., Israel-Syria

2007) because coercion must endeavor to present the target with an opportunity to concede. Israel offered none.

90. Related codings in the literature: Bas and Coe 2016, 2018, and Coe and Vaynman 2015 compile cases of deals struck over nuclear proliferation, but they include a broader set of cases in which counterproliferators did not make threats or impose sanctions. They capture, for instance, cases of signing the NPT that are not necessarily attributable to coercion. Fuhrmann and Kreps (2010) compile a dataset on the use of force (considered or employed) against nuclear programs. Their work emphasizes military prevention but does not capture the bargaining and threat-making that is more common in international nuclear politics.

91. Miller 2014.

92. I have elsewhere considered how secrecy and deniability help to explain why nonproliferation coercion succeeds uncommonly often (Pauly 2021).

93. Saunders 2019, 184 (see also Hal Brands, "Archives and the Study of Nuclear Politics," H-Diplo/ISSF, forum no. 2, June 15, 2014; Francis Gavin, "What We Talk about When We Talk about Nuclear Weapons," H-Diplo/ISSF, forum no. 2, June 15, 2014, http://issforum.org/ISSF/PDF/ISSF-Forum-2.pdf.

94. Mearsheimer 2001.

95. John Lewis Gaddis, Review of *Uncertain Partners: Stalin, Mao and the Korean War* by Sergei N. Goncharov, John W. Lewis, and Xue Litai, *Atlantic Monthly*, May 8, 1994.

96. See Stein 2021, 310.

97. Gibbons 2022.

98. It should be more difficult to get a nuclear weapons state to give up its weapons than to get a potential proliferator to give up its equipment or fissile material (Solingen 2012, 18).

99. In addition to comparing coercion success rates, the timing of coerced concessions is an important outcome to study in the empirical evaluation of coercion (see, e.g., Pape 1997).

100. To bury a proliferation program deeper underground is not to concede but to hide a lack of acquiescence. Still, when a target of coercion altered its planned course of action in a way that significantly slowed its proliferation efforts, I count it as a partial concession.

101. IAEA archives board of governors documents are protected and not made public until at least two years after production.

102. Other important directional changes are sometimes indicated by "lower" and "higher."

103. In the absence of evidence from the target, the codings are more representative of coercer strategies than target perceptions.

104. For a similar approach to exploiting within-case variation, see Bell 2021.

2. "I at Least Want to Be Guilty"

1. M. van Wyk 2010, 52.

2. Liberman 2001. In late 1987 Cuba sent an additional fifteen thousand troops to Africa (A. van Wyk 2010, 114).

3. On nuclear saber-rattling during this period, see J. van Wyk 2014, 14; von Wielligh and von Wielligh-Steyn 2015, 192; Gerzhoy 2014, 188–89; Pabian 1995, 8–9; Richelson 2006, 371–72.

4. Black 1999.

5. For example, Einhorn (2015) writes that "South Africa decided to dismantle the nuclear weapons it had built and join the NPT as a non-nuclear weapon state, not because it received security assurances but because the external security threat motivating its nuclear weapons program had dissipated and President de Klerk was reluctant to put South Africa's nuclear weapons in the hands of the black-majority government that would soon take power." The US government was also concerned about nuclear weapons "in the hands of a government that maintained friendly relations with Libya's Gaddafi and Cuba's Castro" (Purkitt and Burgess 2005, 130).

6. Uri Friedman, "Why One President Gave Up His Country's Nukes," *Atlantic*, September 9, 2017, https://www.theatlantic.com/international/archive/2017/09/north-korea-south-africa/539265/. Also, the South African military wanted more room in the defense budget for

conventional systems (Purkitt and Burgess 2005). Purkitt and Burgess's story is more compelling on South Africa's decision-making to suspend its space launch vehicle program in the 1990s. This missile program was indeed too expensive for the armed forces to sustain.

7. Many scholars explain Pretoria's demand for nuclear technology but minimize in their telling the interaction between South Africa and the international community (Debs and Monteiro 2017b; Liberman 2001; Reiss 1995, 7–44). Liberman (2001, 86) references some coercive assurance dynamics in his case study.

8. For studies focusing on South Africa's motivations for the bomb, see Debs and Monteiro 2017b; Liberman 2001.

9. Pabian 1995, 2.

10. The agreement was renewed in 1967 ("Safeguards in Relation to the South African / USA Agreement of Cooperation," GOV/1210, June 9, 1967, IAEA Archives, Vienna).

11. Stumpf 1995/1996, 3.

12. Stumpf (1995/1996, 3) describes the indigenous enrichment technology as "similar to the German Becker process" (see also von Wielligh and von Wielligh-Steyn 2015, 113.

13. Von Wielligh and von Wielligh-Steyn 2015, 126; Stumpf 1995/1996, 3.

14. Von Wielligh and von Wielligh-Steyn 2015, 121.

15. "The Agency's Verification Activities in South Africa, Report by the Director General," GOV/2684, September 8, 1993, 5, IAEA Archives, Vienna.

16. Von Wielligh and von Wielligh-Steyn 2015, 122.

17. "Agency's Verification Activities," 5.

18. Pabian 1995, 2; Stumpf 1995/1996, 4. In his speech announcing the program's dismantlement, F. W. de Klerk dated South Africa's weapons motivations to "as early as" 1974 (F. W. de Klerk, "Speech on the Nonproliferation Treaty to a Joint Session of Parliament," March 24, 1993, History and Public Policy Program Digital Archive, https://digitalarchive.wilsoncenter. org/document/speech-south-african-president-fw-de-klerk-joint-session-parliment-accession-non, contributed by Jo-Ansie van Wyk. Bleek (2017) codes South African "exploration" as beginning in 1969 because the Pelindaba Nuclear Research Center was designed to produce weapons-grade uranium in its original designs drawn up in 1969 or 1970. However, he codes pursuit as beginning in 1974 with Vorster's approval of PNE hedging. Other scholars prefer to date nuclear weapons ambitions to 1977, when "clear evidence of the program's militarization" appears in the historical record (Liberman 2001, 49).

19. A. van Wyk 2010, 104.

20. In 1975 the United Kingdom had also canceled the Simonstown Agreement on bilateral naval protection in the South Atlantic Ocean.

21. Von Wielligh and von Wielligh-Steyn 2015, 131.

22. Friedman, "Why One President."

23. This chapter unceremoniously skips over much South African history. Especially wanting from this narrative is an economic history—the economic costs of apartheid itself, which exacerbated the economic impact of sanctions. On the history of apartheid, see Beinart 1994; Welsh 2009.

24. A. van Wyk 2010, 101–2.

25. Von Wielligh and von Wielligh-Steyn 2015, 121–23.

26. Von Wielligh and von Wielligh-Steyn 2015, 123–24.

27. M. van Wyk (2017, 199) characterizes it as a "limited measure to appease the newly independent African nations and anti-apartheid movements worldwide that lobbied for punitive measures."

28. In response South Africa began to make its own fuel at the Y-plant, enriching uranium to 45 percent for use as fuel in the Safari-1 reactor (von Wielligh and von Wielligh-Steyn 2015, 107; Pabian 1995, 2; Liberman 2001, 69). The Safari-1 reactor ran on HEU fuel. In the 1970s the United States began a program called Reduced Enrichment for Research and Test Reactors and tried to get South Africa to agree to swap out its HEU for 20 percent enriched fuel, supplied by the US. Safari-1 did not switch to low-enriched uranium (LEU) fuel until 2009 (von Wielligh and von Wielligh-Steyn 2015, 108–9).

29. Taliaferro 2019, 27.

30. M. van Wyk 2010, 52.

31. Thomson 2010, 114.

32. A. van Wyk 2010, 106.

33. India, however, was not removed from the IAEA board of governors after its 1974 PNE, something that did not escape the South Africans' notice (Pabian 1995, 5; Liberman 2001, 69).

34. IAEA Board of Governors, "Record of the Five Hundred and First Meeting," GOV/OR.501, September 19, 1977, IAEA Archives, Vienna. Note that the date of the meeting and the date on the official records are different.

35. J. van Wyk 2014, 11.

36. "Resolution Adopted during the 191st Plenary Meeting on 28 September 1976," GC(XX)/RES/336, November 4, 1976, IAEA Archives, Vienna.

37. J. van Wyk 2012, 186.

38. The final vote tally was 19 in favor and 12 against (including the United States), with 2 abstentions (IAEA Board of Governors, "Record of the Five Hundred and First Meeting").

39. Pabian 1995, 5.

40. Von Wielligh and von Wielligh-Steyn 2015, 136.

41. Richelson 2006, 277–78.

42. A coauthor and I have elsewhere explained why some discoverers of secret wrongdoing share intelligence while others keep discoveries secret (Nutt and Pauly 2021). On the extent of collusion between the United States and the Soviet Union to stem nuclear proliferation, see Coe and Vaynman 2015 (see also Miller and Rabinowitz 2015, 63).

43. *Foreign Relations of the United States* (*FRUS*), 1977–80, vol. 6, *Soviet Union*, doc. 41, "Memorandum from William Hyland of the National Security Council Staff to President Carter," Washington, DC, August 6, 1977, https://history.state.gov/historicaldocuments/frus1977-80v06/d41.

44. "Draft Letter to B. Cardledge on Conversation with U.S. Deputy Undersecretary of State Joseph Nye on South African Nuclear Intentions," September 1977, History and Public Policy Program Digital Archive, UK National Archives, FCO45–2131, http://digitalarchive.wilsoncenter.org/document/116626, contributed by Anna-Mart van Wyk.

45. "TASS Issues Statement on Nuclear Weapons in S. Africa," TASS International Service, August 8, 1977, Foreign Broadcast Information Service (FBIS) Daily Reports, NewsBank database.

46. "TASS Condemns Suppliers of Nuclear Technology to S. Africa," TASS International Service, August 9, 1977, FBIS Daily Reports, NewsBank database.

47. Cable from AMEMBASSY MOSCOW to SECSTATE WASHDC, "Soviet Media on South African Nuclear Test," August 22, 1977, National Archives and Records Administration (NARA), https://aad.archives.gov/aad/createpdf?rid=191055&dt=2532&dl=1629.

48. Cable from AMEMBASSY MOSCOW to SECSTATE WASHDC, August 22, 1977.

49. "Telegram from the Department of State to the Embassy in the Soviet Union," August 11, 1977, *FRUS*, 1977–80, vol. 16, *Southern Africa*, 896–97, https://history.state.gov/historicaldocuments/frus1977-80v16/d288.

50. Cable from SECSTATE WASHDC to WHITE HOUSE, "For the President and the Secretary from Andrew Young, Subject: South African Nuclear Issue," September 22, 1977, NARA, https://aad.archives.gov/aad/createpdf?rid=219729&dt=2532&dl=1629.

51. "Letter, US Ambassador Bowdler to South African Foreign Minister Botha," August 18, 1977, History and Public Policy Program Digital Archive, South African Ministry of Foreign Affairs Archives, Brand Fourie, Atomic Energy, file 2/5/2/1, vols. 1–2, http://digitalarchive.wilsoncenter.org/document/114150, contributed by Anna-Mart van Wyk.

52. "Letter, US Ambassador Bowdler," August 18, 1977.

53. "Unofficial Translation of Aide Memoire from French Embassy in South Africa to Government of South Africa Requesting that South Africa Prove that It Does Not Seek the Ability to Conduct a Nuclear Test," August 18, 1977, South African Foreign Affairs Archives, Brand Fourie, Atomic Energy, file 2/5/2/1, vols. 1–2, https://digitalarchive.wilsoncenter.org/document/114151; Liberman 2001, 50, 69–70.

54. *FRUS*, 1977–80, vol. 16, *Southern Africa*, doc. 294, "Telegram from the Department of State to the Embassies in the United Kingdom and France and the White House," Washington, DC, August 18, 1977.

55. "Letter, US Secretary of State Cyrus Vance to South African Foreign Minister Botha," August 19, 1977, History and Public Policy Program Digital Archive, South African Ministry of Foreign Affairs Archives, Brand Fourie, Atomic Energy, file 2/5/2/1, vols. 1–2, http://digitalarchive.wilsoncenter.org/document/114153, contributed by Anna-Mart van Wyk; "Telegram from the Department of State to the Embassies in South Africa, France, and the United Kingdom," August 19, 1977, *FRUS*, 1977–80, vol. 16, *Southern Africa*, 914–15, https://history.state.gov/historicaldocuments/frus1977-80v16/d295.

56. Pik Botha's recollection gets the date wrong (April instead of August) (Pik Botha, interview with Sue Onslow, December 13, 2012, Pretoria, appendix 1, Institute of Commonwealth Studies, https://commonwealthoralhistories.org/2015/interview-with-rf-pik-botha/). Botha claims they were "Soviet satellite pictures, forwarded to the Americans." Likely they were actually photos taken by the American themselves after the Soviets cued them to look. On August 14 workers at the Kalahari site had reported seeing a small airplane flying very low overhead. It belonged to the US military attaché in Pretoria and was taking pictures to confirm the Soviet satellite images (Richelson 2006, 279).

57. "Memorandum from the President's Assistant for National Security Affairs (Brzezinski) to President Carter," n.d., *FRUS*, 1977–80, vol. 16, *Southern Africa*, 922, https://history.state.gov/historicaldocuments/frus1977-80v16/d301.

58. "Memorandum from the President's Assistant."

59. "Memorandum from the President's Assistant."

60. Cable from AMEMBASSY PRETORIA to SECSTATE WASHDC, "Subject: Possible South African Weapons Program," August 21, 1977, NARA, https://aad.archives.gov/aad/createpdf?rid=190545&dt=2532&dl=1629; Cable from SECSTATE WASHDC to USDEL SECRETARY and WHITE HOUSE, "Subject: Possible South African Nuclear Program," August 22, 1977, NARA, https://aad.archives.gov/aad/createpdf?rid=191238&dt=2532&dl=1629.

61. Fourie provided all three requested statements, acknowledged in "Cable from South African Secretary for Foreign Affairs Brand Fourie to all South African heads of mission outlining the South African Government's position on recent nuclear testing charges," August 26, 1977, South African Foreign Affairs Archives, Brand Fourie, Atomic Energy, file 2/5/2/1, vols. 1–2, contributed by Anna-Mart van Wyk to the Nuclear Proliferation International History Project. Carter's press conference on August 23 included all three requested assurances. He said, "South Africa has informed us that they do not have and do not intend to develop nuclear explosive devices for any purpose, either peaceful or as weapons, that the Kalahari test site which has been in question is not designed for use to test nuclear explosives and that no nuclear explosive tests will be taken in South Africa now or in the future." "Cable from South African Embassy in the U.S. to South African Foreign Ministry on U.S. President Carter's press conference on the Kalahari nuclear test site and related U.S. media coverage," August 23, 1977, South African Foreign Affairs Archives, Brand Fourie, Atomic Energy, file 2/5/2/1 vols. 1–2, contributed by Anna-Mart van Wyk to the Nuclear Proliferation International History Project.

62. "Cable from South African Embassy in the U.S. to South African Foreign Ministry on U.S. President Carter's press conference," August 23, 1977.

63. See "Cable from South African Secretary for Foreign Affairs Brand Fourie," August 26, 1977.

64. "Draft Letter and Aide Memoire from South African Foreign Minister R. F. Botha to US Secretary of State Cyrus Vance," September 30, 1977, History and Public Policy Program Digital Archive, South African Foreign Affairs Archives, http://digitalarchive.wilsoncenter.org/document/116635, contributed by Anna-Mart van Wyk.

65. Looking back in 1983, the CIA assessed the coercion had succeeded in 1977: "International uproar reportedly caused Prime Minister Vorster to order a halt to further nuclear weapons development." But the CIA was thereafter in the dark. "We have had no direct indication of any subsequent activities in the weapons program" after 1977, they assessed. This proved incorrect (CIA Directorate of Intelligence, "New Information on South Africa's Nuclear

Program and South African–Israeli Nuclear and Military Cooperation," March 30, 1983, History and Public Policy Program Digital Archive, National Security Archive, https://digital archive.wilsoncenter.org/document/cia-report-new-information-south-africas-nuclear-program-and-south-african-israeli-nuclear, contributed by Sasha Polakow-Suransky).

66. "Cable from South African Embassy in the US to the South African Secretary for Foreign Affairs on South Africa and the Bomb," August 31, 1977, History and Public Policy Program Digital Archive, http://digitalarchive.wilsoncenter.org/document/114181, contributed by Anna-Mart van Wyk.

67. Pabian 1995, 3.

68. "Cable from South African Embassy in the US to the South African Secretary for Foreign Affairs on South Africa and the Bomb," August 31, 1977.

69. Richelson 2006, 281.

70. Pik Botha, interview with Sue Onslow, December 13, 2012.

71. "Cable from South African Embassy in the US to the South African Secretary for Foreign Affairs on South Africa and the Bomb," August 31, 1977.

72. Andre Buys, interview by Mark Bell and Noel Anderson, July 1, 2014, Pretoria.

73. Buys, interview, July 1, 2014.

74. Neil Barnard, "The Deterrent Strategy and Nuclear Weapons," *Journal for Contemporary History and International Relations* 2 (September 1977): 74–97 (quoted in Pabian 1995, 3).

75. "Cable from South African Embassy in the US to the South African Secretary for Foreign Affairs on South Africa and the Bomb," August 31, 1977.

76. "Cable from South African Embassy in the US to the South African Secretary for Foreign Affairs on South Africa and the Bomb," August 31, 1977.

77. "Cable from South African Embassy in the US to the South African Secretary for Foreign Affairs on South Africa and the Bomb," August 31, 1977.

78. "Cable from South African Embassy in the US to the South African Secretary for Foreign Affairs on South Africa and the Bomb," August 31, 1977.

79. Von Wielligh and von Wielligh-Steyn 2015, 133.

80. Stumpf 1995/1996, 5 (see also Waldo Stumpf, presentation at the conference "50 Years after Hiroshima," organized by Unione Scienziati per il Disarmo, Castiglioncello, Italy, September 28–October 2, 1995, https://fas.org/nuke/guide/rsa/nuke/stumpf.htm).

81. Buys, interview, July 1, 2014.

82. UNSC Resolution 418, 1977 (quoted in Pabian 1995, 7).

83. Von Wielligh and von Wielligh-Steyn 2015, 164.

84. Matthew Nimetz through Warren Christopher to the Secretary, "South African Nuclear Problem," September 8, 1980, with memorandum from Warren Christopher attached: "South African Nuclear Problem," September 27, 1980, National Security Archive, https://nsarchive.gwu.edu/document/22353-40.

85. Cable from SECSTATE WASHDC to WHITE HOUSE, "South African Nuclear Issue," September 22, 1977.

86. Liberman 2001, 69.

87. M. van Wyk 2010, 54.

88. Stumpf 1995/1996, 4. On Koeberg safeguards, see "Safeguards in relation to an agreement of cooperation between France and South Africa for the construction of a nuclear power station," GOV/1805, August 20, 1976, IAEA Archives, Vienna.

89. "The Agency's Verification Activities in South Africa, Report by the Director General," GOV/2684, September 8, 1993, 6, IAEA Archives, Vienna; von Wielligh and von Wielligh-Steyn 2015, 166; Stumpf 1995/1996, 5; Pabian 1995, 6.

90. Liberman 2001, 54; von Wielligh and von Wielligh-Steyn 2015, 149; Stumpf 1995/1996, 5.

91. Heinonen 2016, 150. Earlier, in 1977, the AEB had constructed a gun-type nuclear device but without an HEU core ("The Agency's Verification Activities in South Africa, Report by the Director General," GOV/2684, September 8, 1993, 5, IAEA Archives, Vienna).

92. J. van Wyk and A. van Wyk 2015, 40; Heinonen 2016, 150.

93. A. van Wyk 2010, 112; Stumpf 1995/1996), 7.

94. CIA, "South Africa's Nuclear Options and Decisionmaking Structures," interagency intelligence memorandum, 1978, National Security Archive, https://nsarchive.gwu.edu/ document/29879-document-2-director-central-intelligence-interagency-intelligence-memorandum-south.

95. CIA, "South Africa's Nuclear Options," ii.

96. CIA, "New Information on South Africa's Nuclear Program and South African-Israeli Nuclear and Military Cooperation," March 30, 1983, http://nsarchive.gwu.edu/NSAEBB/ NSAEBB181/sa26.pdf (also discussed in Richelson 2006, 375).

97. M. van Wyk 2010, 58.

98. On "catalytic" nuclear postures, see Narang 2014, 208.

99. Quoted in Narang 2014, 213.

100. M. van Wyk 2010, 55.

101. "Notes on Meeting between South African Minister of Foreign Affairs R. F. Botha and U.S. President Reagan," May 15, 1981, History and Public Policy Program Digital Archive, South African Foreign Affairs Archive, file 137/10/02 vol. 9, doc. 82214/006772, http:// digitalarchive.wilsoncenter.org/document/116764, contributed by Or Rabinowitz.

102. "Notes on Meeting between R. F. Botha and Reagan," May 15, 1981.

103. "Notes on Meeting between R. F. Botha and Reagan," May 15, 1981. This version of the story is largely confirmed by Pik Botha's recollections (Pik Botha, interview, December 13, 2012).

104. Pik Botha, interview, December 13, 2012. On nuclear testing, see also Miller and Rabinowitz 2015, 61; Rabinowitz 2014.

105. American firms, acting legally but skirting US law, brokered the deal to acquire uranium from Switzerland and Belgium and have a French firm enrich it and sell it to Pretoria. The State Department was infuriated by this deal. Reagan also agreed to the export of some civilian nuclear technology to South Africa in 1982 and maintenance contracts for the Koeberg facility in 1983 (M. van Wyk 2010, 56–57; Stumpf 1995/1996, 4).

106. M. van Wyk 2010, 57–60. A February 1984 communication with the IAEA noted that South Africa had "become aware of United States concern about its intentions," and Pretoria sought to stall by beginning negotiations on safeguarding a semicommercial enrichment plant ("Communication received from South Africa," IAEA Archives, INFCIRC/314, February 1984, https://www.iaea.org/sites/default/files/infcirc314.pdf).

107. Jonathan Fuerbringer, "Senate Approves Economic Moves against S. Africa," *New York Times*, July 12, 1985, http://www.nytimes.com/1985/07/12/us/senate-approves-economic-moves-against-s-africa-senate-confirmed-23-nominees-for.html.

108. Passage of a bill in the Senate was a key roadblock that, once breached, signaled a significant legislative impediment to Reagan's foreign policy vis-à-vis South Africa. For the legislative details, see Branaman 1987.

109. M. van Wyk 2010, 61.

110. Baker 2000, 106.

111. "Comprehensive Anti-Apartheid Act of 1986," Pub. L. No. 99–440, October 2, 1986, 99th Congress, https://www.govinfo.gov/content/pkg/STATUTE-100/pdf/STATUTE-100-Pg1086.pdf (see also Albright and Zamora 1991, 27; Pabian 1995, 7).

112. "Comprehensive Anti-Apartheid Act of 1986."

113. M. van Wyk 2010, 61.

114. Baker 2000, 111; von Wielligh and von Wielligh-Steyn 2015, 179.

115. Baker 2000, 109 (citing Giliomee 1997, 127).

116. Baker 2000, 109.

117. Becker and Hofmeyr, 1990.

118. Baker 2000, 109 (citing Schrire 1991).

119. Pretoria's limits on capital flows and import-substitution policies led the economy to shrink by 20–35 percent (Baker 2000, 112).

120. Von Wielligh and von Wielligh-Steyn 2015, 180.

121. "Meeting of the Ad Hoc Cabinet Committee Under the Chairmanship of the Honourable the State President on Tuesday 3 September 1985 at 15h00," document reproduced in von

Wielligh and von Wielligh-Steyn 2015, 480–83. The Atomic Energy Corporation was the new name for the Atomic Energy Board.

122. "Meeting of the Ad Hoc Cabinet Committee."

123. "Meeting of the Ad Hoc Cabinet Committee."

124. Albright 1994, 45.

125. Giliomee 2012.

126. "Address by State President P. W. Botha at the Opening of the National Party Natal Congress Durban," August 15, 1985. https://www.nelsonmandela.org/omalley/index.php/site/q/03lv01538/04lv01600/05lv01638/06lv01639.htm.

127. Stumpf 1995/1996, 6.

128. "Communication Received from South Africa, Received January 31, 1984," INFCIRC/314, February 1984, IAEA Archives, Vienna.

129. Möser 2020, 4. See also Möser 2024.

130. Möser (2020) cites "Overview of Discussions with the IAEA on International Nuclear Safeguards on the Semi-commercial Enrichment Plant," November 13, 1985, PV203, file PS 6/13/3, Archive of Contemporary Affairs, Bloemfontein.

131. Möser 2020.

132. "South Africa's Nuclear Capabilities: Annex D," IAEA, GOV/INF/523, June 2, 1987, IAEA Archives, Vienna.

133. "South Africa's Nuclear Capabilities: Annex C," Letter from the Permanent Mission of South Africa to the IAEA, February 25, 1987, GOV/INF/523, IAEA Archives, Vienna.

134. "South Africa's Nuclear Capabilities: Annex C."

135. "Prohibition of the Participation of a Delegation of South Africa in CAS Meetings," GOV/2054, September 13, 1981, IAEA Archives, Vienna.

136. See IAEA Board of Governors, "Record of the Six Hundred and Sixteenth Meeting," February 22, 1984, GOV/OR.616, IAEA Archives, Vienna; IAEA Board of Governors, "Record of the Six Hundred and Twenty-Fourth Meeting," June 8, 1984, GOV/OR.624, IAEA Archives, Vienna; IAEA Board of Governors, "Record of the Six Hundred and Fifty-Eighth Meeting," September 23, 1986, GOV/OR.658, IAEA Archives, Vienna.

137. IAEA Board of Governors, "Record of the Six Hundred and Sixteenth Meeting"; IAEA Board of Governors, "Record of the Six Hundred and Twenty-Fourth Meeting."

138. IAEA Board of Governors, "Record of the Six Hundred and Sixteenth Meeting."

139. IAEA Board of Governors, "Record of the Six Hundred and Forty-First Meeting," IAEA Board of Governors Meeting, September 19, 1985, GOV/OR.641, February 1986, IAEA Archives, Vienna.

140. "Record of the Six Hundred and Forty-First Meeting."

141. "Record of the Six Hundred and Forty-First Meeting" On occasion, the United States sought to separate the issue of apartheid from debate about South African removal from IAEA membership. "[The US] Government had consistently condemned the policy of apartheid," said Ambassador Kennedy in the June 1985 board of governors meeting, but "that was not the issue at stake." Such appeals were drowned out. IAEA Board of Governors, "Record of the Six Hundred and Thirty-Ninth Meeting," June 13, 1985, GOV/OR.639, September 1985, IAEA Archives, Vienna; IAEA Board of Governors, "Record of the Six Hundred and Twenty-Fourth Meeting."

142. On October 14, 1983, the general conference of the IAEA adopted Resolution 408 ("Resolution adopted during the 256th plenary meeting on 14 October 1983, South Africa's nuclear capabilities," GC(XXVII)/RES/408, November 9, 1983, IAEA Archives, Vienna). In September 1984, the general conference adopted Resolution 423, GC(XXVIII)/RES/423 (cited in J. van Wyk 2014, 12).

143. "South Africa's Nuclear Capabilities: Resolution adopted during the 292nd plenary meeting," October 3, 1986, GC(XXX)/RES/468, IAEA Archives, Vienna.

144. J. van Wyk 2014, 12.

145. M. van Wyk 2010, 62; J. van Wyk 2014, 13.

146. "Pretoria Says It Can Build A-Arms," Reuters, August 13, 1988, http://www.nytimes.com/1988/08/14/world/pretoria-says-it-can-build-a-arms.html.

147. South African Department of Foreign Affairs, *A Balanced Approach to the NPT: Armscor/AEC Concerns Viewed from a DFA Standpoint*, September 1, 1988, History and Public Policy Program Digital Archive, South African Foreign Affairs Archives, NPT-IAEA Agreement/Negotiations on Full-Scope Safeguards, http://digitalarchive.wilsoncenter.org/document/114185, contributed by Anna-Mart van Wyk.

148. Von Wielligh and von Wielligh-Steyn 2015, 189.

149. Purkitt and Burgess 2005, 123–24.

150. Purkitt and Burgess 2005, 124.

151. Liberman 2001, 73–74; Waldo Stumpf, "Foreword," in von Wielligh and von Wielligh-Steyn 2015, iii–iv; Giliomee 2012.

152. Stumpf, "Foreword," in von Wielligh and von Wielligh-Steyn 2015, iii–iv.

153. Giliomee 2012, 302–3. Other South African policymakers agreed that the economic sanctions situation was dire but not critical. "From a financial point of view, South Africa did not have to negotiate in 1990, but conditions were tightening," judged Derek Keys, minister of finance from 1992 to 1994. These views are consistent with framework of compellence—it is not only the current pain but the threat of more punishment to come that generates coercive leverage (Giliomee 2012, 317).

154. Möser 2020, 9.

155. Stumpf 1995/1996, 6.

156. Giliomee 2012, 309.

157. The Y-plant ceased production on February 1, 1990. However, the formal order from De Klerk to shut it down was not received until February 26, 1990, so Stumpf (1995/1996, 6) cites that date as the official closing date (see also Purkitt and Burgess 2005, 125–26).

158. Quoted in Purkitt and Burgess 2005, 124.

159. Thomson 2008, 161.

160. Giliomee 2012, 269.

161. "Participation of South Africa in CAS Meetings, Resolution Adopted by the Board on September 14, 1994," GOV/2763, September 14, 1994, IAEA Archives, Vienna; Reiss 1995, 19.

162. Liberman 2001, 73–74.

163. Von Wielligh and von Wielligh-Steyn 2015, 216.

164. Von Wielligh and von Wielligh-Steyn 2015, 255.

165. Stumpf 1995/1996, 7. A similar Stumpf quote is reported in Albright 1994, 38. Reiss (1995, 23) also notes these perceptions.

166. Waldo Stumpf, interview by Mark Bell and Noel Anderson, June 11, 2014, Pretoria (see also Albright 1994, 38).

167. "Letter, Richard Carter to Herbert Beukes," November 17, 1989, History and Public Policy Program Digital Archive, South African Foreign Affairs Archives, http://digitalarchive.wilsoncenter.org/document/116003, contributed by Anna-Mart van Wyk.

168. "Letter, Carter to Beukes," November 17, 1989.

169. "Letter, Carter to Beukes," November 17, 1989.

170. "Letter, Carter to Beukes," November 17, 1989.

171. South Africa at the time had six nuclear weapons, plus a seventh under construction—not five.

172. "Phasing out of the RSA's Nuclear Weapons Capability," AEC, February 15, 1990, document reproduced in von Wielligh and von Wielligh-Steyn 2015, 506–11.

173. Von Wielligh and von Wielligh-Steyn 2015, 234.

174. Stumpf 1995/1996, 6.

175. According to Reiss (1995, 19), not all uranium metal in the nuclear cores had been melted down and reshaped by the time South Africa signed the NPT, but the task was complete before Pretoria sign the comprehensive safeguards agreement.

176. J. van Wyk 2012, 183.

177. Pauly 2021.

178. Heinonen 2014.

179. Von Wielligh and von Wielligh-Steyn 2015, 241. Von Wielligh claims that "Waldo Stumpf said years later that he did have permission from F. W. de Klerk to disclose what the

highly enriched uranium had been used for in the past in response to a direct question. But nobody on the IAEA team asked this specific question and so Stumpf kept the information to himself."

180. Von Wielligh and von Wielligh-Steyn 2015, 241.

181. Heinonen 2016, 152.

182. South Africa had three facilities already under IAEA safeguards in 1991: Koeberg (two reactors), the Safari-1 research reactor, and a hot-cell facility at Pelindaba. In signing the NPT and accepting full safeguards, South Africa opened up the following facilities: the pilot enrichment facility at Valindaba (the Y-plant), the Kentron Circle / Advena Facility, the Building 5000 complex at Pelindaba, a semicommercial enrichment plant (the Z-plant), a uranium-conversion facility, an HEU-fuel-fabrication facility, an LEU-fuel-fabrication facility, decontamination and waste-storage facilities at Pelindaba, and two spent-fuel and radioactive-waste-disposal facilities (Heinonen 2016, 149).

183. "Report on the Completeness of the Inventory of South Africa's Nuclear Installations and Material," GOV/2609 Attachment, September 3, 1992, 5–6, IAEA Archives, Vienna (see also "Safeguards: Reports on the Implementation of Safeguards Agreements: Agreement between the Agency and South Africa for the Application of Safeguards in Connection with the Treaty on the Non-proliferation of Nuclear Weapons," IAEA, GOV/2609, September 3, 1992, paras. 15 and 17, IAEA Archives, Vienna). The Y-plant was dismantled before accession to the NPT. The Z-plant was decommissioned in 1995.

184. Heinonen 2016, 153.

185. Von Baeckmann, Dillon, and Perricos 1995, 46.

186. Stumpf reports that he recommended revealing the full nuclear dismantlement in 1992, only to be rebuffed by De Klerk, who said the timing was not right. When Stumpf made a second request at transparency in January 1993, De Klerk agreed (Reiss 1995, 23).

187. "De Klerk Discloses Nuclear Capability to Parliament," Johannesburg Radio South Africa Network in English, FBIS-AFR-93–056, March 25, 1993.

188. "Speech by South African President F. W. De Klerk to a Joint Session of Parliament on Accession to the Nonproliferation Treaty," March 24, 1993, History and Policy Program Digital Archive, Archives.un.org, http://digitalarchive.wilsoncenter.org/document/116789, contributed by Jo-Ansie van Wyk.

189. "De Klerk Holds News Conference on Speech," Johannesburg SABC TV 1 Network in English, FBIS-AFR-93–056, March 25, 1993. Stumpf (1995/1996, 7) asserts the same privilege.

190. Heinonen 2014.

191. The shafts were destroyed by "back-filling with sand and casting in place of reinforced concrete plugs at various levels" ("The Agency's Verification Activities in South Africa, Report by the Director General," GOV/2684, September 8, 1993, 10, IAEA Archives, Vienna).

192. "Agency's Verification Activities in South Africa," 10.

193. Einhorn 2015; Purkitt and Burgess 2005, 130. However, De Klerk did hand over to the ANC government a large stockpile of highly enriched uranium. South Africa today retains enough weapons-grade uranium for up to six nuclear devices.

3. "Sanctions with Inspectors"

1. "U.S. Persuades Nations to Join Plan for Tighter Iraq Sanctions," *New York Times*, June 22, 1997.

2. David Rieff, "Were Sanctions Right?" *New York Times*, July 27, 2003, https://www.nytimes.com/2003/07/27/magazine/were-sanctions-right.html.

3. Byman and Waxman 2002, 93; McCoy 2011/2012, 173; Woods, Lacey, and Murray 2006, 15–16. Saddam made such calculations during the Gulf War—for instance, citing the United States' relative casualty aversion as a theory of victory. Iraq could suffer war casualties at a ratio of "four for one" and win, Saddam calculated (Woods, Palkki, and Stout 2011, 195). He also declared victory after the 1991 war.

4. Kenneth M. Pollack, "Why Iraq Can't Be Deterred," Brookings, September 26, 2002, https://www.brookings.edu/articles/why-iraq-cant-be-deterred/; Ewen MacAskill, "Irrational, Illogical, Unpredictable: 24 Years on, the World Awaits Saddam's Next Move," *Guardian*, March 18, 2003, https://www.theguardian.com/world/2003/mar/19/iraq.ewenmacaskill.

5. Woods and Stout 2010.

6. Duelfer and Dyson 2011; Lake 2010/2011 (see also on intelligence failure Jervis 2010; Rovner 2011).

7. McCoy 2011/2012, 173–74.

8. Koblentz 2018.

9. Charles Duelfer, who led the Iraq Survey Group, the mission to find evidence of WMDs in Iraq after the US-led invasion, made the argument that Saddam feared coming clean about his lack of WMDs in the eye of those he was trying to deter. *Comprehensive Report of the Special Advisor to the DCI on Iraq's WMD* (Duelfer Report), vol. 1 (Washington, DC: Central Intelligence Agency, 2004), https://www.govinfo.gov/app/details/GPO-DUELFERREPORT (see also Freedman 2004a; Lake 2010/2011). Braut-Hegghammer (2020) calls this conventional wisdom the "deterrence bluff."

10. Braut-Hegghammer 2020 (see also Coll 2024).

11. Braut-Hegghammer 2016, 28.

12. Braut-Hegghammer 2016, 44.

13. Braut-Hegghammer 2016, 52–53.

14. Braut-Hegghammer 2016, 57.

15. Braut-Hegghammer 2016, 61.

16. Braut-Hegghammer 2016, 62.

17. Braut-Hegghammer 2016, 46.

18. Braut-Hegghammer 2016, 64.

19. Braut-Hegghammer 2016, 61; Sadot 2016, 657.

20. Perlmutter, Handel, and Bar-Joseph 2003; cited in Fuhrmann and Kreps 2010, dataset.

21. Fuhrmann and Kreps 2010, dataset. The attack bore the fingerprints of Mossad (Sadot 2016, 657).

22. Iran also used force against the Iraqi nuclear program. I do not consider this a separate case, however, because it occurred in wartime. As the Iran-Iraq War began, Iranian jets bombed the Osirak facility on September 27, 1980, but did not cause significant damage. Saddam appears to have concluded even at this early attack that Iraq would forge ahead even if its facilities were damaged or destroyed. They could be rebuilt, replaced, or resupplied. The effort would not stop. Braut-Hegghammer 2016, 68.

23. Fuhrmann and Kreps 2010.

24. Målfrid Braut-Hegghammer 2016, 61.

25. Målfrid Braut-Hegghammer 2016, 115–16.

26. Israel assessed that the Osirak reactor would go critical in mid-1981. In September 1980 the Israeli security cabinet authorized an air strike, delegating the timing to Prime Minister Begin (Sadot 2016, 661).

27. Leonard S. Spector and Avner Cohen, "Israel's Airstrike on Syria's Reactor: Implications for the Nonproliferation Regime," *Arms Control Today* 38, no. 6 (July/August 2008): 15–21, https://www.armscontrol.org/act/2008_07-08/SpectorCohen.

28. Spector and Cohen, "Israel's Airstrike."

29. Braut-Hegghammer 2016, 73.

30. Sadot 2016, 663.

31. Braut-Hegghammer 2016, 75.

32. Note that there is a rich debate about whether the Osirak strike was worthwhile— whether it delayed the Iraqi program long enough for Saddam to commit a strategic blunder (invading Kuwait in 1990) or merely caused him to pursue a nuclear deterrent with more vigor and secrecy (see Sadot 2016; Braut-Hegghammer 2016).

33. Braut-Hegghammer 2016, 83.

34. Braut-Hegghammer 2016, 92.

35. Braut-Hegghammer 2016, 96.

36. Braut-Hegghammer 2016, 102.

37. It was a pipe dream. Part of the plan was to divert irradiated fuel from a safeguarded facility (Braut-Hegghammer 2016, 117).

38. Avey 2019, 50. Avey's is an excellent empirical account, but it does not distinguish between threat credibility, assurance credibility, and demand severity as causes of failure.

39. Avey 2019, 50. He cites Woods 2008,109; SH-PDWN-D-000–533, "Meeting between Saddam Hussein and the Soviet Delegation," October 6–10, 1990, Conflict Records Research Center (CRRC), Washington, DC, 18–20.

40. Gause 2002, 60.

41. Gause 2002, 60.

42. Gause 2002, 60; Obeidi and Pitzer 2004.

43. Braut-Hegghammer 2016, 122; Harrer 2014, 3.

44. Sadot 2016, 649.

45. Sadot 2016, 655.

46. ElBaradei 2011, 10.

47. Harrer 2014.

48. "GDP—Iraq," World Bank, https://data.worldbank.org/indicator/NY.GDP.MKTP.CD?locations=IQ.

49. "GDP—Iraq."

50. Obeidi and Pitzer 2004, 138–39.

51. Obeidi and Pitzer 2004, 146.

52. Braut-Hegghammer 2020, 62.

53. Coll 2024, 239.

54. Braut-Hegghammer 2020, 66.

55. CIA, "Misreading Intentions: Iraq's Reaction to Inspections Created Picture of Deception," Iraq WMD Retrospective Series, January 5, 2006, CIA CREST, doc. 0005567895, 1–2. Iraq also destroyed "much of the paperwork that could have verified the destruction."

56. CIA, "Misreading Intentions," i.

57. "Saddam and His Inner Circle Discussing Upheaval and the Communist Coup Attempt in the Soviet Union," SH-SHTP-A-001–210, n.d. (ca. August 19–21, 1991), in Woods, Palkki, and Stout 2011, 257–58.

58. CIA, "Misreading Intentions," v.

59. CIA, "Misreading Intentions," i.

60. Ekéus 2016, 137–38.

61. Obeidi and Pitzer 2004, 146.

62. Obeidi and Pitzer 2004, 154.

63. Obeidi and Pitzer 2004, 155.

64. CIA, "Misreading Intentions," page number redacted.

65. Obeidi and Pitzer 2004, 149.

66. Obeidi and Pitzer 2004, 169.

67. Blix 2004, 30.

68. CIA, "Misreading Intentions," 4.

69. CIA, "Misreading Intentions," 4.

70. In 1993 the US had launched additional cruise missiles against the Zaa'faraniya complex.

71. UN Resolution 687, paragraph 22 spelled out that upon "Council agreement that Iraq has completed all actions contemplated in paragraphs 8 to 13 [on inspections], the prohibitions against the import of commodities and products originating in Iraq and the prohibitions against financial transactions related thereto contained in resolution 661 (1990) shall have no further force or effect" (UN Resolution 687, April 3, 1991, http://unscr.com/en/resolutions/doc/687).

72. Woods, Palkki, and Stout 2011, 255.

73. SH-SHTP-A-001–253, "Saddam and Top Political Advisers Discussing Relations with Saudi Arabia and Other Neighbors," n.d. (ca. October 9–10, 1994), in Woods, Palkki, and Stout 2011, 266–69.

74. SH-SHTP-A-001–255, "Saddam and Top Political Advisers Discussing the Agricultural Situation in Iraq and UN Inspections Teams," n.d. (ca. January/February 1995), in Woods, Palkki, and Stout 2011, 271–74.

75. SH-SHTP-A-001–255.

76. SH-SHTP-A-001–295, "Saddam Meeting with Ba'ath Party Members to Discuss the Results of the UN Inspectors' Mission to Look for WMD," June 19, 1995, CRRC.

77. SH-MISC-V-001–426, "Meeting between UN Biological Inspectors and Iraqi Officials Including Dr. Rihab Taha," ca. 1993–98, CRRC.

78. SH-SHTP-A-001–254, "Meeting between Saddam Hussein and Top Political Advisors Concerning Diplomacy with the United States and Russia," n.d., CRRC.

79. SH-SHTP-A-001–254.

80. CIA, "Misreading Intentions," 4.

81. Robin Wright, "Hussein Vows No Cooperation if Sanctions Stay," Los Angeles Times, July 18, 1995.

82. SH-SHTP-001–011, "Saddam and High Ranking Officials Discussing Iraqi Biological and Nuclear Weapons Programs," May 2, 1995, in Woods, Palkki, and Stout 2011, 275–79.

83. SH-SHTP-A-001–254.

84. SH-SHTP-A-001–254.

85. Woods, Palkki, and Stout 2011, 298. They cite SH-INMD-D-000–657, "Report from Husam Mohammad Amin, Director of the National Monitoring Directorate, on Hussein Kamil," August 14, 1995 (see also Obeidi and Pitzer 2004, 166).

86. UN Special Commission on Iraq, Report to the UN Security Council, S/1995/864, October 11, 1995, https://www.un.org/depts/unscom/sres95-864.htm.

87. CIA, "Misreading Intentions," 5.

88. Woods, Palkki, and Stout 2011, 298, which cites SH-INMD-D-000–657.

89. Obeidi and Pitzer 2004, 167 (see also Blix 2004, 29–30).

90. CIA, "Misreading Intentions," 4.

91. CIA, "Misreading Intentions," 7.

92. CIA, "Misreading Intentions," 5.

93. SH-SHTP-A-001–256, "Saddam and Top Political Advisers Discuss a Visit by Prime Minister Tariq Aziz to the United Nations Delegates," n.d. (ca. November 1995), in Woods, Palkki, and Stout 2011, 279–83.

94. CIA, "Misreading Intentions," 7.

95. CIA, "Misreading Intentions," 4.

96. CIA, "Misreading Intentions," 7.

97. Office of the Press Secretary, "Vice President Speaks at VFW 103rd National Convention," August 26, 2002, https://georgewbush-whitehouse.archives.gov/news/releases/2002/08/20020826.html.

98. Patrick E. Tyler, "U.S. Is Pressuring Inspectors in Iraq to Aid Defections." New York Times, December 6, 2002, https://www.nytimes.com/2002/12/06/international/middleeast/us-is-pressuring-inspectors-in-iraq-to-aid.html.

99. "After 1995, Iraqi leaders solidified their belief that inspections would not end and sanctions would not be lifted, especially when Iraq's new disclosures did not lead to any relief from restrictions." CIA, "Misreading Intentions," 7.

100. CIA, "Misreading Intentions," 7.

101. CIA, "Misreading Intentions," i. These suspicions were even further exacerbated in 1997 when Richard Butler took over the directorship of UNSCOM from Rolf Ekéus and the Iraqis accused him of facilitating CIA electronic surveillance, essentially a perception that UNSCOM was collecting targeting data for a future US attack (ElBaradei 2011, 33).

102. Comprehensive Report of the Special Advisor to the DCI on Iraq's WMD (Duelfer Report), vol. 1 (Washington, DC: Central Intelligence Agency, 2004), 61, https://www.govinfo.gov/app/details/GPO-DUELFERREPORT (quoted in Palkki and Smith 2012, 283).

103. CIA, "Misreading Intentions," 8.
104. SH-SHTP-A-000–789, "Meeting between Saddam Hussein and the Revolutionary Council Regarding the Sanctions Placed on Iraq and Tariq Aziz's Trip to the UN Security Council," ca. November 8, 1995, to December 28, 1995, CRRC.
105. SH-SHTP-A-000–789.
106. David Rieff, "Were Sanctions Right?," *New York Times*, July 27, 2003, https://www.nytimes.com/2003/07/27/magazine/were-sanctions-right.html.
107. Rolf Ekéus, unpublished paper, summarized in Sagan 2013, 6.
108. Madeleine K. Albright, "Policy Speech on Iraq," Georgetown University, March 26, 1997.
109. Albright, "Policy Speech on Iraq."
110. William J. Clinton, "Statement on Signing the Iraq Liberation Act of 1998," October 31, 1998, American Presidency Project, https://www.presidency.ucsb.edu/documents/statement-signing-the-iraq-liberation-act-1998.
111. Palkki and Smith 2012, 283. Litwak (2007, 121) similarly argues that US policymakers' statements about pursuing regime change in Iraq "priced the administration out of the reassurance market."
112. CIA, "Misreading Intentions," 7.
113. Fuhrmann and Kreps 2010, dataset.
114. CIA, "Misreading Intentions," 8.
115. SH-SHTP-A-001–198, "Saddam and His Advisers Discussing United Nations Rules and the UN Security Council," n.d. (ca. late November 1998), in Woods, Palkki, and Stout 2011, 292–95.
116. SH-SHTP-A-001–198.
117. Obeidi and Pitzer 2004, 175.
118. Quoted in Blix 2004, 36.
119. Rice 2011, 172.
120. Rice 2011, 172 (see also Bush 2010, 232).
121. Quoted in Leffler 2023, 105.
122. Leffler 2003, 246.
123. Coll 2024, 423.
124. Advisers such as Jafar D. Jafar were, according to Braut-Hegghammer (2020, 85), "increasingly concerned that the United States would launch a war."
125. Blix 2004, 10.
126. "First Stop, Iraq," *Time*, March 31, 2002 (see also Butt 2019).
127. Quoted in Leffler 2023, 117.
128. Richard N. Haass, "Haass: Former Bush Aide's Dilemma over Iraq," *Newsweek*, May 1, 2009, https://www.newsweek.com/haass-former-bush-aides-dilemma-over-iraq-79875.
129. Leffler 2023, 191.
130. Bush 2010, 242 (quoted in Coll 2024, 441).
131. Leffler 2023, 184.
132. Leffler 2023, 199.
133. "The Final Ultimatum," *Economist*, March 18, 2003, https://www.economist.com/news/2003/03/18/the-final-ultimatum. Why the administration even issued an ultimatum right before the invasion is unclear. There was reportedly some debate about whether to issue an ultimatum at all since the war plan was to be executed anyway.
134. Woodward 2004, 369. Earlier, on January 31, 2003, after meeting with military leaders and his cabinet, President Bush resolved that military preparations should no longer be in support of pressuring Saddam but aimed at their ultimate execution in mid-March (Leffler 2023, 192).
135. Leffler (2023) pushes back against the rush-to-war theory.
136. Obeidi and Pitzer 2004, 9–10.
137. Obeidi and Pitzer 2004, 191.
138. ElBaradei 2011, 2.
139. CIA, "Misreading Intentions," 8.
140. Rieff, "Were Sanctions Right?"

4. "They Will Laugh at Us"

1. Braut-Hegghammer 2016.
2. Tobey 2018, 10.
3. Braut-Hegghammer 2016, 5.
4. See also Bowen 2006, 50–51.
5. "Transcript of the Candidates' First Debate in the Presidential Campaign," *New York Times*, October 1, 2004.
6. Cheney remarks in vice presidential debate in 2004, quoted in Jentleson and Whytock 2005/2006.
7. "Vice President's Remarks and Q&A at a Town Hall Meeting in Minnesota, Cabela's Sporting Goods Store, East Grand Forks, Minnesota," August 6, 2004, Office of the Vice President, https://georgewbush-whitehouse.archives.gov/news/releases/2004/08/20040806-15. html (see also "Vice President's Remarks in Xenia, Ohio, Greene County Fair & Expo Center, Xenia, Ohio," October 19, 2004, Office of the Vice President, https://georgewbush-whitehouse. archives.gov/news/releases/2004/10/20041019-12.html).
8. Braut-Hegghammer 2016, 183.
9. Hymans 2012, 242–43.
10. Bowen 2006, 33.
11. The Libyans recognized that they had purchased low-quality goods from the North Koreans as well. In negotiations, when Donald Mahley, a deputy assistant secretary in the State Department's Nonproliferation Bureau, asked the Libyans for a statement saying that they would not buy any more North Korean missiles, a Libyan official responded, "If you think we are going to buy that crap again, you are mistaken" (William H. Tobey, interview by author, March 14, 2018, Cambridge, MA).
12. Bowen 2006, 8.
13. Qaddafi often invoked Israeli nuclear weapons as a justification for a countervailing "Arab bomb" (Bowen 2006, 21). Braut-Hegghammer (2016, 138–40) calls it a "desire for regional status," especially considering the Israeli nuclear arsenal.
14. Braut-Hegghammer 2016, 139.
15. Tobey 2014.
16. Braut-Hegghammer (2016, 141) says there is no evidence that Abdessalam Jalloud (a Libyan representative sent to China in 1970) asked explicitly to buy a nuclear weapon at this time. Other sources claim Libya offered to buy a nuclear weapon (Cirincione, Wolfstahl, and Rajkumar 2002, 307).
17. Gerzhoy 2014, 127. Braut-Hegghammer (2016, 159) puts the figure at $133 million and 450 tons of yellowcake uranium.
18. This Libya-Pakistan arrangement is worthy of future research. The details of the episode are murky.
19. Braut-Hegghammer 2016, 141.
20. "Libya Country Profile," Nuclear Threat Initiative (hereafter NTI), https://www.nti. org/learn/countries/libya/; Braut-Hegghammer 2016, 158.
21. Libya acquired Soviet fighters and bombers, tanks, and missiles (Bowen 2006, 15).
22. Braut-Hegghammer 2016, 163.
23. Libya had already signed the NPT in 1968 under the government of King Idris.
24. Braut-Hegghammer 2016, 161.
25. Braut-Hegghammer 2016, 161.
26. "Travel Report: Programming Mission to Libya, 1–8 November 1981," interoffice memorandum, November 9, 1981, 2–3, IAEA Archives, Vienna.
27. "Travel Report."
28. Gerzhoy 2014, 128.
29. Gerzhoy 2014, 128.
30. Tobey 2014.
31. Reynolds and Wan (2012, 65) attribute the lack of official nuclear proliferation justification for sanctions to deep secrecy. They write, "Libya's efforts to acquire WMD officially provided an additional justification for sanctions only toward the end of the 1990s."

32. Braut-Hegghammer 2016, 179, citing US Directorate of Intelligence, *The Libyan Nuclear Program: A Technical Perspective*, intelligence assessment, February 1985, National Security Archive, 1–2.

33. Braut-Hegghammer 2016, 171, citing Bowen 2006, 15.

34. Braut-Hegghammer 2016, 185.

35. Braut-Hegghammer 2016, 187.

36. Japan is identified as the supplier in Braut-Hegghammer 2016, but Japan was not identified as the supplier in the IAEA report on Libya's program.

37. Braut-Hegghammer 2016, 189.

38. Braut-Hegghammer 2016, 189. This "undisclosed" country was likely China or the Soviet Union ("Libya Country Profile," NTI).

39. Bowen 2006, 16.

40. "Libya Country Profile," NTI.

41. Although I focus on nuclear technology, constraining Libya's chemical and biological weapons ambitions was also part of US coercive strategy. Reagan publicly said Libya was manufacturing chemical weapons at a facility in Rabta in December 1987. George H. W. Bush threatened military action against Libyan chemical weapons facilities in 1991. And in 1996 Secretary of Defense William Perry threatened military strikes against a Libyan chemical weapons facility under construction.

42. The whereabouts and histories of these components were discovered by IAEA inspectors in 2004 (Bowen 2006, 22). As additional evidence that the nuclear program did not slow down, it has been reported that in the 1980s a "foreign expert," a former employee of a German firm, worked at the Tajoura facility on a project to produce gas centrifuges. According to Libyan disclosures to the IAEA, this "foreign expert" departed in 1992. From 1984 to 1990, Libya experimented with uranium targets at Tajoura, ultimately extracting small amounts of plutonium from two of them (see "Libya Country Profile," NTI; Bowen 2006, 32–33).

43. Quoted in Zimmermann 1994, 203. Braut-Hegghammer (2016, 170) also claims that Reagan altered US policy on Libya to be one of regime change.

44. Gerzhoy 2014, 133.

45. Braut-Hegghammer 2006, 53, citing an interview with a "formerly central figure in the Revolutionary Committee system," Tripoli, June 15, 2005.

46. Burns 2019, 191.

47. UNSC Resolutions 748 (1992) and 831 (1993) were the only multilateral sanctions against Libya. The measures imposed an arms embargo, an air embargo, travel restrictions, oil-sector restrictions, and a financial assets freeze. Nuclear weapons technologies would have fallen under the arms embargo in Resolution 748, but neither resolution banned peaceful nuclear cooperation. These UN sanctions were lifted in 2003 with Resolution 1506 (Reynolds and Wan 2012, 65).

48. In 1992 Libya through back channels (Undersecretary of State William Rogers and Senator Gary Hart) offered a compromise to allow the two indicted Lockerbie bombing suspects to be tried in a neutral country. Jentleson and Whytock (2005/2006) attribute the Bush administration's decision not to engage to pressure from Lockerbie victims' families.

49. The legislation sanctioned any foreign firm with significant ($40 million, later $20 million) investments in Libya or Iran's oil sectors. The Iran-Libya Sanctions Act was renewed in 2001 (Reynolds and Wan 2012, 64).

50. Reynolds and Wan 2012, 64.

51. Braut-Hegghammer 2016, 196.

52. A. Q. Khan supposedly sold the rest of the P-1 centrifuges to Iran in 1993. In addition to its black-market connection to Khan, Libya also connected with South Africa. When the South African nuclear weapons program was dismantled at the end of the 1980s, some South African companies engaged in illicit trade with Libya. One company built a UF6 feeding system in Libya and was exposed when the Khan network was undone in 2003 (Heinonen 2014, 172).

53. Braut-Hegghammer 2016, 203.

54. This "reinvigoration" language comes from the February 2004 IAEA report. Braut-Hegghammer (2016) pushes back against this narrative, arguing that the new strategic effort was fairly consistent from the 1989 reorganization onward.

55. Braut-Hegghammer 2006, 53, citing an interview conducted in Tripoli, June 16, 2005.

56. Braut-Hegghammer 2006, 53, citing an interview conducted in Tripoli, June 15, 2005.

57. The Bush administration understood the same barriers: "It needed to be one step completed, before the next could begin," said a senior State Department official involved in talks with Libya (quoted in Ron Suskind, "The Tyrant Who Came in from the Cold," *Washington Monthly*, October 1, 2006, 19–23).

58. Burns 2019, 193.

59. Bowen 2006, 59–61; Flynt L. Leverett, "Why Libya Gave Up the Bomb," Brookings, January 23, 2004, https://www.brookings.edu/opinions/why-libya-gave-up-on-the-bomb/.

60. Burns 2019, 191.

61. The Lockerbie trials of the indicted Libyans had concluded in January 2001. Abdel Baset Ali Al-Megrahi was convicted, and Lamen Khalifa Fhimah was acquitted.

62. US assistant secretary of state Martin Indyk claimed that the Libyans officially put the chemical weapons program on the table (with Qaddafi's permission) at this first meeting in Geneva. The US agreed but countered that the negotiations should address Lockerbie before tackling WMD issues. The US also had Libya agree to stop lobbying for sanctions relief if the negotiations were to continue (Braut-Hegghammer 2016, 211).

63. Braut-Hegghammer 2016, 211.

64. Reynolds and Wan 2012, 66.

65. William H. Tobey, interview by author, March 14, 2018, Cambridge, MA.

66. Cigar 2012.

67. Suskind, "Tyrant Who Came in from the Cold."

68. Braut-Hegghammer 2016, 204.

69. The UF6 reportedly originated in North Korea (David Sanger and William Broad, "Evidence Is Cited Linking Koreans to Libya Uranium," *New York Times*, May 23, 2004, https://www.nytimes.com/2004/05/23/world/evidence-is-cited-linking-koreans-to-libya-uranium.html).

70. Busch and Pilat 2017, 117.

71. Burns 2019, 191.

72. Libya kicked out the Abu Nidal terrorist organization in 1999 and cooperated with regional partners (Egypt, Jordan, and Yemen) on counterterrorism. After 9/11 Tripoli provided intelligence to Washington on al-Qaeda threats (Bowen 2006, 57).

73. In May 2002 they agreed to an amount of up to $10 million per family. Payments were made over the next few years as litigation continued. Seif al Islam Qaddafi arranged for the Qaddafi International Foundation for Charity Associations to pay the restitution, which "the regime itself claimed did not come from the government" (Bowen 2006, 62). Libya's letter accepting responsibility for the bombing was submitted to the UNSC in August 2003.

74. Burns 2019, 192.

75. Burns 2019, 194.

76. Braut-Hegghammer 2016, 212.

77. Tobey 2014.

78. Corera 2006.

79. Bowen 2006, 54.

80. Burns 2019, 191. In a meeting with President George W. Bush in 2003, Stephen Kappes, a key US negotiator involved in secret talks with Qaddafi, noted Libya's desperate need for foreign investment, which the United States could offer (Tenet and Harlow 2007, 293).

81. Bowen 2006, 54.

82. Braut-Hegghammer, citing an interview with the British ambassador to Libya, Anthony Layden, similarly points out that "with regards to persuading Libya to end its nuclear programme, the important decisions appear to have been made before the invasion of Iraq in March 2003" (Braut-Hegghammer 2006, 53).

83. Scott MacLeod, "Behind Gaddafi's Diplomatic Turnaround," *Time*, May 18, 2006, https://content.time.com/time/world/article/0,8599,1195852,00.html.

84. Charles Lambroschini, "Interview: Libyan Leader Muammar al-Qaddafi," *Le Figaro*, March 11, 2003, https://www.worldpress.org/europe/989.cfm.

85. Lambroschini, "Interview."

86. Pargeter 2012, 188.

87. Pargeter 2012, 187.

88. Gordon Corera, "Behind Closed Doors: The Bewildering Dance between Gaddafi and MI6," *Independent*, August 25, 2011, https://www.independent.co.uk/news/world/africa/behind-closed-doors-the-bewildering-dance-between-gaddafi-and-mi6-2343218.html.

89. Corera, 184–85.

90. Tobey 2014.

91. Suskind, "Tyrant Who Came in from the Cold." Tenet and Harlow (2007, 293) write that Tenet finally briefed Colin Powell, Richard Armitage, and William Burns on the Libya negotiations sometime after Kappes's September meeting with Qaddafi.

92. Tobey 2014.

93. Tobey, interview, March 14, 2018.

94. Bowen 2006, 65.

95. ElBaradei 2011, 150.

96. Leverett, "Why Libya Gave Up the Bomb."

97. Jentleson and Whytock 2005/2006, 76.

98. The secrecy is even more puzzling as a choice, given scholarship that expects publicity of norm violators for the purpose of enforcing and defending normative regimes (Carnegie and Carson 2018). I find no evidence in the record that concealing the seizure of the *BBC China* was meant to uphold the perception that the nonproliferation norm remained strong. According to Carnegie and Carson's theory, the United States should have publicized Libya's violation of nonproliferation norms. This is because Libya was likely to comply with US demands and because there was a low risk of reactive proliferation in the region. See their coding of Libya in Carnegie and Carson 2018, appendix, 20, https://acarson.uchicago.edu/sites/acarson.uchicago.edu/files/uploads/Spotlight_IO_publish.pdf.

99. In light of newly available clandestine intelligence, the CIA in late 2001 revised its assessment of the Libyan program. Reporting from Congress indicates that a still-classified 1999 national intelligence estimate had set 2015 as the earliest threshold by which Libya might be capable of building a bomb (see *Report of the Commission on the Intelligence Capabilities of the United States Regarding Weapons of Mass Destruction* [Washington, DC: Government Printing Office, 2005], 260). In December 2001 the CIA warned in a secret (i.e., nonpublic) assessment that Libya could "produce enough weapons grade uranium for a nuclear warhead as early as 2007." With the help of their moles inside the Khan network, the CIA and MI6 had gained critical insight into Khan's activities in Dubai and Malaysia in 2001 and 2002, where he was arranging for the production of equipment to be delivered to Tripoli. Until early 2003 the CIA did not provide US leaders with the kind of high-confidence information that would have allowed Washington to go public about Libya's misbehavior.

100. CIA, "Attachment A: Unclassified Report to Congress on the Acquisition of Technology Relating to Weapons of Mass Destruction and Advanced Conventional Munitions," January 1–June 30, 2003, Federation of American Scientists, https://fas.org/irp/threat/cia_jan_jun2003.htm.

101. CIA, "Attachment A: Unclassified Report to Congress on the Acquisition of Technology Relating to Weapons of Mass Destruction and Advanced Conventional Munitions," July 1–December 31, 2003, Federation of American Scientists, https://irp.fas.org/threat/july_dec2003.htm (see also Office of the Director of National Intelligence, "Unclassified Report to Congress on the Acquisition of Technology Relating to Weapons of Mass Destruction and Advanced Conventional Munitions," January 1–December 31, 2004, ODNI, 3–4, https://www.dni.gov/files/documents/Newsroom/Reports%20and%20Pubs/2004_unclass_report_to_NIC_DO_16Nov04.pdf).

102. "Libya's disclosures revealed that the A. Q. Khan network had provided Libya with designs for Pakistan's older centrifuges, as well as designs for more advanced and efficient

models, and components" (CIA, "Attachment A: Unclassified Report to Congress on the Acquisition of Technology Relating to Weapons of Mass Destruction and Advanced Conventional Munitions," July 1–December 31, 2003, Federation of American Scientists, https://irp.fas.org/threat/july_dec2003.htm).

103. Bowen 2006, 20.

104. Tobey 2014.

105. Raviv and Melman 2014.

106. *The Committee of Enquiry into the Intelligence System in Light of the War in Iraq*, March 2004, http://www.knesset.gov.il/committees/eng/docs/intelligence_complete.pdf (see also Nutt and Pauly 2021; Nutt 2019; Katz 2019, 33).

107. Some accounts report that the United States shared some vague intelligence with Israel early on in their uncovering of the A. Q. Khan network in 2002. We know about this because of complaints that a September 2002 public statement by Ariel Sharon about potential Libyan proliferation caused consternation in Washington. Regardless of what or if anything was shared, all accounts report that the US did not share anything else with Israel after the Sharon comments. The United States kept Israel in the dark for the duration of the coercive bargaining over WMDs that began in 2003 (see "Libya Denies Sharon Charge It Is Developing Nuclear Weapons," *Haaretz*, September 5, 2002; Ze'ev Schiff, "Libya Intelligence Failure Needs Answers," *Haaretz*, March 31, 2004; Yossi Melman, "Spy vs Spy," *Haaretz*, February 17, 2005, https://www.haaretz.com/2005-02-17/ty-article/spy-vs-spy/0000017f-da7b-d938-a17f-fe7bbeaf0000; Amos Harel, "Senior Officer: Sharon's Slip of the Tongue Made US Hide Libya Talks," *Haaretz*, April 1, 2004, https://www.haaretz.com/2004-04-01/ty-article/senior-officer-sharons-slip-of-the-tongue-made-u-s-hide-libya-talks/0000017f-dbd9-d3a5-af7f-fbff73d00000; "Israel: Army Officer Says No Apparent Change in Hamas, Hezbollah Policy," BBC Monitoring Middle East, March 31, 2004).

108. Corera, "Behind Closed Doors."

109. *Report of the Commission on the Intelligence Capabilities of the United States Regarding Weapons of Mass Destruction*, 257.

110. *Report of the Commission on the Intelligence Capabilities of the United States Regarding Weapons of Mass Destruction*, 260.

111. Burns 2019, 193.

112. Tobey 2014.

113. Tobey 2018, 3.

114. Tobey 2018, 3.

115. The ship was tracked from Malaysia to Dubai and then rerouted to Italy from its planned route of Dubai to Tripoli.

116. Tobey 2014.

117. Tobey, interview, March 14, 2018.

118. Tenet and Harlow 2007, 293–94.

119. Joseph 2009, 7.

120. David Ignatius, "The CIA's Mission Possible," *Washington Post*, March 10, 2006, https://www.washingtonpost.com/archive/opinions/2006/05/10/the-cias-mission-possible/aae3360d-6b1a-49f5-b90d-d1ba757833ac/.

121. Tobey 2014.

122. MacLeod, "Behind Gaddafi's Diplomatic Turnaround." Word of the *BBC China*'s seizure and its broader significance did not surface in the world press for almost two months— this is despite the fact that governments and security services in Germany, Italy, the United Kingdom, and the United States were involved in the operation. On December 31, twelve days after Libya's announcement about voluntary disarmament, the *Wall Street Journal* finally broke the news about the high-seas interception of the illicit centrifuges, citing unnamed "U.S. officials" ("Cargo Seizure Fueled Libya Arms Shift," *Wall Street Journal*, December 31, 2003).

123. *Report of the Commission on the Intelligence Capabilities of the United States regarding Weapons of Mass Destruction*, 258. In his memoir, the State Department's William Burns echoes these sentiments (Burns 2019, 192).

124. House of Commons, *Review of Intelligence on Weapons of Mass Destruction* (London: The Stationery Office, 2004), 21.

125. Ten days is the length reported in Corera, "Behind Closed Doors."
126. Tobey 2014.
127. Tenet and Harlow 2007, 295. This meeting took place on October 21.
128. CIA, "The Worldwide Threat 2004: Challenges in a Changing Global Context," testimony of Director of Central Intelligence George Tenet before the Senate Select Committee on Intelligence, February 24, 2004, https://media.nti.org/pdfs/10.pdf.
129. Albright 2010, 211 (see also Bowen 2006, 66, which says that the BBC China episode "demonstrated to the Libyans that their British and American partners trusted them enough to share very sensitive information at a time when the A. Q. Khan network remained under investigation and its existence had yet to be publicly acknowledged.").
130. Correra 2006,189–90.
131. Correra 2006, 296.
132. Deborah Haynes, "How a Little Cotswold Hotel Became the Rendezvous for Gaddafi's Nuclear Climbdown," Times (London), November 1, 2011, https://www.proquest.com/docview/901188441/27F93D4F0AE44539PQ/1.
133. Haynes, "How a Little Cotswold Hotel."
134. Kappes is quoted in Haynes, "How a Little Cotswold Hotel."
135. Haynes, "How a Little Cotswold Hotel."
136. Haynes, "How a Little Cotswold Hotel."
137. Corera, "Behind Closed Doors," reports that the second technical visit began on December 9.
138. Braut-Hegghammer 2016, 215.
139. Braut-Hegghammer, Tobey, and others agree the call took place on December 17.
140. Tobey, interview, March 14, 2018.
141. Tobey 2014. Joseph (2009, 63) recounts the same fears expressed by Qaddafi on the call: concern about "the appearance of the Libyan decision being portrayed as caving in to pressure" and "the prospect that Libya would be attacked because it had now admitted that it possessed WMD programs."
142. Tobey 2014. According to another account, Blair gave "reassurances that if Gadaffi supported the statement there would be an immediate and positive response from London and Washington. But it had to be absolutely clear what Gadaffi was saying. No more WMD" (Peter Beaumont, Kamal Ahmed, and Martin Bright, "The Meeting That Brought Libya in from the Cold," Observer, December 21, 2003, http://www.globalsecurity.org/org/news/2003/031221-libya-meeting.htm).
143. Tobey 2014.
144. "Libyan WMD: Tripoli's Statement in Full," BBC, December 20, 2003, http://news.bbc.co.uk/2/hi/africa/3336139.stm.
145. Tobey 2014.
146. Tobey, interview, March 14, 2018.
147. "Full Transcript: Blair's Libya Statement," BBC, December 19, 2003, http://news.bbc.co.uk/2/hi/uk_news/politics/3336073.stm.
148. "Bush's Remarks on Arms Agreement with Libya," New York Times, December 19, 2003, http://www.nytimes.com/2003/12/19/international/bushs-remarks-on-arms-agreement-with-libya.html.
149. For details of how the United States pulled off this massive logistical effort, see Tobey 2014.
150. Tobey, interview, March 14, 2018.
151. Joseph 2009, 17.
152. Burns 2019, 195.
153. Burns 2019, 195. "I always thought that was part of the answer but only part, and not necessarily the decisive part," Burns concluded.
154. "Communication Received from the Permanent Mission of the Libyan Arab Jamahiriya to the Agency," INFCIRC/679, July 26, 2006, IAEA Archives, Vienna. The letter was signed by the Libyan secretary of European Affairs, Abdulai Ibrahim Al Obidi, and the British minister of state at the Foreign and Commonwealth Office, Kim Howells. The letter also

reiterated the application of a security assurance issued by Britain in 1995 to come to the aid of non-nuclear-weapons states that are victims of nuclear attack. The assurance was extended to chemical and biological weapons as well.

155. Megan Specia and David E. Sanger, "How the 'Libya Model' Became a Sticking Point in North Korea Nuclear Talks," *New York Times*, May 16, 2018, https://www.nytimes.com/2018/05/16/world/asia/north-korea-libya-model.html.

156. Clinton 2014; Rice 2019; Power 2019; Rhodes 2018; Burns 2019; Obama 2020.

157. Rice 2019, 283.

158. Obama 2020, 657.

159. Burns 2019, 313.

160. Rhodes 2018, 115.

161. The true causes of the 2011 intervention are even more complicated, especially as Obama himself describes how in his decision to intervene he felt "jammed" by European allies who had gone public with calls for intervention.

162. Obama 2020, 660. The president's team did not even wait to fix a malfunctioning mobile communication system while on a trip to Brazil in order to give the "go" order over a secure line. They used an unsecured cell phone instead.

163. Tobey, interview, March 14, 2018.

164. Tobey, interview, March 14, 2018.

165. Bowen 2006, 59–60.

166. Tobey, interview, March 14, 2018.

167. The timing of Saddam's capture was exogenous to negotiations with Libya.

168. MacLeod, "Behind Gaddafi's Diplomatic Turnaround."

5. "We Knew That They Knew We Knew"

1. Faith Karimi and Deirdre Walsh, "Iran: No Signing Final Nuclear Deal unless Economic Sanctions Are Lifted," CNN, April 9, 2015, http://www.cnn.com/2015/04/09/politics/iran-nuclear-bill/.

2. In Nicholas Miller's account, the credibility of threats alone explains Iranian decisions: Tehran pursued the bomb when it was less dependent upon the Western economy and only ceased pursuit when a tough multilateral sanctions regime coalesced (Miller 2018).

3. In 2013 Jervis assessed the barriers to credible threats and promises in the Iran case. Some of the promises he discusses are carrots, and some are better conceptualized as coercive assurance (Jervis 2013).

4. Semira N. Nikou, "Timeline of Iran's Nuclear Activities," United States Institute of Peace, August 17, 2021, https://iranprimer.usip.org/resource/timeline-irans-nuclear-activities.

5. Bleek 2017. As a Western ally, Iran pursued its ambitions through links to major nuclear suppliers. In 1967 the United States supplied Tehran with a nuclear research center and a five-megawatt research reactor (the Tehran Research Reactor). Tehran invested in a French enrichment firm and bought a stake in a Namibian uranium mine. The shah also purchased yellowcake from South Africa ("Iran: Country Profile," NTI, updated May 2018, https://www.nti.org/learn/countries/iran/nuclear/).

6. Miller 2018, 218. Tabatabai cites Akbar Etemad as well (Tabatabai 2017, 227).

7. Miller 2018, 225.

8. Construction at ongoing nuclear projects such as Bushehr was suspended ("Iran: Country Profile").

9. Debs and Monteiro 2017b; Tabatabai 2017, 235 (see also Miller 2018, 227, which cites Bowen and Kidd 2004, 263–64).

10. Director General, IAEA Board of Governors, *Implementation of the NPT Safeguards Agreement in the Islamic Republic of Iran*, GOV/2003/75, November 10, 2003, annex 1, 8.

11. Michael Laufer, "A. Q. Khan Nuclear Chronology," Carnegie Endowment for International Peace, September 7, 2005, https://carnegieendowment.org/2005/09/07/a.-q.-khan-

nuclear-chronology-pub-17420; Fitzpatrick 2006, 529 (see also IAEA Board of Governors, GOV/OR.1148, IAEA Archives, Vienna).

12. "Iran: Country Profile."

13. Fitzpatrick 2006, 533.

14. IAEA Board of Governors, *Implementation of the NPT Safeguards*, GOV/2003/75, annex 1, 1.

15. A project begun and abandoned by Germany.

16. Miller 2018, 228.

17. Miller 2018, 229.

18. Miller 2018, 230.

19. Fitzpatrick 2006, 528.

20. On motivations, see also Miller 2018, 227.

21. Tabatabai 2017, 235–36. Tabatabai suggested that this narrative "politicized" the issue of enrichment such that it was more difficult for Iranian negotiators to make concessions on enrichment.

22. Nader 2012, 213.

23. Reynolds and Wan 2012, 78.

24. Reynolds and Wan 2012, 78.

25. "Iran: Country Profile"; Reynolds and Wan 2012, 78.

26. Miller 2018, 229.

27. Major US policies included the Foreign Appropriations Act (1990), the Iran-Iraq Arms Non-Proliferation Act (1992, amended in 1996), the Iran-Libya Sanctions Act (1996), the Iran Nonproliferation Act (2000), and Executive Orders 12938, 12957, 12959, and 13059 (Samore 2015; Reynolds and Wan 2012, 78).

28. Miller 2018, 229, citing Chris Hedges, "Iran May Be Able to Build an Atomic Bomb in 5 Years, U.S. and Israeli Officials Fear," *New York Times*, January 5, 1995, https://www.nytimes.com/1995/01/05/world/iran-may-be-able-build-atomic-bomb-5-years-us-israeli-officials-fear.html.

29. The Libya sanctions were lifted separately in 2006 (Samore 2015; Nader 2012, 214).

30. Miller 2018, 230.

31. Miller 2018, 231 (see also "Iran: Country Profile").

32. "Iran: Country Profile."

33. Iran, however, "disagreed with the IAEA on the actual scope of the suspension and continued to produce uranium hexafluoride, the feed material for gas centrifuges" (Reynolds and Wan 2012, 80).

34. Director General, IAEA Board of Governors, *Implementation of the NPT Safeguards Agreement and Relevant Provisions of Security Council Resolutions in the Islamic Republic of Iran*, GOV/2011/65, November 8, 2011, annex, 5.

35. Money was also allocated for the acquisition of HEU from abroad, but there is no evidence HEU was actually acquired from abroad (Aaron Arnold's notes from Israeli intelligence briefing, unpublished, January 2019).

36. Arnold et al. 2019. Some experts have argued that over the course of the extended Iranian nuclear crisis, Tehran never intended to pursue nuclear weapons or, at least, that nuclear weapons research was limited to a rogue IRGC operation and compartmentalized without the support or knowledge of civilian leadership (see, e.g., Nader 2012, 220). This theory of the case is contradicted by evidence from the atomic archive. For more details on the former Iranian nuclear weapons program, see this chapter's section "Concluding the JCPOA with Shared Knowledge."

37. National Intelligence Council, "Iran: Nuclear Intentions and Capabilities," NIE, November 2007, https://www.dni.gov/files/documents/Newsroom/Reports%20and%20Pubs/20071203_release.pdf (see also "Background Briefing with Senior U.S. Officials on Syria's Covert Nuclear Reactor and North Korea's Involvement," April 24, 2008, https://fas.org/irp/news/2008/04/odni042408.pdf). Sometimes scholars take this to mean that Iran suspended its pursuit of the bomb in 2003, which is not accurate. Iran continued to hedge by developing its fissile-material production capacity. It was not until 2015 that Iran accepted verifiable limits on its nuclear ambitions.

38. Kreps and Pasha 2012, 200.

39. Quoted in Kreps and Pasha 2012, 198.

40. Kreps and Pasha 2012, 200. Iran seems to have feared US military force until the United States became bogged down fighting insurgencies in Iraq and Afghanistan. "The US is stuck up in Iraq and cannot dare attack Iran," said a member of the Iranian Parliament, Parviz Sourori (quoted in Kreps and Pasha 2012, 202).

41. Patrikarakos 2012, 188; de Bellaigue 2007, 55; Mousavian 2012, 99–100.

42. This so-called atomic archive evidence is filtered through an intelligence community hostile to Iran and should be interpreted as such. See the section of this chapter "Concluding the JCPOA with Shared Knowledge" for more discussion of these documents and their biases.

43. Arnold et al. 2019.

44. Arnold et al. 2019.

45. The IAEA's 2015 PMD report indicated that "from around 2006 onwards, Iran embarked on a four-year programme on the validation of shock-driven neutron source design, including through the use of non-nuclear material to avoid contamination" (IAEA Board of Governors, *Final Assessment on Past and Present Outstanding Issues Regarding Iran's Nuclear Programme*, GOV/2015/68, December 2, 2015, 12; see also Arnold et al. 2019).

46. See IAEA Board of Governors, *Implementation of the NPT Safeguards*, GOV/2011/65, annex, 5; IAEA Board of Governors, *Final Assessment*," GOV/2015/68, 15.

47. ElBaradei says the "grand bargain" offer from Iran was real: "I had brought with me a written message from Hassan Rowhani, on behalf of the Iranian regime, saying that Iran was ready to enter into dialogue with the United States on all issues, including both Iran's nuclear program and broader matters of regional security. The message was on a single sheet of paper, without a letterhead or signature, as it had been delivered to me. I handed the note to Bush, explaining its origin" (see ElBaradei 2011, 132).

48. Iran's Proposal for a "Grand Bargain," *New York Times*, https://static01.nyt.com/packages/pdf/opinion/20070429_iran-memo-3.pdf.

49. Much remains in doubt about the 2003 grand bargain offer. Nicholas Miller (2018, 231) takes the offer seriously (see also Litwak 2008, 101–2). However, William Tobey, who served on the NSC staff at the time, recalled, "I don't know anyone who took the 2003 grand bargain letter seriously. It was not bona fide. The Iranians could have proposed a bargain in a bona fide way—there were bona fide methods of passing along the message—but they did not do so" (William H. Tobey, interview by author, March 14, 2018, Cambridge, MA).

50. Miller 2018, 232.

51. Miller 2018, 232.

52. Notably, during the 2003–5 E3 talks, Hassan Rouhani was the secretary of the Supreme National Security Council, and Javad Zarif was the ambassador to the United Nations. Both men also played a key role in negotiations that led to the JCPOA in 2015.

53. "Iran: Country Profile."

54. Tabatabai 2017, 228.

55. IAEA Board of Governors, "Record of the 1071st Meeting," June 18, 2003, GOV/OR.1071, 9–10, IAEA Archives, Vienna.

56. IAEA Board of Governors, "Record of the 1115th Meeting," November 29, 2004, GOV/OR.1115, 14, IAEA Archives, Vienna.

57. IAEA Board of Governors, "Record of the 1072nd Meeting," June 19, 2003, GOV/OR.1072, 9, IAEA Archives, Vienna.

58. IAEA Board of Governors, "Record of the 1077th Meeting," September 9, 2003, GOV/OR.1077, 11, IAEA Archives, Vienna.

59. IAEA Board of Governors, "Record of the 1109th Meeting," September 18, 2004, GOV/OR.1109, 16–17, IAEA Archives, Vienna.

60. ElBaradei 2011, 211–12.

61. Braut-Hegghammer 2020.

62. IAEA Board of Governors, "Record of the 1071st Meeting," 9–10.

63. IAEA Board of Governors, "Record of the 1081st Meeting," September 12, 2003, GOV/OR.1081, 1, IAEA Archives, Vienna.

64. Iranian presidential elections are not actually democratic. Freedom House writes that the elections "fall short of democratic standards due in part to the influence of the hard-line Guardian Council, an unelected body that disqualifies all candidates it deems insufficiently loyal to the clerical establishment. Ultimate power rests in the hands of the country's supreme leader." See "Iran Profile," Freedom House, https://freedomhouse.org/report/freedom-world/2018/iran.

65. Miller 2018, 233.

66. "Iran: Country Profile."

67. The IAEA board of governors discussed a September 24, 2005, resolution (GOV/2005/77) that found Iran to be in noncompliance but delayed referral as a last chance for Iran (IAEA Board of Governors, "Record of the 1150th Meeting," GOV/OR.1150, IAEA Archives, Vienna).

68. The report on Iran's nuclear program was formally sent to the UNSC on March 8, 2006. For a helpful timeline, see "IAEA and Iran: Chronology of Key Events," IAEA, https://www.iaea.org/newscenter/focus/iran/chronology-of-key-events.

69. Miller 2018, 233.

70. Litwak 2008, 104.

71. Peter Crail, "Iran Presented with Revamped Incentives," *Arms Control Today*, August 7, 2008, https://www.armscontrol.org/act/2008_07-08/IranIncentives.

72. Paul Kerr, "U.S., Allies Await Iran's Response to Nuclear Offer," *Arms Control Today*, July 1, 2006, https://www.armscontrol.org/act/2006_07-08/IranResponse.

73. Kerr, "U.S., Allies Await Iran's Response" (see also Reardon 2012, 17–18).

74. IAEA Board of Governors, "Record of the 1148th Meeting," February 2, 2006, GOV/OR.1148, 8, IAEA Archives, Vienna.

75. Miller (2018, 233), agreeing with Sauer (2007), thinks that the threat of painful UN sanctions was likely not credible because Iran felt it would be protected from the worst by Russia and China.

76. ElBaradei 2011, 195.

77. In November 2007 Director General ElBaradei said the IAEA could not certify the absence of undeclared nuclear material and activities in Iran. Iran's coercers were able to turn this conclusion into another UN sanctions resolution in March 2008, Resolution 1803. In September 2008 Resolution 1835 reaffirmed Resolutions 1696, 1737, 1747, and 1803 (see Miller 2018, 234).

78. Nader 2012, 214.

79. Reynolds and Wan 2012, 79.

80. IAEA Board of Governors, "Record of the 1199th Meeting," November 23, 2007, GOV/OR.1199, 4, IAEA Archives, Vienna.

81. IAEA Board of Governors, "Record of the 1199th Meeting," 4.

82. IAEA Board of Governors, "Record of the 1225th Meeting," November 27, 2008, GOV/OR.1225, 18, IAEA Archives, Vienna.

83. "Videotaped Remarks by the President in Celebration of Nowruz," White House, March 20, 2009, https://obamawhitehouse.archives.gov/blog/2009/03/19/a-new-year-a-new-beginning.

84. Colin Kahl, interview by author, November 2, 2018, Stanford, CA.

85. Ewen MacAskill, "Obama Sent Letter to Khamenei before the Election, Report Says," *Guardian*, June 24, 2009; "Obama Sent Second Letter to Khamenei," *Washington Times*, September 3, 2009; Burns 2019, 348.

86. Sobelman 2018.

87. IAEA Board of Governors, "Record of the 1273rd Meeting," June 9, 2010, GOV/OR.1273, 4, IAEA Archives, Vienna.

88. Reynolds and Wan 2012, 83.

89. The IAEA demand came in a November 2009 board of governors resolution (IAEA Board of Governors, "Implementation of the NPT Safeguards Agreement and Relevant Provisions of Security Council Resolutions 1737 [2006], 1747 [2007], 1803 [2008] and 1835 [2008] in the Islamic Republic of Iran," GOV/2009/82, November 27, 2009, IAEA Archives, Vienna).

90. IAEA Board of Governors, "Record of the 1258th Meeting," November 27, 2009, GOV/OR.1258, 11, IAEA Archives, Vienna.

91. The Stuxnet cyberattack was a brute force attack rather than a coercive strategy chosen by states attempting to prevent Iranian proliferation. However, it was not all that effective. The case of counterproliferation against Iran is overall much more coercive than directly violent (Lindsay 2013). The same can be said of Israel's covert campaign to assassinate Iranian nuclear scientists. Ehud Barak (2018, 417) opaquely writes that "certain steps were taken to delay them [the Iranians]." Much earlier in the case, Iraq also carried out a brute force attack against Iranian nuclear facilities in 1984, during the Iran-Iraq War.

92. The deeply buried enrichment facility near the city of Qom was discovered by US intelligence and only disclosed to the IAEA in September 2009. It had been under development since 2006 and was originally conceived as part of the AMAD Plan (see also Bowen and Brewer 2011, 927–28).

93. Overall, there were six key UNSC resolutions against Iran: 1696 (July 2006), 1737 (December 2006), 1747 (March 2007), 1803 (March 2008), 1835 (June 2010), and 1929 (June 2010) (Samore 2015, 7).

94. Miller 2018, 235.

95. This language was "the potential connection between Iran's revenues derived from its energy sector and the funding of Iran's proliferation sensitive nuclear activities" (Samore 2015, 6).

96. Samore 2015, 8, 9. "SWIFT" stands for the Society for Worldwide Interbank Financial Telecommunication.

97. The United States also closed the "U-turn" loophole, which had allowed non-American banks to conduct transactions with each other in US dollars by clearing them through banks subject to US jurisdiction. Other major American sanctions measures included Executive Orders 13438, 13553, 13572, 13590, 13599, 13606, 13608, 13622, and 13628. And in 2011 the US designated the entire Iranian financial sector a money-laundering concern under the USA PATRIOT Act (Samore 2015, 10–11).

98. Samore 2015, 8.

99. Nephew 2018b; Zarate 2013.

100. Ronen Bergman, "Will Israel Attack Iran?," *New York Times Magazine*, January 25, 2012.

101. "The Iran Primer: Iran's Economy, by the Numbers," United States Institute of Peace, May 11, 2015, https://iranprimer.usip.org/blog/2015/may/11/irans-economy-numbers.

102. "Iran Primer."

103. "Iran Primer."

104. Nephew 2018b, 139.

105. Tabatabai 2017, 233 (see also "Iran Primer.").

106. Such factors include "overreliance on oil exports for revenues; state dominance of the economy where the government or state-affiliated entities own approximately 65–70% of the economy; a poor tax base that provides only 7% of GDP; rampant tax evasion; high subsidies accounting for approximately 18–30% of GDP; the favoring of high-technology industries (e.g. nuclear energy and space technologies) to the detriment of more traditional, labor-intensive industries; and the existence of a black market economy that accounts for approximately 20% of GDP" (Reynolds and Wan 2012, 80).

107. Note that the threats of military force and sanctions were inextricably linked. Partner nations, such as Russia and China, would likely not have agreed to impose and abide by multilateral sanctions had they not believed that the alternative to sanctions was war.

108. Jake Sullivan, telephone interview by author, March 27, 2018.

109. Sullivan, interview, March 27, 2018.

110. Miller 2018, 236; David Sanger and Steven Erlanger, "US Defines Its Demands for Iran Talks," *New York Times*, April 7, 2012.

111. IAEA Board of Governors, *Implementation of the NPT Safeguards*, GOV/2011/65.

112. IAEA Board of Governors, "Record of the 1324th Meeting," March 8, 2012, GOV/OR.1324, 10, IAEA Archives, Vienna.

113. Burns 2019, 376; Kerry 2018, 494–95.

114. *Politico* reports the date of this Oman meeting as July 2012 (Michael Crowley, "Hillary Clinton's Secret Iran Man," *Politico*, April 3, 2015).

115. William Burns and Jake Sullivan made this offer to an Iranian delegation in Oman in August 2013 (Sherman 2018, 34–35; see also Kerry 2018, 496).

116. Sherman 2018, 37.

117. Karl Vick, "The 3 Things the Ayatollah Wanted to Achieve in His Defiant Speech," *Time*, April 15, 2015, http://time.com/3823976/ayatullah-khamenei-speech-iran-negotations/.

118. Karimi and Walsh, "Iran."

119. Tabatabai 2017, 238.

120. Kay Serjoie, "U.S. Cannot Be Trusted, Iran's Supreme Leader Says," *Time*, April 9, 2015, http://time.com/3815110/us-iran-khamenei-lausanne/.

121. Sherman 2018, 26.

122. Sherman 2018, 63.

123. Burns 2019, 361.

124. Sullivan, interview, March 27, 2018.

125. Vaez 2013.

126. Samore 2015, 19.

127. Robert Einhorn, interview by author, March 22, 2018, Washington, DC.

128. Gary Samore, interview by author, February 26, 2019, Cambridge, MA.

129. Amb. Wendy Sherman, interview by author, March 18, 2019, Cambridge, MA.

130. Samore, interview, February 26, 2019.

131. The basis of this money-laundering charge was a whole basket of "Iran's support for terrorism; pursuit of weapons of mass destruction (WMD); reliance on state-owned or controlled agencies to facilitate WMD proliferation; and the illicit and deceptive financial activities that Iranian financial institutions—including the Central Bank of Iran—and other state-controlled entities engage in to facilitate Iran's illicit conduct and evade sanctions" (US Department of the Treasury, "Fact Sheet: New Sanctions on Iran," November 21, 2011, https://www.treasury.gov/press-center/press-releases/Pages/tg1367.aspx). The Obama administration also pointed to the recommendations of the Financial Action Task Force—"a multilateral standard-setting body for anti-money laundering and combating the financing of terrorism"—when it issued the designation ("Iran Sanctions," Congressional Research Service, February 4, 2019, https://fas.org/sgp/crs/mideast/RS20871.pdf).

132. Samore 2015, 23–24.

133. Samore, interview, February 26, 2019.

134. After JCPOA, Iran was also allowed to make progress toward eliminating punishments associated with the money-laundering designation. On June 24, 2016, Iran filed an "action plan" with the Financial Action Task Force, which suspended "countermeasures" and reupped the suspension in June and November 2017 and February 2018. Iran unsuccessfully sought an exception for its support to Hezbollah and Hamas ("Iran Sanctions," Congressional Research Service).

135. This final agreement on the UN resolution was made on July 12, 2015 (Sherman 2018, xii, 63). In accordance with this final agreement, the unanimously adopted UNSC Resolution 2231 provided for an eight-year restriction on Iranian (nuclear-capable) ballistic missile activities and a five-year ban on conventional arms transfers ("Addressing Iran's Ballistic Missiles in the JCPOA and UNSC Resolution," Arms Control Association, July 27, 2015, https://www.armscontrol.org/issue-briefs/2015-07/addressing-irans-ballistic-missiles-jcpoa-unsc-resolution).

136. US Department of State, "Joint Comprehensive Plan of Action," https://www.state.gov/e/eb/tfs/spi/iran/jcpoa/.

137. Jon Wolfsthal, telephone interview by author, March 21, 2018.

138. "The Iranians were skeptical of this," Einhorn recalled (Einhorn, interview, March 22, 2018).

139. Quoted in Tabatabai 2017, 239.

140. Suzanne Maloney, "Reading between the Red Lines: An Anatomy of Iran's Eleventh-Hour Nuclear Negotiating Strategy," Brookings, October 16, 2014, https://www.brookings.

edu/articles/reading-between-the-red-lines-an-anatomy-of-irans-eleventh-hour-nuclear-negotiating-strategy/.

141. Cited in Tabatabai 2017, 239.

142. Sherman 2018, 200.

143. Sullivan, interview, March 27, 2018.

144. Rhodes 2018, 325.

145. "The Iran Primer: Iran's Troubled Economy, by the Numbers," United States Institute of Peace, January 10, 2018, https://iranprimer.usip.org/blog/2018/jan/10/iran's-troubled-economy-numbers.

146. Bozorgmehr Sharafedin, "Iran Says May Withdraw from Nuclear Deal If Banks Continue to Stay Away," Reuters, February 22, 2018, https://www.reuters.com/article/us-iran-usa-nuclear/iran-says-may-withdraw-from-nuclear-deal-if-banks-continue-to-stay-away-idUSKCN1G610S.

147. "Iran Leader Accuses US of Reneging on Nuclear Deal," *Times of Israel*, March 20, 2016, http://www.timesofisrael.com/iran-leader-accuses-us-of-reneging-on-nuclear-deal/.

148. Einhorn, interview, March 22, 2018.

149. Samore 2015, 24–25. There were also domestic reasons why business was slower to return than expected, such as the fact that the Iranian economy was rife with corruption, a stifling bureaucracy, and a lack of transparency.

150. Wolfsthal, interview, March 21, 2018.

151. Nephew 2018b, 131.

152. In an attempt to overcome this problem, the US Treasury issued an update to legal guidance in late 2016 that clarified that "transactions with IRGC-controlled entities might not necessarily be sanctionable" after JCPOA. Nephew called it an "extraordinary step" (Nephew 2018b, 132). Robert Einhorn, too, pointed to the problem of the IRGC in sanctions relief: "Sanctions against the IRGC remain. The problem is that the IRGC has vast economic interests in Iran. So, you don't know if you're dealing with the IRGC. There is a lack of transparency in the Iranian economy" (Einhorn, interview, March 22, 2018).

153. Richard Nephew, interview by author, April 16, 2018, Cambridge, MA.

154. Nephew, interview, April 16, 2018.

155. Samore 2015, 20.

156. Samore 2015, 19.

157. Samore 2015, 20.

158. This fact in itself made any coercive bargain less likely to be durable, but it did not prevent a bargain nor make coercive assurance impossible. For reviews of debates about compliance with treaties and alternative agreements, see Simmons 2010; Simmons 1998.

159. Samore 2015.

160. Nephew, interview, April 16, 2018.

161. "Letter from Senate Republicans to the Leaders of Iran." *New York Times*, March 9, 2015, https://www.nytimes.com/interactive/2015/03/09/world/middleeast/document-the-letter-senate-republicans-addressed-to-the-leaders-of-iran.html. John Kerry (2018, 505) reports that Zarif confronted him with a copy of this letter the next day.

162. Nephew, interview, April 16, 2018.

163. Sherman 2018, 170.

164. Sherman writes that the administration and the negotiating team had "largely ignored the question of congressional approval" until the Lausanne framework was agreed to in March 2015. Then the end game began (Sherman 2018, 174).

165. Ultimately, the actual INARA legislation only required the president to periodically recertify Iranian compliance with the JCPOA.

166. Sherman 2018, 175.

167. Sherman 2018, 198.

168. Kahl, interview, November 2, 2018.

169. Kahl, interview, November 2, 2018.

170. Sen. Tom Cotton, organizer of the earlier letter to Iran from forty-seven senators, was the lone nay vote.

171. Albeit with recurring waivers and congressional oversight. But Iran had already seen such waivers work in the JPOA interim agreement, which allowed by presidential waiver the sale of some crude oil, the export of petrochemicals, gold, and precious metals, suspended some automotive industry sanctions, and unfroze about $700 million monthly (about $12 billion by the end of the interim agreement).

172. Wolfsthal, interview, March 21, 2018.

173. Einhorn, interview, March 22, 2018.

174. Sherman 2018, 61.

175. Sherman 2018, 62.

176. Kahl, interview, November 2, 2018.

177. Sherman 2018, 64.

178. Miller 2018, 239.

179. William Burns, telephone interview with Daniel Sobelman, June 15, 2017 (quoted in Sobelman 2018).

180. Wolfsthal, interview, March 21, 2018.

181. Kahl, interview, November 2, 2018.

182. On the leak to the National Resistance Council, see Bergman "Will Israel Attack Iran?"

183. Barak 2018, 417.

184. Gates, 2014, 190.

185. Barak 2018, 417. Sobelman also writes that in May 2008 Bush denied Israeli prime minister Olmert a "green light" to attack Iran's nuclear sites (Sobelman 2018).

186. Barak 2018, 418. The analysis in this section considers both Israeli capabilities and intent. Even if Israel was incapable of a strike, its leaders may have seen political value in a military option beyond its kinetic effects. For instance, the target of an Israeli strike may not have been the Iranian facilities themselves but the whole prospect of successful coercive diplomacy. Some contend that Israel was never serious about striking Iran—that it was a bluff directed at reducing American freedom of action. It is nearly impossible to know today whether Israel was bluffing in 2011–12. Israeli leaders themselves may disagree.

187. Barak 2018, 424–25.

188. Barak 2018, 425.

189. Under Israeli law, major national security decisions must be approved by either a majority of the full thirty-member cabinet or by a ministerial committee on national security (also called the Security Cabinet, made up of fifteen members of the full cabinet). (Membership in the Security Cabinet has fluctuated as cabinet members changed. It may have up to fifteen members, and it had fourteen or fifteen members for the period I am most concerned with.) In effect, this means that eight votes carry the day, so an "Octet" meets to discuss sensitive decisions before there is a vote. It operates by informal consensus. Fail to convince the Group of Eight, and you did not get to strike Iran. In March 2012 the Group of Eight consisted of Benjamin Netanyahu, Eli Yishai (ultra-Orthodox Shas party leader), Ehud Barak (defense minister), Dan Meridor (Likud party; a deputy prime minister and minister of intelligence and atomic energy), Moshe Ya'alon (Likud party; a deputy prime minister and minister of strategic affairs), Benny Begin (Likud party; minister without portfolio), Yuval Steinitz (Likud party; finance minister), and Avigdor Lieberman (leader of the Yisrael Beytenu party; foreign minister) (Eli Lake, "Meet the Israeli 'Octet' That Would Decide an Iran Attack," *Daily Beast*, March 9, 2012). The Octet remained unchanged in September 2012. The rest of the National Security Cabinet included Silvan Shalom (vice prime minister and regional development minister), Yitzhak Aharonovitch (internal security minister), Yaakov Ne'eman (justice minister), Gideon Sa'ar (education minister), Uzi Landau (national infrastructure minister), and Ariel Atlas (housing and construction minister) (Zanotti et al. 2012, 24).

190. See, e.g., Anshel Pfeffer, "Will They?," *Tablet*, November 18, 2001; Jodi Rudoren and David E. Sanger, "Report on Iran Puts Israel in a Box," *New York Times*, August 30, 2012; Nathaniel Kern and Matthew M. Reed, "Netanyahu's Divided Cabinet, Foreign Reports Bulletin," Middle East Policy Council, September 19, 2012.

191. Lake, "Meet the Israeli 'Octet.'"

192. Barak 2018, 425.

193. Barak 2018. Other ministers' views vacillated over time. For instance, a November 2011 report said that Benny Begin and Moshe Ya'alon were "currently opposed to an attack," citing Iranian retaliation (Pfeffer, "Will They?").

194. The chief of staff, the head of military intelligence, and the commander of the air force also attended the meeting.

195. Barak 2018, 427.

196. Bergman, "Will Israel Attack Iran?," 2012.

197. Lake, "Meet the Israeli 'Octet.'" See also Pardo's reported opposition to a strike in 2011 (Chris Pleasance, "It Was Not a Drill," *Daily Mail*, May 31, 2018, https://www.dailymail. co.uk/news/article-5790089/Ex-Israeli-spy-chief-Netanyahu-planned-Iran-strike-2011.html).

198. Zanotti et al. 2012, 26. In March 2012 Gantz was still reported to be against a strike (see Lake, "Meet the Israeli 'Octet'").

199. According to Barak, in late 2011 "there were still voices of opposition within the inner group of eight: not just Dan Meridor and Benny Begin by the minister for strategic affairs, Boogie Ya'alon, and Finance Minister Yuval Steinitz. This meant that we could not count on passing a resolution to go ahead with the operation" (Barak 2018, 429; see also Barak Ravid, "Barak: Steinitz, Ya'alon Thwarted Iran Strike in 2011," *Ha'aretz*, August 23, 2015).

200. See also Sobelman 2018.

201. Kahl, interview, November 2, 2018.

202. Burns 2019, 355.

203. Samore, interview, February 26, 2019.

204. Among what surely would have been a longer target list for an air strike were Iran's four major nuclear complexes: the Natanz pilot and commercial centrifuge facilities, the Fordow centrifuge facility, the Esfahan uranium conversion facility, and the heavy-water reactor and heavy-water-production facility at Arak. The light-water reactor at Bushehr and the research reactor in Tehran could have been added to the target list—perhaps also certain suspicious buildings at Parchin in addition to various air defense sites.

205. In 2013 the Israeli Air Force had 252 ground-attack fighter aircraft and 143 other fighters of F-15 and F-16 varieties. None was capable of ranging one thousand miles without refueling ("Chapter Seven: Middle East and North Africa," *Military Balance* 113 (1): 385). In 2012 Israel had available only two KC-130 tankers and seven KC-707s (Zanotti et al. 2012, 37).

206. Zanotti et al., 14; Bergman, "Will Israel Attack Iran?," 2012.

207. In 2012 Israeli ordnance included GBU-27 two-thousand-pound bombs that could penetrate more than six feet of reinforced concrete and GBU-28 five-thousand-pound bombs that could penetrate twenty feet of concrete and one hundred feet of earth (Zanotti et al. 2012, 38). For a weaponeering assessment of munitions against a facility such as Natanz, see Raas and Long 2007, 15–20.

208. Adam Entous and Julian Barnes, "Pentagon Seeks Mightier Bomb vs. Iran," *Wall Street Journal*, January 28, 2012.

209. Sobelman 2018.

210. Rudoren and Sanger, "Report on Iran."

211. "Remarks by the President at AIPAC Policy Conference," March 4, 2012, Washington, DC, https://obamawhitehouse.archives.gov/the-press-office/2012/03/04/remarks-president-aipac-policy-conference-0. AIPAC is the American Israel Public Affairs Committee.

212. Kahl, interview, November 2, 2018.

213. Barak 2018, 433.

214. Barak 2018, 433.

215. Maj. Gen. (Res.) Yaakov Amidror, December 6, 2017, Cambridge, MA. Amidror added that he thought President Obama had later lost credibility in 2013 when he did not order a strike on Syria to punish Syrian dictator Bashar al-Assad for using chemical weapons.

216. Jeffrey Heller, "Israel's Peres against Any Solo Iran Attack, Trusts Obama," Reuters, August 16, 2012, https://www.reuters.com/article/us-israel-iran/israels-peres-against-any-solo-iran-attack-trusts-obama-idUSBRE87F0M620120816 (cited in Sobelman 2018).

217. Heller, "Israel's Peres against Attack."

218. Sobelman 2018.

219. Zanotti et al. 2012, 1.

220. Sobelman 2018.

221. Samore, interview, February 26, 2019.

222. Sobelman 2018; on these meetings, see Kerry 2018, 503.

223. This view did not, however, preclude the covert sabotage of the Iranian nuclear program (Lindsay 2013).

224. Quoted in Rudoren and Sanger, "Report on Iran." President Obama articulated this logic in a 2013 press briefing as well—striking Iran preventively would push the Iranian regime to pursue a nuclear weapon "even more vigorously" ("Statement by the President on the Affordable Care Act," November 14, 2013, White House, http://www.whitehouse.gov/the-press-office/2013/11/14/statement-president-affordable-care-act). And Robert Gates agreed in his memoir that he was "convinced that a foreign military attack would . . . rally the Iranian people behind their government" (Gates 2014, 389).

225. Sobelman 2018.

226. Bergman, "Will Israel Attack Iran?," 2012.

227. David Ignatius, "Of a Mind to Attack Iran," *Washington Post*, February 3, 2012.

228. Sobelman 2018.

229. Sobelman 2018, 430–33.

230. Barak 2018, 435. The informal Group of Eight constitutes a majority of the Security Cabinet.

231. Brig. Gen. (Res.) Yaacov Nagel, interview by author, December 5, 2017, Cambridge, MA. Nagel was clear to add that Israel was not party to the JCPOA and that he opposed it.

232. Kahl, interview, November 2, 2018.

233. Sullivan, interview, March 27, 2018.

234. Iran maintains that the documents are forgeries. Israel has shared them with other intelligence services, including the United States, and the documents have been given to the IAEA. For longstanding Iranian denials, see "Communication Dated 28 September 2008 Received from the Permanent Mission of the Islamic Republic of Iran to the Agency," INFCIRC/737, October 1, 2008, IAEA Archives, Vienna.

235. For a journalistic account, see Ronen Bergman, "Iran's Great Nuclear Deception," *Ynetnews Magazine*, November 23, 2018, https://www.ynetnews.com/articles/0,7340,L-5412157,00.html (see also Institute for Science and International Security, Reports on Iran, http://isis-online.org/countries/category/iran).

236. Israel acknowledges that it has held back some material due to proliferation sensitivity. One should also assume that they could have held back exculpatory evidence.

237. The "alleged studies documentation" (a.k.a. the "laptop documents" or the "laptop of death") was a trove of intelligence that was passed to the IAEA in July 2005 (officially by an unnamed member state). The documents came from a laptop reportedly acquired by the CIA from an Iranian informant—a "walk-in defector at an embassy in the Middle East" (Fitzpatrick 2006, 529; see also Dafna Linzer, "Strong Leads and Dead Ends in Nuclear Case against Iran," *Washington Post*, February 8, 2006; William Broad and David Sanger, "Relying on Computer, U.S. Seeks to Prove Iran's Nuclear Aims," *New York Times*, November 13, 2015). The cache consisted of over one thousand pages of documentation, including "correspondence, reports, view graphs from presentations, videos and engineering drawing," and "working level correspondence consistent with the day to day implementation of a formal programme." The IAEA reported that it had close contact with the United States to verify this intelligence (IAEA Board of Governors, *Implementation of the NPT Safeguards*, GOV/2011/65, annex, 3).

238. This additional information overall corroborated the US intelligence as well as shed light on "activities substantially beyond those identified in that [alleged studies] documentation" (IAEA Board of Governors, *Implementation of the NPT Safeguards*, GOV/2011/65, annex, 3).

239. IAEA Board of Governors, *Implementation of the NPT Safeguards*, GOV/2011/65, 8.

240. IAEA Board of Governors, *Implementation of the NPT Safeguards*, GOV/2011/65, annex, 6–12.

241. IAEA Board of Governors, *Implementation of the NPT Safeguards*, GOV/2011/65, 8.

242. IAEA Board of Governors, *Implementation of the NPT Safeguards*, GOV/2011/65, annex, 4–6.

243. IAEA Board of Governors, *Implementation of the NPT Safeguards*, GOV/2011/65, 8 (see also IAEA Board of Governors, *Final Assessment*, GOV/2015/68, 10, https://www.iaea.org/sites/default/files/documents/gov-2015-68.pdf).

244. The final PMD report also mentions knowledge of Iran's "preparatory experimentation relevant to testing a nuclear explosive device" in 2002–3, including "a number of practical tests to see whether its EBW detonator-firing component would function satisfactorily over a long distance between the firing point and a test device located down a deep shaft" (IAEA Board of Governors, *Final Assessment*, GOV/2015/68, 12).

245. IAEA Board of Governors, *Implementation of the NPT Safeguards*, GOV/2011/65, annex, 11.

246. IAEA Board of Governors, *Implementation of the NPT Safeguards*, GOV/2011/65, attachment 1.

247. IAEA Board of Governors, *Implementation of the NPT Safeguards*, GOV/2011/65, annex, 12.

248. IAEA Board of Governors, *Implementation of the NPT Safeguards*, GOV/2011/65, annex, 9–11 (see also IAEA Board of Governors, *Final Assessment*, GOV/2015/68, 10).

249. The 2007 NIE was declassified at the request of the White House (Fingar 2011, 89–125).

250. National Intelligence Council, "Iran."

251. IAEA Board of Governors, *Final Assessment*, GOV/2015/68, 15.

252. In one of its most accommodating sentences, which had not appeared in the 2011 annex, the final report stated that "these activities did not advance beyond feasibility and scientific studies, and the acquisition of certain relevant technical competences and capabilities." The IAEA's own findings belie this diplomatic wording (IAEA Board of Governors, *Final Assessment*, GOV/2015/68, 14).

253. IAEA Board of Governors, *Implementation of the NPT Safeguards*, GOV/2011/65, annex, 2.

254. Iran granted the IAEA "managed access" to the controversial Parchin site by allowing IAEA inspectors to watch as Iranians took environmental samples themselves. So long as the chain of custody could be verified, the IAEA was content with the arrangement (IAEA, "Roadmap for the Clarification of Past and Present Outstanding Issues regarding Iran's Nuclear Program," GOV/INF/2015/14, July 14, 2015).

255. IAEA Board of Governors, *Final Assessment*, GOV/2015/68, 10.

256. IAEA Board of Governors, *Final Assessment*, GOV/2015/68, 10.

257. IAEA Board of Governors, *Final Assessment*, GOV/2015/68, 11.

258. Toosi, Nahal Toosi, "Kerry: Iran Doesn't Have to Account for Past Nuclear Weapons Research," *Politico*, June 16, 2015, http://www.politico.com/story/2015/06/kerry-iran-doesnt-have-to-account-for-past-nuclear-weapons-research-119074.

259. Amb. Wendy Sherman, interview by author, May 18, 2019, Cambridge, MA.

260. Sullivan, interview, March 27, 2018.

261. Hayden 2016, 290–301.

262. Wolfsthal, interview, March 21, 2018.

263. Sullivan, interview, March 27, 2018.

264. Arnold et al. 2019.

265. A senior representative of the Foreign Ministry may also have sat on the council (Arnold et al. 2019).

266. Aaron Arnold's notes from Israeli intelligence briefing, January 2019. Money was also allocated for the acquisition of HEU from abroad. There is no evidence HEU was acquired from abroad.

267. Arnold et al. 2019.

268. Material to feed this cascade was to come from the Gchine uranium mine.

269. Arnold et al. 2019.

270. Arnold et al. 2019.

271. IAEA Board of Governors, *Final Assessment*, GOV/2015/68, 12.

272. Fitzpatrick 2006, 530.

273. Arnold et al. 2019.
274. Arnold et al. 2019.
275. Arnold et al. 2019.
276. Arnold et al. 2019.
277. Arnold et al. 2019.
278. Albright, Heinonen, and Stricker 2018.
279. National Intelligence Council, "Iran."
280. IAEA Board of Governors, *Implementation of the NPT Safeguards*, GOV/2011/65, annex, 5.
281. IAEA Board of Governors, *Implementation of the NPT Safeguards*, GOV/2011/65, annex, 5. The IAEA also continued to track Fakhrizadeh: "In February 2011, Mr Fakhrizadeh moved his seat of operations from MUT [Malek Ashtar University of Technology] to an adjacent location known as the Modjeh Site, and that he now leads the Organization of Defensive Innovation and Research" (IAEA Board of Governors, *Implementation of the NPT Safeguards*, GOV/2011/65, annex, 5). (The Organization of Defensive Innovation and Research is also known by the acronym "SPND.")
282. IAEA Board of Governors, *Final Assessment*, GOV/2015/68, 12.
283. IAEA Board of Governors, *Final Assessment*, GOV/2015/68, 6.
284. Miller 2018, 236 (see also David Sanger and William Broad, "U.S. Sees Window to Pressure Iran on Nuclear Fuel," *New York Times*, January 3, 2010.
285. The State Department's arms control, verification, and compliance report in April 2019 used this language: "Information contained in the nuclear archive . . . provide[s] greater detail to our understanding of Iran's previous nuclear weapons-related efforts" (US State Department, *Adherence to and Compliance with Arms Control, Nonproliferation, and Disarmament Agreements and Commitments*, August 2019, https://2017-2021.state.gov/wp-content/uploads/2019/08/Compliance-Report-2019-August-19-Unclassified-Final.pdf). It is worth considering what details could emerge about Iran's nuclear program that would change the finding of this research. If, in conjunction with signing the JCPOA, Iran successfully hid from the P5+1 a clandestine stockpile or fissile material or a parallel fuel cycle for the production of fissile material, one could no longer say that Tehran and Washington shared knowledge based on available documents.
286. Iran long said that the "alleged studies documentation" was forged. Some analysts agreed, pointing a finger at Israel (see Porter 2010).
287. We know much less about Tehran's decision to preserve its scientific knowledge in a warehouse in 2015. Sometime around the conclusion of the JCPOA, someone gave the order to aggregate all of the files related to nuclear weapons work and store them in safes on mobile flatbed trailers. Most likely Iran sought to retain nuclear know-how, much in the way that roughly 70 percent of the staff on the AMAD Plan still worked for Fakhrizadeh at SPND. (Estimate attributed to Israeli intelligence officials in Arnold et al. 2019.) It would be consistent with a nuclear hedging strategy. Nonetheless, it is also possible that the purpose of the warehouse was to consolidate the information so that no inspectors could come across it. Saddam Hussein pursued such a strategy with Iraq's WMD programs, and it led to vast misperceptions. For instance, Saddam sent military personnel to old WMD production and storage sites to ensure that no stores of chemical agents remained, only to have American intelligence perceive satellite images of trucks at those facilities to be evidence of renewed activity (Sagan 2013; see also Woods, Lacey, and Murray 2006). It is unclear whether the United States or other coercers knew about the Iranian warehouse before the Israeli operation in 2018. Some press reporting suggests that they did. An anonymous US intelligence official told Reuters, "We have known about this facility for some time" (John Irish and Arshad Mohammed, "Netanyahu, in U.N. Speech, Claims Secret Iranian Nuclear Site," Reuters, September 27, 2018, https://www.reuters.com/article/us-un-assembly-israel-iran/israel-accuses-iran-of-concealing-nuclear-material-for-weapons-program-idUSKCN1M72FZ).
288. Some further maintain that the JCPOA was not a coercive bargain at all—that sanctions were not effective in compelling any concessions from Iran (Hossein Mousavian, "It Was Not Sanctions That Brought Iran to the Table," *Financial Times*, November 19, 2013; Trita Parsi, "No, Sanctions Didn't Force Iran to Make a Deal," *Foreign Policy*, May 14, 2014). Tabatabai (2017, 226)

reviews these arguments, including a similar assertion by Zarif, but she concludes that sanctions did play a role in making Iran return to the negotiating table in 2012. And while Iranian elections are not democratic, the election of Rouhani itself can also be seen as evidence of an Iranian desire for coercive sanctions relief. Rouhani campaigned on providing such economic relief.

289. In a related argument, Tabatabai (2017) tracks how Iranian domestic politics shaped the terms of the JCPOA. That is, the important things that varied were within Iran. The four Iranian domestic constraints she identifies are public opinion, the legislative branch, the supreme leader, and the security establishment. Rouhani also took actions to remove bureaucratic roadblocks within Iran: "He stacked his cabinet with many of the individuals who had supported his efforts to reach a deal with the E3 in 2003–2005," including Zarif, and "he moved the nuclear file from the SNSC to the Foreign Ministry and placed it under Zarif's supervision . . . as Rouhani had authority over the composition of the Foreign Ministry, but not that of the SNSC, which includes members of the legislative and judiciary branches, the supreme leader's office, and the armed forces" (Tabatabai 2017, 230).

290. On carrots, see Jervis 2013.

291. Kerr, "U.S., Allies Await Iran's Response"; IAEA Board of Governors, "Record of the 1148th Meeting" 8 (see also Reardon 2012, 17–18).

292. Nephew, interview, April 16, 2018.

293. Burns 2019, 361.

294. Miller 2018, 242–43. However, Miller does not consider maintaining a limited enrichment capacity as an inducement.

295. Peter Baker, "Trump Recertifies Iran Nuclear Deal, but Only Reluctantly," *New York Times*, July 17, 2017, https://www.nytimes.com/2017/07/17/us/politics/trump-iran-nuclear-deal-recertify.html.

296. "Statement by the President on the Iran Nuclear Deal," White House, January 12, 2018, https://www.whitehouse.gov/briefings-statements/statement-president-iran-nuclear-deal/.

297. For a similar argument, see Sahar Nowrouzzadeh, Reid Pauly, and Mahsa Rouhi, "This Is Why Trump's Strategy for Iran Will Fail," *National Interest*, December 21, 2017.

298. See, e.g., reporting that the White House sought ways to declare that Iran was in violation of the JCPOA (David E. Sanger, "Trump Seeks Way to Declare Iran in Violation of Nuclear Deal," *New York Times*, July 27, 2017, https://www.nytimes.com/2017/07/27/world/middleeast/trump-iran-nuclear-agreement.html).

299. Iran has long refused to engage in negotiations over its ballistic missile development. The reason is that Iran relies on its conventional missiles for deterrence, believing it must maintain the capacity to strike Israel and US bases in the region, directly or through proxies. Referring to ballistic missiles as Iran's "defensive power," Iranian leaders consistently place them off limits to talks ("Iranian Leader Refuses Any Negotiation over Ballistic Missiles," *Al-Monitor*, October 25, 2017; "Rouhani: Iran Has No Need to Negotiate over Its Defense," *Al-Monitor*, February 5, 2018).

300. "Iran Accuses U.S. of Brazen Plan to Change Its Government," CNBC, June 28, 2017, https://www.cnbc.com/2017/06/28/iran-accuses-us-of-brazen-plan-to-change-its-government.html.

301. See @khamenei.ir, tweet, January 17, 2018, Twitter, https://twitter.com/khamenei_ir/status/953654085672161280/video/1.

302. John Bolton, "Beyond the Iran Nuclear Deal," *Wall Street Journal*, January 15, 2018, https://www.wsj.com/articles/beyond-the-iran-nuclear-deal-1516044178.

303. Caitlin Oprysko, "Pompeo Announces New Team for Iran Strategy," *Politico*, August 16, 2018, https://www.politico.com/story/2018/08/16/mike-pompeo-iran-action-group-780110.

304. John Bolton, tweet, January 16, 2019, Twitter, https://twitter.com/ambjohnbolton/status/1085547855446720512.

305. "Crude Oil Exports for Iran, Islamic Republic of," Federal Reserve Bank of St. Louis, Economic Research, https://fred.stlouisfed.org/series/IRNNXGOCMBD.

306. "Crude Oil Exports for Iran."

307. Drezner 2021.

308. Aresu Eqbali and Sune Engel Rasmussen, "Iran's Rouhani Says No Talks with U.S. While 'Maximum Pressure' Campaign Is On," *Wall Street Journal*, February 16, 2020, https://www.wsj.com/articles/irans-rouhani-says-no-talks-with-u-s-while-maximum-pressure-campaign-is-on-11581881292.

309. Bozorgmehr Sharafedin, "No Negotiations with U.S., Says Iran's Supreme Leader," Reuters, May 29, 2019, https://www.reuters.com/article/us-usa-iran-rouhani/no-negotiations-with-u-s-says-irans-supreme-leader-idUSKCN1SZ12M.

310. "Trump Says He 'Couldn't Care Less' if Iran Agrees to Negotiate," Reuters, January 12, 2020, https://www.reuters.com/article/us-iran-crsah-trump/trump-says-he-couldnt-care-less-if-iran-agrees-to-negotiate-idUSKBN1ZC013.

311. John Bolton, tweet, January 12, 2020, Twitter, https://twitter.com/ambjohnbolton/status/1216334443880775680.

312. Some accounts suggest that Trump considered attacking Iran during the 2020–21 presidential transition (Susan B. Glasser, " 'You're Gonna Have a Fucking War': Mark Milley's Fight to Stop Trump from Striking Iran," *New Yorker*, July 15, 2021).

313. Sanger David E. and Farnaz Fassihi, "For Biden, Iranian Hard-liner May Be Best Path to Restoring Nuclear Deal," *New York Times*, June 19, 2021, https://www.nytimes.com/2021/06/19/world/middleeast/iran-nuclear-deal-Ebrahim-Raisi.html.

314. Jonathan Tirone, "Nuclear Monitors Deal with Iran Gives Diplomacy a Chance," Bloomberg, March 4, 2021, https://www.bloomberg.com/news/articles/2021-03-04/iran-and-u-s-get-time-for-diplomacy-as-atomic-censure-withdrawn.

315. "Iran Says Nuclear Talks Closer to Deal, Russia Says Much Work Remains," Reuters, June 17, 2021, https://www.reuters.com/world/middle-east/nuclear-talks-closer-than-ever-deal-important-issues-remain-top-iran-delegate-2021-06-17/. The second sticking point nearing the end of Biden-Rouhani talks was a US demand to immediately begin further talks upon reconstitution of the JCPOA pertaining to other issues. This did not entangle issues; in fact, it disentangled. Still, Iranians took exception to it.

316. Sanger and Fassihi, "For Biden, Iranian Hard-liner."

317. Sanger and Fassihi, "For Biden, Iranian Hard-liner"; Laura Rozen, "Iran's Khamenei Complains US Seeking Follow-on Talks, as US Urges Return to Vienna Negotiations," Diplomatic Substack, July 28, 2021, https://diplomatic.substack.com/p/irans-khamenei-complains-us-seeking.

318. Amir Vahdat and Jon Gambrell, "Iran's Supreme Leader Criticizes U.S. as Nuclear Talks Stalled," CTV News, July 28, 2021, https://www.ctvnews.ca/world/iran-s-supreme-leader-criticizes-u-s-as-nuclear-talks-stalled-1.5526018.

319. Vahdat and Gambrell, "Iran's Supreme Leader Criticizes U.S."

320. David E. Sanger, Lara Jakes, and Farnaz Fassihi, "Biden Promised to Restore the Iran Nuclear Deal. Now It Risks Derailment," *New York Times*, July 31, 2021, https://www.nytimes.com/2021/07/31/us/politics/biden-iran-nuclear-deal.html.

321. Sherman (2018, x) writes that they were "the longest an American secretary of state (or an Iranian one for that matter) had spent in one place [Vienna]."

322. Burns 2019, 365.

Conclusion

1. Freedman 2004b, 7.

2. Exodus 1:10.

3. See also Pauly 2021; Nutt and Pauly 2021.

4. Paul Mozur, Mark Scott, and Vindu Goel, "Victims Call Hackers' Bluff as Payoff Deadline Nears in Ransomware Attack," *New York Times*, May 20, 2017, https://www.nytimes.com/2017/05/19/business/hacking-malware-wanncry-ransomware-deadline.html.

5. Ellen Nakashima, "The NSA Has Linked the WannaCry Computer Worm to North Korea," *Washington Post*, June 14, 2017, https://www.washingtonpost.com/world/national-security/the-nsa-has-linked-the-wannacry-computer-worm-to-north-korea/2017/06/14/101395a2–508e-11e7-be25–3a519335381c_story.html.

6. Sheera Frenkel, Mark Scott, and Paul Mozur, "Mystery of Motive for a Ransomware Attack: Money, Mayhem or a Message?," *New York Times*, June 28, 2017, https://www.nytimes.com/2017/06/28/business/ramsonware-hackers-cybersecurity-petya-impact.html.

7. Frenkel, Scott and Mozur, "Mystery of Motive."

8. Andy Greenberg, "The Untold Story of NotPetya, the Most Devastating Cyber Attack in History," *Wired*, January 22, 2018, https://cyber-peace.org/wp-content/uploads/2018/10/The-Untold-Story-of-NotPetya-the-Most-Devastating-Cyberattack-in-History-_-WIRED.pdf.

9. Greenberg, "Untold Story of NotPetya."

10. Manny Fernandez, David E. Sanger, and Marina Trahan Martinez, "Ransomware Attacks Are Testing Resolve of Cities Across America," *New York Times*, August 22, 2019, https://www.nytimes.com/2019/08/22/us/ransomware-attacks-hacking.html.

11. For instance, Colonial Pipeline, a company with $3.1 billion of assets and approximately $500 million of net income, paid $5 million to decrypt its data in a 2021 ransomware attack (William Turton, Michael Riley, and Jennifer Jacobs, "Colonial Pipeline Paid Hackers Nearly $5 Million in Ransom," Bloomberg, May 13, 2021, https://www.bloomberg.com/news/articles/2021-05-13/colonial-pipeline-paid-hackers-nearly-5-million-in-ransom.

12. See Danielle Gilbert, "Ransomware Lessons for a Nation Held Hostage," Lawfare, September 12, 2021, https://www.lawfareblog.com/ransomware-lessons-nation-held-hostage. Ransomware insurance is becoming increasingly common, though it makes one even more of a target (Fernandez, Sanger, and Martinez, "Ransomware Attacks Are Testing Resolve"). Some ransom payments are even tax deductible (Tarah Wheeler and Ciaran Martin, "Should Ransomware Payments Be Banned?," Brookings, July 26, 2021, https://www.brookings.edu/techstream/should-ransomware-payments-be-banned/.

13. Ekelund et al. 2006.

14. Becker 1968.

15. Simmons and Danner (2010) also argue that states join the International Criminal Court as a hand-tying mechanism to signal to rebels that the government will not engage in atrocities after signing a peace deal.

16. Miller 2022.

17. Adlai Stevenson, for instance, was branded "an appeaser" for taking a dovish stance during the Cuban missile crisis, and the administration was happy to hang him out to dry while in secret it had negotiated a missile trade (see Beschloss 1991, 468, 553, 569; see also Michael Dobbs, "The Price of a 50-Year Myth," *New York Times*, October 16, 2012).

18. Dobbs 2008, 88.

19. Jervis 2015; Robert Kennedy (1969) discussed the missile trade in an indirect way in his posthumous memoir, published seven years after the crisis.

20. Kirpichevsky and Lipscy n.d.

21. Fursenko and Naftali 1997, 284, see also 259, 263.

22. Jervis 2015, 29, following quote on 31. Though I do not use the term "trust," Jervis calls the Cuban missile crisis "an instance of unusual trust, one that it hard to explain by standard IR theories. But perhaps there was more trust in the Cold War than most of our accounts would have it."

23. The US noninvasion assurance was perhaps made more credible by the ability of both sides to renege (i.e., the Soviet Union to reintroduce missiles and the US to invade) (see Garthoff 2001, 180; Lebow and Stein 1994, 130).

24. Copeland 2015, 208–9.

25. Scott Sagan (1988) argues that Roosevelt's intended policy was made more aggressive by a hawkish bureaucracy. When the president approved oil-export restrictions, he authorized the Treasury Department to grant licenses on a case-by-case basis up to 1935–36 export levels. By August, however, hawks in the administration had implemented the policy so fully that it was now a full oil embargo. Having made his own assessment that "no rational Japanese could believe that an attack on us could result in anything but disaster for his country," Assistant Secretary of State Dean Acheson confidently strangled Japan. Dale Copeland disagrees and finds that Roosevelt knew of and approved the total embargo to restrain Japan from attacking the Soviet Union while Moscow fought off the German invasion (Copeland 2015, 186).

26. Sagan 1988, 893–922; Goodwin 1994, 266.

27. Copeland 2015, 214–15.
28. Copeland 2015, 216.
29. Copeland 2015, 222–23.
30. Quoted in Copeland 2015, 236.
31. Copeland 2015, 237.
32. Copeland (2015) attributes Roosevelt's pendular diplomacy to the progress of the German invasion of the Soviet Union. When it looked like Moscow was near defeat, Roosevelt refused to restart the flow of oil to Japan lest it unleash a second front on the Soviets. Defeating Nazism was the priority.
33. Sagan 1988, 895, 907.
34. Sagan 1988, 893.
35. Byman and Waxman 2002; Luttwak 1996; Klarevas 2002.
36. Avey 2019; Sechser and Fuhrmann 2017.
37. Chamberlain 2016; Post 2019 (see also Sisson, Siebens, and Blechman 2020).
38. Brooks 2002; Major 2012.
39. Miller 2014; Solingen 2007.
40. Hufbauer, Schott, and Elliott 2011.
41. Cortright and Lopez 2002.
42. Farrell and Newman 2019.
43. The study of economic coercion is ahead of the study of military coercion in appreciating the role of coercive assurance (see Drezner 2021, 2022; Feaver and Lorber 2010).
44. Monteiro (2009) in his dissertation formally proves the logic of assurance in deterrence.
45. Snyder and Borghard 2011; Lin-Greenberg 2019.
46. "Do Audience Costs Exist? A Symposium," *Security Studies* 21 (3): 369–555.
47. In a seminal study, Downes and Sechser (2012) confirm empirically that democracies were no more effective coercers than nondemocracies. This was puzzling for audience costs theory. Schultz (2001) makes a compelling argument for democracies as effective coercers by taking into account selection effects: democracies make more selective threats because of domestic political opposition, thus when they do make threats they are unified politically and their threats are more credible.
48. Weeks (2008) finds that democracies are no more successful at coercive diplomacy than autocracies, which she attributes to autocrats generating their own audience costs to make credible threats.
49. Sartori (2005) argues that the fear of acquiring a reputation makes states eschew bluffing. Rationalist theory on the causes of war also assumes that states acquire reputations for reneging on commitments (see Powell 2006, 1999). For another argument affirming the impact of reputation on signals, see Trager 2012.
50. Press (2005) argues that states cannot form reputations for making empty threats. Harvey and Mitton (2016) dissent and argue that states derive reputational benefits from fighting for credibility.
51. Mercer (1996) argues that reputations for resolve are not worth fighting for because adversaries attribute past backing-down to (context-specific) situational factors. Thus, adversaries can sometimes get reputations for having resolve but not for lacking resolve, and allies can sometimes get reputations for lacking resolve but cannot get reputations for having resolve. See also Lupton (2020), who argues that leaders develop personal reputations for threat credibility. Tomz (2007) finds evidence of reputational effects in sovereign debt markets. Dafoe and Caughey (2016) show that leaders who are more concerned with reputation and honor are more likely to use force in international politics. Weisiger and Yarhi-Milo (2015) show that backing down in crises increases your probability of being challenged again in the future. For a review of this literature, see Dafoe, Renshon, and Huth 2014.
52. For another good review of the reputation literature, see Jervis, Yarhi-Milo, and Casler 2021.
53. "Rotterdam," War over Holland, http://www.waroverholland.nl/index.php?page=rotterdam-4. I thank Erik Sand for this example.
54. I thank Steve Walt for this example.

55. The study of "linkage" concentrates on positive inducements—trading a thing you want for a thing I want. The literature regards it as a type of side payment (Poast 2012, 280; Sebenius 1983; Ritter 2002; see also Stein 1980).

56. Elsewhere Oye calls these "backscratching," "blackmailing," and "bracketing" (Oye 1992, 43–45).

57. Oye (1992, 49), like most of the studies that touch on assurance, turns to reputations developed in past interactions to explain the credibility of future promises.

58. Castle 1999, 77.

59. On the strategy of coercive engineered migration, see Greenhill 2010. She also points to one assurance flaw in the strategy: coercive engineered migration "can be difficult to undo" once it begins (Greenhill 2010, 36).

60. "Turkey's Erdogan Threatened to Flood Europe with Migrants: Greek Website," Reuters, February 8, 2016, https://www.reuters.com/article/us-europe-migrants-eu-turkey/turkey serdogan-threatened-to-flood-europe-with-migrants-greek-website-idUSKCN0VH1R0.

61. Taking a page out of Schelling's distinction between compellence and deterrence, it is generally more difficult to change the status quo than it is to maintain it.

62. "Bush Delivers Ultimatum," CNN, September 21, 2001, http://edition.cnn.com/2001/WORLD/asiapcf/central/09/20/ret.afghan.bush/.

63. Bush 2010, 193.

64. "Statement by the President after Briefing at the National Counterterrorism Center," White House, Office of the Press Secretary, December 17, 2015, https://obamawhitehouse. archives.gov/the-press-office/2015/12/17/statement-president-after-briefing-national-counterterrorism-center (see also Graham Allison, "Why ISIS Fears Israel," *National Interest*, August 8, 2016). I thank Graham Allison for this example.

65. "Statement by the President after Briefing."

66. Steven Pifer, "The Budapest Memorandum and U.S. Obligations," Brookings, December 4, 2014, https://www.brookings.edu/blog/up-front/2014/12/04/the-budapest-memorandum-and-u-s-obligations/ (see also the Budapest Memorandum: "Memorandum on Security Assurances in Connection with Ukraine's Accession to the Treaty on the NPT," United Nations, December 19, 1994, https://www.msz.gov.pl/en/p/wiedenobwe_at_s_en/news/memorandum_on_security_assurances_in_connection_with_ukraine_s_accession_to_the_treaty_on_the_npt).

67. Jentleson and Whytock 2005/2006.

68. ElBaradei 2011, 2.

69. Burns 2019, 315.

70. Sagan 1988; Goodwin 1994, 266.

71. Emanuele Ottolenghi and Mark Dubowitz, "Tightening the Sanctions Noose on Tehran," *Wall Street Journal Europe*, July 19, 2010, https://www.fdd.org/analysis/2010/07/19/tightening-the-sanctions-noose-on-tehran/.

72. Nicholas Kristof, "In Hong Kong, Playing Tennis with Tear-Gas Grenades," *New York Times*, August 30, 2019, https://www.nytimes.com/2019/08/30/opinion/sunday/hong-kong-protests.html.

73. Zegart 2020.

74. Kim and Trump also met once at the Demilitarized Zone in June 2019.

75. Some scholars have made similar arguments in their analyses of relations between the US, South Korea, and North Korea. Andrew Kydd writes about the deficit of trust between the US and North Korea. I intentionally do not use the word "trust." But Kydd points to fundamentally incompatible interests—for example, regime change versus regime survival—as the source of mistrust (Andrew Kydd, "Promises on North Korea Are Easy to Make but Hard to Keep. Here's Why," *Washington Post*, June 7, 2018, https://www.washingtonpost.com/news/monkey-cage/wp/2018/06/07/promises-on-north-korea-are-easy-to-make-but-hard-to-keep-heres-why/.

76. Choe Sang-Hun, "North Korea Accuses Washington of Weaponizing Human Rights as Nuclear Talks Stall," *New York Times*, November 29, 2018, https://www.nytimes.com/2018/11/29/world/asia/north-korea-human-rights.html.

77. Choe Sang-Hun, "Hard-Line U.S. Tactics Will 'Block' Path to Denuclearization, North Korea Warns," *New York Times*, December 16, 2018, https://www.nytimes.com/2018/12/16/world/asia/north-korea-nuclear-talks-us.html.

78. "Statement by H. E. Ri Yong Ho, Minister for Foreign Affairs of the Democratic People's Republic of Korea at the General Debate of the 73rd Session of the General Assembly of the United Nations," September 29, 2018, https://gadebate.un.org/sites/default/files/gastatements/73/kp_en.pdf.

79. The 1994 Agreed Framework, for instance, did not require Congress to appropriate funds for the Korean Peninsula Energy Development Organization light-water reactor project in North Korea.

80. For example, Anonymous, "I Am Part of the Resistance inside the Trump Administration," *New York Times*, September 5, 2018, https://www.nytimes.com/2018/09/05/opinion/trump-white-house-anonymous-resistance.html.

81. Jim Mattis and Rex Tillerson, "We're Holding Pyongyang to Account," *Wall Street Journal*, August 13, 2017.

82. Evan Osnos, "The Risk of Nuclear War with North Korea," *New Yorker*, September 18, 2017. Thank you to Tyler Jost for bringing this example to my attention.

83. Jeffrey Lewis, "John Bolton to Kim Jong Un: Give Up Your Nukes like Gaddafi Did—before We Killed Him," *Daily Beast*, March 29, 2018, https://www.thedailybeast.com/john-bolton-to-kim-jong-un-give-up-your-nukes-like-gaddafi-didbefore-we-killed-him.

84. "Full Statement by North Korea's Vice-Foreign Minister and Nuclear Negotiator Choe Son Hui," *Strait Times*, May 24, 2018, https://www.straitstimes.com/asia/east-asia/full-statement-by-north-koreas-vice-foreign-minister-and-nuclear-negotiator-choe-son.

85. Choe Son-hui, "We Must Confront the Imperialist Front," *Rodong Sinmun*, May 29, 2018, trans. Grace Liu, reprinted in Joshua Pollack, "Friendship without Benefits: North Korea Doesn't Want Uncle Sam's Dollar," Arms Control Wonk, May 30, 2018, https://www.armscontrolwonk.com/archive/1205313/friendship-without-benefits-north-korea-doesnt-want-uncle-sams-dollars/.

86. Drezner 2022; Nephew 2018a; Vaez 2013.

87. Economic sanctions were historically intended to be coercive: threatened but rarely employed (Mulder 2022).

88. Morgan, Bapat, and Kobayashi 2014.

89. "The Treasury 2021 Sanctions Review," US Treasury Department, October 2021, https://home.treasury.gov/system/files/136/Treasury-2021-sanctions-review.pdf.

90. Data gathered by the Center for a New American Security from the Office of Foreign Assets Control, US Department of the Treasury (see Johnpatrick Imperiale, "Sanctions by the Numbers: U.S. Sanctions Designations and Delistings, 2009–2019," Center for a New American Security, February 27, 2020, https://www.cnas.org/publications/reports/sanctions-by-the-numbers).

91. Feaver and Lorber (2010, 7), writing of the challenge of "unwinding" complex sanctions once the target has complied, advise that sanctions "stickiness" makes them "more effective in the short run, but counterproductive in the long run."

92. Richard Nephew, interview by author, April 16, 2018, Cambridge, MA.

93. Boon 2014.

94. Peter Baker and Andrew Higgins, "White House Signals Acceptance of Russia Sanctions Bill," *New York Times*, June 23, 2017.

95. Baker and Higgins, "White House Signals Acceptance."

96. An implication by US Secretary of Defense Lloyd Austin that sanctions were an attempt to "weaken" Russia into the future was not coercively assuring (Missy Ryan and Annabelle Timsit, "U.S. Wants Russian Military 'Weakened' from Ukraine Invasion, Austin Says," *Washington Post*, April 25, 2022, https://www.washingtonpost.com/world/2022/04/25/russia-weakened-lloyd-austin-ukraine-visit/.

97. Drezner 2021; Batmanghelidj and Rouhi 2021.

98. "Treasury 2021 Sanctions Review."

99. "Joint Statement Following Discussions with Leaders of the People's Republic of China," Shanghai, February 27, 1972, *FRUS, 1969–76*, vol. 17, *China, 1969–1972*, doc. 203, https://history.state.gov/historicaldocuments/frus1969-76v17/d203.

100. The Trump administration did so in US Department of Defense, *Indo-Pacific Strategy Report*, June 1, 2019, https://media.defense.gov/2019/Jul/01/2002152311/-1/-1/1/DEPARTMENT-OF-DEFENSE-INDO-PACIFIC-STRATEGY-REPORT-2019.PDF (referenced in Glaser, Weiss, and Christensen 2024).

101. Christian Shepherd and Vic Chiang, "How Chinese Aggression Is Increasing the Risk of War in the Taiwan Strait," *Washington Post*, November 13, 2023, https://www.washington post.com/world/2023/11/13/china-biden-xi-meeting-apec-taiwan/.

102. Glaser, Weiss, and Christensen 2024.

References

Abrahms, Max. 2013. "The Credibility Paradox: Violence as a Double-Edged Sword in International Politics." *International Studies Quarterly* 57 (4): 660–71. https://doi.org/10.1111/isqu.12098.

Albright, David. 1994. "South Africa and the Affordable Bomb." *Bulletin of the Atomic Scientists* 50 (4): 37–47. https://doi.org/10.1080/00963402.1994.11456538.

——. 2010. *Peddling Peril: How the Secret Nuclear Trade Arms America's Enemies.* New York: Free Press.

Albright, David, Olli Heinonen, and Andrea Stricker. 2018. "Breaking Up and Reorienting Iran's Nuclear Weapons Program: Iran's Nuclear Archive Shows the 2003 Restructuring of Its Nuclear Weapons Program, Then Called the AMAD Program, into Covert and Overt Parts." *Institute for Science and International Security*, October 29. https://isis-online.org/isis-reports/detail/breaking-up-and-reorienting-irans-nuclear-weapons-program.

Albright, David, and Tom Zamora. 1991. "South Africa Flirts with the NPT." *Bulletin of the Atomic Scientists* 47 (1): 27–31.

Arnold, Aaron, Matthew Bunn, Caitlin Chase, Steven E. Miller, Rolf Mowatt-Larssen, and William H. Tobey. 2019. "The Iran Nuclear Archive: Impressions and Implications." Harvard Kennedy School Belfer Center for Science and International Affairs. https://www.belfercenter.org/publication/iran-nuclear-archive-impressions-and-implications.

Art, Robert J. 2003. "Coercive Diplomacy: What Do We Know?" In Art and Cronin 2003, 359–421.

Art, Robert J., and Patrick M. Cronin, eds. 2003. *The United States and Coercive Diplomacy.* Washington DC: United States Institute of Peace Press.

Art, Robert J., and Kelly M. Greenhill. 2018. "Coercion: An Analytical Overview." In Greenhill and Krause 2018, 3–32.

Avey, Paul. 2019. *Tempting Fate: Why Nonnuclear States Confront Nuclear Opponents.* Ithaca, NY: Cornell University Press.

Axelrod, Robert. 1984. *The Evolution of Cooperation.* New York: Basic Books.

Baker, Pauline H. 2000. "The United States and South Africa: Persuasion and Coercion." In Haass and O'Sullivan 2000, 95–119.

Barak, Ehud. 2018. *My Country, My Life: Fighting for Israel, Searching for Peace.* New York: St. Martin's.

Bas, Muhammet A., and Andrew J Coe. 2018. "Give Peace a (Second) Chance: A Theory of Nonproliferation Deals." *International Studies Quarterly* 62 (3): 606–17. https://doi.org/10.1093/isq/sqy015.

Batmanghelidj, Esfandyar, and Mahsa Rouhi. 2021. "The Iran Nuclear Deal and Sanctions Relief: Implications for US Policy." *Survival* 63 (4): 183–98.

Becker, Charles M., and J. H. Hofmeyr. 1990. *The Impact of Sanctions on South Africa, Part 1: The Economy.* Washington, DC: Investor Responsibility Research Center.

Becker, Gary S. 1968. "Crime and Punishment: An Economic Approach." *Journal of Political Economy* 76 (2): 169–217. https://www.jstor.org/stable/1830482.

Beinart, William. 1994. *Twentieth-Century South Africa.* New York: Oxford University Press.

Bell, Mark. 2021. *Nuclear Reactions.* Ithaca, NY: Cornell University Press.

Beschloss, Michael R. 1991. *The Crisis Years: Kennedy and Khrushchev.* New York: HarperCollins.

Biddle, Tami Davis. 2020. "Coercion Theory: A Basic Introduction for Practitioners." *Texas National Security Review* 3 (2): 94–109. http://dx.doi.org/10.26153/tsw/8864.

Black, David. 1999. "The Long and Winding Road: International Norms and Domestic Political Change in South Africa." In *The Power of Human Rights: International Norms and Domestic Change,* edited by Thomas Risse, Stephen C. Ropp, and Kathryn Sikkink, 78–108. Cambridge: Cambridge University Press.

Blechman, Barry and Stephen Kaplan. 1978. *Force without War: U.S. Armed Forces as a Political Instrument.* Washington, DC: Brookings Institution.

Bleek, Philipp C. 2017. "When Did (and Didn't) States Proliferate? Chronicling the Spread of Nuclear Weapons." Cambridge, MA: Belfer Center, Harvard Kennedy School. https://www.belfercenter.org/publication/when-did-and-didnt-states-proliferate.

Blix, Hans. 2004. *Disarming Iraq.* New York: Pantheon Books.

Boon, Kristen E. 2014. *Terminating Security Council Sanctions.* New York: International Peace Institute.

Bowen, W. Q. 2006. "Libya and Nuclear Proliferation: Stepping Back from the Brink." *Adelphi Papers* (380): 7–83.

Bowen, Wyn Q., and Jonathan Brewer. 2011. "Iran's Nuclear Challenge: Nine Years and Counting." *International Affairs* 87 (4): 923–43. https://www.jstor.org/stable/20869766.

Bowen, W. Q., and J. Kidd. 2004. "The Iranian Nuclear Challenge." *International Affairs* 80 (2): 257–76. https://doi.org/10.1111/j.1468-2346.2004.00382.x.

Bowen, Wyn Q., Jeffrey Knopf, and Matthew Moran. 2020. "The Obama Administration and Syrian Chemical Weapons: Deterrence, Compellence, and the Limits of the 'Resolve plus Bombs' Formula." *Security Studies* 29 (5): 797–831. https://doi.org/10.1080/09636412.2020.1859130.

——. 2021. "The Obama Administration's Response to the Use of Chemical Weapons in Syria: An Exchange." *Security Studies* 30 (2): 302–24. https://doi.org/10.1080/09636412.2021.1944723.

Branaman, Brenda M. 1987. *Sanctions against South Africa: Activities of the 99th Congress*. Congressional Research Service. Report No. 87–200 F. February 13. https://digital.library.unt.edu/ark:/67531/metacrs8421/m1/1/high_res_d/87-200F_1987Feb13.pdf.

Braut-Hegghammer, Målfrid. 2006. "Libya's Nuclear Turnaround." *RUSI Journal* 151 (6): 52–55. https://doi.org/10.1080/03071840608522858.

———. 2016. *Unclear Physics: Why Iraq and Libya Failed to Build Nuclear Weapons.* Ithaca, NY: Cornell University Press.

———. 2020. "Cheater's Dilemma: Iraq, Weapons of Mass Destruction, and the Path to War." *International Security* 45 (1): 51–89. https://doi.org/10.1162/isec_a_00382.

Brodie, Bernard. 1959. *Strategy in the Missile Age.* Princeton, NJ: Princeton University Press.

Brooks, Risa. 2002. "Sanctions and Regime Type." *Security Studies* 11 (4): 1–50. https://doi.org/10.1080/714005349.

Burns, William J. 2019. *The Back Channel: A Memoir of American Diplomacy and the Case for Its Renewal.* New York: Random House.

Busch, Nathan E., and Joseph F. Pilat. 2017. *The Politics of Weapons Inspections: Assessing WMD Monitoring and Verification Regimes.* Stanford, CA: Stanford University Press.

Bush, George W. 2010. *Decision Points.* New York: Crown.

Butt, Ahsan I. 2019. "Why Did the United States Invade Iraq in 2003?" *Security Studies* 28 (2): 250–85. https://doi.org/10.1080/09636412.2019.1551567.

Byman, Daniel, and Matthew Waxman. 2002. *The Dynamics of Coercion.* New York: Cambridge University Press.

Carnegie, Allison. 2015. *Power Plays: How International Institutions Reshape Coercive Diplomacy.* New York: Cambridge University Press.

Carnegie, Allison, and Austin Carson. 2018. "The Spotlight's Harsh Glare: Rethinking Publicity and International Order." *International Organization* 72 (3): 627–57. https://doi.org/10.1017/S0020818318000176.

———. 2019. "The Disclosure Dilemma: Nuclear Intelligence and International Organizations." *American Journal of Political Science* 63 (2): 269–85. https://www.jstor.org/stable/45132477.

Castle, Alfred L. 1999. "U.S. Commercial Policy and Hawai'i, 1890–1894." *Hawaiian Journal of History* 33: 69–81. https://evols.library.manoa.hawaii.edu/items/6f13de30-32c8-4558-95df-9b86e8f395ff.

Cebul, Matthew D., Allan Dafoe, and Nuno P. Monteiro. 2021. "Coercion and the Credibility of Assurances." *Journal of Politics* 83 (3): 975–91. https://doi.org/10.1086/711132.

Chamberlain, Dianne Pfundstein. 2016. *Cheap Threats: Why the United States Struggles to Coerce Weak States.* Washington, DC: Georgetown University Press.

"Chapter Seven: Middle East and North Africa." 2013. *The Military Balance* 113 (1): 353–414. https://doi.org/10.1080/04597222.2013.757003.

Christensen, Thomas. 2011. *Worse Than a Monolith: Alliance Politics and the Problem of Coercive Diplomacy in Asia.* Princeton, NJ: Princeton University Press.

Cigar, Norman L. 2012. *Libya's Nuclear Disarmament: Lessons and Implications for Nuclear Proliferation.* Quantico, VA: Middle East Studies, Marine Corps University. archive.org/details/libyasnucleardis00norm.

Cirincione, Joseph, Jon Wolfstahl, and Miriam Rajkumar. 2002. *Deadly Arsenals: Tracking Weapons of Mass Destruction.* Washington, DC: Carnegie Endowment for International Peace.

Clinton, Hillary. 2014. *Hard Choices.* New York: Simon & Schuster.

Coe, Andrew J., and Jane Vaynman. 2015. "Collusion and the Nuclear Nonproliferation Regime." *Journal of Politics* 77 (4): 983–97. https://doi.org/10.1086/682080.

Colgan, Jeff D. 2021. *Partial Hegemony: Oil Politics and International Order.* New York: Oxford University Press.

Coll, Steve. 2024. *The Achilles Trap: Saddam Hussein, the CIA, and the Origins of America's Invasion of Iraq.* New York: Penguin.

Cooper, James Fenimore. 1826. *The Last of the Mohicans: A Narrative of 1757.* Philadelphia: H. C. Carey & I. Lea.

Copeland, Dale C. 2000. *The Origins of Major War.* Ithaca, NY: Cornell University Press.

———. 2015. *Economic Interdependence and War.* Princeton, NJ: Princeton University Press.

Corera, Gordon. 2006. *Shopping for Bombs: Nuclear Proliferation, Global Insecurity, and the Rise and Fall of the A. Q. Khan Network.* Oxford: Oxford University Press.

Cortright, David, and George Lopez. 2002. *Smart Sanctions.* Lanham, MD: Rowman & Littlefield.

Dafoe, Allan, and Devin Caughey. 2016. "Honor and War: Southern U.S. Presidents and the Effects of Concern for Reputation." *World Politics* 68 (2): 341–81. https://doi.org/10.1017/s0043887115000416.

Dafoe, Allan, Jonathan Renshon, and Paul Huth. 2014. "Reputation and Status as Motives for War." *Annual Review of Political Science* 17 (1): 371–93. https://doi.org/10.1146/annurev-polisci-071112-213421.

Davis, James W. 2000. *Threats and Promises: The Pursuit of International Influence.* Baltimore: Johns Hopkins University Press.

de Bellaigue, Christopher. 2007. *The Struggle for Iran.* New York: New York Review Books.

Debs, Alexandre, and Nuno P. Monteiro. 2017a. "Conflict and Cooperation on Nuclear Nonproliferation." *Annual Review of Political Science* 20: 331–49. https://doi.org/10.1146/annurev-polisci-051215-022839.

———. 2017b. *Nuclear Politics: The Strategic Causes of Proliferation.* New York: Cambridge University Press.

"Do Audience Costs Exist? A Symposium." 2012. *Security Studies* 21 (3): 369–555.

Dobbs, Michael. 2008. *One Minute to Midnight: Kennedy, Khrushchev, and Castro on the Brink of Nuclear War.* New York: Vintage Books.

Dorussen, Han. 2001."Mixing Carrots with Sticks: Evaluating the Effectiveness of Positive Inducements." *Journal of Peace Research* 38 (2): 251–62. https://www.jstor.org/stable/425499.

Downes, Alexander B. 2018. "Step Aside or Face the Consequences." In Greenhill and Krause 2018, 93–116.

Downes, Alexander B., and Todd S. Sechser. 2012. "The Illusion of Democratic Credibility." *International Organization* 66 (3): 457–89. https://doi.org/10.1017/S0020818312000161.

Drezner, Daniel W. 2021. "The United States of Sanctions: The Use and Abuse of Economic Coercion." *Foreign Affairs* 100 (5): 142–54.

——. 2022. "How Not to Sanction." *International Affairs* 98 (5): 1533–52. https://doi.org/10.1093/ia/iiac065.

Duelfer, Charles A., and Stephen Benedict Dyson. 2011. "Chronic Misperception and International Conflict: The U.S.-Iraq Experience." *International Security* 36 (1): 73–100. https://doi.org/10.1162/ISEC_a_00045.

Early, Bryan. 2011. "Unmasking the Black Knights." *Foreign Policy Analysis* 7 (4): 381–402. https://doi.org/10.1111/j.1743-8594.2011.00143.x.

Edelstein, David M. 2017. *Over the Horizon: Time, Uncertainty, and the Rise of Great Powers*. Ithaca, NY: Cornell University Press.

Einhorn, Robert. 2015. "Ukraine, Security Assurances, and Nonproliferation." *Washington Quarterly* 38 (1): 47–72. https://doi.org/10.1080/0163660X.2015.1038174.

Ekelund, Robert B., John D. Jackson, Rand W. Ressler, and Robert D. Tollison. 2006. "Marginal Deterrence and Multiple Murders." *Southern Economic Journal* 72 (3): 521–41. https://doi.org/10.1002/j.2325-8012.2006.tb00718.x.

Ekéus, Rolf. 2016. "Lessons from UNSCOM and Iraq." *Nonproliferation Review* 23 (1–2): 131–46. https://doi.org/10.1080/10736700.2016.1186875.

ElBaradei, Mohamed. 2011. *The Age of Deception: Nuclear Diplomacy in Treacherous Times*. London: Picador.

Evans, Gary. 1964. "Effect of Unilateral Promises and Value of Rewards upon Cooperation and Trust." *Journal of Abnormal and Social Psychology* 69: 587–90. https://psycnet.apa.org/doi/10.1037/h0042023.

Farrell, Henry, and Abraham Newman. 2019. "Weaponized Interdependence." *International Security* 44 (1): 42–79. https://doi.org/10.1162/isec_a_00351.

——. 2023. *Underground Empire: How America Weaponized the World Economy*. New York: Henry Holt.

Fearon, James D. 1994. "Domestic Political Audiences and the Escalation of International Disputes." *American Political Science Review* 88 (3): 577–92. https://doi.org/10.2307/2944796.

——. 1995. "Rationalist Explanations for War." *International Organization* 49 (3): 379–414. http://www.jstor.org/stable/2706903.

——. 1997. "Signaling Foreign Policy Interests: Tying Hands versus Sinking Costs." *Journal of Conflict Resolution* 41 (1): 68–90. https://www.jstor.org/stable/174487.

——. 2002. "Selection Effects and Deterrence." *International Interactions* 28 (5): 5–29. https://doi.org/10.1080/03050620210390.

——. 2011. "Two States, Two Types, Two Actions." *Security Studies* 20 (3): 431–40. https://doi.org/10.1080/09636412.2011.599192.

Feaver, Peter D., and Eric B. Lorber. 2010. *Coercive Diplomacy: Evaluating the Consequences of Financial Sanctions*. London: Legatum Institute.

Finel, Bernard I., and Kristin M. Lord, eds. 2002. *Power and Conflict in the Age of Transparency*. London: Palgrave Macmillan.

Fingar, Thomas. 2011. *Reducing Uncertainty: Intelligence Analysis and National Security*. Stanford, CA: Stanford University Press.

Fitzpatrick, Mark. 2006. "Lessons Learned from Iran's Pursuit of Nuclear Weapons." *Nonproliferation Review* 13 (3): 527–37. https://doi.org/10.1080/10736700601071603.

Fortna, Virginia Page. 2004. *Peace Time: Cease-Fire Agreements and the Durability of Peace*. Princeton, NJ: Princeton University Press.

Freedman, Lawrence. 2004a. "War in Iraq: Selling the Threat." *Survival* 4 (2): 7–49. https://doi.org/10.1080/00396338.2004.9688597.

——. 2004b. *Deterrence*. Malden, MA: Polity Press.

Fuhrmann, Matthew. 2009. "Taking a Walk on the Supply Side: The Determinants of Civilian Nuclear Cooperation." *Journal of Conflict Resolution* 53 (2): 181–208. https://doi.org/10.1177/0022002708330288.

Fuhrmann, Matthew, and Sarah E. Kreps. 2010. "Targeting Nuclear Programs in War and Peace: A Quantitative Empirical Analysis, 1941–2000." *Journal of Conflict Resolution* 54 (6): 831–59. https://www.jstor.org/stable/25780757.

Fuhrmann, Matthew, and Todd S. Sechser. 2014. "Signaling Alliance Commitments: Hand-Tying and Sunk Costs in Extended Nuclear Deterrence." *American Journal of Political Science*, 58 (4): 919–35. https://doi.org/10.1111/ajps.12082.

Fursenko, Aleksandr, and Timothy Naftali. 1997. *"One Hell of a Gamble": The Secret History of the Cuban Missile Crisis*. New York: W. W. Norton.

Gahagan, James P., and James T. Tedeschi. 1968. "Strategy and the Credibility of Promises in the Prisoner's Dilemma Game." *Journal of Conflict Resolution* 12 (2): 224–34. https://doi.org/10.1177/002200276801200208.

Gambetta, Diego. 2011. "Signaling." In *The Oxford Handbook of Analytical Sociology*, edited by Peter Bearman and Peter Hedstrom, 168–94. Oxford: Oxford University Press. https://doi.org/10.1093/oxfordhb/9780199215362.013.8.

Garthoff, Raymond L. 2001. *A Journey through the Cold War: A Memoir of Containment and Coexistence*. Washington, DC: Brookings Institution Press.

Gates, Robert M. 2014. *Duty: Memoirs of a Secretary at War*. New York: Alfred A Knopf.

Gause, F. Gregory, III. 2002. "Iraq's Decision to Go to War." *Middle East Journal* 56 (1): 47–70. https://www.jstor.org/stable/4329720.

Gavin, Francis J. 2014. "What We Talk about When We Talk about Nuclear Weapons." H-Diplo/ISSF, Forum No. 2, June 15, 11–36. http://issforum.org/ISSF/PDF/ISSF-Forum-2.pdf.

——. 2015. "Strategies of Inhibition: US Grand Strategy, the Nuclear Revolution, and Nonproliferation." *International Security* 40 (1): 9–46. https://doi.org/10.1162/ISEC_a_00205.

George, Alexander L., and William Simons, eds. 1994. *The Limits of Coercive Diplomacy*, 2nd ed. Boulder, CO: Westview.

George, Alexander L., and Richard Smoke. 1974. *Deterrence in American Foreign Policy: Theory and Practice*. New York: Columbia University Press.

Georghe, Eliza. 2019. "Proliferation and the Logic of the Nuclear Market." *International Security* 43 (4): 88–127. https://doi.org/10.1162/isec_a_00344.

Gerzhoy, Gene. 2014. "Coercive Nonproliferation: Security, Leverage, and Nuclear Reversals." PhD diss., University of Chicago.

——. 2015. "Alliance Coercion and Nuclear Restraint: How the United States Thwarted West Germany's Nuclear Ambitions." *International Security* 39 (4): 91–129. https://www.jstor.org/stable/24480608.

Gibbons, Rebecca Davis. 2022. *The Hegemon's Tool Kit: US Leadership and the Politics of the Nuclear Nonproliferation Regime*. Ithaca, NY: Cornell University Press.

Giliomee, Hermann. 1997. "Surrender without Defeat: Afrikaners and the South African 'Miracle.'" *Daedalus* 126 (2): 113–46. https://www.jstor.org/stable/20027431.

———. 2012. *The Last Afrikaner Leaders: A Supreme Test of Power*. Charlottesville: University of Virginia Press.

Gilpin, Robert. 1981. *War and Change in World Politics*. New York: Cambridge University Press.

Glaser, Bonnie S., Jessica Chen Weiss, and Thomas J. Christensen. 2024. "Taiwan and the True Sources of Deterrence: Why America Must Reassure, Not Just Threaten, China." *Foreign Affairs* 103 (1): 88–100.

Glaser, Charles L. 2010. *Rational Theory of International Politics*. Princeton, NJ: Princeton University Press.

Goemens, Hein. 2000. *War and Punishment: The Causes of War Termination and the First World War*. Princeton, NJ: Princeton University Press.

Goodwin, Doris Kearns. 1994. *No Ordinary Time*. New York: Simon & Schuster.

Greenhill, Kelly M. 2010. *Weapons of Mass Migration: Forced Displacement, Coercion, and Foreign Policy*. Ithaca, NY: Cornell University Press.

Greenhill, Kelly M., and Peter Krause, eds. 2018. *Coercion: The Power to Hurt in International Politics*. New York: Oxford University Press.

Haass, Richard N., and Meghan L. O'Sullivan, eds. 2000. *Honey and Vinegar: Incentives, Sanctions, and Foreign Policy*. Washington, DC: Brookings Institution Press.

Harrer, Gudrun. 2014. *Dismantling the Iraqi Nuclear Programme: The Inspections of the International Atomic Energy Agency, 1991–1998*. New York: Routledge.

Harvey, Frank P., and John Mitton. 2016. *Fighting for Credibility: U.S. Reputation and International Politics*. Toronto: University of Toronto Press.

Haun, Phil. 2015. *Coercion, Survival, and War: Why Weak States Resist the United States*. Stanford, CA: Stanford University Press.

Hayden, Michael V. 2016. *Playing to the Edge*. New York: Penguin Random House.

Healey, Denis. 1989. *The Time of My Life*. London: Michael Joseph.

Heinonen, Olli. 2014. "Verifying the Dismantlement of South Africa's Nuclear Weapons Program." In Sokolski 2014, 163–83.

———. 2016. "Lessons Learned from Dismantlement of South Africa's Biological, Chemical, and Nuclear Weapons Programs." *Nonproliferation Review* 23 (1–2): 147–62. https://doi.org/10.1080/10736700.2016.1182685.

Howard, Michael. 1982. "Reassurance and Deterrence: Western Defense in the 1980s." *Foreign Affairs* 61 (2): 309–24. https://doi.org/10.2307/20041437.

Hufbauer, Gary, Jeffrey Schott, and Kimberley Elliott. 1990. *Economic Sanctions Reconsidered*. Washington, DC: Institute for International Economics.

Huth, Paul, and Bruce Russett. 1984. "What Makes Deterrence Work? Cases from 1900 to 1980." *World Politics* 36 (4): 496–526. https://doi.org/10.2307/2010184.

———. 1988. "Deterrence Failure and Crisis Escalation." *International Studies Quarterly* 32 (1): 29–45. https://doi.org/10.2307/2600411.

Hymans, Jacques E. C. 2012. *Achieving Nuclear Ambitions: Scientists, Politicians, and Proliferation*. New York: Cambridge University Press.

Jentleson, Bruce W., and Christopher A. Whytock. 2005/2006. "Who 'Won' Libya? The Force-Diplomacy Debate and Its Implications for Theory and Policy." *International Security* 30 (3): 47–86. https://doi.org/10.1162/isec.2005.30.3.47.

Jervis, Robert. 1968. "Hypotheses on Misperception." *World Politics* 20 (3): 454–79. https://doi.org/10.2307/2009777.

———. 1970. *The Logic of Images in International Relations*. Princeton, NJ: Princeton University Press.

——. 1976. *Perception and Misperception in International Politics*. Princeton, NJ: Princeton University Press.

——. 1978. "Cooperation under the Security Dilemma." *World Politics* 30 (2): 167–214. https://doi.org/10.2307/2009958.

——. 2010. *Why Intelligence Fails*. Ithaca, NY: Cornell University Press.

——. 2013. "Getting to Yes with Iran: The Challenges of Coercive Diplomacy." *Foreign Affairs* 92 (1): 105–15.

——. 2015. "The Cuban Missile Crisis: What Can We Know, Why Did It Start, and How Did It End?" In *The Cuban Missile Crisis: A Critical Reappraisal*, edited by Len Scott and R. Gerald Hughes, 1–39. New York: Routledge.

Jervis, Robert, Keren Yarhi-Milo, and Don Casler. 2021. "Redefining the Debate over Reputation and Credibility in International Security: Promises and Limits of New Scholarship." *World Politics* 73 (1): 167–203. https://doi.org/10.1017/S0043887120000246.

Jo, Dong-Joon, and Erik Gartzke. 2007. "Determinants of Nuclear Weapons Proliferation." *Journal of Conflict Resolution* 51 (1): 167–94. https://doi.org/10.1177/0022002706296158.

Joseph, Robert G. 2009. *Countering WMD: The Libyan Experience*. Fairfax, VA: National Institute Press.

Kahn, Herman. 1960. *On Thermonuclear War*. Princeton, NJ: Princeton University Press.

Katz, Yaakov. 2019. *Shadow Strike*. New York: St. Martin's.

Katzenstein, Peter J., ed. 1996. *The Culture of National Security: Norms and Identity in World Politics*. New York: Columbia University Press.

Kaufmann, William W. 1954. *The Requirements of Deterrence*. Princeton, NJ: Princeton Center of International Studies.

Kemp, R. Scott. 2014. "The Nonproliferation Emperor Has No Clothes." *International Security* 38 (4): 39–78. https://www.jstor.org/stable/24481100.

Kennedy, Robert F. 1969. *Thirteen Days: A Memoir of the Cuban Missile Crisis*. New York: W. W. Norton.

Keohane, Robert. 2005. *After Hegemony*. Princeton, NJ: Princeton University Press.

Kerry, John. 2018. *Every Day Is Extra*. New York: Simon and Schuster.

Kirpichevsky, Yevgeniy, and Phillip Lipscy. n.d. "The Dark Side of Democratic Advantage: International Crises and Secret Agreements." Working paper. https://www.lipscy.org/papersecretagreements.pdf.

Klarevas, Louis. 2002. "The 'Essential Domino' of Military Operations: American Public Opinion and the Use of Force." *International Studies Perspectives* 3 (4): 417–37. https://www.jstor.org/stable/44218233.

Knopf, Jeffrey W., ed. 2012a. *Security Assurances and Nuclear Nonproliferation*. Stanford, CA: Stanford University Press.

——. 2012b. "Varieties of Assurance." *Journal of Strategic Studies* 35 (3): 375–99. https://doi.org/10.1080/01402390.2011.643567.

Koblentz, Gregory D. 2018. "Saddam versus the Inspectors: The Impact of Regime Security on the Verification of Iraq's WMD Disarmament." *Journal of Strategic Studies* 41 (3): 372–409. https://doi.org/10.1080/01402390.2016.1224764.

Koch, Lisa Langdon. 2023. *Nuclear Decisions: Changing the Course of Nuclear Weapons Programs*. New York: Oxford University Press.

Kreps, Sarah, and Zain Pasha. 2012. "Threats for Peace? The Domestic Distributional Effects of Military Threats." In Solingen 2012, 174–210.

Kroenig, Matthew. 2010. *Exporting the Bomb: Technology Transfer and the Spread of Nuclear Weapons*. Ithaca, NY: Cornell University Press.

Kydd, Andrew, and Roseanne McManus. 2017. "Threats and Assurances in Crisis Bargaining." *Journal of Conflict Resolution* 61 (2): 325–48. https://www.jstor.org/stable/26363885.

Lake, David A. 2010/2011. "Two Cheers for Bargaining Theory: Assessing Rationalist Explanations of the Iraq War." *International Security* 35 (3): 7–52. https://doi.org/10.1162/ISEC_a_00029.

Lanoszka, Alexander. 2018. *Atomic Assurance: The Alliance Politics of Nuclear Proliferation*. Ithaca, NY: Cornell University Press.

Lebow, Richard Ned. 2001. "Deterrence and Reassurance: Lessons from the Cold War." *Global Dialogue* 3 (4): 119–32.

Lebow, Richard Ned, and Janice Gross Stein. 1987. "Beyond Deterrence." *Journal of Social Issues* 43 (4): 5–71. https://doi.org/10.1111/j.1540-4560.1987.tb00252.x.

——. 1989. "Rational Deterrence Theory: I Think, Therefore I Deter." *World Politics* 41 (2): 208–24. https://doi.org/10.2307/2010408.

——. 1990. "Deterrence: The Elusive Dependent Variable." *World Politics* 42 (3): 336–69. https://doi.org/10.2307/2010415.

——. 1994. *We All Lost the Cold War*. Princeton, NJ: Princeton University Press.

Leffler, Melvyn P. 2023. *Confronting Saddam Hussein: George W. Bush and the Invasion of Iraq*. New York: Oxford University Press.

Lessing, Benjamin. 2018. *Making Peace in Drug Wars: Crackdowns and Cartels in Latin America*. New York: Cambridge University Press.

Levite, Ariel E. 2002/2003. "Never Say Never Again: Nuclear Reversal Revisited." *International Security* 27 (3): 59–88. https://www.jstor.org/stable/3092114.

Levy, Jack S. 2003. "Applications of Prospect Theory to Political Science." *Synthese* 135 (2): 215–41. https://doi.org/10.1023/A:1023413007698.

Liberman, Peter. 2001. "The Rise and Fall of the South African Bomb." *International Security* 26 (2): 45–86. https://doi.org/10.1162/016228801753191132.

Lin-Greenberg, Erik. 2019. "Backing Up, Not Backing Down: Mitigating Audience Costs through Policy Substitution." *Journal of Peace Research* 56 (4): 559–74. https://doi.org/10.1177/0022343319832641.

Lindsay, Jon R. 2013. "Stuxnet and the Limits of Cyber Warfare." *Security Studies* 22 (3): 365–404. https://doi.org/10.1080/09636412.2013.816122.

Litwak, Robert S. 2007. *Regime Change: U.S. Strategy through the Prism of 9/11*. Washington, DC: Woodrow Wilson Center Press.

——. 2008. "Living with Ambiguity: Nuclear Deals with Iran and North Korea." *Survival* 50 (1): 91–118. https://doi.org/10.1080/00396330801899496.

Lupton, Danielle. 2020. *Reputation for Resolve: How Leaders Signal Determination in International Politics*. Ithaca, NY: Cornell University Press.

Luttwak, Edward. 1996. "A Post-Heroic Military Policy." *Foreign Affairs* 75 (4): 33–44.

Major, Solomon. 2012. "Timing Is Everything: Economic Sanctions, Regime Type, and Domestic Instability." *International Interactions* 38 (1): 79–110. https://doi.org/10.1080/03050629.2012.640253.

Martin, Lisa L. 1992. *Coercive Cooperation: Explaining Multilateral Economic Sanctions*. Princeton, NJ: Princeton University Press.

Mastro, Oriana Skylar. 2019. *The Costs of Conversation: Obstacles to Peace Talks in Wartime*. Ithaca, NY: Cornell University Press.

McCoy, Michael K. 2011/2012. "Correspondence: Bargaining Theory and Rationalist Explanations for the Iraq War." *International Security* 36 (3): 172–78. https://doi.org/10.1162/ISEC_c_00069.

McDermott, Rose. 1998. *Prospect Theory in American Foreign Policy.* Ann Arbor: University of Michigan Press.

McManus, Roseanne. 2021. "Crazy like a Fox? Are Leaders with Reputations for Madness More Successful at International Coercion?" *British Journal of Political Science* 51 (1): 275–93. https://doi.org/10.1017/S0007123419000401.

Mearsheimer, John J. 1983. *Conventional Deterrence.* Ithaca, NY: Cornell University Press.

——. 2001. *The Tragedy of Great Power Politics.* New York: W. W. Norton.

Mehta, Rupal N. 2020. *Delaying Doomsday: The Politics of Nuclear Reversal.* New York: Oxford University Press.

Mercer, Jonathan. 1996. *Reputation and International Politics.* Ithaca, NY: Cornell University Press.

——. 2005. "Prospect Theory and Political Science." *Annual Review of Political Science* 8 (1): 1–21. https://doi.org/10.1146/annurev.polisci.8.082103.104911.

Miller, Andrew. 2022. "Without an Army: How ICC Indictments Reduce Atrocities." *Journal of Peace Research* 60 (4): 573–87. https://doi.org/10.1177/00223433221088692.

Miller, Nicholas L. 2014. "Secret Success of Nonproliferation Sanctions." *International Organization* 68 (4): 913–44. https://www.jstor.org/stable/43283283.

——. 2018. *Stopping the Bomb: The Sources and Effectiveness of U.S. Nonproliferation Policy.* Ithaca, NY: Cornell University Press.

Miller, Nicholas L., and Or Rabinowitz. 2015. "Keeping the Bombs in the Basement: US Nonproliferation Policy toward Israel, South Africa, and Pakistan." *International Security* 40 (1): 47–86. https://www.jstor.org/stable/24480595.

Milner, Helen V. 1997. *Interests, Institutions, and Information: Domestic Politics and International Relations.* Princeton, NJ: Princeton University Press.

Monteiro, Nuno. 2009. "Three Essays on Unipolarity." PhD diss., University of Chicago.

Monteiro, Nuno P., and Alexandre Debs. 2014. "The Strategic Logic of Nuclear Proliferation." *International Security* 39 (2): 7–51. https://doi.org/10.1162/ISEC_a_00177.

Morgan, T. Clifton, Navin Bapat, and Yoshi Kobayashi. 2014. "The Threat and Imposition of Sanctions: Updating the TIES Dataset." *Conflict Management and Peace Science* 31 (5): 541–58. https://doi.org/10.1177/0738894213520379.

Morrow, James D. 1989. "Capabilities, Uncertainty, and Resolve: A Limited Information Model of Crisis Bargaining." *American Journal of Political Science* 33 (4): 941–72. https://doi.org/10.2307/2111116.

Möser, Robin. 2020. "'The Major Prize': Apartheid South Africa's Accession to the Treaty on the Prohibition of Nuclear Weapons, 1988–91." *Nonproliferation Review* 26 (5–6): 559–73. https://doi.org/10.1080/10736700.2019.1696543.

——. 2024. *Disarming Apartheid: The End of South Africa's Nuclear Weapons Programme and Accession to the Treaty on the Non-Proliferation of Nuclear Weapons, 1968–1991.* New York: Cambridge University Press.

Mousavian, Seyyed Hossein. 2012. *The Iranian Nuclear Crisis: A Memoir.* Washington, DC: Carnegie Endowment for International Peace.

Mulder, Nicholas. 2022. *The Economic Weapon*. New Haven, CT: Yale University Press.

Myrick, Rachel. 2021. "Partisan Polarization and International Politics." PhD diss., Stanford University.

Nader, Alireza. 2012. "Influencing Iran's Nuclear Decisions." In Solingen 2012, 211–31.

Narang, Vipin. 2014. *Nuclear Strategy in the Modern Era*. Princeton, NJ: Princeton University Press.

——. 2016/2017. "Strategies of Nuclear Proliferation: How States Pursue the Bomb." *International Security* 4 (3): 110–50. https://doi.org/10.1162/ISEC_a_00268.

Nephew, Richard. 2018a. "The Hard Part: The Art of Sanctions Relief." *Washington Quarterly* 41 (2): 63–77. https://doi.org/10.1080/0163660X.2018.1484225.

——. 2018b. *The Art of Sanctions*. New York: Columbia University Press.

Nutt, Cullen G. 2019. "Proof of the Bomb: The Influence of Previous Failure on Intelligence Judgments of Nuclear Programs." *Security Studies* 28 (2): 321–59. https://doi.org/10.1080/09636412.2019.1551569.

Nutt, Cullen G., and Reid B. C. Pauly. 2021. "Caught Red-Handed: How States Wield Proof to Coerce Wrongdoers." *International Security* 46 (2): 7–50. https://doi.org/10.1162/isec_a_00421.

Obama, Barack. 2020. *A Promised Land*. New York: Crown.

Obeidi, Mahdi, and Kurt Pitzer. 2004. *The Bomb in My Garden*. Hoboken, NJ: John Wiley & Sons.

Osgood, Charles E. 1962. *An Alternative to War or Surrender*. New York: Cromwell-Collier.

Oye, Kenneth A. 1992. *Economic Discrimination and Political Exchange*. Princeton, NJ: Princeton University Press.

Pabian, Frank. 1995. "South Africa's Nuclear Weapons Program: Lessons for U.S. Nonproliferation Policy." *Nonproliferation Review* 3 (1): 1–19. https://www.nonproliferation.org/wp-content/uploads/npr/31pabian.pdf.

Palkki, David D., and Shane Smith. 2012. "Contrasting Causal Mechanisms: Iraq and Libya." In Solingen 2012, 261–96.

Pape, Robert A. 1996. *Bombing to Win: Air Power and Coercion in War*. Ithaca, NY: Cornell University Press.

——. 1997. "Why Economic Sanctions Do Not Work." *International Security* 22 (2): 90–136. https://doi.org/10.1162/isec.22.2.90.

Pargeter, Alison. 2012. *Libya: The Rise and Fall of Qaddafi*. New Haven, CT: Yale University Press.

Parsi, Trita. 2014. "No, Sanctions Didn't Force Iran to Make a Deal." *Foreign Policy*, May 14. https://foreignpolicy.com/2014/05/14/no-sanctions-didnt-force-iran-to-make-a-deal/.

Patrikarakos, David. 2012. *Nuclear Iran: The Birth of an Atomic State*. New York: I. B. Tauris.

Pauly, Reid B. C. 2021. "Deniability in the Nuclear Nonproliferation Regime." *International Studies Quarterly* 66 (1). https://doi.org/10.1093/isq/sqab036.

——. 2024. "Damned If They Do, Damned If They Don't: The Assurance Dilemma in International Coercion." *International Security* 49 (1): 91–132. https://doi.org/10.1162/isec_a_00488.

Pauly, Reid B. C., and Rose McDermott. 2023. "The Psychology of Nuclear Brink-manship." *International Security* 47 (3): 9–51. https://doi.org/10.1162/isec_a_00451.

Perlmutter, Amos, Michael I. Handel, and Uri Bar-Joseph. 2003. *Two Minutes over Baghdad*. London: Routledge.

Petrovics, Ariel. 2019. "Inducing Nuclear Reversal: Foreign Policy Effectiveness and Deproliferation." PhD diss., University of California, Davis.

Poast, Paul. 2012. "Does Issue Linkage Work? Evidence from European Alliance Negotiations, 1860 to 1945." *International Organization* 66 (2): 277–310. https://doi.org/10.1017/S0020818312000069.

Porter, Gareth. 2010. "The Iran Nuclear 'Alleged Studies' Documents: The Evidence of Fraud." *Middle East Policy* 17 (4): 23–39. https://doi.org/10.1111/j.1475-4967.2010.00460.x.

Posen, Barry R. 1991. *Inadvertent Escalation*. Ithaca, NY: Cornell University Press.

——. 1996. "Military Responses to Refugee Disasters." *International Security* 21 (1): 72–111. https://doi.org/10.2307/2539109.

Post, Abigail. 2019. "Flying to Fail: Costly Signals and Air Power in Crisis Bargaining." *Journal of Conflict Resolution* 63 (4): 869–95. https://doi.org/10.1177/0022002718777043.

Powell, Robert. 1999. *In the Shadow of Power: States and Strategies in International Relations*. Princeton, NJ: Princeton University Press.

——. 2004. "Bargaining and Learning while Fighting." *American Journal of Political Science* 48 (2): 344–61. https://doi.org/10.1111/j.0092-5853.2004.00074.x.

——. 2006. "War as a Commitment Problem." *International Organization* 60 (1): 169–203. https://www.jstor.org/stable/3877871.

Power, Samantha. 2019. *Education of an Idealist: A Memoir*. New York: HarperCollins.

Press, Daryl G. 2005. *Calculating Credibility*. Ithaca, NY: Cornell University Press.

Purkitt, Helen E., and Stephen F. Burgess. 2005. *South Africa's Weapons of Mass Destruction*. Bloomington: Indiana University Press.

Putnam, Robert D. 1988. "Diplomacy and Domestic Politics: The Logic of Two-Level Games." *International Organization* 42 (3): 427–60. https://doi.org/10.1017/S0020818300027697.

Raas, Whitney and Austin Long. 2007. "Osirak Redux? Assessing Israeli Capabilities to Destroy Iranian Nuclear Facilities." *International Security* 31 (4): 7–33. https://muse.jhu.edu/article/213649.

Rabinowitz, Or. 2014. *Bargaining on Nuclear Tests: Washington and Its Cold War Deals*. New York: Oxford University Press.

Ramsay, Kristopher. 2004. "Politics at the Water's Edge: Crisis Bargaining and Electoral Competition." *Journal of Conflict Resolution* 48 (4): 459–86. https://www.jstor.org/stable/4149804.

Raviv, Dan, and Yossi Melman. 2014. *Spies against Armageddon*. 2nd ed. Sea Cliff, NY: Levant Books.

Reardon, Robert J. 2012. *Containing Iran: Strategies for Addressing the Iranian Nuclear Challenge*. Santa Monica, CA: RAND Corp.

Reiss, Mitchell. 1995. *Bridled Ambition: Why Countries Constrain their Nuclear Capabilities*. Washington, DC: Woodrow Wilson Center Press.

Reynolds, Celia L., and Wilfred T. Wan. 2012. "Empirical Trends in Sanctions and Positive Inducements." In Solingen 2012, 56–124.

Rhodes, Ben. 2018. *The World as It Is: A Memoir of the Obama White House*. New York: Random House.

Rice, Condoleezza. 2011. *No Higher Honor: A Memoir of My Years in Washington*. New York: Crown.

Rice, Susan. 2019. *Tough Love: My Story of the Things Worth Fighting For*. New York: Simon & Schuster.

Richelson, Jeffrey T. 2006. *Spying on the Bomb: American Nuclear Intelligence from Nazi Germany to Iran and North Korea*. New York: W. W. Norton.

Ritter, Jeffery M. 2002. "Know Thine Enemy." In Finel and Lord 2002, 83–113. New York: Palgrave Macmillan.

Rovner, Joshua. 2011. *Fixing the Facts: National Security and the Politics of Intelligence*. Ithaca, NY: Cornell University Press.

Russett, Bruce M. 1963. "The Calculus of Deterrence." *Journal of Conflict Resolution* 7 (2): 97–109. https://doi.org/10.1177/002200276300700201.

Sadot, Uri. 2016. "Osirak and the Counter-Proliferation Puzzle." *Security Studies* 25 (4): 646–76. https://doi.org/10.1080/09636412.2016.1220206.

Sagan, Scott D. 1988. "Origins of the Pacific War." *Journal of Interdisciplinary History* 18 (4): 893–922. https://doi.org/10.2307/204828.

——. 1996. "Why Do States Build Nuclear Weapons? Three Models in Search of a Bomb." *International Security* 21 (3): 54–86. https://doi.org/10.1162/isec.21.3.54.

——. 2013. "Deterring Rogue Regimes: Rethinking Deterrence Theory and Practice." Monterey, CA: Center on Contemporary Conflict, Naval Postgraduate School. http://hdl.handle.net/10945/34336.

Samore, Gary, ed. 2015. "Sanctions against Iran: A Guide to Targets, Terms, and Timetables." Cambridge, MA: Belfer Center, Harvard Kennedy School. https://www.belfercenter.org/publication/sanctions-against-iran-guide-targets-terms-and-timetables.

Sartori, Anne. 2005. *Deterrence by Diplomacy*. Princeton, NJ: Princeton University Press.

Sauer, Tom. 2007. "Coercive Diplomacy by the EU: The Iranian Nuclear Weapons Crisis." *Third World Quarterly* 28 (3): 613–33. https://www.jstor.org/stable/20454949.

Saunders, Elizabeth N. 2019. "The Domestic Politics of Nuclear Choices: A Review Essay." *International Security* 44 (2): 146–84. https://doi.org/10.1162/isec_a_00361.

Schelling, Thomas C. 1956. "An Essay on Bargaining." *American Economic Review* 46 (3): 281–306. https://www.jstor.org/stable/1805498.

——. 1960. *Strategy of Conflict*. Cambridge, MA: Harvard University Press.

——. 1965. "Signals and Feedback in the Arms Dialogue." *Bulletin of the Atomic Scientists* 21 (1): 5–10.

——. 1966. *Arms and Influence*. New Haven, CT: Yale University Press,

——. 1984. "Confidence in Crisis." *International Security* 8 (4): 55–66. https://doi.org/10.2307/2538562.

——. 1989. "Promises." *Negotiation Journal* 5 (2): 113–18. https://doi.org/10.1007/BF01000723.

——. 2006. *Strategies of Commitment and Other Essays*. Cambridge, MA: Harvard University Press.

Schrire, Robert. 1991. *Adapt or Die: The End of White Politics in South Africa*. New York: Ford Foundation / Foreign Policy Association.

Schultz, Kenneth A. 1998. "Domestic Opposition and Signaling in International Crises." *American Political Science Review* 92 (4): 829–944. https://doi.org/10.2307/2586306.

——. 2001. *Democracy and Coercive Diplomacy*. New York: Cambridge University Press.

——. 2017. "Perils of Polarization for U.S. Foreign Policy." *Washington Quarterly* 40 (4): 7–28. https://doi.org/10.1080/0163660X.2017.1406705.

Sebenius, James K. 1983. "Negotiation Arithmetic." *International Organization* 37 (2): 281–316. https://doi.org/10.1017/S002081830003438X.

Sechser, Todd S. 2010. "Goliath's Curse: Coercive Threats and Asymmetric Power." *International Organization* 64 (4): 627–60. https://doi.org/10.1017/S0020818310000214.

——. 2011. "Militarized Compellent Threats, 1918–2001." *Conflict Management and Peace Science* 28 (4): 377–401. https://doi.org/10.1177/0738894211413066.

——. 2018. "A Bargaining Theory of Coercion." In Greenhill and Krause 2018, 55–76.

Sechser, Todd S., and Matthew Fuhrmann. 2017. *Nuclear Weapons and Coercive Diplomacy*. New York: Cambridge University Press.

Sherman, Wendy R. 2018. *Not for the Faint of Heart: Lessons in Courage, Power, and Persistence*. New York: PublicAffairs.

Simmons, Beth A. 1998. "Compliance with International Agreements." *Annual Review of Political Science* 1 (1): 75–93. https://doi.org/10.1146/annurev.polisci.1.1.75.

Simmons, Beth A. 2010. "Treaty Compliance and Violation." *Annual Review of Political Science* 13 (1): 273–96. https://doi.org/10.1146/annurev.polisci.12.040907.132713.

Simmons, Beth A., and Allison Danner. 2010. "Credible Commitments and the International Criminal Court." *International Organization* 64 (2): 225–56. https://doi.org/10.1017/S0020818310000044.

Singh, Sonali, and Christopher R. Way. 2004. "The Correlates of Nuclear Proliferation: A Quantitative Test." *Journal of Conflict Resolution* 48 (6): 859–85. https://www.jstor.org/stable/4149798.

Sisson, Melanie W., James A. Siebens, and Barry M. Blechman, eds. 2020. *Military Coercion and U.S. Foreign Policy: The Use of Force Short of War*. New York: Routledge.

Slantchev, Branislav. 2005. "Military Coercion in Interstate Crises." *American Political Science Review* 99 (4): 533–47. https://doi.org/10.1017/S0003055405051865.

Snyder, Glenn H. 1961. *Deterrence and Defense: Toward a Theory of National Security*. Princeton, NJ: Princeton University Press.

Snyder, Jack, and Erica D. Borghard. 2011. "The Cost of Empty Threats: A Penny, Not a Pound." *American Political Science Review* 105 (3): 437–56. https://doi.org/10.1017/S000305541100027X.

Sobelman, Daniel. 2018. "Restraining an Ally: Israel, the United States, and Iran's Nuclear Program, 2011–2012." *Texas National Security Review* 1 (4): 10–38. http://doi.org/10.15781/T23T9DS99.

Sokolski, Henry D., ed. 2014. *Nuclear Weapons Materials Gone Missing: What Does History Teach?* Carlisle, PA: Strategic Studies Institute, US Army War College.

Solingen, Etel. 2007. *Nuclear Logics: Contrasting Paths in East Asia and the Middle East.* Princeton, NJ: Princeton University Press.

——, ed. 2012. *Sanctions, Statecraft, and Nuclear Proliferation.* New York: Cambridge University Press.

Spence, Michael. 1973. "Job Market Signaling." *Quarterly Journal of Economics* 87 (3): 355–74. https://doi.org/10.2307/1882010.

Steele, Ian K. 1990. *Betrayals: Fort William Henry and the "Massacre."* New York: Oxford University Press.

Stein, Arthur A. 1980. "The Politics of Linkage." *World Politics* 33 (1): 62–81. https://doi.org/10.2307/2010255.

Stein, Janice Gross. 1991."Deterrence and Reassurance." In *Behavior, Society, and Nuclear War, Volume II*, edited by Philip E. Tetlock, Jo L. Husbands, Robert Jervis, Paul C. Stern, and Charles Tilly, 8–72. New York: Oxford University Press.

——. 2012. "The Psychology of Assurance: An Emotional Tale." In Knopf 2012a, 39–57.

——. 2021. In "The Obama Administration's Response to the Use of Chemical Weapons in Syria: An Exchange." *Security Studies* 30 (2): 302–24. https://doi.org/10.1080/09636412.2021.1944723.

Stumpf, Waldo. 1995/1996. "South Africa's Nuclear Weapons Program: From Deterrence to Dismantlement." *Arms Control Today* 25 (10): 3–8. https://www.jstor.org/stable/23625371.

Tabatabai, Ariane. 2017. "Negotiating the 'Iran Talks' in Tehran: The Iranian drivers that shaped the Joint Comprehensive Plan of Action." *Nonproliferation Review* 24 (3–4): 225–42. https://doi.org/10.1080/10736700.2018.1426180.

Taliaferro, Jeffrey W. 2019. *Defending Frenemies: Alliances, Politics, and Nuclear Nonproliferation in US Foreign Policy.* New York: Oxford University Press.

Tenet, George, and Bill Harlow. 2007. *At the Center of the Storm: My Years at the CIA.* New York: HarperCollins.

Thompson, Alexander. 2009. *Channels of Power: The UN Security Council and U.S. Statecraft in Iraq.* Ithaca, NY: Cornell University Press.

Thomson, Alex. 2008. *U.S. Foreign Policy towards Apartheid South Africa, 1948–1994.* London: Palgrave Macmillan.

——. 2010. "The Diplomacy of Impasse: The Carter Administration and Apartheid South Africa." *Diplomacy and Statecraft* 21 (1): 107–24. https://doi.org/10.1080/09592290903577775.

Tobey, William. 2014. "A Message from Tripoli: How Libya Gave Up Its WMD, Parts 1–5." *Bulletin of the Atomic Scientists*, December 3–8. https://thebulletin.org/2014/12/a-message-from-tripoli-how-libya-gave-up-its-wmd/; https://thebulletin.org/2014/12/a-message-from-tripoli-part-2-how-libya-gave-up-its-wmd/; https://thebulletin.org/2014/12/a-message-from-tripoli-part-3-how-libya-gave-up-its-wmd/; https://thebulletin.org/2014/12/a-message-from-tripoli-part-4-how-libya-gave-up-its-wmd/; https://thebulletin.org/2014/12/a-message-from-tripoli-part-5-how-libya-gave-up-its-wmd/.

——. 2018. "Intelligence and Policy Community Cooperation in the Libya WMD Disarmament Case." Occasional Paper 1802. Nonproliferation Policy Education

Center, June. https://npolicy.org/intelligence-and-policy-community-cooperation-in-the-libya-wmd-disarmament-case-occasional-paper-1802/.

Tomz, Michael. 2007. *Reputation and International Cooperation: Sovereign Debt across Three Centuries*. Princeton, NJ: Princeton University Press.

Trachtenberg, Marc. 1999. *A Constructed Peace: The Making of the European Settlement, 1945–1963*. Princeton, NJ: Princeton University Press.

Trager, Robert F. 2012. "Long-Term Consequences of Aggressive Diplomacy: European Relations after Austrian Crimean War Threats." *Security Studies* 21 (2): 232–65. https://doi.org/10.1080/09636412.2012.679204.

Tsebelis, George. 2002. *Veto Players: How Political Institutions Work*. Princeton, NJ: Princeton University Press.

Vaez, Ali. 2013. *Spider Web: The Making and Unmaking of Iran Sanctions*. Brussels: International Crisis Group. https://www.crisisgroup.org/middle-east-north-africa/gulf-and-arabian-peninsula/iran/138-spider-web-making-and-unmaking-iran-sanctions.

Van Wyk, Anna-Mart. 2010. "Apartheid's Atomic Bomb: Cold War Perspectives." *South African Historical Journal* 62 (1): 100–20. https://doi.org/10.1080/0258247 1003778367.

van Wyk, Jo-Ansie. 2012. "Nuclear Diplomacy as Niche Diplomacy: South Africa's Post-Apartheid Relations with the International Atomic Energy Agency." *South African Journal of International Affairs* 19 (2): 179–200. https://doi.org/10.1080/10220461.2012.706492.

——. 2014. "Atoms, Apartheid, and the Agency: South Africa's Relations with the IAEA, 1957–1995." *Cold War History* 15 (3): 395–416. https://doi.org/10.1080/14682745.2014.897697.

van Wyk, Martha S. 2007. "Ally or Critic? The United States' Response to South African Nuclear Development, 1949–1980." *Cold War History* 7 (2): 195–225. https://doi.org/10.1080/14682740701284124.

——. 2010. "Sunset over Atomic Apartheid: United States–South African Nuclear Relations, 1981–93." *Cold War History* 10 (1): 51–79. https://doi.org/10.1080/14682740902764569.

Volpe, Tristan A. 2017. "Atomic Leverage: Compellence with Nuclear Latency." *Security Studies* 26 (3): 517–44. https://doi.org/10.1080/09636412.2017.1306398.

——. 2023. *Leveraging Latency: How the Weak Compel the Strong with Nuclear Technology*. New York: Oxford University Press.

von Baeckmann, Adolf, Garry Dillon, and Demetrius Perricos, 1995. "Nuclear Verification in South Africa." *IAEA Bulletin* 1. https://www.iaea.org/sites/default/files/publications/magazines/bulletin/bull37-1/37105394248.pdf.

von Wielligh, Nic, and Lydia von Wielligh-Steyn. 2015. *The Bomb: South Africa's Nuclear Weapons Programme*. Pretoria: Litera Publications.

Wagner, R. Harrison. 2000. "Bargaining and War." *American Journal of Political Science* 33 (3): 469–84. https://doi.org/10.2307/2669259.

Walter, Barbara. 1997. "The Critical Barrier to Civil War Settlement." *International Organization* 51 (3): 335–64. https://doi.org/10.1162/002081897550384.

Waltz, Kenneth N. 1979. *Theory of International Politics*. Long Grove, IL: Waveland.

Weeks, Jessica L. 2008. "Autocratic Audience Costs: Regime Type and Signaling Resolve." *International Organization* 62 (1): 35–64. https://www.jstor.org/stable/40071874.

Weisiger, Alex. 2013. *Logics of War: Explanations for Limited and Unlimited Conflicts*. Ithaca, NY: Cornell University Press.

Weisiger, Alex, and Keren Yarhi-Milo. 2015. "Revisiting Reputation: How Past Actions Matter in International Politics." *International Organization* 69 (2): 473–95. https://doi.org/10.1017/S0020818314000393.

Welsh, David. 2009. *The Rise and Fall of Apartheid*. Charlottesville: University of Virginia Press.

Whitlark, Rachel. 2021. *All Options on the Table: Leaders, Preventive War, and Nuclear Proliferation*. Ithaca, NY: Cornell University Press.

Wohlstetter, Albert. 1959. "The Delicate Balance of Terror." *Foreign Affairs* 37 (2): 211–34.

Woods, Kevin M. 2008. *The Mother of All Battles: Saddam Hussein's Strategic Plan for the Persian Gulf War*. Annapolis, MD: Naval Institute Press.

Woods, Kevin M., James Lacey, and Williamson Murray. 2006. "Saddam's Delusions: The View from the Inside." *Foreign Affairs* 85 (3): 2–26. https://doi.org/10.2307/20031964.

Woods, Kevin M., David D. Palkki, and Mark E. Stout, eds. 2011. *The Saddam Tapes: The Inner Workings of a Tyrant's Regime*. New York: Cambridge University Press.

Woods, Kevin M., with Michael R. Pease, Mark E. Stout, Williamson Murray, and James G. Lacey. 2006. *Iraqi Perspectives Project: A View of Operation Iraqi Freedom from Saddam's Senior Leadership*. Norfolk, VA: Joint Center for Operational Analysis, US Joint Forces Command.

Woods, Kevin M., and Mark E. Stout. 2010. "Saddam's Perceptions and Misperceptions: The Case of 'Desert Storm.'" *Journal of Strategic Studies* 33 (1): 5–41. https://doi.org/10.1080/01402391003603433.

Woodward, Bob. 2004. *Plan of Attack*. New York: Simon & Schuster.

Zanotti, Jim, Kenneth Katzman, Jeremiah Gertler, and Steven A. Hildreth. 2012. "Israel: Possible Military Strike against Iran's Nuclear Facilities." Congressional Research Service. Report No. R42443. September 28. https://crsreports.congress.gov/product/pdf/R/R42443.

Zarate, Juan C. 2013. *Treasury's War: The Unleashing of a New Era of Financial Warfare*. New York: PublicAffairs.

Zegart, Amy. 2020. "Cheap Fights, Credible Threats: The Future of Armed Drones and Coercion." *Journal of Strategic Studies* 43 (1): 6–46. https://doi.org/10.1080/01402390.2018.1439747.

Zimmermann, Tim. 1994. "Coercive Diplomacy and Libya." In George and Simons, 1994, 201–28.

Index

Figures and tables are indicated by "f" and "t" following page numbers.